The history of the life of Marcus Tullius Cicero. By Conyers Middleton, ... The fifth edition. Volume 2 of 3

Conyers Middleton

ECCO
PRINT EDITIONS

Eighteenth Century
Collections Online
Print Editions

Gale ECCO Print Editions

Relive history with *Eighteenth Century Collections Online*, now available in print for the independent historian and collector. This series includes the most significant English-language and foreign-language works printed in Great Britain during the eighteenth century, and is organized in seven different subject areas including literature and language; medicine, science, and technology; and religion and philosophy. The collection also includes thousands of important works from the Americas.

The eighteenth century has been called "The Age of Enlightenment." It was a period of rapid advance in print culture and publishing, in world exploration, and in the rapid growth of science and technology – all of which had a profound impact on the political and cultural landscape. At the end of the century the American Revolution, French Revolution and Industrial Revolution, perhaps three of the most significant events in modern history, set in motion developments that eventually dominated world political, economic, and social life.

In a groundbreaking effort, Gale initiated a revolution of its own: digitization of epic proportions to preserve these invaluable works in the largest online archive of its kind. Contributions from major world libraries constitute over 175,000 original printed works. Scanned images of the actual pages, rather than transcriptions, recreate the works *as they first appeared.*

Now for the first time, these high-quality digital scans of original works are available via print-on-demand, making them readily accessible to libraries, students, independent scholars, and readers of all ages.

For our initial release we have created seven robust collections to form one the world's most comprehensive catalogs of 18th century works.

Initial Gale ECCO Print Editions collections include:

History and Geography
Rich in titles on English life and social history, this collection spans the world as it was known to eighteenth-century historians and explorers. Titles include a wealth of travel accounts and diaries, histories of nations from throughout the world, and maps and charts of a world that was still being discovered. Students of the War of American Independence will find fascinating accounts from the British side of conflict.

Social Science

Delve into what it was like to live during the eighteenth century by reading the first-hand accounts of everyday people, including city dwellers and farmers, businessmen and bankers, artisans and merchants, artists and their patrons, politicians and their constituents. Original texts make the American, French, and Industrial revolutions vividly contemporary.

Medicine, Science and Technology

Medical theory and practice of the 1700s developed rapidly, as is evidenced by the extensive collection, which includes descriptions of diseases, their conditions, and treatments. Books on science and technology, agriculture, military technology, natural philosophy, even cookbooks, are all contained here.

Literature and Language

Western literary study flows out of eighteenth-century works by Alexander Pope, Daniel Defoe, Henry Fielding, Frances Burney, Denis Diderot, Johann Gottfried Herder, Johann Wolfgang von Goethe, and others. Experience the birth of the modern novel, or compare the development of language using dictionaries and grammar discourses.

Religion and Philosophy

The Age of Enlightenment profoundly enriched religious and philosophical understanding and continues to influence present-day thinking. Works collected here include masterpieces by David Hume, Immanuel Kant, and Jean-Jacques Rousseau, as well as religious sermons and moral debates on the issues of the day, such as the slave trade. The Age of Reason saw conflict between Protestantism and Catholicism transformed into one between faith and logic -- a debate that continues in the twenty-first century.

Law and Reference

This collection reveals the history of English common law and Empire law in a vastly changing world of British expansion. Dominating the legal field is the *Commentaries of the Law of England* by Sir William Blackstone, which first appeared in 1765. Reference works such as almanacs and catalogues continue to educate us by revealing the day-to-day workings of society.

Fine Arts

The eighteenth-century fascination with Greek and Roman antiquity followed the systematic excavation of the ruins at Pompeii and Herculaneum in southern Italy; and after 1750 a neoclassical style dominated all artistic fields. The titles here trace developments in mostly English-language works on painting, sculpture, architecture, music, theater, and other disciplines. Instructional works on musical instruments, catalogs of art objects, comic operas, and more are also included.

The BiblioLife Network

This project was made possible in part by the BiblioLife Network (BLN), a project aimed at addressing some of the huge challenges facing book preservationists around the world. The BLN includes libraries, library networks, archives, subject matter experts, online communities and library service providers. We believe every book ever published should be available as a high-quality print reproduction; printed on-demand anywhere in the world. This insures the ongoing accessibility of the content and helps generate sustainable revenue for the libraries and organizations that work to preserve these important materials.

The following book is in the "public domain" and represents an authentic reproduction of the text as printed by the original publisher. While we have attempted to accurately maintain the integrity of the original work, there are sometimes problems with the original work or the micro-film from which the books were digitized. This can result in minor errors in reproduction. Possible imperfections include missing and blurred pages, poor pictures, markings and other reproduction issues beyond our control. Because this work is culturally important, we have made it available as part of our commitment to protecting, preserving, and promoting the world's literature.

GUIDE TO FOLD-OUTS MAPS and OVERSIZED IMAGES

The book you are reading was digitized from microfilm captured over the past thirty to forty years. Years after the creation of the original microfilm, the book was converted to digital files and made available in an online database.

In an online database, page images do not need to conform to the size restrictions found in a printed book. When converting these images back into a printed bound book, the page sizes are standardized in ways that maintain the detail of the original. For large images, such as fold-out maps, the original page image is split into two or more pages

Guidelines used to determine how to split the page image follows:

• Some images are split vertically; large images require vertical and horizontal splits.
• For horizontal splits, the content is split left to right.
• For vertical splits, the content is split from top to bottom.
• For both vertical and horizontal splits, the image is processed from top left to bottom right.

THE

HISTORY

OF THE

LIFE

OF

Marcus Tullius Cicero.

Hunc igitur spectemus   Hoc propositum sic nobis exemplum.
Ille se profecisse sciat, cui CICERO *valde placebit*
                    QUINTIL. Inftit l x. 1.

By CONYERS MIDDLETON, D. D.
Principal Library-keeper of the Univerfity of *Cambridge.*

VOL. II.

The SIXTH EDITION.

LONDON·
Printed for W. INNYS and J. RICHARDSON in *Pater-*
nofter-Row, R. MANBY in the *Old-Bailey* near *Lud-*
gate-hill, and H. S. COX in *Pater-nofter-Row.*
MDCCLV.

THE
HISTORY
OF THE
LIFE
OF
M.TULLIUS CICERO.

SECT VI.

Cᴵᴄᴇʀᴏ's return was, what he himself truly calls it, *the beginning of a new life* to him [a], which was to be governed by new maxims, and a new kind of policy, yet so as not to forfeit his old character He had been made to feel in what hands the weight of power lay, and what little dependence was to be placed on the help and support of his Aristocratical friends Pompey had served him on this important occasion very sincerely, and with the concurrence also of Cæsar, so as to make it a point

A Urb 696
Cic 50
Coss
P Cᴏʀɴᴇʟɪᴜs
Lᴇɴᴛᴜʟᴜs
Sᴘɪɴᴛʜᴇʀ,
Q Cæᴄɪʟɪᴜs
Mᴇᴛᴇʟʟᴜs
Nᴇᴘᴏs

[a] Alterius vitæ quoddam initium ordimur [ad Att 4 1] In another place, he calls his restoration to his former dignity, παλιγγενεσίαν, [ad Att 6 6] or a new birth, a word borrowed probably from the *Pythagorean* school, and applied afterwards by the sacred Writers to the renovation of our nature by Baptism, as well as our restoration to life, after death, in the general resurrection Matt xix 29 Tit iii 5

A. Urb 695
Cic 50
Coſſ
P Cor elius
Lentulus
Spinther,
Q Cecilius
Metellus
Nepos

of gratitude, as well as prudence, to be more ob-
ſervant of them than he had hitherto been　the
ſenate, on the other hand, with the Magiſtrates,
and the honeſt of all ranks, were zealous in his
cauſe, and the *Conful Lentulus* above all ſeemed
to make it *the ſole end and glory of his adminiſtra-*
tion [b] This uncommon conſent of oppoſite
parties in promoting his reſtoration, drew upon
him *a variety of obligations, which muſt needs often*
croſs and interfere with each other, and which it
was his part ſtill to manage ſo, as to make them
conſiſtent with his honour, his ſafety, his private,
and his public duty　theſe were to be the ſprings
and motives of his *new life*, the hinges on which
his future conduct was to turn, and to do juſtice
ſeverally to them all, and aſſign to each *its proper*
weight and meaſure of influence, required his utmoſt ſkill and addreſs [c]

The day after his arrival, *on the fifth of Sep-*
tember, the Conſuls ſummoned the Senate, to
give him an opportunity of paying his thanks to
them in public for their late ſervices, where,
after a general profeſſion of his obligations to them
all, he made his particular acknowledgments to
each Magiſtrate by name, *to the Conſuls, the*
Tribuns, the Praetors　he addreſſed himſelf *to*
the Tribuns, before the *Praetors*, not for the dignity of their office, for in that they were inferior,
but for their greater authority in making laws;
and conſequently, their greater merit in carrying

[b] Hoc ſpecimen virtu-
tis, vel cum am....... vere la-
mentis ....
.... me minim a men... in
Populo redduntur —— Poſt
red in ſen. i

[c] Sed cum ſaepe conſi-
deres, prop... eorum de me
meritor... .... ſo conten-
tiones, ut eodem tempore in
omnes vereor ne vix poſſim
gratus videri　Sed ego hoc
nec ponderibus exam nabo,
non ſolum quid cuique de-
beam, ſed etiam quid cujuſ-
que merit, & quid a me cu-
jaſque tempſ poſcat　Pro
Plancio 32

his law into effect The number of his private
friends *was too great to make it possible for him to*
enumerate or thank them all, so that he confined
himself to the Magistrates, with exception only to
Pompey [d], whom for the eminence of his character, though at present only a private man, he
took care to distinguish by a personal address and
compliment But as Lentulus was the first in
office, and had served him with the greatest affection, so he gives him *the first share of his praise*,
and in the overflowing of his gratitude stiles him,
the Parent and the God of his life and fortunes [e]
The next day he paid his thanks likewise to the
people, in a speech from *the Rostra*, where he
dwelt chiefly on the same topics which he had
used in the senate, celebrating the particular
merits and services of his principal friends, especially *of Pompey*, whom he declares to be the
greatest man for virtue, wisdom, glory, who was
then living, or had lived, or ever would live, and
that he owed more to him on this occasion, than it
was even lawful almost, for one man to owe to an-
other [f]

A Urb 696.
Cic 50
Coss
P Cornelius
Ifniulus
Spinther,
Q Cæcilius
Metellus
Nepos.

[d] Cum perpaucis nomi-
natim gratias egissem, quod
omnes enumerari nullo modo
possent, scelus autem esset
quenquam præteriri ―ib 30
  Hodierno autem die nominatim a me Magistratibus sta-
tui gratias esse agendas, & de
privatis uni, qui pro salute mea
municipia, coloniasque adi-
isset ―Post red in Sen 12
  [e] Princeps P *Lentulus*,
parens ac *Deus* nostræ vitæ,
fortunæ, &c ib 4 It was a
kind of maxim among the
ancients that *to do good to a*
mortal, was to be a God to a
mortal Deus est mortali ju-
vare mortalem [Plin H
2 7] Thus *Cicero*, as he
calls *Lentulus* here his *God*, so
on other occasions gives the
same appellation to *Plato*
Deus ille noster Plato― [ad
Att 4 16] to express the
highest sense of the benefits
received from them
  [f] Cn Pompeius, vir
omnium qui sunt, fuerunt,
erunt, princeps virtute, sa-
pientia, ac gloria ― Huic
ego homini Quirites, tantum
debeo quantum hominem ho-
mini debere vix fas est Post
red ad Quir 7

A. U. C. 696
C c 56
C c T
P. Cornelius
Lentulus
Spinther,
Q. Cæcilius
Metellus
Nepos

BOTH these speeches are still extant, and a passage or two from each will illustrate the temper and disposition in which he returned—in speaking to the Senate, after a particular recital of the services of his friends, he adds, " as I have a pleasure in enumerating these, so I willingly pass over in silence what others wickedly acted against me—it is not my present business to remember injuries, which if it were in my power to revenge, I should chuse to forget, my life shall be applied to other purposes, to repay the good offices of those who have deserved it of me, to hold fast the friendships which have been tried as it were in the fire, to wage war with declared enemies, to pardon my timorous, nor yet expose my treacherous friends, and to balance the misery of my exil by the dignity of my return—[g] " To the people he observes, " that there were four sorts of enemies, who concurred to oppress him—the first, who, out of hatred to the Republic, were mortal enemies to him for having saved it—the second, who, under a false pretence of friendship, infamously betrayed him—the third, who, through their inability to obtain what he had acquired, were envious of his dignity—the fourth, who, though by office they ought to have been the guardians of the Republic, bartered away his safety, the peace of the City, and the dignity of the Empire, which were committed to their trust—I will take my revenge, says he, on each of them, agreeably to the different manner of their provocation, on the bad Citizens, by defending the Republic strenuously, on my perfidious friends, by never trusting them again, on the envious, by continuing my steady pursuit of virtue and

                                                  " glory,

" gloiy, on thofe Merchants of Piovinces, by
" calling them home to give an account of their
" adminiftration but I am moie follicitous how
" to acquit myfelf of my obligations to you, for
" your great fervices, than to refent the injuries
" and cruelties of my enemies for it is much
" eafiei to revenge an injury than to iepay a
" kindnefs. and much lefs trouble to get the
" better of bad men than to equal the good [*h*] "

A Urb 696.
Cic 50
Coff
P Cornelius
Lentulus
Spinther,
Q Cæcilius
Metflius
Nepos.

This affair being happily ovei, the Senate had leifure again to attend to public bufinefs, and there was now a cafe before them of a very urgent nature, which required a prefent remedy; *an unufual fcarcity of corn and piovifions* in the City, which had been greatly encreafed by the late concourfe of people from all parts of *Italy*, on Cicero's account, and was now felt very feveiely by the poor Citizens They had born it with much patience while Cicero's return was in agitation, comforting themfelves with a notion, that if he was once ieftored, plenty would be reftored with him, but finding the one at laft effected without the other, they began to grow clamorous, and unable to endure their hunger any longer

Clodius could not let flip fo fair an opportunity of exciting fome new difturbance, and cieate ing frefh trouble to Cicero, by charging the calamity to his *fcore* · for this end he employed a number of young fellows to run all night about the ftreets, making a lamentable outcry for bread, and calling upon Cicero to relieve them from the famine to which he had reduced them, as if he had got fome hidden ftore or magazine of corn, fecreted fiom common ufe [*i*]. He
fent

[*h*] Poft red ad Quir 9 ad imperitorum animos inci-
[*i*] Qui facultate oblata, tandos, renovaturum te illa
funefta

B 3

sent his mob also to the Theatre, in which *the Prætor Cæcilius*, Cicero's particular friend, was exhibiting *the Apolhoman frews*, where they raised such a terror that they drove the whole company out of it then, in the same tumultuous manner, they marched to the Temple of CONCORD, whither Metellus had summoned the Senate, but happening to meet with Metellus in the way, they presently attacked him with vollies of stones, with some of which they wounded even the Conful himself, who, for the greater security, immediately adjourned the Senate into the *Capitol.* They were led on by two desperate Ruffians, their usual commanders, M Lollius and M. Sergius the first of whom had in Clodius's Tribunate undertaken the task of killing Pompey; the second had been Captain of the Guard to Catiline, and was probably of his family [k] but Clodius, encouraged by this hopeful beginning, put himself at their head in person, and pursued the Senate into the *Capito'*, in order to disturb their debates, and prevent their providing any relief for the present evil, and above all, to excite the meaner fort *to some violence against Cicero.*

funesta introic r a ob arronæ ca. . . . puta isti Pro dom 5

Q . puerorum i la con-cur o ned ura nam a e p. . t. . me frumentam fag abent Quasi vero ego au ru fumentar æ præfuifer au con pre sum aliquod f un ea um tencrem Ib 6

[ ] Cum nomines ad I he ction pri mo, a nde ad Senatum con cur sient impulia Coch Ad at . . .

Concurs s et ad Templum Corcures facu, Senatum h uc ecante M. ello— qui

sunt homines a Q Metello, in Senatu palam nominati, a quibus ille se lapidibus appetium, etiam percusfam esse dixit —Quis est iste Lollius? Qui te Tribuno pleb —Cn Pompeium interfic endum depoposcit —Quis est Sergius? armiger Catilinæ, stipa ur tui corporis, signifer seditionis—h s atque hujosmodi ducibus, cum tu in annona caritate in Consules, in Senatum— repen nos impetu, comparares —pro dem 5

But he foon found, to his great difappointment, that Cicero was too ftrong in the affections of the City to be hurt again fo foon for the people themfelves faw through his defign, and were fo provoked at it, *that they turned univerfally againft him, and drove him out of the field, with all his mercenaries,* when perceiving that Cicero *was not prefent in the Senate, they called out upon him by name with one voice, and would not be quieted till he came in perfon to undertake their caufe, and propofe fome expedient for their relief* He had kept *his houfe all that day, and refolved to do fo, till he faw the iffue of the tumult,* but when he underftood that Clodius *was repulfed, and that his prefence was univerfally required by the Confuls, the Senate, and the whole People, he came to the Senatehoufe, in the midft of their debates, and being prefently afked his opinion,* propofed, *that Pompey fhould be entreated to undertake the province of reftoring plenty to the City, and, to enable him to execute it with effect, fhould be invefted with an abfolute power over all the public ftores and corn-rents of the Empire through all the Provinces* the motion *was readily accepted, and a vote immediately paffed, that a law fhould be prepared for that purpofe, and offered to the people* [*l*]. *All the Confular Senators*

B 4   *were*

A Urb 696.
Cic 50
Coff
P CORNELIUS
LENTULUS
SPINTHER,
Q CÆCILIUS
METELLUS
NEPOS.

[*l*] Ego vero domi me tenui, quamdiu turbulentum tempus fuit— cum fervos tuos ad rapinam, ad bonorum cædem paratos— armatos etiam in Capitolium tecum venife conftabat— fcio me domi manfiffe —— pofteaquam mihi nunciatum eft, populum Romanum in Capitolium— convenife, miniftros autem fcelerum tuorum perterritos, partim amiffis gladiis, partim ereptis diffugiffe, veni non folum fine ullis copiis, ac manu, verum etiam cum paucis amicis —Ib 3

Ego denique — a populo Romano univerfo, qui tum in Capitolium convenerat, cum illo die minus valerem, nominatim in Senatum vocabar Veni expectatus, multis jam fententiis dictis, rogatus fum fententiam, dixi Reipub faluberrimam, mihi neceffarium Ib 7

Factum

A Urb 696
Cic o
Coſſ
P CORNELIUS
LENTULUS
SPINTHER,
Q CÆCILIUS
METELLUS
NEPOS

were abſent, except *Meſſala and Afranius* they pretended to be afraid of the mob, but the real cauſe was their unwillingneſs to concur in granting this commiſſion to *Pompey* The Conſuls carried the decree with them *into the Roſtra*, and read it publicly to the people, *who on the mention of Cicero's name, in which it was drawn, gave an univerſal ſhout of applauſe, upon which, at the deſire of all the Magiſtrates, Cicero made a ſpeech to them,* ſetting forth the reaſons and neceſſity of the decree, and giving them the comfort of a ſpeedy relief, from the vigilance and authority of Pompey [m] The abſence however of the Conſular Senators gave a handle to reflect upon the act, *as not free and valid, but extorted by fear, and without the intervention of the principal members,* the very next day, in a fuller Houſe, when all *the Senators were preſent, and a motion was made for re ſame decree, it was* unanimouſly rejected [n], and the Conſuls were ordered to draw up a law conformable to it, by which *the whole adminiſtration of the corn and proviſions of the Republic was to be granted to Pompey for five years, with a power of chuſing fifteen Lieutenants to aſſiſt him in it.*

This furniſhed Clodius with freſh matter of abuſe upon Cicero he charged him *with ingratitude, and the deſertion of the Senate, which had*

Factum eſt S C in meam ſententiam, ut cum Pompeio ageretur ut eam rem ſuſciperet leſque ferretur Ad Att 4 1

[m] Cum abeſſent Conſules q od tuto ſe negarent poſſe ſe commendare, propter Meſſalam & Afranium It u

Q o S C recitato cum continuo more noc inſullo & ſoſo plauſum, nico nomine

rec tando dediſſet, habui concionem ————Ibid

[n] At enim l berum Senatus judicium propter metum non fu t Pro dom 4

Poſtridie Senatus frequens, & omnes Conſulares nihil Pompeio poſtulanti negarunt Ad Att 4 1

Cum omnes adeſſent, captum eſt referri de inducendo S C ab univerſo Senatu reclamatum eſt Pro dom 4
always

always been firm to him, in order to pay his court to
a man, who had betrayed him · and that he was so
silly, as not to know his own strength and credit in
the City, and how able he was to maintain his authority without the help of Pompey [o] But Cicero defended himself by saying, " that they must
" not expect to play the same game upon him
" now that he was restored, with which they
" had ruined him before, by raising jealousies
" between him and Pompey that he had smarted
" for it too severely already, to be caught again
" in the same trap , that, in decreeing this com-
" mission to Pompey, he had discharged both
" his private obligations to a friend, and his pub-
" lic duty to the State , that those who grudged
" all extraordinary power to Pompey, must
" grudge the victories, the triumphs, the ac-
" cession of dominion and revenue, which their
" former grants of this sort had procured to the
" Empire; that the success of those shewed,
" what fruit they were to expect from this [p] "

BUT what authority soever this law conferred
on Pompey, his creatures were not yet satisfied
with it, so that Messius, one of the Tribuns,
proposed another, to give him the additional
power *of raising what money, fleets, and armes he*

A Urb 696
Cic 50.
Coss
P CORNELIUS
LENTULUS
SPINTHER,
Q CÆCILIUS
METELLUS
NEPOS

[o] Tune es ille, inquit,
quo Senatus carere non potuit ꞓ—quo restituto, Senatus
auctoritatem restitutam puta-
bamus ? quam primum adve-
niens prodidisti Ib 2

Nescit quantum auctoritate
valeat, quas res gesserit, qua
dignitate sit restitutus Cur
ornat cum a quo desertus est?
Ib 11

[p] Desinant homines iis-
dem machinis sperare me re-
stitutum posse labefactari,qui-
bus antea stantem perculerunt
—data merces est erroris mei
magna, ut me non solum pi-
geat stultitia meæ, sed etiam
pudeat Ib 11

Cn Pompeio——maxima
terra marique bella extra ordinem esse commissa quarum
rerum si quem pœniteat, eum
victoria populi Romani necesse est pœnitere Ib 8

thought

A Urb 696
C.c 50
Cof.
P CORNELIUS
LENTULUS
SPINTER,
Q CÆCILIUS
METELLUS
NEPOS

thought fit , with a greater command through all the Provinces, than their proper Governors had in each Cicero's laws feemed modeft in comparifon of Meffius's: Pompey pretended to be content with the firft, whilft all his dependents were pufhing for the laft; they expected that Cicero would come over to them; but he continued filent, nor would ftir a ftep farther, for his affairs were ftill in fuch a ftate, as obliged him to act with caution, and to manage both the Senate and the men of power · the conclufion was, that Cicero's law was received by all parties, *and Pompey named him for his firft Lieutenant, declaring that he fhould confider him as a fecond felf, and act nothing without his advice* [q]. *Cicero accepted the employment, on condition that he might be at liberty to ufe or refign it at pleafure, as he found it convenient to his affairs* [r] but he foon after quitted it to his Brother, and chofe to continue in the city; where he had the pleafure to fee the end of his law effectually anfwered for the credit of Pompey's name immediately reduced the price of victuals in the markets; and his vigor and diligence in profecuting the affair foon eftablifhed a general plenty.

CICERO was reftored to his former dignity, but not to his former fortunes, nor was any fatiffaction yet made to him for the ruin of his

---

[q] Legem Confules confcripferunt—alteram Meffius, qua omnis pecuræ dat poteftatem, & adjungit claffem & exercitum, & majus imperium in provinciis quam fit eorum, qui eas obtinent Illa noftra lex Confularis nunc modefta videtur, hæc Meffii non ferenda Pompeius illam velle fe dicit, Familiares hanc Confulares duce Favonio fremunt, nos tace-

mus, & eo magis quod de domo noftra nihil adhuc Pontifices refponderunt —

Ille legatos quindecim cum poftularet, me principem nominavit, & ad omnia me alterum fe fore dixit ——Ad Att 4 1

[r] Ego me a Pompeio legari ita fum paffus, ut nulla re impedirer, quod re fi vellem, mini effet integrum — Id 2

houfes and eftates a full reftitution indeed had
been decreed, but was referved to his return ,
which came now before the Senate to be confidered and fettled by public authority, where it
met ftill with great obftruction The chief difficulty was about his *Palatin houfe*, which he valued above all the reft, and which Clodius, for
that reafon, had contrived to alienate, as he hoped,
irretrievably , by demolifhing the Fabric, *and*
dedicating a Temple upon the area to the Goddefs
Liberty where, to make his work the more complete, he pulled down alfo the adjoining *portico*
of Catullus, that he might build it up anew, of
the fame order with his Temple ; and by blend-
ing the public with private property, and *confe-*
crating the whole to Religion, might make it impoffible to feparate or reftore any part to Cicero ;
fince a confecration, legally performed, made the
thing confecrated unapplicable ever after to any
private ufe

THIS portico was built, as has been faid, on the
fpot where Fulvius Flaccus formerly lived, whofe
houfe was publicly demolifhed, for the treafon
of its mafter , and it was Clodius's defign *to join*
Cicero's to it under the fame denomination , as the
perpetual memorial of a difgrace and punifhment in-
flicted by the people [s] When he had finifhed the
portico therefore, and annexed his Temple to it,
which took up but a fmall part, *fcarce a tenth, of*
Cicero's houfe, he left the reft of the area void,
in order *to plant a grove, or walks of pleafure upon*
it, as has been ufual in fuch cafes , where, as it
has been obferved, he was profecuting a particular intereft, as well as indulging his malice in ob-
ftructing the reftitution of it to Cicero.

[s] Ut domus M Tullii publicc conftitutæ conjuncta
Ciceronis cum domo Fulvii efte videatur Pro dom 38
Flacci ad memoriam pœnæ

A Urb 696
Cic 50
Coff
P CORNELIUS
LENTULUS
SPINTHER,
Q CÆCILIUS
METELLUS
NEPOS

THE

A U b 696
Cic 50
Coſſ
P CORNELIUS
LENTULUS
SPINTHER,
Q CECILIUS
METELLUS
NEPOS

THE affair was to be determined by *the college of Priests*, who were the Judges in all cafes relating to religion for the Senate could only make a provifional decree, *that if the Priefts difcharged the ground from the fervice of religion, then the Confuls fhould take an eftimate of the damage, and make a contract for rebuilding the whole ct the public charge, fo as to reftore it to Cicero in the condition in which he left it* [t] The *Priefts* therefore of all orders were called together *on the laft of September*, to hear this caufe, which Cicero pleaded in perfon before them they were men of the firft dignity and families in the Republic, and there never was, as Cicero tells us, *fo full an appearance of them in any caufe, fince the foundation of the City* he reckons up *nineteen* by name, a great part of whom were of *Confular rank* [u] His firft care, before he entered into the merits of the queftion, was to remove the prejudices, which his enemies had been labouring to inftil, on the account of his late conduct in favour of Pompey, by explaining the motives, and fhewing the neceffity of it, contriving at the fame time to turn the odium on the other fide, by running over *the hiftory of Clodius's Tribunate*, and painting all its violences in the moft lively colours, but the queftion on which the caufe fingly turned, *was about the efficacy of the pretended confecration of the houfe, and the dedication of the Temple:* to fhew the nullity therefore of this act, he endeavours to overthrow the very foundation of it, " and prove Clodius s Tribunate to be original-

[t] Qui fi fuftulerint religiorem, aream præclaram habebimus fuperficiem Confules ex S C æftimabunt — Aa Att 4 1

[u] Nego unquam poft facra conftituta, quorum eadem eft antiquitas, quæ ipfius urbis, ulla de re, ne de capite quidem Virginum Veftalium, tam frequens collegium judicaffe De Harufp refp 6, 7

" ly

A. Urb 696.
Cic 50
Coſſ
P Cornelius
Lentulus
Spinther,
Q Cæcilius
Metellus
Nepos

" ly null and void, from the *invalidity of his*
" *adoption,* on which it was entirely grounded ."
he ſhews, " that the ſole end of adoption, which
" the laws acknowledged, was to ſupply the
" want of children, by borrowing them as it
" were from other families, that it was an eſſen-
" tial condition of it, that he who adopted had
" no children of his own, nor was in condition
" to have any · that the parties concerned were
" obliged to appear before the Prieſts to ſignify
" their conſent, the cauſe of the adoption, the
" circumſtances of the families intereſted in it,
" and the nature of their religious rites, that the
" Prieſts might judge of the whole, and ſee that
" there was no fraud or deceit in it, nor any diſ-
" honour to any family or perſon concerned ·
" that nothing of all this had been obſerved in
" the caſe of Clodius . that the Adopter was not
" full twenty years old, when he adopted a Se-
" nator, who was old enough to be his father :
" that he had no occaſion to adopt, ſince he had
" a wife and children, and would probably have
" more, which he muſt neceſſarily diſinherit by
" this adoption, if it was real   that Clodius had
" no other view, than, by the pretence of an
" adoption, to make himſelf *a Plebeian* and *Tri-*
" *bun,* in order to overturn the State, that the
" act itſelf, which confirmed the adoption, was
" null and illegal, being tranſacted while Bibu-
" lus was obſerving the Auſpices, which was
" contrary to expreſs law, and huddled over in
" three hours by Cæſar, when it ought to have
" been publiſhed for three market days ſucceſ-
" ſively, at the interval of nine days each [x]
" that if the adoption was irregular and illegal,
" as it certainly was, the Tribunate muſt needs

[x] Pro dom   14, 15, 16

" be

A Urb 696
C.c 50.
Coss
P Cornelius
Lentulus
Spinther,
Q Cæcilius
Metellus
Nepo.

" be so too, which was intirely built upon it .
" but granting the Tribunate after all to be valid,
" because some eminent men would have it so,
" yet the act made afterwards for his banishment
" could not possibly be considered as a law, but
" as a *Privilege* only, made against a particular
" person, which the sacred laws, and the laws
" of the twelve Tables had utterly prohibited ·
" that it was contrary to the very constitution of
" the Republic, to punish any Citizen either in
" body or goods, till he had been accused in
" proper form, and condemned of some crime
" by competent judges that *Privileges*, or laws
" to inflict penalties on single persons by name,
" without a legal trial, were cruel and pernicious,
" and nothing better than proscriptions, and of
" all things not to be endured in their City [y]."
Then in entering upon the question of his house
he declares, " that the whole effect of his resto-
" ration depended upon it, that if it was not
" given back to him, but suffered to remain a
" monument of triumph to his enemy, of grief
" and calamity to himself, he could not consider
" it as a restoration, but a perpetual punishment:
" that his house stood in the view of the whole
" people, and if it must continue in its present
" state, he should be forced to remove to some
" other place, and could never endure to live in
" that City, in which he must always see tro-
" phies erected both against himself and the Re-
" public the house of Sp Melius," says he,
" who affected a Tyranny, was levelled, and
" by the name of *Æquimelium*, given to the place,
" the people confirmed the Equity of his punish-
" ment the house of Sp Cassius was overturn-

[y] . . . . est injustius? de Legib.
. . . .
. . . .

" ed

A Urb 696.
Cic 50
Coff
P Cornelius
Lentulus
Spinther,
Q Cæcilius
Meteilus
Nepos

" ed alfo for the fame caufe, and a Temple raif-
" ed upon it to Tellus · M. Vaccus's houfe was
" confifcated and levelled , and, to perpetuate
" the memory of his treafon, the place is ftill
" called Vaccus's meadows · M Manlius like-
" wife, after he had repulfed the *Gauls* from the
" *Capitol,* not content with the glory of that
" fervice, was adjudged to aim at dominion , fo
" that his houfe was demolifhed, where you now
" fee the two groves planted muft I therefore
" fuffer that punifhment, which our Anceftors
" inflicted as the greateft, on wicked and traite-
" rous Citizens , that pofterity may confider me,
" not as the oppreffor, but the author and captain
" of the Confpiracy [z] ?" When he comes to
fpeak to the dedication itfelf, he obferves, " that
" the Goddefs LIBERTY, to which the Temple
" was dedicated, was the known ftatue of a cele-
" brated ftrumpet, which Appius brought from
" *Greece* for the ornament of his Ædilefhip : and
" upon dropping the thoughts of that magiftra-
" cy, gave to his brother Clodius, to be advan-
" ced into a Deity [a] that the ceremony was
" performed without any licence or judgement
" obtained from the College of Priefts, by the
" fingle miniftry of a raw young man, the bro-
" ther-in-law of Clodius, who had been made
" Prieft but a few days before , a mere novice
" in his bufinefs, and forced into the fervice [b]:
" but if all had been tranfacted regularly, and
" in due form, that it could not poffibly have
" any force, as being contrary to the ftanding
" laws of the Republic for there was an old
" Tribunician law, made by Q Papirius, which
" prohibited the confecration of houfes, lands, or
" altars, without the exprefs command of the

[z] Pro dom 37, 38   [b] Ib 45.
[a] Ib 43

" people;

A Urb 695
Cic 50
Coſ
P Cornelius
Lentulus
Spinther,
Q Cæcilius
Metellus
Nepos

" people, which was not obtained, nor even
" pretended in the present case [c]. that great
" regard had always been paid to this law in se-
" veral instances of the gravest kind that Q.
" Marcius, the Censor, erected a Statue of Con-
" cord in a public part of the City, which C
" Caſſius afterwards, when Censor, removed into
" the Senate-house, and consulted the College
" of Priests, whether he might not dedicate the
" statue, and the house also itself, to Concord.
" upon which M Æmilius, the High-Priest,
" gave answer in the name of the College, that
" unless the people had deputed him by name,
" and he acted in it by their authority, they
" were of opinion, that he could not rightly de-
" dicate them [d] that Licinia also, a vestal
" virgin, dedicated an altar, and a little temple,
" under the sacred Rock upon which S. Julius
" the Prætor, by order of the Senate, consulted
" the College of Priests, for whom P Scævola,
" the High-Priest, gave answer, that what Li-
" cinia had dedicated in a public place, without
" any order of the people, could not be consi-
" dered as sacred so that the Senate injoined
" the Prætor to see it desecrated, and to efface
" whatever had been inscribed upon it after all
" this, it was to no purpose, he tells them, to
" mention, what he had proposed to speak to in
" the last place, that the dedication was not per-
" formed with any of the solemn words and rites
" which such a function required, but by the ig-
" norant young man before-mentioned, without
" the help of his Collegues, his books, or any
" to prompt him especially when Clodius, who
" directed him, that impure enemy of all reli-
" gion, who often acted the woman among
" men, as well as the man among women, hud-

[c] Pro dom 49 [d] Ib 50, 53

" dled

" dled over the whole ceremony in a blundering,
" precipitate manner, faultring and confounded
" in mind, voice, and speech, often recalling
" himself, doubting, fearing, hesitating, and
" performing every thing quite contrary to what
" the sacred books prescribed nor is it strange,
" says he, that, in an act so mad and villainous,
" his audaciousness could not get the better of
" his fears. for what Pirate, though ever so
" barbarous, after he had been plundering Tem-
" ples, when pricked by a dream, or scruple of
" religion, he came to consecrate some altar on
" a desert shore, was not terrified in his mind, on
" being forced to appease that Deity by his pray-
" ers, whom he had provoked by his sacrilege?
" In what horrors then, think you, must this
" man needs be, the plunderer of all Temples,
" houses, and the whole City, when for the ex-
" piation of so many impieties, he was wickedly
" consecrating one single altar [e]? Then after a
" solemn invocation and appeal to all the Gods,
" who peculiarly favoured and protected that City,
" to bear witness to the integrity of his zeal and
" love to the Republic, and that, in all his labours
" and struggles, he had constantly preferred the
" public benefit to his own, he commits the
" justice of his cause to the judgement of the
" venerable Bench "

HE was particularly pleased with the composition of this speech, which he published immediately, and says upon it, that if ever he made
any figure in speaking, his indignation, and the
sense of his injuries, had inspired him with new
force and spirit in this cause [f]. The sentence
of

A Urb 696
Cic 50
Cosl
P CORNELIUS
LENTULUS
SPINTHER,
Q CÆCILIUS
METELLUS
NEPOS

---

[e] Pro dom 54, 55   a nobis, & si urquam in di-
[f] Acta res est accurate   cendo fuimus aliquid, aut

A Urb 696
Cic 50
Coſſ
P Corelius
Lentulus
Spinther
Q Cæcilius
Metellus
Nepos

of the Prieſts turned wholly on what Cicero had alledged about the force of *the Papirian law*; viz. *that if he, who performed the office of conſecration, had not been ſpecially authoriſed and perſonally appointed to it by the people, then the area in queſtion might, without any ſcruple of religion, be reſtored to Cicero.* This though it ſeemed ſomewhat evaſive, was ſufficient for Cicero's purpoſe, *and his friends congratulated him upon it, as upon a clear victory*, while Clodius interpreted it ſtill in favour of himſelf, and being produced *into the Roſtra*, by his Brother Appius, acquainted the people, *that the Prieſts had given judgement for him, but that Cicero was preparing to recover poſſeſſion by force, and exhorted them therefore to follow him and Appius in the defence of their liberties.* But his ſpeech made no impreſſion on the audience; *ſome wondred at his impudence, others laughed at his folly, and Cicero reſolved not to trouble himſelf, or the people about it, till the Conſuls, by a decree of the Senate, had contracted for rebuilding the portico of Catulus* [g].

THE Senate met the next day, in a full houſe, to put an end to this affair, when Marcellinus,

---

etiam ſi unquam alias fuimus, tum profecto dolor & magnitudo vim quandam nobis dicendi dedit itaque Oratio invertuti noſtræ deberi non poteſt Ad Att 4 2

[g] Cum Pontifices decreſſent, ita ſi neque populi juſſu, reque plebis ſcitu, is qui ſe dicaſſe diceret, nominatim ei rei præfectus eſſet, neque populi juſſu neque plebis ſcito id facere juſſus eſſet videri poſſe ſine religione eam partem area mihi reſtitui

Mihi facta ſtatim eſt gratulatio nemo enim dubitat, quin domus nobis eſſet adjudicata Tum ſubito ille in concionem aſcendit, quam Appius ei dedit nunciat jam populo, Pontifices ſecundum ſe decreviſſe, me autem vi conari in poſſeſſionem venire hortatur, ut ſe & Appium ſequantur, & ſuam libertatem id defendant Hic cum etiam illi infimi partim admirarentur, partim irriderent hominis amentiam —Ad Att 4 2

one of the Confuls elect, being called upon to
fpeak firft, addreffed himfelf *to the Priefts, and
defired them to give an account of the grounds and
meaning of their fentence* upon which Lucullus,
in the name of the reft, declared, *that the Priefts
were indeed the Judges of religion, but the Senate of
the law; that they therefore had determined only
what related to the point of religion, and left it to
the Senate to determine whether any obftacle remained in point of law* all the other priefts fpoke
largely after him in favor of Cicero's caufe when
Clodius rofe afterwards to fpeak, he endeavoured
to waft the time fo, as to hinder their coming to
any refolution that day, but after he had been
fpeaking *for three hours* fucceffively, the affembly
grew fo impatient, and made fuch a noife and
hiffing, that he was forced to give over. yet
when they were going to pafs a decree, in *the
words of Marcellinus, Serranus put his negative
upon it ·* this raifed an univerfal indignation, and
a frefh debate began, at the motion of the Two
Confuls, *on the merit of the Tribun's interceffion,*
when after many warm fpeeches, they came to
the following vote; *that it was the refolution of
that Senate, that Cicero's houfe fhould be reftored to
him, and Catulus's portico rebuilt, as it had been
before, and that this vote fhould be defended by all
the Magiftrates, and if any violence or obftruction
was offered to it, that the Senate would look upon it,
as offered by him, who had interpofed his negative.*
This ftaggered Serranus, and the late Farce was
played over again, *his father threw himfelf at his
feet, to beg him to defift, he defired a night's time;*
which at firft was refufed, but, on Cicero's requeft, granted, and the next day he revoked his
negative, and, without farther oppofition, fuffered the Senate to pafs a decree, *that Cicero's da-*

A Urb 966
Cic 50
Coff
P Cornelius
Lentulus
Spinther,
Q Cæcilius
Metellus
Nepo

mage

A. U. C. 696
Cic. 50
Coss.
P. Cornelius
Lentulus
Spinther,
Q. Caecilius
Metellus
Nepos.

ing should be made good to him, and his houses re-
vived at the public charge [h]

THE Consuls began presently to put the decree in execution, and having contracted for the rebuilding *Catulus's portico,* set men to work, *upon clearing the ground, and demolishing what had been built by Clodius* but as to Cicero's buildings, it was agreed to take an estimate of his damage, and pay the amount of it to himself, to be laid out according to his own fancy in which *his Palatin house was valued at sixteen thousand pounds; his Tusculan at four thousand, his Formian only at two thousand* This was a very deficient and shameful valuation, *which all the world cried out upon,* for *the Palatin house* had cost him, not long before, near twice that sum. but Cicero would not give himself any trouble about it, or make any exceptions, which gave the Consuls a handle to throw the blame upon *his own modesty, for not remonstrating against it, and seeming to be satisfied with what was awarded* but the true reason was, as he himself declares, *that those, who had clipt his wings, had no mind to let them grow again; and though they had been his advocates when absent, began now to be secretly angry, and openly envious of him when present* [i].

---

[h] Ad Att. 4. 2
[i] Nobis superficiem ædium Coss. de consilii senten-tiâ æstimârunt HS vicies, cætera valde illiberaliter, Tusculanam villam quingen-tis millibus, Formianam du-centis quinquaginta millibus, quæ æstimatio non modo ab optimo quoque sed etiam a plebe reprehenditur Dices,

quid igitur causæ fuit? Di-cunt illi quidem pudorem meum, quod neque negarim, neque vehementius postula-rim Sed non est id, nam hoc quidem etiam profuisset Verum idem, mi Pomponi, idem inquam illi, qui mihi pennas inciderunt, nolunt e-asdem renasci—Ibid

BUT

BUT as he was never covetous, this affair gave him no great uneasiness, though, through the late ruin of his fortunes, he was now in such want of money, that he resolved *to expose his Tusculan Villa to sale*, but soon changed his mind and built it up again with much more magnificence than before, and, for the beauty of its situation, and neighbourhood to the City, took more pleasure in it ever after, than in any other of his country seats But he had some domestic grievances about this time, which touched him more nearly, and which, as he signifies obscurely to Atticus, *were of too delicate a nature to be explained by a letter* [k] they arose chiefly from the petulant humor of his wife, which began to give him frequent occasions of chagrin, and, by a series of repeated provocations, confirmed in him that settled disgust, which ended at last in a divorce

As he was now restored to the possession both of his dignity and fortunes, so he was desirous to destroy all the public monuments of his late disgrace, nor to suffer the *law of his exil* to remain, with the other acts of *Clodius's Tribunate*, hanging up *in the Capitol*, engraved, as usual, on tables of brass . watching therefore the opportunity of Clodius's absence, *he went to the Capitol, with a strong body of his friends, and taking the tables down conveyed them to his own house* This occasioned a sharp contest in the Senate between him and Clodius, about *the validity of those acts*, and drew Cato also into the debate ; who, for the sake of *his Cyprian commission, thought himself obliged to defend their legality against Cicero, which*

A Urb 696.
Cic 50
Coss
P CORNELIUS
LENTULUS
SPINTHER,
Q CÆCILIUS
METELLUS
NEPOS

[*l*] Tusculanum proscripsi suburbano non facile careo -- cetera, quæ me sollicitant, νενικωτ-αα sunt Amamur a fratie & sua Ibid

created

A Urb 696
Cic 50
Coff
P Cornelius
Lentulus
Spinther,
Q Cæcilius
Metellus
Nepos

created some little coldness between them, and gave no small pleasure to the common enemies of them both [*l*]

BUT Cicero's chief concern at present was, how to support his former authority in the City, and provide for his future safety; as well against the malice of declared enemies, as the envy of pretended friends, which he perceived to be growing up afresh against him. he had thoughts of putting in for *the Censorship*, *or of procuring one of those honorary Lieutenancies*, which gave a public character to private Senators, with intent to make a progress through *Italy*, *or a kind of religious pilgrimage to all the Temples, Groves, and sacred places, on pretence of a vow, made in his exile.* This would give him an opportunity of shewing himself every where in a light, which naturally attracts the afection of the multitude, by testifying a pious regard to the favourite superstitions and local religions of the Country, as the Great, in the same Country, still pay their court to the vulgar, by visiting the shrines and altars of the Saints, which are most in vogue· he mentions these projects to Atticus, as designed to be executed in the spring, resolving in the mean while to cherish the good inclination of the people towards him, by keeping himself perpetually in the view of the City [*m*]

Catulus's portico, and Cicero's house, were rising again apace, and carried up almost to the roof; when Clodius, without any warning, attacked them, *on the second of November, with a band of*

[*l*] Plutarch in Cic Dio p 1co

[*r*] Ut nulla re impedirer, quod ne civellem mihi esset integrum aut secum a Censorum proximi Consules haberent, petere posse, aut Votiam Legationem sumsisse prope omnium Fanorum, lucorum Ad Att 4 2

armed

A Urb 696
Cic 50
Coff
P CORNELIUS
LENTULUS
SPINTHER.
Q CECILIUS
METELLUS
NEPOS.

armed men, who demolished the portico, and drove the workmen out of Cicero's ground, and with the stones and rubbish of the place began to batter Quintus's house, with whom Cicero then lived, and at last set fire to it, so that the two Brothers, with their families, were forced to save themseves by a hasty flight. Milo had already accused Clodius for his former violences, and resolved, if possible, to bring him to justice Clodius, on the other hand, was suing for *the Ædileship*, to secure himself, for one year more at least, from any prosecution he was sure of being condemned, if ever he was brought to trial, *so that whatever mischief he did in the mean time was all clear gain, and could not make his cause the worse* [*n*] · he now therefore gave a free course to his natural fury, was perpetually scouring the streets with his incendiaries, *and threatning fire and sword to the City itself, if an assembly was not called for the election of Ædiles* In this humor, about a week after his last outrage, *on the eleventh of November*, happening to meet with Cicero, in the sacred street, he presently assaulted him *with stones, clubs, and drawn swords* · Cicero was not prepared for the encounter, and took refuge in the Vestibule of the next house, where his attendants rallying in his defence, beat off the assailants, *and could easily have killed their Leader, but that Cicero was willing*, he says, *to cure by diet, rather than Surgery* The day following Clodius

---

[*r*] Armatis hominibus ante diem III Non Novemb expulsi sunt fabri de area nostra, disturbata porticus Catuli—Quæ ad tectum pœne pervenerat Quinti fratris domus primo fracta conjectu lapidum, ex area nostra, deinde jussu Clodii inflammata, inspectante Urbe, conjectis ignibus —— Videt, si omnes quos vult palam occiderit, nihilo suam causam difficiliorem, quam adhuc sit, in judicio futuram —— Ad Att 4. 3

attacked

A Urb 696
C.c :o
Coſ
P Cornelius
Lentulus
Spinter,
Q Cæcilius
Metellus
Nepos.

attacked *Milo's houſe, with ſword in hand, and lighted Flambeaus, with intent to ſtorm and burn it.* but Milo was never unprovided for him, and Q. Flaccus, ſallying out with a ſtrong band of ſtout fellows killed ſeveral of his men, *and would have killed Clodius too, if he had not hid himſelf in the inner apartments of P Sylla's houſe, which he made uſe of on this occaſion as his Fortreſs* [o]

THE Senate met, on the fourteenth, to take theſe diſorders into conſideration ; *Clodius did not think fit to appear there,* but *Sylla* came, to clear himſelf, probably from the ſuſpicion of encouraging him in theſe violences, on account of the freedom which he had taken with his houſe [p]. Many ſevere ſpeeches were made, and vigorous counſils propoſed, Marcellinus's opinion was, *that Clodius ſhould be impeached anew for theſe laſt charges, and that no election of Ædiles ſhould be ſuffered, till he was brought to a trial* Milo declared, *that as long as he continued in office, the Conſul Metellus ſhould make no election, for he would take the aſpices every day, on which an aſſembly could be held, but Metellus contrived to waſt the day in ſpeaking, ſo that they were forced to break up without making any decree* Milo was as good as his word, and, having gathered a ſuperior force, took care to obſtruct the election, though the Conſul Me-

---

[o] Ante diem tertium Id Novemb cum ſacra via deſcenderem, inſecutus eſt me cum ſuis. Clamor lapides, fuſtes, gladii, hæc improviſa omnia Diſceſſimus in veſtibulum Tetti Damionis qui erant mecum facile operas acuras prohibuerint Ipſe occiſi potuit ſed ego diæta & cubiculo, chirurgiæ me-

det— Mironis domum pridie id expugnare & incendere ita conatus eſt, ut palam hora quinta cum ſcutis homines, eductis gladiis, alios cum accenſis facibus adduxerit Ipſe domum P Syllæ pro caſtris ad eam impugnationem ſumpſerat &c Ad Att 4 3

[p] Sylla ſe in Senatu poſtridie Idus domi Clodius Ib

tellus

tellus employed all his power and art to elude his
vigilance, and procure an assembly by stratagem,
calling it to one place, and holding it in another,
sometimes in the field of Mars, sometimes in the
Forum, but Milo was ever beforehand with him;
and, keeping a constant guard in the field, from
midnight to noon, was always at hand to inhibit
his procedings, by *obnouncing*, as it was called, or
declaring, that he was *taking the auspices on that
day*, so that the three Brothers were baffled and
disappointed, though they were perpetually haranguing and labouring to inflame the people
against those, who interrupted their assemblies and
right of electing, *where Metellus's speeches were
turbulent, Appius's rash, Clodius's furious.* Cicero,
who gives this account to Atticus, was of opinion,
*that there would be no election, and that Clodius
would be brought to trial, if he was not first killed
by Milo*, which was likely to be his fate: Milo,
says he, *makes no scruple to own it, being not deterred by my misfortune, and having no envious or
perfidious counsellors about him, nor any lazy Nobles
to discourage him it is commonly given out by the
other side, that what he does, is all done by my advice, but they little know, how much conduct, as
well as courage, there is in this Hero* [q]

YOUNG

A Urb 696.
Cic 50
Coss
P CORNELIUS
LENTULUS
SPINTHER,
Q CÆCILIUS
METELLUS
NEPOS.

[q] Egregius Marcellinus,
omnes acies, Metellus ca-
lumnia dicendi tempus ex-
emit conciones turbulentæ
Metelli, temeraria Appii,
furiosissimæ Clodii hæc tamen summa, nisi Milo in
Campum obnunciasset, Co-
mitia futura — Comitia fore
non arbitror, reum Publi-
um, nisi ante occisus erit,
fore a Milone puto Si se
inter viam obtulerit, occisum
iri ab ipso Milone video
Non dubitat facere, præ se
fert, casum illum nostrum
non extimescit, &c
  Meo consilio omnia illi
fieri querebantur ignari quantum in illo heroe esset animi,
quantum etiam consilii ——
Ad Att 4. 3
  N B From these facts it
appears, that what is said
above.

A Urb 696
Cic 50
Coſſ
P Cornelius
Lentulus
Spinther,
Q Cæcilius
Metellus
Nepos

Young Lentulus, the ſon of the Conſul, was, by the intereſt of his father, and the recommendation of his noble birth, *choſen into the College of Augurs* this ſummer, though not yet *ſeventeen years old, having but juſt changed his puerile for the manly gown* [r] Cicero was invited to the inauguration feaſt, where, by eating too freely of *ſome vegetables*, which happened to pleaſe his palate, he was ſeized with a violent pain of the bowels, and *diarrhæa*; of which he ſends the following account to his friend Gallus.

Cicero to Gallus.

" After I had been labouring for ten days, with
" a cruel diſorder in my bowels, yet could not
" convince thoſe, who wanted me at the bar,
" that I was ill, becauſe I had no fever, I ran
" away to *Tuſculum* having kept ſo ſtrict a faſt
" for two days before, that I did not taſte ſo
" much as water being worn out therefore with
" illneſs and faſting, I wanted rather to ſee you
" than imagined, that you expected a viſit from
" me. for my part, I am afraid, I confeſs, of
" all diſtempers, but eſpecially of thoſe, for
" which the *Stoics* abuſe your Epicurus, when
" he complains of *the ſtrangury* and *dyſentery*,
" the one of which they take to be the effect of

above of Clodius's repealing the *Ælian and Fuſian Laws*, and prohibiting the Magiſtrates from obſtructing the Aſſemblies of the people, is to be underſtood only in a partial ſenſe, and that his new law extended no farther than to hinder the Magiſtrates from diſſolving an Aſſembly after it was actually convened

and had entered upon buſineſs, for it was ſtill unlawful, we ſee, to convene an Aſſembly, while the Magiſtrate was in the act of obſerving the heavens

[r] Cui ſuperior annus idem & virilem patris & prætextam populi judicio togam dederit — Pr Sext 69 it Dio l 39 p 99

" gluttony,

" gluttony ; the other of a more fcandalous in-
" temperance I was apprehenfive indeed of a
" *dyfentery* ; but feem to have found benefit, ei-
" ther from the change of air, or the relaxation
" of my mind, or the remiffion of the difeafe
" itfelf . but that you may not be furprifed, how
" this fhould happen, and what I have been
" doing to bring it upon me , the fumptuary
" law, which feems to introduce a fimplicity of
" diet, did me all this mifchief For fince our
" men of tafte are grown fo fond of covering
" their tables with the productions of the Earth,
" which are excepted by the law, they have
" found a way of dreffing mufhrooms, and all
" other vegetables, fo palatably, that nothing
" can be more delicious . I happened to fall
" upon thefe at Lentulus's Augural fupper, and
" was taken with fo violent a flux, that this
" is the firft day on which it has begun to give
" me any eafe. Thus I, who ufed to command
" myfelf fo eafily in *oyfters and lampreys,* was
" caught with *bete and mallows ,* but I fhall be
" more cautious for the future you, however,
" who muft have heard of my illnefs from Ani-
" cius, for he faw me in a fit of vomiting, had
" a juft reafon, not only for fending, but for
" coming yourfelf to fee me. I think to ftay
" here till I recruit myfelf, for I have loft
" both my ftrength and my flefh , but, if I once
" get rid of my diftemper, it will be eafy, I
" hope, to recover the reft [s] "

A Urb 696.
Cic 50
Cofl
P Cornelius
Lentulus
Spinther,
Q Cæcilius
Metellus
Nepos

KING

[s] Ep Fam 7 26
N B Pliny fays, that the
colum, by which he is fuppofed to mean *the Cholic, was*
not known at Rome *till the*
eign of Tiberius but the cafe
defcribed in this Letter feems
to come fo very near to it,
that he muft be underftood
rather of the name than
the thing, as the learned
Le Clerk has obferved in
Hifto y

A Urb 696
C.c 50
Coff
P CORNELIUS
LENTULUS
SPINTHER,
Q CECILIUS
METELLUS
NEPOS,

KING Ptolemy *left Rome* about this time, after he had diftributed immenfe fums among the Great, to purchafe his reftoration by *a Roman army*. The people of *Ægypt* had fent deputies alfo after him, to plead their caufe before the Senate, and to explain the reafons of their expelling him, but the King contrived to get them all affaffinated on the road, before they reached the City. This piece of villainy, and the notion of his having bribed all the Magiftrates, had raifed fo general an averfion to him among the people, that he found it advifeable to quit the City, and leave the management of his intereft to his Agents. The Conful Lentulus, who had obtained the province *of Cilicia and Cyprus*, whither he was preparing to fet forward, was very defirous to be charged with the commiffion *of replacing him on his Throne*: for which he had already procured *a vote of the Senate* the opportunity of a command, almoft in fight of *Ægypt*, made him generally thought to have the beft pretenfions to that charge; and he was affured of Cicero's warm affiftance in foliciting the confirmation of it.

IN this fituation of affairs the new Tribuns entered into office. C Cato, of the fame family with his namefake *Marcus*, was one of the number, a bold turbulent man, of no temper or prudence, yet a tolerable fpeaker, and generally on the better fide in politics. Before he had born any public office, he attempted *to impeach Gabinius of*

History of Medicine —Plin l 26 1 Le Cler Hift. par 2 l 4 fect 2 c 4

The mention likewife of the διουρικα ταξι, or the Strangury of Epicurus and the cenfure, which the Stoic paffed upon it, would make one apt to fufpect, that fome diforders of *a general kind* were not unknown to the ancients

bribery

bribery and corruption; but not being able to get an audience of the Prætors, he had the hardness to mount the Rostra, which was never allowed to a private Citizen, and, in a speech to the people, *declared Pompey Dictator* but his presumption had like to have cost him dear, for it raised such an indignation in the audience, *that he had much difficulty to escape with his life* [t]. He opened his present magistracy by declaring loudly against *King Ptolemy,* and all who favoured him; especially Lentulus, whom he supposed to be under some private engagement with him, and for that reason, was determined to baffle all their schemes.

A Urb 696.
Cic 50.
Coss
P Cornelius
Lentulus
Spinther,
Q Cæcilius
Metellus
Nepos.

Lupus likewise, one of his collegues, summoned the Senate, and raised an expectation of some uncommon proposal from him it was indeed of an extraordinary nature, *to revise and annull that famed act of Cæsar's Confulship, for the division of the Campanian lands. he spoke long and well upon it, and was heard with much attention; gave great praises to Cicero, with severe reflections on Cæsar, and expostulations with Pompey,* who was now abroad in the execution of his late commission: in the conclusion he told them, *that he would not demand the opinions of the particular Senators, because he had no mind to expose them to the resentment and animosity of any, but from the ill humour, which he remembered, when that act first passed, and the favour, with which he was now heard, he could easily collect the sense of the House.*

[t] Ut Cato, adolescens nullius consilii,——vix vivus efugeret, quod cum Gabinium de ambitu vellet postulare, neque Prætores diebus aliquot adiri possent, vel potestatem suam facerent, in concionem adscendit, & Pompeium privatus Dictatorem appellavit Propius nihil est factum, quam ut occideretur Ep ad Quint Frat. 1. 2

Upon

A Urb 696
Cic 50
Coſſ
P CORNELIUS
LENTULUS
SPINTHER,
Q CÆCILIUS
METELLUS
NEPOS.

Upon which Marcellinus ſaid, *that he muſt not conclude from their ſilence, either what they liked or diſliked that for his own part, and he might anſwer too, he believed, for the reſt, he choſe to ſay nothing on the ſubject at preſent, becauſe he thought, that the cauſe of the Campanian lands ought not to be brought upon the ſtage, in Pompey's abſence.*

THIS affair being dropt, Racilius, another Tribun, roſe up and renewed the debate about Milo's *impeachment of Clodius*, and called upon Marcellinus, the Conſul elect, to give his opinion upon it, who, after inveighing againſt all the violences of Clodius, propoſed, *that, in the firſt place, an allotment of Judges ſhould be made for the trial, and, after that, the election of Ædiles, and if any one attempted to hinder the trial, that he ſhould be deemed a public enemy* The other Conſul elect, Philippus, was of the ſame mind, but the Tribuns, Cato and Caſſius, ſpoke againſt it, *and were for proceeding to an election before any ſtep towards a trial* When Cicero was called upon to ſpeak, *he run through the whole ſeries of Clodius's extravagances, as if he had been accuſing him already at the bar, to the great ſatisfaction of the aſſembly* · Antiſtius, the Tribun, ſeconded him, and declared, *that no buſineſs ſhould be done before the trial*, and when the houſe was going univerſally into that opinion, *Clodius began to ſpeak, with intent to waſt the reſt of the day, while his ſlaves and followers without, who had ſeized the ſteps and avenues of the ſenate, raiſed ſo great a noiſe of a ſudden, in abuſing ſome of Milo's friends, that the Senate broke up in no ſmall hurry, and with freſh indignation at this new inſult* [u].

THERE

[u] Tum Clodius rogatus —deinde ejus operæ repente
diem dicendo eximere cœpit a Græcoſtaſi & gradibus cla-
                                 mor n

THERE was no more bufinefs done through the remaining part *of December*, which was taken up chiefly with holy days. *Lentulus and Metellus*, whofe confulfhip expired with the year, fet forward for their feveral governments, the one for *Cilicia*, the other for *Spain* Lentulus committed the whole direction of his affairs to Cicero, and Metellus, unwilling to leave him his enemy, made up all matters with him before his departure, and wrote an affectionate letter to him afterwards from *Spain*, in which he acknowledges his fervices, and intimates, *that he had given up his brother Clodius, in exchange for his friendfhip* [x].

CICERO's firft concern, on the opening of the new year, was to get the commiffion, *for reftoring King Ptolemy*, confirmed to Lentulus, which came now under deliberation : The Tribun, Cato, was fierce, againft reftoring him at all, with the greateft part of the Senate on his fide, when taking occafion to confult *the Sibylline books*, on the fubject of *fome late prodigies*, he chanced to find in them certain verfes, *forewarning the Roman people, not to replace an exiled King of Egypt, with an army*. This was fo pat to his purpofe, that there could be no doubt of it's being forged, but *Cato called up the Guardians of the books into the Roftra, to teftify the paffage to be genuin, where it was publicly read and explained to the people* It was laid alfo before the Senate, who greedily received it ; and, after a grave debate on this fcruple of religion, came to a refolution, *that it feemed dangerous to the Republic, that the King*

A Urb 69.
Cic 51
Cof
C. Cornelius Lentulus Marcellinus,
L Marcius Philippus

---

morem fuis magnum fuftulerunt, opinor in Q Sextilium & amicos Milonis incitatæ, eo metu injecto repente magna quermonia omnium difceffimus Ad Quint Fr 2 1

[x] Libenterque commutata perfona, te mihi fratris loco effe duco. Ep Fam 5 3

fhould

A Urb 697
Cc 51
Coſſ
C. CORNE-
LIUS LE-
TULUS
MARCE-
LINUS,
L MARCIUS
PHILIPPUS.

ſhould be reſtored by a multitude [y]   It cannot be imagined, that they laid any real ſtreſs on this admonition of *the Sibyl*, for there was not a man either in or out of the Houſe, *who did not take it for a fiction ·* but it was a fair pretext for defeating a project, which was generally diſliked. They were unwilling to gratify any man's ambition, *of viſiting the rich country of Ægypt, at the head of an army*, and perſuaded, that without an army, no man would be ſollicitous about going thither at all [z].

THIS point being ſettled, the next queſtion was, *in what manner the King ſhould be reſtored.* various opinions were propoſed, Craſſus moved, *that three Embaſſadors, choſen from thoſe who had ſome public command, ſhould be ſent on the errand, which did not exclude Pompey.* Bibulus propoſed, *that three private Senators,* and Volcatius, *that Pompey alone ſhould be charged with it.* but Cicero, Hortenſius, and Lucullus, urged, *that Lentulus, to whom the Senate had already decreed it, and who could execute it with moſt convenience, ſhould reſtore him without an army.* The two firſt opinions were ſoon over-ruled, and the ſtruggle lay between *Lentulus and Pompey.* Cicero, *though he had ſome reaſon to complain of Lentulus, ſince his return,* particularly for the contemptible valuation of his houſes, yet for the great part, which he had born, in reſtoring him, was very

[y] Senatus religionis calumniam, non religione ſed malevolentia, & illius regiæ largitionis invidia comprobat —Ep Fam 1 1

De Rege Alexandrino factum eſt S C cum multitudo eam reducat, periculoſam Reip ſ tanem — Ad Quin Fr 2 2

[z] Hæc tamen opinio eſt populi Romani, a tuis invidis atque obtrectatoribus nomen inductum ficta religionis, non tam ut te impedirent, quam ut nequis, propter exercitus cupiditatem, Alexandriam vellet ire Ep Fam 1 4

deſirous

A Urb 697.
Cic 51
Cofl
Cn Corne-
lius Len-
tulus
Marcel-
linus,
L Marcius
Philippus.

defirous to fhew his gratitude, and refolved to fupport him with all his authority Pompey, who had obligations alfo to Lentulus, acted the fame part towards him, which he had done before towards Cicero, by his own conduct and profeffions, *he feemed to have Lentulus's intereft at heart, yet, by the conduct of all his friends, feemed defirous to procure the employment for himfelf, while the* King's Agents and Creditors, fancying that their bufinefs would be ferved the moft effectually by Pompey, *began openly to follicit, and even to bribe for him* [a] But the Senate, through Cicero's influence, ftood generally inclined to Lentulus. and after a debate, which ended in his favour, Cicero, who had been the manager of it, *happening to fup with Pompey that evening, took occafion to prefs him with much freedom, not to fuffer his name to be ufed in this competition; nor give a handle to his enemies, for reproaching him with the defertion of a friend, as well as an ambition, of engroffing all power to himfelf Pompey feemed touched with the*

[a] Craffus tres legatos decernit, nec excludit Pompeium cenfet enim etiam ex iis, qui cum imperio funt M Bibulus tres legatos ex iis, qui privati funt Huic affentiutur reliqui confulares, præter Servilium, qui omnino reduci negat oportere, & Volcatium, qui decernit Pompeio —

Hortenfii & mea & Luculli fententia—Ex illo S C quod te referente factum cft, tibi decernit, ut reducas regem —

Regis caufâ fi qui funt qui velint, qui pauci funt, omnes rem ad Pompeium deferri volunt Ep Fam 1 1

Reliqui cum effet in Senatu contentio, *Lentulufne an Pompeius reduceret, obtinere caufam Lentulus videbatur* —In ea re Pompeus quid velit non defpicio familiares ejus quid cupiant, omnes vident Creditores vero Regis aperte pecunias fuppeditant contra Lentulum Sine dubio res remota a Lentulo videtur, cum magno meo dolore quamquam multa fecit, quare fi fas effet, jure ei fuccenfere poffumus Ad Quin Fr 2 2

remonstrance, and professed to have no other thought but of serving Lentulus, while his dependents continued still to act so, as to convince every body, that he could not be sincere [b]

WHEN Lentulus's pretensions seemed to be in a hopeful way, C. Cato took a new and effectual method to disappoint them, *by proposing a law to the people, for taking away his government or a recalling him home.* This stroke surprized every body, the Senate condemned it as factious, and Lentulus's *son changed his habit upon it*, in order to move the Citizens, and hinder their offering such an affront to his Father. The Tribun, Caninius, proposed another law at the same time, *for sending Pompey to Egypt* · but this pleased no better than the other, and the Consuls contrived, that neither of them should be brought to the suffrage of the people [c] These new contests gave a fresh interruption *to Ptolemy's cause*, in which Cicero's resolution was, if the commission could not be obtained for Lentulus, *to prevent it's being granted at least to Pompey, and fetch themselves the disgrace of being baffled*

---

[b] Ego to the case and Pompey ... cum tempe hoc regis dominium de ... antea po tuam cessum, is enim eos ... in Senatu, ita cum ... loquar, ut mini videatur ... ab omnia ... cogitatione ad tuam dignitatem, t erdem traducere quem ego ... cum audio, ... cum vero omni suffragiis ... cum auc... omnium ... vide. perspicio, d quod jam omnibus est apertum, totam rem istam jam pridem a certis hominibus, ... in ito Rege ipso — esse corruptum. Ep Fam 1 2

[c] Nos cum maxime consilio, studio, labore, gratia, de causa regia niteremur, subito extorta est nefaria Catonis promulgatio, quæ studia nostra impediret, & animos a minore cura ad summum timorem traduceret. Ibid 5

Suspicor per vim rogationem Caninium perlaturum Ad Quint 2 2

ty a competitor [d] but the senate was grown so sick of the whole affair, that they resolved to leave the King to shift for himself, without interposing at all in his restoration, and so the matter hung, whilst other affairs more interesting were daily rising up at home, and engaging the attention of the City

THE election of *Ædiles*, which had been industriously postponed through all the last summer, could not easily be kept off any longer the City was impatient for its Magistrates and especially for the plays and shews, with which they used to entertain them , and several also of the new Tribuns being zealous for an election, it was held at last *on the twentieth of January*; when Clodius *was chosen Ædile*, without any opposition , so that Cicero began once more to put himself upon his guard, from the certain *expectation of a furious Ædileship* [e].

IT may justly seem strange, how a man so profligate and criminal, as Clodius, whose life was a perpetual insult on all laws, divine and human, should be suffered not only to live without punishment, but to obtain all the honors of a free City in their proper course , and it would be natural to suspect, that we had been deceived in our accounts of him, by taking them from his enemies, did we not find them too firmly supported by facts to be called in question but a little attention to the particular character of the

---

[d] Sed vereor ne aut eripiatur nobis causa regia, aut deferatur — Sed si res coget, est quiddam tertium, quod non — mihi displicebat , ut neque jacere Regem patere mur, nec nobis repugnantibus, ad eum deferri, ad quem prope jam delatum videtur — Ne, si quid non obtinuerimus, repulsi esse videamur Ep Fam 1 5

[e] Sed omnia fiunt tardiora propter furiose Ædilitatis expectationem Ad Quint. 2 2

man,

man, as well as of the times, in which he lived, will enable us to solve the difficulty. First, the splendor of his family, which had born a principal share in all the triumphs of the Republic, from the very foundation of its liberty, was of great force to protect him in all his extravagances: those, who know any thing of *Rome*, know what a strong impression this single circumstance *of illustrious nobility would necessarily make upon the people*. Cicero calls the nobles of this class, *Prætors and Consuls elect from their cradles, by a kind of hereditary right, whose very names were sufficient to advance them to all the dignities of the state* [*f*] Secondly, his personal qualities were peculiarly adapted to endear him to all the meaner sort: his bold and ready wit, his talent at haranguing, his profuse expense, and his being the first of his family, who had pursued popular measures, against the maxims of his Ancestors, who were all stern assertors of *the Aristocratical power*. Thirdly, the contrast of opposite factions, who had each their ends in supporting him, contributed principally to his safety: the Triumvirate willingly permitted, and privately encouraged, his violences, to make their own power not onely the less odious, but even necessary, for controuling the fury of such an incendiary, and though it was often turned against themselves, yet they chose to bear it, and dissemble their ability of repelling it, rather than destroy the man, who was playing their game for them, and by throwing

---

[*f*] Non idem in nobi licet, quibus omnia a majoribus facta sunt, quibus omnia populi Romani beneficia dormientibus deferunt r.——In Verr 5 70

Erat nobilitate ipsa blanda conciliatricula commendatus. Omnes semper boni nobilitati favemus &c.——Pr Sext 9

the Republic into confusion, throwing it of courſe
into their hands the Senate, on the other ſide,
whoſe chief apprehenſions were from the Triumvirate, thought, that the raſhneſs of Clodius might
be of ſome uſe to perplex their meaſures, and ſtir
up the people againſt them on proper occaſions ,
or it humoured their ſpleen at leaſt, *to ſee him of-*
ten inſulting Pompey to his face [g] Laſtly, all,
who envied Cicero, and deſired to leſſen his authority, privately cheriſhed an enemy, who employed all his force to drive him from the adminiſtration of affairs this accidental concurrence
of circumſtances, peculiar to the man and the
times, was the thing that preſerved Clodius,
whoſe inſolence could never have been endured
in any quiet and regular ſtate of the City.

By his obtaining *the Ædileſhip,* the tables
were turned between him and Milo . the one
was armed with the authority of a Magiſtrate ,
the other become a private man the one freed
from all apprehenſion of Judges and a trial, the
other expoſed to all that danger from the power
of his antagoniſt and it was not Clodius's cuſtom
to neglect any advantage againſt an enemy, ſo
that he now accuſed Milo of the ſame crime, of
which Milo had accuſed him , *of public violence*
and breach of the laws, in maintaining a band of
Gladiators to the terror of the City Milo made
his appearance to this accuſation, *on the ſecond of*

A Urb 697
Cic 51
Coſſ
Cn Corne
lius L n-
tulus
Marcel
linus,
L Marcius
Philippus

[g] Vilius igitur nomi-
rem per ſcipſum jam ? dem
affictum ne ? centum, peri-
cioſis Optimatum diſcordiis
eicitari — Ne a Republica
Reipub pellis amoveretur,
reſtiterunt etiam, ne cauſam
diceret etiam ne privatus
eſſet etiamne in ſinu atque
in deliciis quidam optimi viri viperam illam venenatam
ac peſtiferam habere potuerunt ? Quo tandem decepti
monere ? Volo inquiunt, eſſe
qui in concione detrahat de
Pompeio —De Haruſp Reſp.
24

A Urb 697
Cic 51
Coſ
C\. Corne-
lius Len-
tulus
Marcel-
linus,
L Marcius
Philippus

February, when Pompey, Craſſus, and Cicero appeared with him, and M Marcellus, though Clodius's *Collegue in the Ædileſhip, ſpoke for him at Cicero's deſire*, and the whole paſſed quietly and favorably for him on that day The ſecond hearing was appointed *on the ninth*, when Pompey undertook to plead his cauſe, but no ſooner ſtood up to ſpeak, than Clodius's mob began to exert their uſual arts, and *by a continual clamor of reproaches and invectives, endeavoured to hinder him from going on, or at leaſt from being heard*, but Pompey was too firm to be ſo baffled, *and ſpoke for over three hours, with a preſence of mind, which commanded ſilence in ſpite of their attempts* When Clodius roſe up to anſwer him, Milo's party, in their turn, ſo diſturbed and confounded him, that he was not able to ſpeak a word, *while a number of Epigrams and Lampoons upon him and his Siſter were thrown about, and publicly rehearſed among the multitude below, ſo as to make him quite* ... till recollecting himſelf a little, and finding it impoſſible to proceed in his ſpeech, he demanded aloud of his mob, *who it was, that attempted to ſtarve them by famine?* To which they preſently cried out, Pompey he then aſked, *who it was that deſired to be ſent to Ægypt?* They all ecchoed, Pompey : but when he aſked, *who it was that they themſelves had a mind to ſend* They anſwered, Craſſus for the old jealouſy was now breaking out again between him and Pompey, *and though he appeared that day on Milo's ſide, yet he was not*, as Cicero ſays, *a real well-wiſher to him*

THESE warm proceedings among the chiefs, brought on a fray below, among their partiſans, *the Clodians began the attack, but were repulſed by the Pompeians, and Clodius himſelf driven out of the*
th.

the Roftra. Cicero, when he faw the affair procede to blows, thought it high time to retreat, and
make the beft of his way towards home, but no
great harm was done, for Pompey, having cleared
the Forum of his enemies, prefently drew oh his
forces, to prevent any farther mifchief or fcandal from his fide [*h*]

THE Senate was prefently fummoned, to provide fome remedy for thefe diforders, where
Pompey, who had drawn upon himfelf a frefh
envy from his behaviour *in the Ægyptian affair,*
was feverely handled by Bibulus, Curio, Favonius,
*and others, Cicero chofe to be abfent, fince he muft
either have offended Pompey, by faying nothing for
him, or the honeft party, by defending him.* The
fame debate was carried on for feveral days, in

[*h*] Ad diem IIII Non
Febr Milo affuit Ei Pom-
peius advocatus venit Dixit Marcellus a me rogatus
Honefte difceffimus Produc-
tus dies eft in IIII Id Feb
—A D IIII Idem Milo af-
fuit Dixit Pompeius, five
voluit Nam ut furrexit, o-
pera Clodianæ clamorem fuftulerunt idque ei perpetua
oratione contigit, non modo
ut acclamatione, fed ut con-
vicio & maledictis impedire-
tur Qui ut peroravit, nam
in eo fane fortis fuit, non
eft deterritus, dixit omnia,
atque interdum etiam filentio, cum auctoritate perege-
rat, fed ut peroravit, furrexit Clodius ei tantus clamor a noftris, placuerat enim
referre gratiam, ut neque
mente, neque lingua, neque
ore confifteret — Cum omnia

maledicta, tum verfus et an
obfceniffimi in Clodium &
Clodiam dicerentur Ille fu-
rens & exfanguis interroga-
bat fuos in clamore ipfo, quis
effet, qui plebem fame ne-
caret Refpondebant operæ,
Pompeius Quis Alexandri-
am ire cuperet? Refponde-
bant, Pompeius Quem ire
vellent Refpondebant, Craf-
fum Is aderat tum Miloni
animo non amico,———

Hora fere nono, quafi fig-
no dato, Clodiani noftros
confputare cœperunt Exar-
fit dolor, urgere illi ut loco
nos moverent Factus eft a
noftris impetus, fuga opera-
rum Ejectus de Roftris Clodius Ac nos quoque tum
fugimus, ne quid in turba —
Senatus vocatus in Curiam,
Pompeius domum ———Ad
Qu nt Fr 2 3

D 4   which

A Urb 697
Cic 51
Coff
C. CORNE-
LIUS LEN-
TULUS
MARCEL
LINUS,
L MARCIUS
PHILIPPUS

which Pompey was treated very roughly *by the Trium Cato, who inveighed against him with great fierceness, and laid open his perfidy to Cicero, to whom he paid the highest compliments, and was heard with much attention by all Pompey's enemies.*

POMPEY answered him with an unusual vehemence, and *reflecting openly on Crassus, as the author of these affronts, declared, that he would guard his life with more care, than Scipio Africanus did, when Carbo murdered him* —— These warm expressions seemed to open a prospect of some great agitation likely to ensue: Pompey consulted with Cicero on the proper means of his security; and acquainted him with his apprehensions *of a design against his life, that Cato was privately supported, and Clodius furnished with money by Crassus, and both of them encouraged by Curio, Bibulus, and the rest, who envied him, that it was necessary for him to look to himself, since the meaner people were wholly alienated, the nobility and Senate generally disaffected, and the youth corrupted* Cicero readily consented to join forces with him, *and to sum up their clients and friends from all parts of* Italy for though he had no mind to fight his battles in the Senate, he was desirous to defend his person from all violence, especially against Crassus, whom he never loved they resolved likewise to oppose, with united strength, *all the attempts of Clodius and Cato against Lentulus and Mo* [1] Clodius, on the other hand, was not less

---

[1] Neque ego in Senatum, neque de tantis rebus t cerem ac in Pompeio de-
cre nto, nam 's carpebatur
Bibulo, Curone Fa onio,
nru offuo comos bono-
rum Recrem Res in po-
d a est —— Eo
die nihil perfectum —— Ad die II Id —— Cato est vehementer in Pompeium invectus & eum oratione perpetua tanquam reum accusavit De me multa me invito, cum mea summa laude dixit Cum illius in me perfidiam increpavit,

A Urb 697
Cic 51
Coff
Cn Corne-
lius Len-
tulus
Marcel-
linus,
L Marcius
Philippus.

lefs bufy in muftering his friends againft the next hearing of Milo's caufe but as his ftrength was much inferior to that of his adverfary, fo he *had no expectation of getting him condemned, nor any other view, but to teize and harafs him* [k]. for after two hearings, the affair was put off by feveral adjournments *to the beginning of* May, from which time we find no farther mention of it

T H E Conful, Marcellinus, who drew his Collegue, Philippus, along with him, was a refolute oppofer of *the Triumvirate,* as well as of all the violences of the other Magiftrates for which reafon, he refolved to fuffer no affemblies of the people, except fuch as were neceffary for the elections into the annual offices his view was, to prevent Cato's *law for recalling Lentulus, and the monftrous things,* as Cicero calls them, *which fome were attempting at this time in favour of Cæfar.* Cicero gives him the character *of one of the beft Confuls that he had ever known, and blames him only in one thing, for treating Pompey on all occafions too rudely, which made Cicero often abfent himfelf from the Senate, to avoid taking part, either*

increpavit auditus eft magno filentio malevolorum Refpondit ei vehementer Pompeius, Craffumque defcripfit, dixtque aperte, fe munitiorem ad cuftodiendam vitam fuam fore, quam Africanus fuiffet, quem C Carbo interemiffet Itaque magis mihi res moveri videbantur Nam Pompeius hæc intelligit mecumque communicat infidias vitæ fuæ fieri C Catonem a Craffo fuftentari, Clodio pecuniam fuppeditari utrumque & ab eo &

riore, B bulo, cæterifque fuis obtrectatoribus confirmari vehementer effe provide dum ne opprimatur, concionario illo populo, a fe prope alienato, nobilitate inimica, non æquo Senatu Juventute improba, itaque fe comparat, homines ex agris arceffit Operas autem fuas Clodius confirmat Manus ad Quirinalia paratur In eo multo fumus fuperiores, &c Ad Quint 2 3

[?] Vid Dio p 99

A Urb 697
Cic 51
Coff
C Cor E-
L us Len-
tulus
Marcel-
inus,
L Marcus
Philippus

on the one fide or the other [*l*]   For the fupport
therefore of his dignity and intereft in the City,
he refumed his old tafk of pleading caufes, which
was always popular and reputable, and in which
he was fure to find full employment. His firft
caufe was the defence of L. Beftia, on the tenth
of February, who, after the difgrace of a repulfe
from the Prætorfhip in the laft election, was ac
cufed *of bribery and corruption in his fuit for it*,
and, notwithftanding the authority and eloquence
of his advocate, was convicted and banifhed He
was a man extremely corrupt, turbulent, and fe
ditious. had always been an enemy to Cicero,
and fuppofed to be deeply engaged *in Catiline's
plot*, and is one inftance of the truth of what Ci
cero fays, *that he was often forced, againft his will,
to defend certain perfons, who had not deferved it of
him, by the interceffion of thofe who had* [*m*]

CÆSAR, who was now in the career of his
victories in *Gaul*, fent a requeft to the Senate,
*that money might be decreed to him for the payment
of his Army, with a power of chufing ten Lieutenants, for the better management of the war, and
the conquered Provinces, and that his command*

A Urb 697.
Cic 51.
Coſl
Cn Cornf-
lius Len-
tulus
Marcel-
linus,
L Marcius
Philippus.

ſhould be prolonged for five years more The demand was thought very exorbitant; and it seemed ſtrange, that, after all his boaſted Conqueſts, he ſhould not be able to maintain his army without money from home, at a time when the treaſury was greatly exhauſted, and the renewal of a commiſſion, obtained at firſt by violence, and againſt the authority of the Senate, was of hard digeſtion. But Cæſar's intereſt prevailed, and Cicero himſelf was the promoter of it, and procured a decree to his ſatisfaction, yet not without diſguſting the old patriots, who ſtood firm to their maxim of oppoſing all extraordinary grants: but Cicero *alledged the extraordinary ſervices of Cæſar, and that the courſe of his victories ought not to be checked by the want of neceſſary ſupplies, while he was ſo gloriouſly extending the bounds of the Empire, and conquering nations, whoſe names had never been heard before at* Rome *and though it were poſſible for him to maintain his troops without their help, by the ſpoils of the enemy, yet thoſe ſpoils ought to be reſerved for the ſplendor of his Triumph, which it was not juſt to defraud by their unſeaſonable parſimony* [n]

He might think it imprudent perhaps, at this time, to call Cæſar home from an unfiniſhed war, and ſtop the progreſs of his arms in the very height of his ſucceſs, yet the real motive of his conduct ſeems to have flowed, not ſo much from the merits of the cauſe, as a regard to the

---

[n] Illum enim arbitrabar etiam ſine hoc ſubſidio pecuniæ retinere exercitum præda ante parta, & bellum conficere poſſe ſed decus illud & ornamentum Triumphi minuendum noſtra parſimonia non putavi. Et quas regiones, quaſque gentes nulla nobis, antea littera, nulla vox, nulla fama notas fecerat, his noſter Imperator noſter ue exercitus, & populi Romani arma peragrarunt —De Prov Conſul XI 13 —

A Urb 697
Cic 51
Coff
C. CORNE-
LIUS LEN-
TULUS
MARCEL-
LINUS,
L MARCIUS
PHILIPPUS.

condition of the times, and his own circumstan
ces For in his private letters he owns, " tha
" the malevolence and envy of the Aristocrati
" cal chiefs had almost driven him from his ol
" principles . and though not so far as to make
" him forget his dignity, yet so as to take a
" proper care of his safety, both which migh
" be easily consistent, if there was any faith o
" gravity in the Consular Senators . but the
" had managed their matters so ill, that thos
" who were superior to them in power, were be
" come superior too in authority, so as to be abl
" to carry in the Senate, what they could n
" have carried even with the people without vio
" lence that he had learnt from experience,
" what he could not learn so well from books,
" that as no regard was to be had to our safety
" without a regard also to our dignity, so the con
" sideration of dignity ought not to exclude the
" care of our safety [o] " In another letter he says,
" that the state and form of the government wa
" quite changed, and what he had proposed to
" himself, as the end of all his toils, *a dignity an*
" *liberty, of acting and voting*, was quite lost and
" gone, that there was nothing left, but either
" meanly to assent to the few, who governed

[o] Quorum malevolentis-
simis obtrectationibus nos scito
de vetere illa nostra, diu-
turnaque sententia prope jam
esse depulsos non nos quidem ut nostræ dignitatis si-
mus obliti, sed ut habeamus
rationem aliquando etiam salutis Poterat utrumque præclare, si esset fides, si gra-
vitas in hominibus Consula-
ribus —

Nam qui plus opibus, ar-

mis, potentia valent profecisse tantum mihi videntur
stultitia & inconstantia adversariorum, ut etiam auctori-
te jam plus valerent —quod
ipse, litteris omnibus a pue-
ritia deditus, experiundo tamen magis, quam discendi
cognovi,— neque salutis nostra rationem habendam nobis esse sine dignitate, neque
dignitatis sine salute — Ep
fam 1 7

" all

" all, or weakly to oppose them, without doing
" any good   that he had dropt therefore all
" thoughts of that old Consular gravity and
" character of a resolute Senator, and resolved
" to conform himself to Pompy's will, that his
" great affection to Pompey made him begin to
" think all things right, which were useful to
" him, and he comforted himself with reflect-
" ing, that the greatness of his obligations would
" make all the world excuse him, for defending
" what Pompey liked, or, at least, for not op-
" posing it, or else, what of all things he most
" desired, if his friendship with Pompey would
" permit him, for retiring from public business,
" and giving himself wholly up to his books [p] "

B u t he was now engaged in a cause, in
which he was warmly and specially interested, *the
defence of P Sextius,* the late Tribun   *Clodius,
who gave Cicero's friends no respite,* having himself undertaken Milo, assigned the prosecution of
Sextius to one of his confidents, M. Tullius Al-
binovanus, who accused him *of public violence, or
breach of peace in his Tribunate* [q]   Sextius had

A Urb 697.
Cic 51.
Coss.
Cn Corne-
lius Len-
tulus
Marcel-
linus,
L Marcius
Philippus

[p] Tantum enim animi inductio & mehercule amor erga Pompeium apud me valet, ut, quæ illi utilia sunt, & quæ ille vult, ea mihi omnia jam & recta & vera videantur— Me quidem illa res consolatur, quod ego is sum, cui vel maxime concedant omnes, ut vel ea defendam, quæ Pompeius velit, vel taceam, vel etiam, id quod mihi maxime lubet, ad nostra me studia referam litterarum, quod profecto faciam, si mihi per ejusdem amicitiam licebit ——

Quæ enim proposita fuerant nobis, cum & honoribus amplissimis, & laboribus maximis perfuncti essemus, dignitas in sententiis dicendis, libertas in Rep capessenda, ea sublata tota   sed nec mihi magis, quam omnibus Nam aut assentiendum est nulla cum gravitate paucis, aut frustra dissentiendum Ibid 8.

[q] Qui cum omnibus salutis meæ defensoribus bellum sibi esse gerendum judicaverunt. Pr Sext 2

I

been

A Urb 697
Coſ 51
Coſ

C CORNE-
LIUS LEN-
TULUS
MARCEL-
LINUS,

L MARCIUS
PHILIPPUS

been a true friend to Cicero in his diſtreſs; and born a great part in his reſtoration, but as in caſes of eminent ſervice, conferred jointly by many, every one is apt to claim the firſt merit, and expect the firſt ſhare of praiſe, ſo Sextius, naturally moroſe, fanſying himſelf neglected or not ſufficiently requited by Cicero, had behaved very churliſhly towards him ſince his return. but Cicero, who was never forgetful of paſt kindneſſes, inſtead of reſenting his perverſeneſs, having heard, *that Sextius was indiſpoſed, went in perſon to his houſe, and cured him of all his jealouſies, by freely offering his aſſiſtance and patronage in pleading his cauſe* [r]

THIS was a diſappointment to the proſecutors, who flattered themſelves, that Cicero was ſo much diſguſted, that he would not be perſuaded to plead for him, but he entered into the cauſe with a hearty inclination, and made it, as in effect it really was, his own [s]. In his ſpeech, which is ſtill extant, after laying open the hiſtory of his exil, and the motives of his own conduct, through the whole progreſs of it, he ſhews, " that
" the onely ground of proſecuting Sextius was,
" his faithful adherence to him, or rather to the
" Republic, that by condemning Sextius, they
" would in effect condemn him, whom all the or
" ders of the City had declared to be unjuſtly ex-
" pelled, by the very ſame men, who were now
" attempting to expell Sextius that it was a
" banter and ridicule on juſtice itſelf, to accuſe a

[r] Is erat æger domum, ut debuimus ad eum ſtatim venimus eique nos totos tradidimus idque fecimus præter hominum opinionem, qui nos ei jure ſuccenſere putabant, ut humaniſſimi gratiſ-

ſimique & ipſi & omnibus vi deremur itaque faciemus Ad Quint 2 3

[s] P Sextius eſt reus non ſuo ſed meo nomine, &c Pr ſext 13

" man

" man of violence, who had been left for dead
" upon the fpot, by the violence of thofe who
" accufed him, and whofe onely crime it was,
" that he would not fuffer himfelf to be quite
" killed, but prefumed to guard his life againft
" their future attempts " In fhoit he managed
the caufe fo well, that Sextius was acquitted, and
in a mannei the moft honoiable, *by the vnanimous
fuffrages of all the Judges, and with an vniverfal
applaufe of Cicero's humanity and giatitude* [*t*].

A Urb 697.
Cic 51.
Coff
Cn Corne-
lius Len-
tulus
Marcel-
linus,
L Marcius
Philippus.

POMPEY attended this trial as a fiiend to Sextius, while Cæfar's *creature,* Vatinius, appeaied
not onely as an adverfary, but *a witnefs againft
him* which gave Cicero an opportunity of lafh-
ing him, as Sextius particularly defiied, with all
the keenefs of his raillery, *to the gieat diverfion of
the audience,* for inftead of interrogating him in the
ordinary way, about the facts depofed in the trial,
he contrived to teize him with a perpetual feries
of queftions, which revived and expofed the iniquity of his factious Tribunate, and the whole
courfe of his profligate life, from his firft appearance in public; and, in fpite of all his impudence, *quite daunted and confounded him.* Vatinius however made fome feeble effort to defend
himfelf, and rally Cicero in his turn; and
among other things, reproached him *with the
bafenefs of changing fides, and becoming Cæfar's
friend, on account of the fortunate ftate of his af-
faiis* · to which Cicero brifkly replied, though
Pompey himfelf ftood by, *that he ftill preferred*

[*t*] Sextius nofter abfolutus eft A D II. Id. Mart
& quod vehementer interfu t
Reipub nullam videri in ejufmodi caufa diffenfionem effe,
omnibus fententiis abfolutus
eft—Scito nos in eo judicio
confecutos effe, ut omnium
gratiffimi judicaremur. Nam
in defendendo homine mo-
rofo cumulatiffime fatisfeci-
mus.—Ad Quint 2 4—

A Urb 697
Cic 51
Coſſ
C. CORNE-
LIUS LEN-
TULUS
MARCEL-
LINUS,
L MARCIUS
PHILIPPUS

the condition of *Bibulus's Conſulſhip, which Vatinius* thought *abject and miſerable,* to the *victories and triumphs of all men whatſoever.* This ſpeech againſt Vatinius is ſtill remaining, under the title of *the interrogation,* and is nothing elſe but what Cicero himſelf calls it, *a perpetual invective on the Magiſtracy of Vatinius, and the conduct of thoſe who ſupported him* [*u*]

IN the beginning of *April,* the Senate granted *the ſum of three hundred thouſand pounds to Pompey,* to be laid out *in purchaſing corn for the uſe of the City*, where there was ſtill a great ſcarcity, and as great at the ſame time of money ſo that the moving a point ſo tender could not fail of raiſing ſome ill humour in the aſſembly, when Cicero, whoſe old ſpirits ſeemed to have revived in him, from his late ſucceſs in Sextius's cauſe, ſurprized them by propoſing, *that in the preſent inability of the treaſury to purchaſe the Campanian lands, which by Cæſar's act were to be divided to the people, the act itſelf ſhould be reconſidered, and a day appointed for that deliberation.* the motion was received with an univerſal joy, and a kind of tumultuary acclamation : the enemies of *the Triumvirate* were extremely pleaſed with it, in hopes that it would make *a breach between*

[*u*] Vatinium, a quo palam oppugnabatur, arbitratu noſtro concidimus Diis hominibuſque plaudentibus — Quid quæris, Homo petulans & audax Vatinius valde perturbatus, debilitatuſque diſceſſit —Ibid

Ego ſeverre Pompeio, cum ut laudaret P Sextium introdiſſet in urbem, dixiſſetque teſt s Vatinius, me fortuna & felicitate C Cæſaris commotum, illi amicum eſſe cœpiſſe, dixi, me eam Bibuli torturam, quam ille afflictam putaret, omnium triumphis victoriſque anteferre —Tota vero interrogatio mea nihil habuit, niſi reprehenſionem il' us Tribunatus in quo omnia dicta ſunt libertate, animoque maximo.— Ep fam 1. 9

Cicero

A Urb 697
Cic 51
Coſſ
Cn Corne-
lius Len-
tulus
Marcel-
linus,
L Marcius
Philippus

Cicero and Pompey, but it ſerved only for a proof, of what Cicero himſelf obſerves, *that it is very hard for a man to depart from his old ſentiments in politics, when they are right and juſt* [x]

POMPEY, whoſe nature was ſingularly reſerved, expreſſed no uneaſineſs upon it, nor took any notice of it to Cicero, though they met and ſupped together familiarly, as they uſed to do but he ſet forward ſoon after towards *Aſia*, in order to provide corn, and intending to call at *Sardinia*, propoſed to embark at *Piſa* or *Leghorn*, that he might have an interview with *Cæſar*, who was now at *Luca*, the utmoſt limit of his *Gallic Government* He found Cæſar exceedingly out of humor with Cicero, for Craſſus had already been with him at *Ravenna*, and greatly incenſed him by his account of Cicero s late motion, which he complained of ſo heavily, that Pompey promiſed to uſe all his authority, to induce Cicero to drop the purſuit of it, and for that purpoſe ſent away an expreſs to *Rome*, to entreat him, not to proceed any farther in it till his return, and when he came afterwards to *Sardinia*, where his Lieutenant, Q Cicero, then reſided, he entered immediately into an expoſtulation with him about it, " recounting all his ſervices to his " Brother, and that every thing, which he had " done for him, was done with Cæſar's conſent, " and reminding him of a former converſation " between themſelves concerning Cæſar's acts.

---

[x] Pompeio pecunia decreta in rem frumentariam ad HS cccc ſed eodem die vehementer actum de agro Campano, clamore Senatus prope concionali Acriorem cauſam inopia pecuniæ faciebat, & annonæ caritas ——

Ad Quint 2 5
Nonis April mihi eſt Senatus ſſenſus ut de agro Campano, idibus Maiis, frequenti Senatu referretur Num potui magis in arcem illius cauſæ invadere — Ep ram 1 9

A. Urb. 697
Cic 51
Coſſ
C. Corne-
lius Len-
tulus
Marcel-
linus,
L. Marcius
Philippus

" and what Quintus himſelf had undertaken for
" his Brother on that head, and as he then
" made himſelf anſwerable for him, ſo he was
" now obliged to call him to the performance
" of thoſe engagements in ſhort, he begged of
" him, to preſs his Brother to ſupport and de
" fend Cæſar's intereſts and dignity, or if he
" could not perſuade him to that, to engage
" him at leaſt, not to act againſt them [*y*] "

THIS remonſtrance from Pompey, enforced
by his Brother Quintus, ſtaggered Cicero's reſo
lution, and made him enter into a freſh delibera
tion with himſelf about the meaſures of his con
duct, where, after caſting up the ſum of all
his thoughts, and weighing every circumſtance,
which concerned either his own or the public
intereſt, he determined at laſt to drop the affair,
rather than expoſe himſelf again, in his preſent
ſituation, to the animoſity of Pompey and Cæſar
for which he makes the following apology to his
friend Lentulus " that thoſe, who profeſſed the
" ſame principles, and were embarked in the ſame

[*y*] Hoc S. C. in ſententiam meam faćto Pompeio,
cum illa nõ poſuiſſet et ſe
e e officium in Sardiniam
& in Africam porecius eſt,
ceſte tree Iucii ad Cæ
ſaiem ſei ibi multa de
mea ſententia cuſſus eſt Cæ
ſar, cujus qui etiam Ra
venne Craſſum ante vidiſſet,
no eam in me etiam con-
f. Scit molle Pompeia
id ſere conſtabat quod
ego cum nuuſſem ex aliis,
maxim ex fratre meo cog-
novi, quem cum in Sardinia
paucis poſt diebus, quam Lu-

ca diſceſſerat, convenſſet
Te inquit ipſum cupio h
i i opportunus potui acc
cere niſi cum Marco fra
diligenter egeris depende
dum tibi eſt, quod mi i p
illo ſpoſpondiſu quid mi i
Quictus eſt gravter ſua n
rita commemoravit quid
g ſſet ſuo ſine de ætis Cæ
rs cum meo fratre quido
ſi i is de me recepiſſet,
memoriam redegit ſequen
de mea ſalute egiſſet, volu
ti e Cæſaris egiſſe, ipſi
meum fratrem teſtatus eſ
It d

          " ca

"caufe with him, were perpetually envying and
"thwarting him, and more difgufted by the
"fplendor of his life, than pleafed with any
"thing which he did for the public fervice,
"that their only pleafure, and what they could
"not even diffemble, while he was acting with
"them, was to fee him difoblige Pompey, and
"make Cæfar his enemy, when they, at the
"fame time, were continually careffing Clodius
"before his face, on purpofe to mortify him
"that if the Government indeed had fallen into
"wicked and defperate hands, neither hopes nor
"fears, nor gratitude itfelf could have prevailed
"with him to join with them, but when Pom-
"pey held the chief fway, who had acquired it
"by the moft illuftrious merit, whofe dignity
"he had always favoured from his firft fetting
"out in the world, and from whom he had re-
"ceived the greateft obligations, and who, at
"that very time, made his enemy the common
"enemy of them both, he had no reafon to ap-
"prehend the charge of inconftancy, if, on
"fome occafions, he voted and acted a little
"differently from what he ufed to do, in complai-
"fance to fuch a friend that his union with
"Pompey neceffarily included Cæfar, with
"whom both he and his brother had a friend-
"fhip alfo of long ftanding, which they were
"invited to renew by all manner of civilities and
"good offices, freely offered on Cæfar's part.
"that, after Cæfar's great exploits and victories,
"the Republic itfelf feemed to interpofe, and
"forbid him to quarrel with fuch men that
"when he ftood in need of their affiftance, his
"Brother had engaged his word for him to
"Pompey, and Pompey to Cæfar, and he

A Urb 967
Cic 51
Coff
Cn Corne-
lius Len-
tulus
Marcel-
linus,
L Marcius
Philippus

L 2   'thought

" thought himself obliged to make good those
" engagements [z]

THIS was the general state of his political be
haviour he had a much larger view, and more
comprehensive knowledge both of men and
things, than the other chiefs of the Aristocracy
Bibulus, Marcellinus, Cato, Favonius, &c
whose stiffness had ruined their cause, and
brought them into the present subjection *by alie
nating Pompey and the Equestrian order from th
S...* they considered *Cicero's management of
the Triumvirate,* as a mean submission to illega
power, which they were always opposing and ir
ritating, though ever so unseasonable , *wherea
Cicero thought it time to give over fighting, whe
the forces were so unequal. and that the more p
r ...ty they suffered the dominion of their New Ma
fters, the more temperately they would use it* [a]
being

[z] Qui cum illa sentirent
in Repub que ego agebam,
semperque infisissent, me ta
men non satisfacere Pompeio,
Cæfaremque inimicissimum
mini futurum, gaudere se aie-
bant nec mini dolendum
fea illud multo magis quod
inimicum meum — fic ani-
p...bentur — fic se præ
fente osculabantur — Ego fi
no improbus & pravis civi-
b.. Rem ib aerem vacabam
— non modo præmiis — Sed
re per cui squidem his com-
p....— Ad eorum caufam
me adjungerem, rei summa
quidem corum in me merita
commaren Cum autem in
Repub Cn Pompeius prin-
ceps Tu — i..o q..e mini-

cum unum in Civitate habe..
inimicum, non putavi fama
inconstantiæ mihi pertim..
cendam, si quibufdim in fo
tentiis paullum me immuta
fem meamque voluntata
ad fummi viri de meque op
time meriti dignitatem a
gregaffem &c Gravissin
autem me in hac mente a
pai.t, & Pompeii fides, qu..
d me Cæfari dediat, & f..
tris mei, quam Pompeio-
Lp fim i 9

[a] Neque ut ego ar
tror, errarent, si cum pa
efe non poff nt, pignare
iffcrent ———

Commutata to a ratio
Senatus, judiciorum, R...
tius publica Otium ne
exoptan..

being perfuaded, that Pompey, at leaſt, who
was the head of them, had no defigns againſt the
public liberty, unlefs he were provoked and driven to it by the perverfe oppofition of his enemies [b] Thefe were the grounds of that complaifance, which he now generally paid to him,
for the fake both of his own and the public quiet
in confequence of which, when the appointed
day came, for confidering the cafe of *the Compa-
nian lands,* the debate dropt of courfe, when it
was underftood that Cicero, the mover of it,
was abfent, and had changed his mind though it
was not, as he intimates, without fome ftruggle
in his own breaft, that he fubmitted to this ftep,
which was likely to draw upon him an imputation
of levity [c]

His daughter, Tullia, having now lived a
widow about a year, was married *to a fecond hufband, Furius Craſſipes, and the wedding Feaft held
at Cicero's houfe, on the fixth of* April we find
very little faid, of the character or condition of
this Craſſipes, but by Cicero's care in making
the match, the fortune which he paid, and the
congratulation of his friends upon it, he appears
to have been a Nobleman of principal rank and
dignity [d]. Atticus alfo, who was about a year

E 3 younger

A Urb 697
Cc 51
Coff
C CORNE
IIUS LEN-
TULUS
MARCEL
IUS,
L MARCIUS
PHILIPUS

---

c optandum eft quod i, qui
potiunt r rerum, præfici ui
videntur, ſi quidam homines
patientius eorum potentiam
ferre potuerint Dignitatem
quidem illam confularem
fortis & conftantis Senatoris,
nihil eſt, quod cogitarius
Amiſſa eft culpa eorum, qui
a Senatu & ordinem conjunc-
tiffimum, & hominem clarif-

fimum abftrahunt Ibid 8

[b] Lp 1 im 1 9

[c] Quod Idibus & po-
ſtridie fuerit dictum, de A-
gro Campano actum iri, non
eſt actum In hac caufa mihi aqua hæret — Ad Quint.
2 8

[d] De noſtra Tullia —
fpero nos cum Craſſipede con-
feciſſe. Ib 4.

Quod

younger than Cicero, was married this spring to Pilia, and invited him to the wedding [e] As to his domestic affairs, his chief care at present was about rebuilding three of his houses, which were demolished in his exile, and repairing the rest, with that also of his Brother, out of which they were driven in the last attack of Clodius by the hints, which he gives of them, they all seem to have been very magnificent, and built under the direction of the best Architects Clodius gave no farther interruption to them, being forced to quit the pursuit of Cicero, in order to watch the motions of a more dangerous enemy Milo Cicero however was not without a share of uneasiness, within his own walls, *his Brother's wife and his own, neither agreed well with each other, nor the own before as* Quintus's was displeased at her husband's staying so long abroad and Cicero's not disposed to make hers the happier for staying at home His Nephew also *Young Quintus*, a perverse youth, spoiled by a mother's indulgence, added somewhat to his trouble, for he was now charged with the care of his education, in the Father's absence, and had him taught, under his own eye, by *Tyrannio*, a Greek Master, who, with several other learned men of that country, was entertained in his house [f]

KING

Quod mihi de Filia & de Crassipede gratularis—spero q. e. cito nunc coniunctio-rum nobis voluptati fore Ep. Fam. i 7

Vix cum Crassipes praeb. Ad Att. 4 5

[e] Pro Filia, scripsisti, tu laudem. Lectio plurium-

pomium in ejus nuptiis erat cœnaturus Ad Quint. 2 3

[f] Domus utriusque nostrum ædificatur strenue — Id 4 Longilium redempto rem coortatus sum Fidem n. in faciebat, se velle nobis placere Domus erit egregia ib 6

Quin.

A Urb 697
Coss
Cos
Cn CORNE-
IIUS LEN
TULUS
MARCE-
IINUS,
L MARCIUS
PHILIPPUS

KING Ptolemy's affair was no more talked of, Pompey had other bufinefs upon his hands, and was fo ruffled by *the Tribun, Cato,* and *the Conful, Marcellius,* that he laid afide all thoughts of it for himfelf, and wifhed to ferve Lentulus in it The Senate had paffed a vote *againft reftoring him at all, but one of the Tribuns inhibited them from proceding to a decree,* and a former decree was actually fubfifting in favor of Lentulus Cicero therefore, after a confultation with Pompey, fent him their joint and laft advice, " that by his
" command of a Province, fo near to *Ægypt,*
" as he was the beft judge of what he was
" able to do, fo if he found himfelf Mafter
" of the thing, and was affured of fuccefs, he
" might leave the king at Ptolemais, or fome
" other neighbouring City, and procede with-
" out him to *Alexand,* where, if by the in-
" fluence of his fleet and troops he could ap-
" peafe the public diffenfions, and perfuade the
" Inhabitants to receive their King peaceably,
" he might then carry him home, and fo reftore
" him according to the firft decree, yet without
" a multitude, as our religious men, *fays he,*
" tell us, *the Sibyl has injoined* — that it was the
" opinion however of them both, that people
" would judge of the fact by the event if he
" was certain therefore of carrying his point, he
" fhould not defer it, if doubtfull, fhould not
" undertake it for as the world would applaud

Quint. tuus, pater optime
eruditur egregie   Hoc nunc
magis adi adverto   quod
Tyranrio docet apud me —
Ib 4

A D VIII Id Apr
'Sponfalia Craffipedi præbui
Hac convivio puer optimus,

Quintu tuus, quod perlexiter
commotus fuerat, defiit —
Multum is mecum fermonem
habuit & perhumaniter de
difcordiis muuerum nofra
rum— Pomponia rute no e
tiam de te quefta eft —Ib 6

" him.

' him, if he effected it with ease, so a miscar-
" riage might be fatal, on account of the late
" vote of the Senate, and the scruple about re-
' ligion [g] ' But Lentulus, wisely judging
the affair too hazardous for one of his dignity
and fortunes, left it to a man of a more desperate character, Gabinius, who ruined himself
soon after by embarking in it

The Tribun Cato, who was perpetually *inveighing against keeping Gladiators,* like so many
standing armies, to the terror of the Citizens, *had
lately bought a band of them, but finding himself
unable to maintain them,* was contriving to part
with them again without noise or scandal *Milo
got scent of it, and privately employed a person,
one of his own friends, to buy them, and when the
sale was closed, Racilius, another Tribun, taking the act upon himself, and pretending, that they
were bought for him, published a proclamation, that
Cato's company of Gladiators was to be sold by auction;
which gave so much diversion to the City* [h]

MILO'

[g] Te perspicere posse
c Cum reque te-
re a efficere & ud
cerreu possis, & s res fa-
cultatem habitura videatur,
ut al nisi ma que Ægyp-
tum gerere possi, esse & tuæ
inertir imperii dignitatis,
Posem ide aut aliquo pro
tum loco rege collocato,
ut cum classe atque exerciru
profectus Alexandriam ut
cum eam pace præsdisque
firmaris, Ptolemæus redeat
in regnum ut fore, ut per
te restituatur, quemadmo-
cum Senatus initio censuit,
& Ubi collocare oportet,

quemadmodum homines re-
gis& Sibylla placere dixe-
runt Sed hoc sententia ue
& illi & nobis probabatur, ut
excentu homines de tuo con-
filio existimaturos videremu
—Nos eo idem hoc sentimu
si exploratum tibi fit, posse
te regni illius potiri, non
esse cunctandum si dubium,
non esse conandum, &c Ep
Fam 1 7

[h] Ille vindex Gladiato-
rum & Bettiorum emen
—Bettanos— Hos alere non
poterat Itaque vix teneb
Sensit Milo, dedit cuidam
ron familiari negotium, qu
fu

Milo's trial being put off to *the fifth of May*, Cicero took the Benefit of a short vacation, to make an excursion into the Country, and visit his estates and Villa's in different parts of *Italy*. He spent five days at *Arpinum*, whence he proceded to his other houses *at Pompeii and Cumæ*, and stopt a while, on his return, at *Antium*, where he had lately rebuilt his house, and was now disposing and ordering his library, by the direction of Tyrannio, *the remains of which, he says, were more considerable than he expected from the late ruin*. *Atticus lent him two of his Librarians to assist his own*, in taking Catalogues, and placing the books in order, which he calls *the infusion of a soul into the body of his house* [1] During this tour, his old enemy, Gabinius, the Proconsul of *Syria*, having gained some advantage *in Judæa against Aristobulus*, who had been dethroned by Pompey, and on that account was raising troubles in the country, sent *public letters to the Senate to give an account of his victory, and to beg the decree of a Thanksgiving for it* His friends took the opportunity of moving the affair in Cicero's absence, from whose authority they apprehended some obstruction, but the Se-

A Urb 697.
Cic 51.
Coss
Cn Cornt-
ius Len-
tulus
Marcel-
linus,
L Marcius
Philippus

---

fine suspicione emerct eam sim li n a Catone cuæ simulerque abducta est, Rocilius rem patefecit, eosque homines sibi emptos esse dixit ——& tabulam proscripsit, se familiam Catonianam vincturum In eam tabulam magni ri us consequebantur ——Ad Q ii 2 [

[ ] Curiæ designatonem Tyranni us mirificam ariorum meorum Biblio

theca, quorum reliquiæ multo meliores sunt, quam i turim Utnam velim in h mittas de tuis Librariolis duos aliquos, quibus Tyrannio utatur glutinatoribus, & ad cetera administris —Ad Att 4

Postea vero quam Tyrannio mihi libros disposuit, mens addita videtur meis ædibus qui quidem in re, mirifica opera Dionysi & Menophili tui fuit, Ib 8

rate, in a full Houſe, ſlighted his letters and rejected his ſuit an affront, which had never been offered before to any Proconſul Cicero was infinitely delighted with it, calls _the reſolution of_ _that, a d_ was doubly pleas'd for its being a _free a d ge t j dgement of the Senate, without_ _any ſtruggle or influence o his part_, and reproaching Gabinius with it afterwards, ſays, that by that act the Senate had declared, _that they could not_ _believe that he, whom they had always known to_ _be a traitor at home, could ever do any thing abroad_ _that was uſefull to the Republic_ [k]

MANY prodigies were reported to have happened about this time, in the neighbourhood of _Rome horrible noiſes under ground, with claſhing_ _of Arms, and on the Alban hill a little ſhrine of_ _June, which ſtood on a table facing the eaſt, turned_ _ſuddenly of itſelf toward the north_ Theſe terrors alarmed the City, and the Senate conſulted the _Haruſpices_, who were the public Diviners or Prophets of the State, ſkill'd in all the Tuſcan diſcipline of interpreting portentous events, who gave the following anſwer in writing, _that ſup_ _p cations muſt be made to Jupiter, Saturn, Nep_ _t e, and the other Gods that the ſolemn ſhews_ _and plays had been negligently performed and polluted_ _ſacred and religious places made profane Embaſſa_ _dors killed contrary to right and law faith a_

---

[k] Id Ma Senatus fre
q en nt rus ſuit in Supplica-
tio e Gabin o deneganda
and ut Procil us hoc nemini
ac a e Foris valde plau-
citur Mihi cum ſua ſponte
jucundum tam jucundius
q me ſalute, eſt enim
er jac cum, ſine op-
pugnatore, ſine gra a no-

ſti ——— Ad Quin 2 8
4 5

Hoc ſtatuit Senatus, cum
frequens ſupplicationem Ga
b nio denegavit — A prodi
tore atque eo, quem praeſen
tem hoſtem Reipub cogita
ſet, bene Rempub geri non
potuiſſe — De Prov Con
ſul 6

cali

oaths disregarded   ancient and hidden sacrifices care-
lessly performed, and profaned —— that the Gods
gave this warning, left by the discord and dissension
of the better sort, dangers and destruction should fall
upon the Senate and the chiefs of the City, by which
means the provinces would fall under the power of a
single person, their armies be beaten, great loss en-
sue, and honors be heaped on the unworthy and dif-
graced ——[l].

A Urb 697
Cic 51.
Coff
Cn Corne-
lius Len-
tulus
Marcel-
linus,
L Marcius
Philippus.

ONE may obferve from this anfwer, that *the*
Diviners were under the Direction of thofe, who
endeavoured to apply the influence of religion to
the cure of their civil diforders · each party interpreted it according to their own views   Clodius took a handle from it of venting his fpleen
afrefh againft Cicero, and calling the people together for that purpofe, attempted to perfuade
them, *that this divine admonition was defigned par-*
ticularly againft him; and that the article of the
facred and religious places referred to the cafe of his
houfe, which, after a folemn confecration to religion,
was rendered again profane, charging all the dif-
pleafure of the Gods to Cicero's account, who affected
nothing lefs than a tyranny, and the oppreffion of their
liberties [m]

CICERO made a reply to Clodius the next
day in the Senate, where, after a fhort and general invective upon his profligate life, " he leaves
" him, *he fays,* a devoted victim to Milo, who
" feemed to be given to them by heaven, for
" the extinction of fuch a plague, as Scipio
" was for the deftruction of *Carthage* he de-
" clares the prodigy to be one of the moft ex-
" traordinary, which had ever been reported to

A Urb 697
Cic 51
Coſſ
C. Corne-
lius Len-
tulus
Marcel-
linus,
L Marcius
Philippus

" the Senate, but laughs at the abſurdity of ap
" plying any part of it to him, ſince his houſe,
" as he proves at large, was more ſolemnly
" cleared from any ſervice or relation to religion,
" than any other houſe in Rome, by the Judge
" ment of the Prieſts, the Senate, and all the
" orders of the City [*n*] " Then running through
the ſeveral articles of the anſwer, " he ſhews them
" all to tally ſo exactly with the notorious acts
" and impieties of Clodius's life, that they could
" not poſſibly be applied to any thing elſe ——
" That as to the ſports, ſaid to be negligently
" performed and polluted, it clearly denoted the
" pollution of the *Megaleſian play*, the moſt
" venerable and religious of all other ſhews
" which Clodius himſelf, as Ædile, exhibited
" in honor of the Mother of the Gods, where
" when the Magiſtrates and Citizens were ſeated
" to partake of the diverſions, and the uſual
" proclamation was made, to command all ſlaves
" to retire, a vaſt body of them, gathered from
" all parts of the City, by the order of Clodius,
" forced their way upon the ſtage, to the great
" terror of the aſſembly, where much miſchief
" and bloodſhed would have enſued, if the
" Conſul Marcellinus, by his firmneſs and pre
" ſence of mind, had not quieted the tumult
" and in another repreſentation of the ſame
" plays, the ſlaves, encouraged again by Clo
" dius, were ſo audacious and ſucceſsfull in a ſe
" cond irruption, that they drove the whole
" company out of the Theater, and poſſeſſed
" it intirely to themſelves [*o*] that *as to the*
" *profanation of ſacred and religious places*, it
" could not be interpreted of any thing ſo aptly,

[*n*] De Haruſpic reſpon　　[*o*] Ibid 10, 11, 12, 13
&c

" as of what Clodius and his friends had done A Urb 697.
" for that, in the houfe of Q Seius, which he Cic 51
" had bought after murthering the owner, there Coff
" was a chappel and altars, which he had lately Cn Corne-
" demolifhed   that L. Pifo had deftroyed a cele- lius Len-
" brated chappel of Diana, where all that neigh- tulus
" bourhood, and fome even of the Senate, ufed Marcel-
" annually to perform their family facrifices · linus,
" that Serranus alfo had thrown down, burnt, L Marcius
" and profaned feveral confecrated Chappels, and Philippus
" raifed other buildings upon them [p]. that *as*
" *to Embaffadors killed contrary to law and right ,*
" though it was commonly interpreted of thofe
" from *Alexandria*, yet other Embaffadors had
" been murthered, whofe death was no lefs of-
" fenfive to the Gods, as Theodofius, killed
" with the privity and permiffion of Clodius, and
" Plator, by the order of Pifo [q]   as *to the vio-*
" *lation of faith and oaths*, that it related evidently
" to thofe Judges, who had abfolved Clodius,
" as being one of the moft memorable and fla-
" grant perjuries, which *Rome* had ever known ;
" that the anfwer itfelf fuggefted this interpreta-
" tion, when it fubjoined, *that ancient and oc-*
" *cult facrifices were polluted* , which could refer
" to nothing fo properly as to the rites of the
" *Bona Dea*, which were the *moft ancient* and
" *the moft occult* of any in the City , celebrated
" with incredible fecrecy to that Goddefs, whofe
" name it was not lawful for men to know ,
" and with ceremonies, which no man ever
" pried into, but Clodius [r]   Then as to the
" warning, given by the Gods, of *dangers, likely*
" *to enfue from the diffenfions of the principal*

[p] Ibid 14, 15   [r] Ibid 17, 18.
[q] Ibid 16

" *Citizens* ;

A Urb 697
C.c 51
Coss
C. CORNE-
LIUS LEN-
TULUS
MARCEL-
LI US,
L. MARCIU-
PHILIPPUS

" *Citizens*, that there was no man so particular!,
" active, in promoting those dissensions, as Clo
" dius, who was perpetually enflaming one side
" or the other, now pursuing popular, now
" Aristocratical measures, at one time a favorite
" of the Triumvirate, at another of the Senate,
" whose credit was wholly supported by their
" quarrels and animosities He exhorts them
" therefore in the conclusion, to beware of falling
" into those miseries, of which the Gods so evi-
" dently forewarned them, and to take care
" especially, that the form of the Republic was
" not altered, since all civil contests between great
" and powerfull Citizens must necessarily end,
" either in an universal destruction, or a tyran
" ny of the Conqueror that the state was now
" in so tottering a condition, that nothing could
" preserve it but their concord that there was
" no hope of it's being better, while Clodius re-
" mained unpunished and but one degree left
" of being worse, by being wholly ruined and
" enslaved, for the prevention of which, the
" Gods had given them this remarkable admo-
" nition, for they were not to believe, what
" was sometimes represented on the stage, that
" any God ever descended from heaven to con-
" verse familiarly with men, but that these ex-
" traordinary sounds and agitations of the world,
" the air, the elements, were the onely voice
" and speech, which heaven made use of, that
" these admonished them of their danger, and
" pointed out the remedy, and that the Gods,
" by intimating so freely the way of their safety,
" had shewn, how easy it would be to pacify
" them, by pacifying onely their own animosi-
" ties and discords among themselves "

I

ABOUT the middle of the summer, and before the time of chusing new Consuls, which was commonly *in August,* the Senate began to deliberate *on the Provinces,* which were to be assigned to them at the expiration of their office *The Consular Provinces,* about which the debate singly turned, were *the two Gauls,* which Cæsar now held, *Macedonia,* which Piso, and *Syria,* which Gabinius possessed All who spoke before Cicero, excepting Servilius, *were for taking one, or both the* Gauls *from Cæsar,* which was what the Senate generally desired. but when it came to Cicero's turn, he gladly laid hold on the occasion to revenge himself on Piso and Gabinius; and exerted all his authority, to get them recalled with some marks of disgrace, and their Governments assigned to the succeeding Consuls but as for Cæsar, his opinion was, *that his command should be continued to him, till he had finished the war, which he was carrying on with such success, and settled the conquered countries* This gave no small offence. and the *Consul* Philippus could not forbear interrupting and reminding him, *that he had more reason to be angry with Cæsar, than with Gabinius himself, since Cæsar was the author and raiser of all that storm, which had oppressed him* But Cicero replied, *that, in this vote, he was not pursuing his private resentment, but the public good, which had reconciled him to Cæsar, and that he could not be an enemy to one who was deserving so well of his country that a year or two more would complete his conquests, and reduce all Gaul to a state of peacefull subjection. that the cause was widely different between Cæsar and the other two, that Cæsar's administration was beneficial, prosperous, glorious to the Republic, theirs, scandalous, ignominious, hurtfull to their subjects, and*

contemptible

A. Urb 697
Cic 51.
CoÎ
Cn Cornelius Lentulus Marcellinus,
L Marcius Philippus.

A Urb 697
Cc 51
Coll
Cn Corne-
lius Len-
tulus
Marcel-
linus,
L Marcus
Philippus

contemptible to their enemies —— In fhort, he managed the debate fo, that the Senate came fully into his Sentiments, and decreed *the revocation of Pifo and Gabinius* [s]

He was now likewife engaged in pleading two confiderable caufes at the Bar, the one in defence of Cornelius Balbus, the other of M Cælius Balbus was a native of *Gades* in *Spain*, of a fplendid family in that City, who, for his fidelity and fervices to the Roman Generals in that Province, and efpecially *in the Sertorian war, had the freedom of* Rome *conferred upon him by Pompey, in virtue of a law, which authorifed him to grant it to as many as he thought proper*. But Pompey's act was now called in queftion, as originally null and invalid, on a pretence, *that the City of* Gades *was not within the terms of that alliance and relation to* Rome, *which rendered its Citizens capable of that privilege* Pompey and Craffus were his advocates, and, at their defire, Cicero alfo, who had *the third place*, or poft of honor affigned to him, to give the finifhing hand

[ ] Itaque ego idem, qui nunc Confulibus iis, qui defignati erunt, Syriam Macedoniamque decerno — Quod fi effent illi optimi viri tamen ego mea fententia C Cælerio dum fuccedendum putarem Quare dicam, Patres confcripti, quod fentio, atque illam interpellationem familiaris mei, qua paullo ante interrupta eft oratio mea, non pertimefcam Negat me vir optimus inimiciorem debere effe Gabrio, quam Cæfari, omnem enim illam tempeftatem, cui cefferim, Cæfare impulfore atque adjutore effe excitatam Cui fi primum fic refpondeam, me communis utilitatis habere rationem, non doloris mei — Hic me meus in Rempub animus priftinus ac perenni cum C Cælare reducit reconciliat, reftituit in gratiam Quod volent denique homines exiftiment liceat egopoffum effe bene de Republica merenti non amicis — Vid Orat de Provin Conf 8, 9, &c

to the cause [*t*] The profecution was projected, not fo much out of enmity to Balbus, as to his Patrons Pompey and Cæfar, by whofe favor he had acquired great wealth and power, being at this time *General of the Artillery to* Cæfar, and the principal manager or fteward of all his affairs. The Judges gave fentence for him, and confirmed his right to the City, from which foundation he was raifed afterwards, *by Auguftus, to the* Confulate itfelf his Nephew alfo, *Young Balbus, who was made free with him at the fame time, obtained the honor of a triumph, for his victories over the Garamantes*, and, *as* Pliny *tells us, they were the onely inftances of Foreigners, and adopted Citizens, who had ever advanced themfelves to either of thofe honours in* Rome [*u*]

CÆLIUS, whom he next defended, was a young Gentleman *of Equeftrian rank*, of great parts and accomplifhments, trained under the difcipline of Cicero himfelf, to whofe care he was committed by his Father, upon his firft introduction into the Forum before he was of age to hold any Magiftracy, he had diftinguifhed himfelf *by two public impeachments*, the one of C Antonius, Cicero's collegue in the Confulfhip, *for confpiring againft the ftate*, the other of L. Atratinus, *for bribery and corruption* Atra-

---

[*t*] Quo mihi difficilior eft hic extremus perorandi loci —Sed mos eft gerendus, non modo Cornelio, cujus ego voluntati in ejus periculis nullo modo deeffe poffum, fed etiam Cn Pompeio ——— Pr Balbo 1 2 &c

[*u*] Fuit & Balbus Cornelius major Conful — Primus externorum, atque et am in

oceano genitorum ufus illo honore —Hift N 7 43

Garama caput Garamantum omnia armis Romanis fuperata, & a Cornelio Balbo triumphata uno omnium externo curru & Quir ini jure donato qui, pe Gadibus nato Civitas Rom cum Balbo majore patruo data eft Ib 5 5

A Urb 697
Cæ 5,
Cof

C Corne-
lius Le -
tlls
Marcel-
li l,
L Marcll
Philippus

tinus's fon was now revenging his Father's quar
rel, and *accufea Cælius of public violence, for being
concer'd in the affaffination of Dio, the chief of
the Alexandrien embaffy*; *and of an attempt to po,
fon Clodia, the fifter of Clodus* he had been th
Lady's Gallant whofe refentment for her favor
flighted by him, was the real fource of all h
trouble In this fpeech Cicero treats *the chara
ter and geometries of Clodia, her Commerce with
Cælius, and the gaieties and licentiousnefs of youl,
with fuch a circuity of wit and humor*, that make
it one of the moft entertaining, which he has le
to us. Cælius, who was truly *a Libertine*, live
on *the Palatin hill*, in a houfe which he hired
Clodius, and, among the other pioofs of his ex
travagance, it was objected, *that a young man
in no public employment, fhould take a feparate hou
from his Father, at the yearly rent of two hundr
and fifty pounds* to which Cicero replied, *th
Clodius, he perceived, had a mind to fell his hou
by fetting the value of it fo high , whereas, in trut
it was but a little paultry dwelling, of fmall ren
fcarce above eighty pounds per annum* [x] Cæln
was acquitted, and ever after profeffed the high
eft regard for Cicero; with whom he held,
correfpondence of Letters, which will give u
occafion to fpeak more of him, in the fequel
the Hiftory

CICERO feems to have compofed *a little
Poem* about this time, in compliment to Cæfar
and excufes his not fending it to Atticus, "be
"caufe Cæfar preffed to have it, and he had re
"ferved no copy though, to confefs the truth,

[x] Sumptus unius generis
objectus eft, habitationis
tigna miliuus civiftis cum
habitare Nunc denum in-
telligo P Clodii infulam ef
venalem, cujus hic in ædie
us habitet, decem, ut opinor
milibus —Pro Cælio. 7
"l'

" *he says,* he found it very difficult to digest the
" meanness of recanting his old principles But
" adieu, *says he,* to all right, true, honest councils
" it is incredible, what perfidy there is in those,
" who want to be Leaders, and who really
" would be so, if there was any faith in them
" I felt what they were to my cost, when I was
" drawn in, deserted, and betrayed, by them
" I resolved still to act on with them in all
" things, but found them the same as before,
" till by your advice I came at last to a better
" mind You will tell me, that you advised me
" indeed to act, but not to write, 'tis true, but
" I was willing to put myself under a necessity of
" adhering to my new alliance, and preclude the
" possibility of returning to those, who instead
" of pitying me, as they ought, never cease en-
" vying me — But since those, who have no
" power, will not love me, my business is to
" acquire the love of those who have you will
" say, I wish that you had done it long ago, I
" know you wished it, and I was a mere Ass for
" not minding you [*y*]."

A Urb 967.
Cic 51
Coss
Cn Corne-
lius Len-
tulus
Marcel-
linus,
L Marcius
Philippus.

In

[*y*] Urgebar ab eo, ad quem misi, & non habebam exemplar quid? etiam, (dudum circumrodo, quod devorandum est) subtupicula mihi videbatur παλινωδία, sed valeant recta, vera, honesta consilia Non est credibile, quæ sit perfidia in istis principibus, ut volunt esse, & ut essent, si quicquam haberent fidei Senseram, noram, inductus, relictus, projectus ab iis tamen hoc erat in animo, ut cum iis in Rep consenti-

rem Iidem erant, qui fuerant Vix aliquando te auctore resipivi, Dices, ea te monuisse, quæ facerem, non etiam ut scriberem. Ego mehercule mihi necessitatem volui imponere hujus-novæ conjurationis, ne qua mihi liceret labi ad illos, qui etiam tum cum miserei mei debent, non desinunt invidere Sed tamen modici fuimus ὑποθέσει, ut scripsi —— Sed quoniam qui nihil possunt, ii me amare nolunt,

Γ 2   demus

A. Urb. 697. Cic. 51. Coss. C. Cornelius Lentulus Marcellinus, L. Marcius Philippus.

IN this year also, Cicero wrote that celebrated letter to Lucceius, in which he presses him, *to attempt the history of his transactions*. Lucceius was a man of eminent learning and abilities, and had just finished *the history of the Italick and Marsian civil wars*, with intent to carry it down through his own times, and, in the general relation, to include, as he had promised, a particular account of Cicero's acts: but Cicero, who was pleased with his stile and manner of writing, labors to engage him in this letter, to postpone the design of his continued history, and enter directly on that separate period, "from the beginning of his Consulship to his restoration, "comprehending Catiline's conspiracy, and his "own exil." He observes, "that this short "interval was distinguished with such a variety "of incidents, and unexpected turns of fortune, "as furnished the happiest materials, both to "the skill of the writer, and the entertainment "of the reader; that, when an author's attention "was confined to a single and select subject, "he was more capable of adorning it, and displaying his talents, than in the wide and diffusive field of general history; but if he did "not think the facts themselves worth the pain "of adorning, that he would yet allow so much "to friendship, to affection, and even to that "favor, which he had so laudably disclaimed in "his Prefaces, as not to confine himself scrupulously to the strict laws of history, and the "rules of truth —— That, if he would under"take it, he would supply him with some rough

demus operam, ut ab iis, qui possunt, diligamur dices, vellem jampridem. Scio te voluisse, & me asinum germanum fuisse.—Ad Att. 4. 5.

Scribis poema ab eo nostrum probari.—Ad Quint. 2. 15.

"memori-

" memoirs, or commentaries, for the foundation
" of his work, if not, that he himself should be
" forced to do, what many had done before
" him, write his own life, a task liable to
" many exceptions and difficulties, where a
" man would necessarily be restrained by mo-
" desty, on the one hand, or partiality on the
" other, either for blaming, or praising him-
" self, so much as he deserved, &c [z] "

A Urb 697.
Cic 51
Coss
Cn Corne-
lius Len-
tulus
Marcel-
linus,
L Marcius
Philippus.

THIS letter is constantly alledged as a proof
of Cicero's vanity, and excessive love of praise:
but we must consider it as written, not by a philo-
sopher, but a statesman, conscious of the greatest services to his country, for which he had
been barbarously treated, and, on that account,
the more eager to have them represented in an
advantageous light and impatient to taste some
part of that glory when living, which he was
sure to reap from them when dead and as to the
passage which gives the offence, where he presses
his friend *to exceed even the bounds of truth in his*
praises it is urged onely, we see, conditionally,
and upon an absurd or improbable supposition,
that Lucceius did not think the acts themselves really
loudable, or worth praising but whatever exceptions there may be to the morality, there can be
none to the elegance and composition of the letter, which is filled with a variety of beautifull
sentiments, illustrated by examples, drawn from
a perfect knowledge of history, so that it is justly ranked among the capital pieces of the episto-
lary kind, which remain to us from antiquity.
Cicero had employed more than ordinary pains
upon it, and was pleased with his success in it. for
he mentions it to Atticus with no small satisfac-

[z] Ep. fam 12

tion,

tion, and wiſhed him to get a copy of it from their friend Lucceius The effect of it was, that Lucceius *undertook what Cicero deſired,* and probably made ſome progreſs in it, ſince Cicero ſent him *the memoirs,* which he promiſed, and Lucceius lived many years after, in an uninterrupted friendſhip with him, though neither this, nor any other of his writings had the fortune to be preſerved to ſucceeding ages [a]

ALL people's eyes and inclinations began now to turn towards Cæſar, who by the eclat of his victories, ſeemed to rival the fame of Pompey himſelf, and, by his addreſs and generoſity, gained ground upon him daily in authority and influence in public affairs. He ſpent the winter at *Luca*; whither a vaſt concourſe of all ranks reſorted to him from *Rome.* Here Pompey and Craſſus were again made friends by him, and a project formed, *that they ſhould jointly ſeize the Conſulſhip for the next year, though they had not declared themſelves Candidates, within the uſual time.* L. Domitius Ahenobarbus, a profeſſed enemy, was one of the competitors, who thinking himſelf ſure of ſucceſs, could not forbear bragging, *that he would effect, when Conſul, what he could not do when Prætor, reſcind Cæſor's acts, and recall him from his Government* [b], which made them reſolve at all hazards to defeat him.

[a] Epiſtolam, Lucceo quam mi — fac ut ab eo ſumas, valde bella eſt, eumque ut adproperet adhorteris, &, quod mihi ſe ita facturum reſcripſit, agas gratias Ad Att 4 6

Tu Lucceo librorum noſtrum datis Ioin 11

[b] Sed cum L Domitius conſulatus Candidatus palam minaretur, Conſulem ſe effecturum, quod Prætor nequiſſet, adempturum que ei exercitus Craſſum Pompeium que in urbem Provinciæ ſuæ Lucam extractos compulit, ut detrudendi Domitii cauſa alterum Corſulatum peterent— Sueton J Cæſ 24

What

What greatly favored their defign was the ob- A Urb 69·.
Cc 5¹
Coff
ftinacy of the Tribun, C Cato, who, to revenge
himfelf on Marcellinus, for not fuffering him to Cn Cornᴇ-
hold *any affemblies of the people, for promulgating* lius Iᴇɴ-
his laws, would not fuffer the Confuls to hold any, tuʟʟs
for the choice of the Magiftrates [c] The Trium- Marcᴇʟ-
ʟɪɴᴜs,
virate fupported him in this refolution till the ɪ Marcɪᴜs
year expired, and the Government fell into *an* Pʜɪʟɪᴘᴘᴜs
Inter-regnum, when by faction and violence, and
the terror of troops poured into the City, *they*
extorted the Confulfhip out of the hands of Domitius,
and fecured it to themfelves [d]. This made Pompey generally odious, who, in all this heigth of
greatnefs, could not defend himfelf from the
perpetual railleries and infults of his adverfaries,
which yet he bore with fingular temper and patience Marcellinus was conftantly alarming the
City with the danger of his power, and as he
was haranguing one day on that fubject. being encouraged by a general acclamation of the people,
cry out, Citizens, fays he, *cry out while you may,*
for it will not be long in your power to do fo with
fafety [e] Cn Pifo alfo, a Young Nobleman,
who had impeached Manilius Crifpus, a man of
Prætorian rank and notorioufly guilty, being provoked by Pompey's protection of him, turned
his attack againft Pompey himfelf, and charged
him with many crimes againft the State, being
afked therefore by Pompey, why he did not

[c] Conful—dies comitia- | Conful fuerit, Confulem fieri
les exemit omnes — C Cato | non p fl. &c Ad Att 4 8
concionatus et, comitia ha- | Vid Dio p 103
beri non fiturum, fi fibi cum | [e] Acclamate, inquit, Qui-
populo agendi dies effent ex- | rites, acclamate, dum licet
empti Ad Quint 2 6 | jam enim vobis impune face-
   [d] Quid enim hoc miferi | re non licebit —Val Max 6.
us, quam eum, qui tot an- | 2
nos, quod habet, defignatus

chufe

chufe to impeach him rather than the Criminal, he replied briskly, *that he would give bail to ford a trial, a thou raifing a civil war, be would foon bring him before the Judges* [f]

DURING the continuance of thefe tumults, occafioned by the election of the new Confuls, Cicero retired into the country, where he ftaid to the beginning of *May*, much out of humor, and difgufted both with the Republic and himfelf Atticus's conftant advice to him was, *to confult his fafety and interoff, by uniting himfelf with the men of power*, and they on their part, were as conftantly inviting him to it, by all poffible affurances of their affection but in his anfwers to Atticus he obferves, " that their two cafes " were very different, that Atticus, having no " peculiar character, fuffered no peculiar indig- " nity, nothing but what was common to all " the Citizens, whereas his own condition was " fuch, that if he fpoke what he ought to do, he " fhould be looked upon as a madman, if what " was ufefull onely to himfelf, as a flave, if no- " thing at all, as quite oppreffed and fubdued " that his uneafinefs was the greater, becaufe he " could not fhew it without being thought un- " gratefull— fhall I withdraw myfelf then, *fays* " *me*, from bufnefs and retire to the port of " eafe? That will not be allowed to me.   Shall " I follow thefe Leaders to the wars, and, after " having refufed to command, fubmit to be ' commanded? I will do fo, for I fee that it is " your advice, and wifh that I had always fol-

[f] De ... , trades quam de Manlii capite, in R...to... ...ers, concilium judices mittam ...e bellum ... e cha... Ibid ... ... ,

" lowed

" lowed it · or fhall I refume my poft, and enter
" again into affairs? I cannot perfuade myfelf to
" that, but begin to think Philoxenus in the
" right, who chofe to be carried back to pri-
" fon rather than commend the Tyrant's
" verfes This is what I am now meditating,
" to declare my diflike at leaft of what they are
" doing [g]"

A Urb 698
Cic 52
Coff
Cn POMPEI-
us MAG-
NUS II
M LICINIUS
CRASS. II.

SUCH were the agitations of his mind at
this time, as he frequently fignifies in his letters he was now at one of his Villa's, on the
delightfull fhore of *Baiæ*, the chief place of refort and pleafure for the great and rich, *Pompey*
come thither in April, and no fooner arrived, than
he fent him his compliments, and fpent his whole
time with him *they had much difcourfe on public*
affairs, in which Pompey expreffed great uneafinefs,
and owned himfelf diffatisfied with his own part in
them, but Cicero, in his account of the converfation, intimates *fome fufpicion of his fincerity* [h].

In

[g] Tu quidem, etfi es
natura πολιτικός, tamen nullam habes propriam fervitu-
tem communi frueris no-
mine Ego vero, qui, fi lo
quor de Repub quod oportet,
infanus, fi quod opus eft, fer-
vus exiftimor, fi taceo, op-
preffus & captus, quo dolore
effe debeo? quo fum fcilicet
hoc etiam acriore, quod ne
dolere quidem poffum, ut
non ingratus videar Quid
fi ceffare libeat & in otii por-
tum confugere? Nequicquam
Immo etiam in bellum & in
caftra ergo erimus οταδο.,
qui ταγοι effe noluimus? Sic
fac endum eft, tibi enim ipfi,

cui utinam femper paruiffem,
fic video placere. Reliqui
eft, Σταιαν έχει, ταυταν
λισμει, non mehercule poffum & Philoxeno ignofco,
qui reduci in carcerem maluit Veruntamen id ipfum
mecum in his locis commen-
tor, ut ifta improbem — Ad
Att 4 9
The ftory of Dionyfius the
Tyrant of Syracufe, and Philoxenus the Poet, is told by
Diodorus Siculus Lib 15
P 331
[h] Pompeius in Cuma-
num Parilibus venit mifit
ad me ftatim qui falutem
nunciaret ad eum poftridie
mane

A Urb 698
Cic. 52.
Coss
Cn Pompei-
us Mag
nus II
M Licinius
Crassus II

In the midst of this company and diversion, C cero's *entertainment was in his studies*, for he ne ver resided any where without securing to him self the use of a good library· here he had *the command of Faustus's*, the son of Sylla, and son-in law of Pompey, one of the best collections of *Italy*: gathered from the spoils of *Greece*, and especially of *Athens*, from which *Sylla brought away many thousand volumes*. He had no body in the house with him, but Dionysius, a learned *Greek slave*, whom Atticus had made free, and who was entrusted with the instruction of *the two young Cicero's*, the son and the Nephew *with this companion, he was devouring books, since the wretched state of the public had deprived him, as he tells us, of all other pleasures*. I had much rather, says he to Atticus, *be sitting on your little bench, under Aristotle's picture, than in the Curule chair of our great ones, or taking a turn with you in your walks, than with him, whom it must, I see, be my fate to walk with as for the success of that walk, let fortune look to it, or some God, if there be any, who takes care of us* [1]   He mentions in

mane videbam —— Ad Att
4. x
    Nos hic cum Pompeio fuimus sane sibi displicens,
ut loquebatur, sic est enim
in hoc homine dicendum —
In nos vero suavissime effusus
venit etiam ad me in Cumanum a se— Ib 8

[1] Ego hic pascor Bibliotheca Fausti Fortasse tu pu
tabas his rebus Puteolanis &
Lucrinensibus Ne ista quidem desunt Sed mehercule
a caeteris oblectationibus defetor & voleptatibus propter

Rempub sic literis sustentor
& recreor, maloque in illa
tua sedecula, quam habes sub
imagine Aristotelis, sedere,
quam in istorum sella curuli,
tecumque apud te ambulare,
quam cum eo, quocum video
esse ambulandum Sed de
illa ambulatione fors videret,
aut si qui est, qui curet Deus
Ib 10

    Nos hic voramus literas
cum homine mirifico, ita me
hercule sentio, Dionysio. Ib.
11.

the same letter a current report at *Puteoli, that* A Urb 698.
King Ptolemy was restored, and desires to know, Cic 52.
what account they had of it at Rome. the report Coss Cn Pompei-
was very true, for Gabinius, tempted by Ptole- us Mag-
my's gold, and the plunder of *Ægypt*, and en- nus II
couraged also, as some write, *by Pompey himself,* M Licinius
undertook to replace him on the Throne with Crassus II.
his Syrian Army; which he executed with a high
hand, and the destruction of all the King's enemies, *in open defiance of the authority of the Senate,*
and the direction of the Sibyl this made a great
noise at *Rome*, and irritated the people to such a
degree, that they resolved to make him feel their
displeasure for it very severely, at his return [*k*].

HIs Collegue Piso came home the first from
his nearer Government of *Macedonia*, after an
inglorious administration of a Province, *whence no*
Consular Senator had ever returned, but to a tri-
umph For though, on the account of some
trifling advantage in the field, he had procured
himself *to be saluted Emperor by his army*, yet the
occasion was so contemptible, *that he durst not*
send any letters upon it to the Senate but after op-
pressing the subjects, plundering the allies, and
losing the best part of his troops against the neighbouring barbarians, who invaded and laid waste
the country, he ran away in disguise from a mu-
tiny of the soldiers, whom he disbanded at last
without their pay [*l*] When he arrived at
Rome,

[*k*] Vid. Dio l. 39. p
116, &c
 [*l*] Ex qua aliquot Præto-
rio imperio, Consulari quidem nemo redit, qui incolu-
mis fuerit, qui non triumpha-
rit In Pison. 16.

Ut ex ea provincia, quæ
fuit ex omnibus una maxime
triumphalis, nullas sit ad Senatum litteras mittere ausus
—Nuncius ad Senatum missus
est nullus. Ib 19.

Mitto

A Urb 698
Cic. 52
Coss
Cn Pompei-
us Mag-
nus II
M Licinius
Crassus II

Rome, he ftript his Fafces of their laurel, and entered the City obfcurely and ignominioufly, without any other attendance than his own retinue [*m*] On his firft appearance in public, trufting to the authority of his fon-in-law, Cæfar, he had the hardinefs to attack Cicero, and complain to the Senate of his injurious treatment of him but when he began *to reproach him with the difgrace of his exil, the whole Affembly interrupted him by a loud and general clamor* [*n*] Among other things, with which he upbraided Cicero, he told him, *that it was not any envy for what he had done, but the vanity of what he had faid, which had driven him into exil, and that a fingle verfe of his,*

Cedant arma Togæ, concedat laurea linguæ,

was the caufe of all his calamity; by provoking Pompey to make him feel, how much *the power of the General was fuperior to that of the Orator* he put him in mind alfo, *that it was mean and ungenerous to exert his fpleen onely againft fuch, whom he had reafon to contemn, without daring to*

Mitto de amiffa maxima par e exercitus—20 —

Dyrrhachium ut venit decedens obfeffus eft ab iis ipfis militibus—Quibus cum juratus affirmaffet, fe, quæ deberentur, poftero die perfoluturum, domum fe abdidit inde nocte intempefta crepidatus, vefte fervili navem confcendit —38 —

[*m*] Sic ifte— Macedonicus Imperator in urbem fe intulit, ut nullius negotiatoris obfcuriffimi reditus unquam fuerit defertior — 23

Cum tu— detraclam e cruentis fafcibus lauream ad portam Efquilinam abjecifti.— Ib 30

[*n*] Tunc aufus es meum difceffum illum — maledicti & contumeliæ loco ponere Quo quidem tempore cepi, Patres confcripti, fructum immortalem veftri in me amoris— qui non admurmuratione, fed voce & clamore abjecti hominis — petulantiam fregifti —Ib 14.

meddli

meddle with those, who had more power, and where
his resentment was more due [o] But it had been
better for him, to have stifled his complaints and
suffered Cicero to be quiet, who, exasperated by
his imprudent attack, made a Reply to him upon the spot, in *an Invective speech*, the severest
perhaps, that was ever spoken by any man, on
the person, the parts, the whole life and conduct
of Piso, which, as long as the *Roman* name sub-
sists, must deliver down a most detestable character of him to all posterity. As to the verse,
with which he was urged, he ridicules the absur-
dity of Piso's application of it, and tells him,
" that he had contrived a very extraordinary pu-
" nishment for *poor poets*, if they were to be ba-
" nished for every *bad line* · that he was a Critic
" of a new kind, not an Aristarchus, but a
" Grammatical Phalaris, who, instead of ex-
" punging the verse, was for destroying the au-
" thor that the verse itself could not imply any
" affront to any man whatsoever that he was
" an ass, and did not know his letters, to ima-
" gine, that by the Gown, he meant his own
" gown, or by arms, the arms of any particu-
" lar General, and not to see, that he was
" speaking onely in the Poetical stile, and as the
" one was the emblem of peace, the other of
" war, that he could mean nothing else, than
" that the tumults and dangers, with which the
" City had been threatened, must now give way
" to peace and tranquillity that he might have

---

[o] Non ulla tibi, inquit,   Paullo ante dixisti me cum
invidia nocuit, sed versus tui   iis confligere, quos despice-
—Hæc res tibi fluctus illos   rem, non attingere eos, qui
excitavit—Tuæ dicis, inquit,   plus possent, quibus iratus es-
Togæ, summum Imperato-   se deberem —Ib 29, 30, 31
rem esse cessurum —

" stuck

A Urb 698
Cic 52.
Coff
C\ Pompei-
ts M.g-
nts II
M Licinius
Crassus II

" stuck a little indeed in explaining the latter
" part of the verse, if Pifo himfelf had not
" helped him out; who, by trampling his own
" *laurel* under foot at the Gates of *Rome*, had
" declared how much he thought it inferior to
" every other kind of honor —— that as for
" Pompey, it was filly to think that, after the
" volumes, which he had written in his praife,
" one filly verfe fhould make him at laft his ene
" my but that in truth, he never was his ene-
" my, and if, on a certain occafion, he had
" fhewn any coldnefs towards him, it was all
" owing to the perfidy and malice of fuch as
" Pifo, who were continually infufing jealoufies
" and fufpicions into him, till they had removed
" from his confidence all who loved either him,
" or the Republic [*p*] "

About this time, the Theater, which Pompey had built at his own charge, for the ufe and
ornament of the City, was folemnly opened and
dedicated · it is much celebrated by the ancients,
for its grandor and magnificence the plan was
taken from the Theater of *Mytilene,* but greatly

[*p*] Quoniam te non Arif-
tarchum, fed Grammaticum
Phalarim habemus, qui non
rotam apponas ad malum
verfum, fed poetam armis
profequare — Quid nunc te,
Afine, literas doceam ? Non
dixi hanc togam, qua fum
amictus, nec arma, fcutum
& gladium unius Imperato-
ris fed quod pacis eft infig
ne & otii toga, contra autem arma, tumultus ac belli,
more poetarum locutus, hoc
intelligi volui, bellum ac tu-
multum paci atque otio con-
ceffurum — in altero — ita re-
rem, nifi tu expediffes Nam
cum tu— detractam e cruen
tis fafcibus lauream ad portam Efquilinam abjecifti, in-
dicafti, non modo ampliffi-
me, fed etiam minimæ lau-
di lauream conceffiffe— Vis
Pompeium ifto verfu inimi
cum mihi effe factum—Pri-
mo nonne compenfabit cum
uno verficulo tot mea volu
mina laudum fuarum ? Vef-
træ fraudes,— æftræ crimina-
tiones infidiarum mearum—
effecerunt t ego excluderer
—Sc in P fon 30, 31

enlarged,

enlarged, fo as to receive commodioufly *forty thoufand people.* It was furrounded *by a Portico, to fhelter the company in bad weather, and had a Curia, or Senate-houfe, annexed to it; with a Bafilica alfo, or grand Hall, proper for the fittings of Judges,* or any other public bufinefs. which were all finifhed *at Pompey's coft, and adorned with a great number of Images, formed by the ableft mafters, of men and women, famed for fomething very remarkable or prodigious in their lives and characters* [q]. Atticus undertook the care of *placing all thefe ftatues,* for which Pompey charged Cicero *with his thanks to him* [r]   but what made this Fabric the more furprifing and fplendid, was a *beautiful Temple, erected at one end of it to Venus the Conquerefs, and fo contrived, that the feats of the Theater might ferve as ftairs to the Temple*   This was defigned, it is faid, *to avoid the reproach of making fo vaft an expence for the meer ufe of luxury; the Temple being fo placed, that thofe who came to the fhews, might feem to come to worfhip the Goddefs* [s].

[q] Pompeius Magnus in ornamentis Theatri mirabiles fama pofuit imagines, ob id diligentius magnorum artificum ingeniis elaboratas inter quas legitur Eutyche, a viginti liberis rogo illata, enixa triginta partus, Alcippe, Elephantum, Plin   H 7 3

[r] Tibi etiam gratias agebat, quod figna componenda fufcepiffes   Ad Att 4 9

[s] Quum Pompeius, inquit, ædem Victoriæ dedicaturus effet, cujus gradus verem Theatri effent, &c   A

Gell X 1 Vid Tertull de Spectat

Dion Caffius mentions it, as a tradition, that he had met with, that this Theater was not really built by Pompey, but by his Freedman, Demetrius, who had made himfelf richer than his mafter, by attending him in his wars, and to take off the envy of raifing fo vaft an eftate, laid out a confiderable part of it upon the Theater, and gave the honor of it to Pompey   Dio p 107 Senec de Tranq Anim c 8

AT the ſolemnity of this dedication, Pompey entertained the people with *the moſt magnificent ſhews, which had ever been exhibited in Rome in the Theater, where ſtage plays, prizes of muſic, weſtling, and all kinds of bodily exerciſes in the Circus, horſe-races, and huntings of wild beaſts for five days ſucceſſively, in which five hundred lions were killed, and on the laſt day, twenty elephants whoſe lamentable howling, when mortally wounded, raiſed ſuch a commiſeration in the multitude, from a vulgar notion of their great ſenſe and love to man, that it deſtroyed the whole diverſion of the ſhew, and drew curſes on Pompey himſelf, for being the author of ſo much cruelty* [t]. So true it is, what Cicero obſerves of this kind of prodigality, *that there is no real dignity or laſting honor in it, that it ſatiates, while it pleaſes, and is forgotten, as ſoon as it is over* [v] It gives us however a genuin Idea of the wealth and grandor of theſe principal ſubjects of *Rome*, who, from their private revenues, could raiſe ſuch noble buildings, and provide ſuch ſhews, from the ſeveral quarters of the world, which no monarch on earth is now able to exhibit

[t] Magnificentiſſima vero Pompeii nobis munera in ſecundo Conſulatu De Off 2 16

Pompei quoque altero Conſulatu dedicatione Templi Veneris Victricis pugna vere in Circo agitur Elephante —— Amiſſa fugæ ſpe ſenſore animi vulgi renarrori habita ereptes ſuppoſuere quadam iſſe lamentatione complorantes, ſuo populi dolore ut obliti Imperator —— Hic cum

verſus conſurgeret, dirasque Pompeio, quas ille mox luit, pœnas imprecaretur—Plin l 8 7 Vid Dio l 39 p 107 It Plutar in Pomp

[v] In his infinitis—ſumptibus, nihil nos magnopere mirari cum nec neceſſaria ſubveniatur, rec dignitas augeatur ipſaque illa delectatio multitudinis ſit ad breve exiguumque tempus—in quo ſit nec ipſo una cum ſatietate memoria quoque moritur voluptas—De Off 2 16

CICERO, contrary to his cuſtom, was preſent
at theſe ſhews, out of compliment to Pompey,
and gives a particular account of them to his
friend M Marius, who could not be drawn by
them from his books and retreat in the country
" The old actors, *ſays he*, who had left the ſtage,
" came on to it again, in honor to Pompey , but
" for the ſake of their own honour, ought rather
" to have ſtaid away, our friend Æſopus ap-
" peared to be quite ſunk and worn out, ſo that
" all people ſeemed willing to grant him his qui-
" etus for in attempting to raiſe his voice,
" where he had occaſion to ſwear, his ſpeech
" faultered and failed him —— In the other
" plays, the vaſt apparatus, and crouded machi-
" nery, which raiſed the admiration of the mob,
" ſpoiled the entertainment ſix hundred mules,
" infinite treaſures of plate, troops of horſe and
" foot fighting on the ſtage ———The huntings
" indeed were magnificent, but what pleaſure to
" a man of taſt, to ſee a poor weak fellow torn
" to pieces by a fierce beaſt, or a noble beaſt
" ſtruck dead with a ſpear the laſt day's ſhew
" of Elephants, inſtead of delight, raiſed a ge-
" neral compaſſion, and an opinion of ſome re-
" lation between that animal and man but leſt
" you ſhould think me wholly happy, in theſe
" days of diverſion, I have almoſt burſt myſelf
" in the defence of your friend Gallus Caninius
" if the City would be as kind to me, as they
" are to Æſopus, I would willingly quit the
" ſtage, to live with you, and ſuch as you, in a
" polite and liberal eaſe [x] "

THE City continued for a great part of this
ſummer without it's annual Magiſtrates for the

A Urb. 58
Cic 52
Coſſ
CN POM ···
us MAG-
NUS II
M LICINIUS
CRASSUS II.

[x] Ep fam 7 1

elections,

A Urb 698
Cic 52
Coff
C Pompei
ï Mag-
ïus II
M Licin ius
Craffus II

elections, which had been postponed from the
laſt year, were ſtill kept off by the Conſuls, till
they could ſettle them to their minds, and ſecure
them to their own Creatures which they effect
ed at laſt, except in the caſe of *two Tribuns*, who
ſlipt into the office againſt their will but the
moſt remarkable repulſe was, of M Cato *from
the Praetorſhip*, which was given to Vatinius, from
the beſt Citizen, to the worſt. Cato, upon his
return from *the Cyprian* voyage, was compli
mented by the Senate for that ſervice with *the
offer of the Praetorſhip, in an extraordinary manner* [,] But he declined the compliment, think
ing it more agreeable to his character to obtain
it in the ordinary way, by the free choice of the
people but when the election came on, in which
he was thought ſure of ſucceſs, Pompey *broke up
the aſſembly, on pretence of ſomewhat inauſpicious
in the heavens, and, by intrigue and management, got
Vatinius declared Praetor, who had been repulſed the
year before with diſgrace from the Aedileſhip* [z] but
this being carried by force of money, and likely
to produce an impeachment of Vatinius, Afra
nius moved for a decree, *that the Praetors ſhould
not be queſtioned for bribery after their election,*
which paſſed againſt the general humor of the
Senate, *with an exception onely, of ſixty days
in which they were to be conſidered as private men*
The pretence for the decree was, that ſo much
of the year being ſpent, the whole would paſs
without any Praetors at all, if a liberty of im

[,] Cujus in referri grat a
Senatus dictatorem interponi
jubebat ut Praetoris Comi-
tis extra ordinem ratio ejus
haberetur Sed ipſe id fieri
paſſus non eſt —Val Max

ι Plutar in Cato
[z] Proxima dementiae ſuf
fragia — quoniam quem ho
norem Catoni negaverun
Vatinio dare coacti ſunt Va
Max 7 5 Plut in Pomp

peachin

peaching was allowed: *from this moment*, says
Cicero, *they have given the exclusion to* Cato , *and,
being masters of all, resolve that all the world shall
know it* [*a*]

A Urb. 698.
Cic 52
Coss
Cn Pompei-
us Mag-
nus II
M Licinius
Crassus II.

CICERO's *Palatin house*, and the adjoining
Portico of Catulus were now finished , *and as he
and his brother were the Curators likewise of the
repairs of the Temple of Tullus* [*b*], so they seem
to have provided some inscriptions for these
buildings in honor and memory of themselves·
but since no public Inscriptions could be set up,
unless by public authority, they were apprehensive of an opposition from Clodius. Cicero mentioned the case to Pompey, who promised his
assistance, but advised him to talk also with Crassus, which he took occasion to do, as he attended him home one day from the Senate   Crassus
readily undertook the affair, and told him, *that
Clodius had a point to carry for himself, by Pompey's
help and his, and that if Cicero would not oppose
Clodius, he was persuaded that Clodius would not
disturb him , to which Cicero consented*   Clodius's
business was to procure one of those *free or honorary Lieutenencies, that he might go with a public
character to Byzantium, and King Brogitarus,* to
gather the money, which they owed him for past
services   *As it is a mere money matter*, says Cicero, *I shall not concern myself about it, whether I
gain my own point or not, though Pompey and Cras-*

[*a*] A D III id Mais S
C factum est de ambitu in
Afranii sententiam —— Sed
magno cum gemitu Senatus
Consules non sunt persecuti
eorum sententias qui Afra-
nio cum essent assensi addi-
derant, ut Prætores ita crea-
rentur, ut dies LX privati

essent. Eo die Catonem plane repudiarunt Quid mul-
tis Tenet omnia, idque ita
omnes intelligere volunt Ad
Quint 2 6
   [*b*] Quod Ædes Telluris
est curationis meæ De Ha-
rusp resp 14

sus

A Urb 698
Cic 52
Cof
C. Pompe-
i. Mag
nts II
M Licinius
Crassus II.

to have jointly undertaken it but he seems to have obtained what he desired, since besides the intended Inscriptions, he mentions *a statue also of his Brother, which he had actually erected at the Temple of Tellus* [c]

TREBONIUS, one of the Tribuns, in the interest of the Triumvirate, published a law, for the assignment of Provinces to the Consuls for the term of five years to Pompey, Spain *and* Africa to Crassus, Syria, *and the Parthian war, with* power of raising what forces they thought fit and that Cesar's commission should be renew'd also for five years more The law was opposed by the generality of the Senate, and, above all, *by Cato Favonius, a d two of the Tribuns, C. Ateius Capito, and P Aquilius Gallus:* but the superior force of the Consuls and the other Tribuns prevailed, and cleared the Forum by violence of their opponents

THE law no sooner passed, than Crassus began to prepare for his Eastern expedition, and was in such haste to set forward, that he left *Rome* about two months before the expiration of his Consulship his eagerness to involve the Republic in a desperate war, for which *the Parthians* had given no pretext, was generally detested by the City

---

[c] Multa noce cum Vibullio veni ad Pompeium Consule ego egi cum de illis operibus & inscriptionibus, pr m i benigne respondit —Cum Crasso si dixit loqui esse, mihi que, at idem facerem, suasit Crassum Consulem ex Senatu domum recar suscepit rem, d atque ese quod Clodius hoc tempore cuperet se, & per Pompeium consequi Putare si ego eum non impedire posse me adipisci sine contentione quod vellem —&c Quint z 9

Reddita est mihi pervet Epistola —— in qua de A Telluris, & de porticu Catuli me admones Fit utrumque diligenter Ad Tellu e um tuam statuam loca Ib 3 1

Tribun Ateius declared it impious, and prohibited by
all the auspices, and denounced direful imprecations
against it, but finding Craſſus determined to
march in defiance of all religion, he waited for
him at the gates of the City, *and having dreſſed
up a little altar, ſtood ready with a fire and ſacrifice
to devote him to deſtruction* [d] *Aterus was afterwards turned out of the Senate by Appius, when he
was Cenſor, for falſifying the auſpices on this occaſion,* but the miſerable fate of Craſſus ſupported the credit of them, and confirmed the vulgar
opinion *of the inevitable force of thoſe ancient rites,
in drawing down the divine vengeance on all, who
preſumed to contemn them* [e] Appius was one
of *the Augurs* and the onely one of the College,
who maintained *the truth of their auguries, and the
reality of divination, for which he was laughed at
by the reſt,* who charged him alſo with an abſurdity, in the reaſon, which he ſubſcribed, for his
Cenſure upon Ateius, *viz that he had falſified the
auſpices, and brought a great calamity on the Roman
people for if the auſpices, they ſaid, were falſe,
they could not poſſibly have any effect, or be the cauſe
of that calamity* [f] But though they were undoubtedly forged, it is certain however, that
they had a real influence on the overthrow of

---

[d] Dio l 39 p 109
Plut in Craſſ———

[e] M Craſſo quid acci-
derit, videmus, dirarum obnunciatione neglecta — De
Divin 1 16

[f] Solus enim multorum
annorum memoria, non de-
cantandi Augurii, ſed divi-
nandi tenuit diſciplinam
quem irridebant Collega tui,
cumque tum Piſidam, tum

Soranum Augurem eſſe dicebant Quibus nulla videba-
tur in Auguriis aut Auſpiciis
præſentio —Ib 47

In quo Appius, bonus Au-
gur — non ſatis ſcienter——
Civem egregium, Ateium,
cenſor notavit, quod emen-
titam auſpici ſubſcripſe it —
—Quæ ſi falſa fuiſſet nullam
adſc e po un et cauſam cala-
mi atis —Ib 16

G 3   Craſſus:

A Urb 698
Cic 52
Coſſ
Cn Pompei
us Mag-
nus II
M Licinius
Crassus II

Craſſus· for the terror of them had deeply poſ-ſeſſed the minds of the ſoldiers, and made them turn every thing which they ſaw, or heard, *to an omen of their ruin*, ſo that when the enemy appeared in ſight, they were ſtruck with ſuch a panic, that they had not courage or ſpirit enough left to make a tolerable reſiſtance.

Crassus was deſirous, before he left *Rome*, to be reconciled to Cicero. they had never been real friends, but generally oppoſite in party, and Cicero's early engagements with Pompey kept him of courſe at a diſtance from Craſſus their coldneſs was ſtill encreaſed on account of Cati line's *plot*, of which Craſſus was ſtrongly ſuſpect ed; and charged Cicero with being the author of that ſuſpicion they carried it however on both ſides with much decency, out of regard to Craſ-fus s ſon, Publius, a profeſſed admirer and diſci-ple of Cicero; till an accidental debate in the Senate blew up their ſecret grudge into an open quarrel The debate was upon Gabinius, whom Craſſus undertook to defend, with many ſevere reflections upon Cicero, who replied with no leſs acrimony, and gave a free vent *to that old reſent-ment of Craſſus's many injuries, which had been ga-thering,* he ſays, *ſeveral years, but lain dormant ſo long, that he took it to be extinguiſhed, till, from this accident, it burſt out into a flame* The quarrel gave great joy to the chiefs of the Senate, who highly applauded Cicero, in hopes to embroil him with *the Triumvirate*· but Pompey labored hard to make it up, and Cæſar alſo by letter ex-preſſed his uneaſineſs upon it, and begged it of Cicero, as a favor, to be reconciled with Craſſus ſo that he could not hold out againſt an interceſ-ſion ſo powerfull, and ſo well enforced by his affection *to young Craſſus*. their reconciliation was
confirmed

confirmed by mutual professions of a sincere friendship for the future, and Crassus, *to give a public
testimony of it to the City, invited himself, just before his departure, to sup with Cicero, who entertained him in the gardens of his son-in-law, Crassipes* [g]　These gardens were upon *the banks of
the Tiber*, and seem to have been famous for their
beauty and situation [h]　and are the only proof,
which we meet with, of the splendid fortunes and
condition of Crassipes.

Cicero spent a great part of the summer in
the country, in study and retreat; *pleased*, he
says, *that he was out of the way of those squabbles,
where he must either have defended what he did not
approve, or deserted the man whom he ought not to
forsake* [i]　In this retirement, he put the last
hand to his Piece, *on the Complete Orator*, which
he sent to Atticus, and promises also to send to
Lentulus, telling him, *that he had intermitted his
old task of orations, and betaken himself to the milder*

A Urb 698
Cic 51
Coss
Cn Pompei-
us Mag-
nus II
M Licinius
Crassus II.

[g] Repentinam ejus Ga-
binii defensionem —— Si sine
ulla mea contumelia susce-
pisset, tulissem sed cum me
disputantem, non lacessentem
lesisset, exarsi non solum
præsenti, credo, iracundia
(nam ea tam vehemens for-
tasse non fuisset) sed cum in-
clusum illud odium multo-
rum ejus in me injuriarum,
quod ego effudissé me omne
arbitrabar, residuum tamen
insciente me fuisset, omne
repente apparuit —— Cumque
Pompeius ita contendisset, ut
nihil unquam magis, ut cum
Crasso redirem in gratiam,
Cæsarque per literas maxima
se molestia ex illa contentione

affectum ostenderet habui
non temporum solum meo-
rum rationem, sed etiam
naturæ Crassusque ut quasi
testata populo Rom esset non
tan gratia, pæne a meis la-
ribus in provinciam est profectus　Nam cum mihi con-
dixisset, cœnavit apud me in
mei Generi Crassipedis hortis.
——Ep fam 1 9
　[h] Ad Quint 3 7　Ad
Att 4 12
　[i] Ego afuisse me in alter-
cationibus, quas in Senatu
factas audio, fero non moleste, nam aut defendissem
quod non placeret, aut defu-
issem cui non oporteret　Ad
Att 4 13

and gentler studies, in which he had finished, to his satisfaction, three books, by way of dialogue, on the subject of the Orator, in Aristotle's manner, which would be of use to his son, young Lentulus, being drawn, not in the ordinary way of the schools, and the dry method of precepts, but comprehending all that the ancients, and especially Aristotle and Isocrates, had taught on the Institution of an Orator [k]

THE three books contain as many Dialogues, upon the character and Idea of the perfect Orator, the principal speakers were P Crassus, and M Antonius, persons of the first dignity in the Republic, and the greatest Masters of Eloquence, which *Rome* had then known they were near forty years older than *Cicero*, and the first Romans who cou'd pretend to dispute the prize of Oratory with the *Greeks*, and who carried the Latin tongue to a degree of perfection, which left little or no room for any farther improvement [l] The disputation was undertaken at the desire, and for the instruc-

[k] Scripsi etiam, (nam ab orationibus disjungo me fere refero-que ad mansuetiores musas, rescripsi igitur Aristotelio more, quemadmodum quidem volui, tres libros in disputatione & dialogo de Oratore, e os arbitror Lentulo tuo non fore inutiles. Abhorrent enim a communibus præceptis ac omnem articulorum & Aristoteleam & Isocrateam rationem Oratoriam complectantur Ep fam 1 9

[l] Crassus —— quatuor & triginta tum habebat annos, to demque annis mihi ætate præstabat —— Triennio ipso mi-

nor quam Antonius, quod id circo posui, ut dicendi latine prima maturitas qua ætate extitisset, posset notari, & intelligeretur, jam ad summum pæne esse perductam, ut eo nihil ferme quisquam addere posset, nisi qui a Philosophia, a jure civili, ab historia fuisset instructior Brut 275

Nunc ad Antonium, Crassumque pervenimus Nam ego sic existimo hos Oratores fuisse maximos & in his primum cum Græcorum gloria latine dicendi copiam æquatam—Ib 250

tion of two young Orators of great hopes, *C Cotta and P Sulpicius,* who were then beginning to flourish at the bar *Cicero himself was not present at it,* but being informed by *Cotta,* of the principal heads and general argument of the whole, supplied the rest from his own invention, agreeably to the different stile and manner, which those great men were known to pursue, and with design to do honor to the memory of them both, but especially of Craffus, who had been the director of his early studies, and to whom he affigns the defence of that notion, which he himself always entertained, of the character of a confummate Speaker [m]

ATTICUS was exceedingly pleafed with this treatife, and commended it to the fkies, but objected to the propriety *of difmiffing Scævola from the difputation, after he had once been introduced into the firft dialogue* Cicero defends himfelf by the example *of their God,* Plato as he calls him, in his book on Government, where the Scene being laid in the houfe of an old Gentleman, Cephalus, *the old man, after bearing a part in the firft converfation, excufes himfelf, that he muft go to prayers, and returns no more,* Plato not thinking it *fuitable to the character of his age,* to be detained in the Company through *fo long a difcourfe that, with greater reafon therefore, he had ufed the fame caution in the cafe of Scævola, fince it was not decent to fuppofe a perfon of his dignity, extreme age,*

---

[r] Nos enim, qui ipfi fermoni non interfuiffemus, & quibus C Cotta tantummodo locos, ac fententias hujus difputationis tradidiffet, quo in genere orationis utrumque Oratorem cognoveramus, id ipfum fumus in eorum fermone adumbrare conati———De Orat 3 4

Ut ei (Craffo) & fi nequaquam parem illius ingenio, at pro noftro tamen ftudio meritam gratiam debitamque referemus—Ibid ———

and

A. Urb 698.
Cic 52
Coss
C. Pompei-
us Mag-
nus II
M. Licinius
Crassus II

and infirm health, spending several days successively in another man's house that the first day's dialogue related to his particular profession, but the other two turned chiefly on the rules and precepts of the art, where it was not proper for one of Scævola's temper and character to assist onely as a hearer [n].   This admirable work remains intire, a standing monument of Cicero's parts and abilities, which, while it exhibits to us the Idea of a perfect Orator, and marks out the way, by which Cicero formed himself to that character, it explanes the reason likewise why no-body has since equalled him, or ever will, till there be found again united, what will hardly be found single in any man, *the same industry, and the same parts*

CICERO returned to *Rome*, about the middle of November, to assist at Milo's wedding, who married Fausta, a rich and noble Lady, the daughter of *Sylla the Dictator* [o], with whom, as some writers say, he found Sallust *the Historian in bed not long after, and had him soundly lashed, before he dismissed him.* The Consuls, Pompey and Crassus, having reaped all the fruit, which they had proposed from the Consulship, *of securing to themselves the Provinces, which they wanted,* were not much concerned about the choice of their successors, so that, after postponing the election to the end of the year, they gave way at last to their enemy, L Domitius Ahenobarbus, being content to have joined with him their friend, Appius Claudius Pulcher.

[n] Quod in iis libris, quos laudas, personam desideras Scævolæ Non eam temere dimovi, sed feci idem, quod in πολιτεια Deus ille noster, Plato Cum in Piræum Socrates venisset ad Cephalum, locupletem & festivum senem, quoad primus ille sermo haberetur ad est in disputando Senex—&c Ad Att 4 16

[o] Ad Att 4 13 5 8

As foon as the new year came on, Craffus's
enemies began to attack him in the Senate: their
defign was to revoke his commiffion, or abridge
it at leaft of the powei *of making war upon the
Parthians* but Cicero exerted himfelf fo ftrenu-
oufly in his defence, that he baffled their attempts,
after a warm conteft with *the Confuls themfelves,
and feveral of the Confular Senatois* He gave
Craffus an account of the debate by letter, in
which he tells him, *that he had given proof, not
onely to his friends and family, but to the whole
City, of the fincerity of his reconciliation; and af-
fures him of his refolution to ferve him, with all his
pains, advice, authority, inteieft, in every thing
great or fmall, which concerned himfelf, his friends,
or chents, and bids him look upon that Letter as a
league of amity, which on his part fhould be invio-
lably obferved* [p]

THE month of February being generally employed in *giving audience to foreign Princes and
Embaffadors,* Antiochus, *King of* Comagene, *a
territory on the banks of the* Euphrates [q], preferred a petition to the Senate for fome new honour or privilege, which was commonly decreed
to Princes in alliance with the Republic but
Cicero being in a rallying humor, made the petition fo ridiculous, *that the houfe rejected it, and
at his motion, referred likewife out of his jurifdiction one of his principal Towns,* Zeugma; *in which
was the chief bridge and paffage over the* Euphrates Cæfar, in his Coniulfhip, *had granted to this
King the honor of the Prætexta, or the robe of the
Roman Magiftrates;* which was always difagree-

A Urb 699.
Cic 53.
Coff
L DOMITIUS
AHENO-
BARBUS,
A. CLAUDIUS
PULCHER

[p] Has literas velim ex-
iftimes fœdtris habiturus effe
vim, non epiftolæ, meque
ta, quæ tibi promitto ac re-
cipio, fanctiffime effe obfer-
vaturum—Ep fam 5 8
[q] Ep fam. 15 1, 3, 4.

able

A Urb 699
Cic 53.
Coſſ
L. Domitius
Aeno-
barbus,
A Claudius
Pulcher

able to the nobility, who did not care to ſee theſe petty Princes put upon the ſame rank with themſelves ; ſo that Cicero, *calling out upon the nobles, will you*, ſays he, *who refuſed the Prætexta to the King of* Boſtra, *ſuffer this* Comagenian *to ſtrut in purple !* But this diſappointment was not more mortifying to the King, than it was to the Conſuls, whoſe beſt perquiſites were drawn from theſe compliments, which were always repaid by rich preſents, *ſo that Appius, who had been lately reconciled to Cicero, and paid a particular court to him at this time, applied to him by Atticus, and their common friends, to ſuffer the petitions of this ſort to paſs quietly, nor deſtroy the uſual harveſt of the month, and make it quite barren to him* [1]

CICERO made an excurſion this ſpring to viſit his ſeveral ſeats and eſtates in the country, and, in his *Cuman Villa*, began *a Treatiſe on politics, or on the beſt ſtate of a City, and the duties of a Citizen*. he calls it *a great and laborious work, yet worthy of his pains, if he could ſuccede in it , if not, I ſhall throw it*, ſays he, *into that ſea, which is now before me, and attempt ſomething elſe, ſince it is impoſſible for me to be idle* It was drawn up in the form of *a dialogue*, in which the greateſt perſons of the old Republic were intro-

[1] De Comageno Rege, quod rem totam diſcuſſeram, mihi & per ſe & per Pomponium blanditur Appius Videt enim, ſi hoc genere dicendi utar in cæteris, Februarium ſterilem futurum Eumque luſi jocoſe ſatis neque ſolum illud extorſi oppidulum, quod erat poſitum in Euphrate Zeugma, ſed præterea togam ejus prætextam, quam erat adeptus Cæſare Conſule magno hominum riſu cavillatus —— Vos autem homines nobiles, qui Boſtrenum Prætextatum non ferebatis, Comagenum feretis ? —— Multa dixi in ignobilem Regem, quibus totus eſt exploſus Quo genere commotus Appus totum me amplexatur —— Ad Quint 2 12

duced, debating on the origin and beft conftitu- tion of government, Scipio, Lælius, Philus, Manilius, &c. [s] The whole was to be diftributed into nine books, each of them the fubject of one day's difputation when he had finifhed the two firft, they were read in *his Tufculan Villa* to fome of his friends, where Salluft, who was one of the company, advifed him to change his plan, and treat the fubject *in his own perfon, as Ariftotle had done before him, alledging, that the introduction of thofe ancients, inftead of adding gravity, gave an air of Romance to the argument, which would have the greater weight, when delivered from himfelf, as being the work, not of a little Sophift, or contemplative Theorift, but of a Confular Senator, and Statefmen, converfant in the greateft affairs, and writing what his own practice, and the experience of many years, had taught him to be true* Thefe reafons feemed very plaufible, and made him think of altering his fcheme, efpecially fince, by throwing the fcene fo far back, he precluded himfelf from touching on thofe important revolutions of the Republic, which were later than the period, to which he confined himfelf but, after fome deliberation, being unwilling to throw away *the two books*, already finifhed, with which he was much pleafed, he refolved to ftick to the old plan, and as he had

---

[s] Scribebam illa, quæ dixeram πολ]ιτι, fpiffum fane opus & operofum fed fi ex fententia fuccefferit, bene erit opera pofita, fin minus, in illud ipfum mare dejiciemus, quod fcribentes fpectamus, aggrediemur alia, quoniam quiefcere non poffamur Ib 14.

Hanc ego, quam inftitui, de Repub difputationem in Africani perfonam & Phili, & Iælii & Manilii contuli, &c —Rem, quod te non fugit, magnam complexus fum & gravem, & plurimi otii, quod ego maxime egeo Ad Att 4 16

preferred

A Urb 699
Cic 53.
Coſſ
L Domitius
Ahenoba-
barbus,
A Claudius
Pulcher.

preferred it from the firſt, *for the ſake of avoiding offence*, ſo he purſued it without any other alteration, than that of reducing the number of books from *nine to ſix*, in which form they were afterwards publiſhed, and ſurvived him for ſeveral ages, though now unfortunately loſt [*t*]

FROM the fragments of this work, which ſtill remain, it appears to have been a noble performance, and one of his capital pieces, where all the important queſtions in politics and morality were diſcuſſed with the greateſt elegance and accuracy, *of the origin of Society, the nature of law and obligation, the eternal difference of right and wrong, of juſtice being the onely good policy, or foundation either of public or private proſperity* ſo that he calls *his ſix books, ſo many pledges, given to the public, for the integrity of his conduct* [*u*] The younger Scipio was the principal ſpeaker of the Dialogue, whoſe part it was *to aſſert the*

[*t*] Sermo autem in novem & dies & libros diſtributus de optimo ſtatu civitatis & de optimo cive —Hi libri, cum in Tuſculano mihi legerentur, audiente Salluſtio, admonitus ſum ab illo, multo majore auctoritate illis de rebus dici poſſe, ſi ipſe loquerer de Republ. præſertim cum eſſem, non Heraclides Ponticus, ſed conſularis, & is, qui in maximis verſatus in Repub. rebus eſſem quæ tam antiquis hominibus attroderem, ea ſi ſum in ſcita eſſe — Commovit me, & eo magis quod me ipſos modo noſtræ civitatis attingere non poteram, quod erant inferiores, quam illorum ætas qui loquebantur —

Ego autem id ipſum tum eram ſecutus, ne in noſtra tempora incurrens offenderem quempiam — Ad Quint 3 5

This will ſolve that variation which we find in his own account of this work, in different parts of his writings and why Fannius, who in ſome places is declared to be a ſpeaker in it, [Ad Att 4. 16 Ad Quint 3 5] is denied to be ſo in others, being dropt, when the number of books was contracted

[*u*] Cum ſex libris, tanquam prædibus me ipſum obſtrinxerim, quos tibi tam valde probari gaudeo Ad Att 6 1

excellence of the Roman conſtitution, preferably to that of all other ſtates [x]　who, in the ſixth book, under *the fiction of a dream,* which is ſtill preſerved to us, takes occaſion to inculcate *the doctrine of the immortality of the ſoul, and a future ſtate,* in a manner ſo lively and entertaining, that it has been the ſtanding pattern ever ſince to the wits of ſucceeding ages, for attempting the ſame method of inſtilling moral leſſens, in the form of dreams or viſions

A. Urb 699.
Cic 53.
Coſſ
L Domitius
Ahenobarbus,
A Claudius
Pulcher.

HE was now drawn at laſt into a particular intimacy and correſpondence of Letters with Cæſar, who had long been endeavouring to engage him to his friendſhip, and, with that view, had invited *his brother,* Quintus, to be one of *his Lieutenants in Gaul,* where Quintus, to pay his court the better to his General, joined heartily in preſſing his Brother *to an union with him,* inſtead of adhering ſo obſtinately *to Pompey, who,* as he tells him, *was neither ſo ſincere, nor ſo generous a friend as Cæſar* [y]　Cicero did not diſlike the advice, and expreſſed a readineſs to comply with it, of which Balbus gave an intimation to Cæſar, with *a Letter, alſo incloſed, from Cicero himſelf;* but the packet happening to fall into water, the Letters were all deſtroyed, except *a ſcrap or two of Balbus's,* to which Cæſar returned anſwer; *I perceive, that you had written ſomewhat about Cicero, which I could not make out, but as far as I can gueſs, it was ſomething rather to be wiſhed,*

[x] An cenſes, cum in illis de Repub libris perſuadere videatur Africanus, omnium Rerumpub noſtram veterem illam fuiſſe optimam —De leg 2 x vid ib 1 6. 9

[y] De Pompeio aſſentior tibi, vel tu potius mihi, nam, ut ſcis, jampridem, iſtum canto Cæſarem — Ad Quint 2 13

then

A Urb 709
Cic 53
Coſſ
L Do ITIUS
æ E O-
BARBUS,
A CLAUDIUS
PULC-ER

than hoped for [z]   But Cicero ſent another copy of the ſame Letter, which came ſafe to his hands, written, as he ſays, *in the familiar ſtile, yet without departing from his dignity.* Cæſar anſwered him with all imaginable kindneſs, and the offer of every thing, in which his power could ſerve him, telling him, *how agreeable his Brother's company was to him, by the revival of their old affection: and ſince he was now removed to ſuch a diſtance from him, he would take care, that in their mutual want of each other, he ſhould have cauſe at leaſt to rejoice, that his Brother was with him, rather than any one elſe.* He thanks him alſo for ſend-*ing the Lawyer Trebatius to him, and ſays upon it jocoſely, that there was not a man before in his ar-my, who knew how to draw a recognizance.* Ci-cero, in his account of this Letter to his Brother, ſays, " it is kind in you, and like a Brother,
" to preſs me to this friendſhip, though I am
" running that way apace myſelf, and ſhall do,
" what often happens to travellers, who riſing
" later than they intended, yet, by quickening
" their ſpeed, come ſooner to their journey's
" end, than if they had ſet out earlier , ſo I,
" who have over-ſlept myſelf in my obſervance
" of this man, though you were frequently rouſ-
" ing me, will correct my paſt lazineſs by mend-
" ing my pace for the future."——— But as to his

[z] Ille ſcripſit ad Bal-bum, faciculum ſuum Epiſ-tolarum, in quo fuerat & mea & Balbi, totum ſibi aqua ma-cidum eſſe ut ne illud qui-dem ſciat, meam fuſſe ali-quam epiſtolam Sed ex Balbi epiſtola pauca verba intelſexerat ad quæ reſcripſit n. verbis De Cicerone vi-deo te quiddam ſcripſiſſe, quod ego non intellexi, quantum autem conjectura conſequebar id erat hujuſmo-di ut magis optandum, quam ſperandum putarem Ad Quir 2 12

A Urb 699
Cic 53
Coss
L Domitius
Ahexo-
barbus,
A Claudius
Pulcher.

ſeeking any advantage or perſonal benefit from
this alliance, *believe me, ſays he, you who know
me, I have from him already what I moſt value,
the aſſurance of his affection, which I prefer to all
the great things that he offers me——* [a] In another letter he ſays, *I lay no great ſtreſs on his
promiſe, want no farther honours, nor deſire any
more glory, and ſeek nothing more, but the continuance of his eſteem, yet live ſtill in ſuch a courſe of
exertion and fatigue, as if I were expecting what
I do not really aſpire* [b]

But though he made no uſe of Cæſar's generoſity for himſelf, yet he uſed it freely for his
friends, for beſides his brother, who was Cæſar's *Lieutenant*, and Trebatius, who was *his
Lawyer*, he procured an eminent poſt for Orſius,
and a Regiment for Cattius, yet Cæſar was
chiding him all the while *for his reſervedneſs in*

---

[a] Cum Cæſaris literis,
refuſis omni officio diligenter, ſuavitat—Quarum ini-
tium eſt, quam ſuavis erit us
adventus fuerit, & recordatio
veteris amoris, denarce ſe ef
florumum ut ego in medio
dolore ac deſiderio tui, te,
cum in me abuſſes, potiſſimum
ſecum eſſet mter——Trebati-
um quod ad ſum ſerim per-
ſuade & his parter etiam gra-
es impigit negre erit in
tanta multitudine eo uri qui
uniſſent quenpam fuiſſe,
qui ad nomium concipere
poſſe——

Quare ſicis tu quidem fra-
terne, quod me hortar, ſed
mehercule currentem nunc

quidem, ut omnia mea ſtudia
in ſumum conteram, &c

Sed mihi crede, quem
noſti, quod in his rebus ego
plurum ero jam habeo
——vide Cæſaris orationem in
me merere, quam omnibus
his honoribus, quos me ſe
expectare velt, ntepeno——
Ad Quint z 15

[b] Promiſſionibus, quæ oſ-
tendit, non valde pendeo;
nec honores ſito nec deſide-
ro gloriam mariſque ejus voluntatis perpetuitatem, quam
promiſſorum exitum expecto.
Vive tamen in ea ambitione
& labore, tanquam id, quod
non poſtulo, expectem ib.
3 5.

A Uro 693
Cic 53
Cof.
L Domitius
Aeno-
Barbus,
A Claud Is
Pulcher

Anno [a] His recommendatory Letter of Trebatius, will fhew both what a fhare he poſſeſſed
at this time of Cæfar's confidence, and with what
an affectionate zeal he uſed to recommend his
friends

"Cicero to Cæfar Emperor.

"SEE, how I have perfuaded myſelf to con-
"fider you as a ſecond ſelf, not onely in what
"affects my own intereſt, but in what conceins
"my friends   I had refolved, whitherfoever I
"went abroad, to carry C. Trebatius along with
"me, that I might bring him home, adorned
"with the fruits of my caie and kindneſs · but
"fince Pompey's ftay in *Rome* has been longer
"than I expected, and my own irrefolution, to
"which you are no ftranger, will either wholly
"hinder, or at leaſt retard, my going abroad at
"all, fee, what I have taken upon myſelf
'I began prefently to refolve, that Trebatius
"fhould expect the fame things from you,
"which he had been hoping for from me   nor
"did I aſſure him with leſs franknefs of your
"good will, than I uſed to do of my own   but
"a wonderfull incident fell out, both as a tefti-
"mony of my opinion, and a pledge of your
"humanity, for while I was talking of this
"very Trebatius at my houfe, with our friend
"Balbus, your Letter was delivered to me, in
"the end of which you faid, *as to M Orfius*,
"*whom you recommended to me, I will make him*
"*even king of Gaul, or Lieutenant to* Lepta, *fend*

---

[a] M Curtio Tribunatum
a te co peti ·—Ib 2 15 Ep
fam 7 5
De Trebatio— mihi ipfe

Cæfer non inat m Curtio paratum eſſe refcripfit meamque in rogando verecundium
objurgavit Ad Quin 3 1

"*me*

" *me another therefore, if you please, whom I may*
" *prefer* We lifted up our hands, both I and
" Balbus, the occasion was so pat, that it seem-
" ed not to be accidental, but divine I send
" you therefore Trebatius, and send him so, as
" at first indeed I designed, of my own accord,
" but now also by your invitation embrace him,
" my dear Cæsar, with all your usual courtesy,
" and whatever you could be induced to do for
" my friends, out of your regard to me, confer
" it all singly upon him I will be answerable
" for the man, not in my former stile, which
" you justly rallied, when I wrote to you about
" Milo, but in the true Roman phrase, which
" men of sense use, that there is not an *honester*,
" *worthier, modester, man living* I must add,
" what makes the principal part of his character,
" that he has a singular memory, and perfect
" knowledge of the civil Law. I ask for him,
" neither a Regiment nor Government, nor any
" certain piece of preferment, I ask your bene-
" volence and generosity, yet am not against
" the adorning him, whenever you shall think
" proper, with those trappings also of glory in
' short, I deliver the whole man to you, from
' my hand, as we say, into yours, illustrious
" for victory and faith But I am more impor
" tunate than I need be to you, yet I know
' you will excuse it Take care of your health,
" and continue to love me, as you now do [d] "

TREBATIUS was of a lazy, indolent, studious temper, a lover of books and good company, eagerly fond of the pleasures of *Rome*,
and wholly out of his element in a Camp and
because Cæsar, through the infinite hurry of his

A Urb 699
Cic 53.
Coss
L Domitius
Aheno-
barbus,
A Claudius
Pulcher

[d] Ep fam 7 5

affairs,

A ... ... could not ... ... admit him to his ... ... and ... him so soon as he expected, he was tired of the drudgery of attending him and ... ... to be at home again. Under these circumstances, there is a series of Letters to him from Cicero, written not only with the disinterested affection of a friend, but the follicitude ... of a parent, employing all the arts of infinuation, as well of the grave, as of the facetious kind, to hinder him from ... his hopes and ... ... by his imprudence. " He laughs at ... ... into the City ; bids him ... ... for which he went abroad, ... it with constancy, observes from ... ... *and L....* ... that many had served themselves ... of the public ... at a distance from their Country, where others, by spending ... ... at home, had lived and died ... ignobly; of which number, *says he*, you ... ... had been one, if we had not thrust you ... out ; and fince I am now acting *Judge*, take ... this other advice from me, *that he, who is not ... ...* [e]" He ... ... on their " imprudence, ... he had carried a bond, not a Letter to " Cicero, and thought that he had nothing to " do but to take his money, and return home

[e] Tum ... ... propterea funt in ... ...

Quo in numero tu cer fam, nisi excussiffemu — & quando Medeam ago ... ... cap, hoc semper memento ... ... qui ipfe fibi sapiens prod ... ... non quit, nequicquam sapi ... ... Ip ... ...

A Urb 699
Cic 53
Coſſ
L DOMITIUS
AHENO-
BARBUS
A CLAUDIUS
PULCHER

" not recollecting, that even thoſe, who follow-
' ed King Ptolemy with bonds to *Alexandria*,
" had not yet brought back a penny of mo-
' ney [f] You write me word, *Joshua*, that
" Cæſar now conſults you, I had rather hear,
" that he conſults your Intereſt [g] Let me
" die, If I do not believe, ſuch is your vanity,
' that you had rather be conſulted, than enrich-
" ed by him [h] By theſe raileries and perpetual admonitions he made Trebatius aſhamed of
his ſoftneſs, and content to ſtay with Cæſar, by
whoſe favor and generoſity he was cured at laſt
of all his uneaſineſs, and having here laid the
foundation of his fortunes, floriſhed afterwards
in the court of Auguſtus, with the character of
the moſt learned Lawyer of that age [i]

CÆSAR was now upon his ſecond expedition
into *Britain*, which raiſed much talk and expectation at *Rome*, and gave CICERO *no ſuch concern*
for the ſafety of his Brother, who, as one *of
Cæſar's Lieutenants*, was to bear a conſiderable
part in it [k] But the accounts which he received from the place, ſoon caſed him of his apprehenſions, by informing him, *that there was
nothing either to fear or to hope from the attempt,*

[f] Sibi imprudens vide-
... tanquam eam f. ngu-
... ad Imper ...em, non
... attuliſſe ſic, pe-
... ab'ata, ... mum redire
... Nec tibi in men-
... veniebat, eos pio, qui
cum ſyngraphis veniſſent A-
lexandriam nummam a ... c
... um afferre pot... Ib

...] Conſuli qu ... em ... a
... reſcribis ſed ... ...
... illo con ... ...

Ib ...

[g] Moneri me qua tua
gloria eſt, puto te malle a
Cæſare conſuli, quam inau-
rari Ib ...

[h] — Nii quid tu, docte
Trebati

Diſſentis —Hor Sat 2 1 79

[k] Ex Quinti fratris literis ſuſpicor jam eum eſſe in
Britannia ſuſpenſo animo
expecto quid agit— Ad Att
4 15

A Urb 699
Cic 53
Coſſ
L Domitius
Aeno-
barbus,
A Claudius
Pulcher

, *no danger from the people, no ſpoils from the Coun-try* [*l*]   In a letter to Atticus, *we are in ſuſ-penſe,* ſays he, *about the Britiſh war   it is certain, that the acceſs of the Iſland is ſtrongly fortified, and it is known alſo already, that there is not a grain of ſilver in it, nor any thing elſe but ſlaves, of whom you will ſcarce expect any, I dare ſay, ſkilled in muſic or Letters* [*m*]   In another to Trebatius, *I hear, that there is not either gold or ſilver in the Iſland   if ſo, you have nothing to do but to take one of their chariots, and fly back to us* [*n*]

FROM their railleries of this kind on *the bar-barity and ſtupidity of our Iſland,* one cannot help reflecting on the ſurpriſing fate and revolutions of Kingdoms   how *Rome,* once the miſtreſs of the world, the ſeat of arts, empire, and glory, now lyes ſunk in ſloth, ignorance, and poverty, enſlaved to the moſt cruel, as well as to the moſt contemptible of Tyrants, *Superſtition and religious Impoſture*   while this remote Country anciently the jeſt and contempt of *the polite Ro-mans,* is become the happy ſeat of liberty, plen-ty, and letters, floriſhing in all the arts and re-finements of civil life, yet running perhaps the ſame courſe, which *Rome* itſelf had run before it,

---

[*l*] O ſuperdes mihi tuas de Britannia literas ! Time-bam oceanum, timebam lit-tus Inſulæ   Reliqua non e-quidem contemno——Ad Quint i 16

De Britannicis rebus cog noſco ex tuis literis, nihil eſſe nec quod metuamus, nec quod gaudeamus —Ib 3 i

[*m*] Britannici belli exitus expectatur   Conſtat enim aditus inſulæ muniros eſſe mirificis molibus   Etiam il-

led jam cognitum eſt, neque argenti ſcrupulum eſſe ullum in illa inſula, neque ullam ſpem prædæ, niſi ex mancipi is , ex quibus nullos puto te literis, aut muſicis erudi tos e pectare   Ad Att 4 16

[ ] In Britannia nihil eſſe audio neque auri neque ar genti   Id ſi ita eſt, eſſedum aliquod ſuadeo capias, & ad nos quam primum recurras Ep Fam 7 7

from virtuous industry to wealth, from wealth to luxury from luxury to an impatience of difcipline, and corruption of morals, till by a total degeneracy and lofs of virtue, being grown ripe for destruction, it falls a prey at laft to fome hardy oppreffor, and, with the lofs of liberty, lofing every thing elfe that is valuable, finks gradually again into its original barbarifm

CICERO taking it for granted, that Trebatius followed Cæfar *into Britain,* began to joke with him upon *the wonderfull figure that a Britifh Lawyer wou'd make at* Rome, *and, as it was his profeffion to guard other people's fafety, bids him beware that he himfelf was not caught by the Britifh chariots* [o] But Trebatius, it feems, knew how to take care of himfelf without Cicero's advice, and when Cæfar paffed over to *Britain,* chofe to ftay behind in *Gaul* this gave a frefh handle for raillery, and Cicero *congratulates him,* " upon being arrived at laft into a country, " where he was thought to know fomething, ' that if he had gone over alfo to *Britain,* there " would not have been a man in all that great " Ifland, wifer than himfelf.—" He obferves, ' that he was much more cautious in military, " than in civil contefts, and wonders, that be" ing fuch *a lover of fwimming,* he could not be " perfuaded to *fwim* in the Ocean, and when " he could not be kept away from every fhew " of Gladitors at *Rome,* had not the curiofity ' to fee *the Britifh chariots* he rejoices how" ever, after all, that he did not go, fince they

A Urb 699
Cc 53
Coff
L DOMITIUS
AHENO
BARBUS,
A CLAUDIUS
PULCHER

[o] Mira enim perfona indari poteft Britannici Juris confulti Ep Iam 7 xi
Tu, qui cæteris cavere di
et cifti, in Britannia ne ab effedariis decipiaris caveto Ib 6

H 4   " fhould

A. U. 699   " hou'd not now be troubled with the imperti-
       " nence of his Brain-bones [*e*] '

     QUINTUS CICERO, who had a genius for
poetry, was projecting the plan of a poem, upon
    his four days journey, and begged his Brother's
     Cicero approved the design, and
    upon it, that the *stature and structure
of   age, the manners of the people, their
       and the General himself Cæsar,
     subjects for poetry   so to his assi-
       to Athens that Quin-
     for Tragedies as soon de,
     the help of some other way, else
his Electra or the Troades [*f*].*   In other letters,
                he

[*e*] ...

                Ep. 21. v 8.

[*f*] ...

he answers more seriously, *that it was impossible
to conceive, how much he wanted leisure for versify-
ing; that to write verses required an ease and cheer-
fulness of mind, which the times had taken from
him, and that his poetical flame was quite extinguished by the sad prospect of things before them* [r]

Hr had sent Cæsar his Greek Poem, in three
books, on the History of his Consulship, and Cæsar's
judgment upon it was, *that the beginning of it
was as good as any thing, which he had ever seen
in that language, but that the following lines, to a
certain place, were not equal in accuracy and spirit.*
Cicero desires therefore to know of his Brother,
*what Cæsar really thought of the whole, whether the
matter or the stile displeased him,* and begs that he
*would tell him the truth freely, since whether Cæ-
sar liked it or not, he should not,* he says, *be a jot
the less pleased with himself* [s].   He began however

A Urb 699
Cic 53
Coss
L Domitius
Ahevo-
tarbus,
A Claudius
Pulcher

Troem & Troaden scrip-
turus ——Ib 3 6.

N B These few Tragedi-
es said to be written in
seven days, cannot be supposed to have been original
productions, but translations
from some of the Greek Poets of which Quintus was a
great Master, finished by him
in haft for the entertainment
of the Camp   for the word
Troas in the text, the name
of one of them, should most
probably be *Troades* the title
of one of Euripides's Plays,
as the *Electra* also was

[ ] Quod me de faciendis
verfibus rogas   incredible
eſt, mi frater, quantum egeam
tempore —— Facerem ta-

mer ut possim sed —— opus
eſt ad poema quadam animi
alacritate, quam plane mihi
tempora eripiunt——Ib 3 5

De versibus —— deeſt mihi
opera quæ non modo tem-
pus, sed etiam animum ab
omni cura vacuum deſiderat
sed abeſt etiam *ψυχαγωγία*
——So Ib 4

[s] Sed heus tu celari videor a te, quomodonam mi
frater de noſtris verſibus Cæsar? Nam primum librum
se legiſse scripſit ad me ante
& prima sic ut neget se ne
Græca quidem meliora legiſse, reliqua ad quendam locum σραθυμότερα. Hoc enim
utar verbo   Dic mihi verum num aut res eum aut
Z χαρακτὴρ

A Urb 699
Coß 53
Coff
L Domitio
Aheno-
barbo,
A Claudio
Pulcher

ever another Poem, at his Brother's earneſt re queſt, to be addreſſed to Cæſar, but after ſome progreſs was ſo diſſatisfied with it, that he tore it [*t*] yet Quintus ſtill urging, and ſignifying, *that he had acquainted Cæſar with the deſign,* he was obliged to reſume it, and actually finiſhed an *Epic Poem in honour of Cæſar,* *which he promiſes* to ſend as ſoon as he could find a proper convey ance, *that it might not be loſt, as Quintus's Tragedy of Eringces in coming from* Gaul, *the only thing,* ſays he, *which had not found a ſafe paſſage, ſince Cæſar governed that Province* [*u*].

While Cicero was expreſſing no ſmall diſ ſatisfaction at the meaſures, which his preſent ſitu ation obliged him to purſue, Cæſar was doing every thing in his power, to make him eaſy *he treated his Brother with as much kindneſs, as if Cicero himſelf had been his general, gave him the choice of his winter quarters, and the Legion, which he beſt liked* [*x*] *and Clodius happening to write to him from* Rome, *he ſhewed the Letter to Quintus, and declared that he would not anſwer it,*

γ...ῖς non delectat? Ni hil eſt quod vereare Ego enim ne pilo quidem minus me amabo ——Ib 16

[*t*] Poema ad Cæſarem, quod compoſueram, incidi ——Ib 5 1 § 4

[ ] Quod me inſtitutum ad illum Poema jubes perfi cere, etſi diſtentus tum ope ra, tum animo ſum multo magis quoniam ex epiſtola, quam ad te miſeram, cogno vit Cæſar me aliquid eſſe exo rſum, revertar ad inſti tutum ——Ib

Quod me hortaris

folvam, habeo abſolutum ſua ve, mihi quidem uti videtur *ἐπικόν* ad Cæſarem Sed quæ ro locupletem tabellarium, ne accidat quod Erigonæ tuæ, cui ſoli, Cæſare Imperatore, iter ex Gallia tutum non fuit Ib 9

[*x*] Quintum meum —— Dii boni! quemadmodum tractat, honore, dignitate, gratia? Non ſecus ac ſi ego eſſem Imperator Hibernem Legionem eligendi optio de lata commodum ut ad me ſcribis ——ad Att 4 18

though

though Quintus civilly preſſed him not to put ſuch an affront upon Clodius, for their ſakes [y] In the midſt of all his hurry in *Britain*, he ſent frequent accounts to Cicero, in his own hand, of his progreſs and ſucceſs, and, at the inſtant of quitting the Iſland, *wrote to him from the very ſhore, of the embarkment of the troops, and his having taken hoſtages, and impoſed a Tribute · and leſt he ſhould be ſurprized at having no Letters at the ſame time from his Brother,* he acquaints him, *that Quintus was then at a diſtance from him, and could not take the benefit of that expreſs.* Cicero received all *theſe Letters at* Rome, *in leſs than a month after date, and takes notice in one of them, that it arrived on the twentieth day*, a diſpatch equal to that of our preſent Couriers by the poſt [z]

As to the news of the City this ſummer, Cicero tells his Brother, " that there were ſome " hopes of an election of Magiſtrates, but thoſe " uncertain, ſome ſuſpicion of a Dictator, yet " that not more certain, a great calm in the " Forum, but of a City, ſeemed to be quieted " rather by the effects of age, than of concord:

A Urb 699
Cic 53
Coſſ
L Domitius
Aheno-
barbus,
A Claudius
Pulcher.

[y] In qua primum eſt de Clodii ad Cæſarem literis, in quo Cæſaris conſilium probo, quod tibi amantiſſime petenti veniam non dedit, ut ullum ad illam Furiam verbum reſcriberet— Ad Quint 3 1 § 4

[z] Ab Quinto fratre & a Cæſare accepi A D IX Kal Nov literas, confecta Britannia, obſidibus acceptis, nulla præda, imperata tamen pecunia, datas a littoribus Britanniæ, proximo A D VI Kal Octob exercitum Britannia reportabant Ad Att 4 17

Ex Britannia Cæſar ad me Kal Sept dedit literas quas ego accepi A D IIII Kal Octob ſatis commodas de Britannicis rebus quibus, ne admirer, quod a te nullas acceperim, ſcribit ſe ſine te fuiſſe, cum ad mare acceſſerit Ad Quint 3 1 § 7

Cum hanc jam Epiſtolam complicarem, tabellarii a vobis venerunt ad D XI Kal Sept viceſimo die Ib 3 1 § 5

" that

A U·b. 699
C 5.
Cc?
L Do iT·us
·· ·o-
·····, ,
A C·····s
P··c ··

" that his own conduct, as well in public, as in
" private, was just what Quintus had advised,
" softer than the tip of his ear, and his votes
" in the Senate such, as pleased others, rather
" than himself

" Such ills does wretched war and discord breed,

" that bribery was never carried so high, as at
" this time, by the Consular candidates, Mem-
" mius, Domitius, Scaurus, Messala, that they
" were all alike, no eminence in any, for mo
" ney levelled the dignity of them all   that
" above eighty thousand pounds was promised
" to the first Tribe, and money grown so scarce,
" by this profusion of it, that interest was risen
" from four to eight per Cent [*e*]."

MEMMIUS and Cn Domitius, who joined
their interests, made a strange sort of contract
with the Consuls, which was drawn up in writing, and attested in proper form by many of
their friends on both sides, by which, " the
" Consuls obliged themselves, to serve them
" with all their power in the ensuing election
" and they on their part undertook, when elect-
" ed, to procure for the Consuls what Provinces

[ ] Res Romanæ sic se
habebant Prætor··· a spes
com tiorum, sed incerta e-
rat aliqua suspic·o Dictatu-
ræ ne··· qu·d in ce·ia sum-
m··m o·u·· f·e··· sed
·····en s m··g·s ·u tho·,
c·am·d·q··c·cn· ··r n-
·· ····m ··t··· ·e·t··
· ··cd···a···ci··o·
··· ··· ·, ····· ····

Τοια ἦ ὁ τλἥμων –?ευ ε ἕ
εἢ α ζέʃα· Ευrip Ικ·τ·d

Ambitus recit immanis nun
quam par fuit Ad Q·m
z 15

Sequere me nunc in Cam
pum Ard t an itus ··
μ·d··· ·· ω, sanus est·
ente Idib Quint f·ctum e··
n·····—·c· ·· in n·llo··,
p cu··a om·ium c·gni·ion
····?··—·d ··· ; 15
                      " th ;

A Urb 699
Cic 53
Coss
L Domitius
Aheno-
barbus,
A Claudius
Pulcher.

' they defired, and gave a Bond of above
" 3000 *l* to provide three Augurs, who fhould
" teftify, that they were prefent at making
" a law for granting them thofe Provinces,
' when no fuch law had ever been made, and
" two Confular Senators, who fhould affirm,
' that they were prefent likewife at paffing a de-
" cree of the Senate, for furnifhing the fame
" provinces with arms and money, when the
' Senate had never been confulted about it [*b*] "
Memmius, *who was ftrongly fupported by Cæfar [c]*, finding fome reafon to diflike his bargain, refolved to break it, and, by Pompey's *advice, gave an account of it to the Senate* Pompey was pleafed with the opportunity of mortifying *the Conful* Domitius, and willing likewife
to take fome revenge on Appius, who, though his
near relation, *did not enter fo fully as he expected
into his meafures* [*d*] but Cæfar *was much out of
humor at this ftep* [*e*], as it was likely to raife
great fcandal in the City, and ftrengthen the intereft of thofe who were endeavouring to reftrain that infamous corruption, which was the

[*b*] Confules flagrant in-
f a, quod C Memmius
candidatus pactionem in Senatu recitav t, qu m ipfe &
fuus competitor Domitius cum
Confulibus fecifent, uti ambo HS quadragena Confu
lis darent, fi effent pfi
Confules f c, nifi tres Augures dedinent, qui fe ad
fuit dicerent, cum lex cu
ita ferretur quæ lata non
effet, & duo Confulares qui
fe dicerent in ornandis provinciis confularibus fcribendo affuifle, cum omnino ne

Senatus quidem fuiffet Hac
pacto non verbis fed no-
minibus & periculi proribus,
multorum tabulis cum effe
facta diceretur, prolata a
Memmio eft nominibus in-
ductis auctore Pompeio ——
Ad Att 15

[*c*] Memmium Cefaris
o nes opes confirmant ——
Io 15 1

[*d*] Dio l 39 p 118

[*e*] Ut quidam intelligo-
bimur eam rationem illam
Memmui valde Cæfari dipli-
c re —— d Att 4 16

main

A Urb 699
Cc 53
Coſ
L Domitius
Aheno-
barbus,
A C aldius
Pulcher

main inſtrument of advancing his power. Ap
pius *never changed countenance, nor loſt any cred.t
by the diſcovery, but his collegue Domitius, who*
affected the character of a Patriot, *was extremely
diſcompoſed, and Memmius, now grown deſperate,
reſolved to promote the general diſorder and the crea
tion of a Dictator* [ƒ].

QUINTUS ſent his Brother word from Gaul,
*that it was reported there, that he was preſent at
this contract* but Cicero aſſures him that it was
falſe, and *that the bargain was of ſuch a nature,
as Memmius had opened it to the Senate, that no
honeſt man could have been preſent at it* [g] The
Senate was highly incenſed, and to check the
inſolence of the parties concerned, *paſſed a decree,
that their conduct ſhould be inquired into by what
they called a private or ſilent judgement,* where
the Sentence was not to be declared till after the
election, yet ſo, as to make void the election of
thoſe who ſhould be found guilty this they
reſolved to execute with rigor, and *made an allotment of Judges for that purpoſe* but ſome of
the Tribuns were prevailed with *to interpoſe their
negative, on pretence of hindering all inquiſitions,
not ſpecially authorized by the people* [h].

THIS

[ƒ] Hic Appius erat i-
dem, nihil ſane jacturæ
Corruerat alter, & plane, inquam, jacebat Memmius
autem — plane refrixerat, &
eo magis nunc cogitare dictaturam, tum fa ere juſtitio &
omnium rerum licentiæ.——
I 18

[g] Quod ſcribis te au-
diſſe, in Candidatorum Con-
ſularium coitione me inter-
fuiſſe, id falſum eſt Ejuſ-

modi enim pactiones in iſta
coitione factæ ſunt, quas po
ſtea Memmius patefecit, ut
nemo bonus intereſſe debue
rit—Ad Quint 3 1 § 5

[h] At Senatus decrevit ut
tacitum judicium ante comi
tia fieret —— Magnus timor
Candidatorum Sed quidam
Judices—Tribunos pl appel
larunt, ne injuſſu populi ju
dicarent, Res cedit, comi
tia dilata ex S C dum lex de
tacito

· THIS detestable bargain of forging laws and decrees at pleasure, in which so many of the first rank were concerned, either as Principals or witnesses, is alledged by an ingenious *French* writer, as a flagrant instance of *that Libertinism, which hastened the destruction* of Rome [*i*] So far are *private vices from being public benefits*, that this great Republic, of all others the most free and florishing, owed the loss of its Liberty to nothing else but a general defection of its Citizens, from the probity and discipline of their ancestors Cicero often foretells their approaching ruin from this very cause, and, when he bewails the wretchedness of the times, usually joins *the wickedness of their morals*, as the genuin source of it [*k*]

BUT lest these corrupt Candidates should escape without punishment, they were all publicly impeached by different Prosecutors, and the City was now in a great ferment about them, *since, as* Cicero says, *either the men or the law must necessarily perish· yet they will all*, says he, *be acquitted, for trials are now managed so corruptly, that no man will ever be condemned for the future, unless for murder* [*l*].   But Q. Scævola, one of

A Urb 699.
Cic 53
Coss
L DOMITIUS
AHENO-
BARBUS,
A CLAUDIUS
PULCHER.

---

tacito judicio ferretur Venit legi dies   Terentius intercess. ——— Ad Att 4 16

[*i*] Considerations sur les causes de la grandeur, &c de Romains C X

[*k*] His præsertim moribus atque temporibus, quibus ita prolapsa Resp est, ut omnium opibus refrerenda, ac coercenda sit De Divin 2 2

Qui sit Remp afflictam & oppressam miseris temporibus, ac perditis moribus, in

veterem dignitatem & libertatem vindicaturus ——— Ep Fam 2 5

[*l*] De ambitu postulati sunt omnes, qui consulatum petant——Magno res in motu est Propterea quod aut hominum aut legum interitus ostendetur——Ad Quin 3 2

Sed omnes absolventur, nec posthæc quisquam damnabitur, nisi qui hominem occiderit Ad Att. 4 16

the

the Tribuns, took a more effectual way to mortify them, by refolving to hinder any election
Confuls during his Magiftracy, in which he per-
fevered, and by his authority *diffolved all the c*
fembles, convened for that purpofe [m] T
Tribunian Candidates however were remarkab
modeft this year for they made an agreem
among themfelves, which they all confirmed
an oath, " that in profecuting their feveral i
" terefts, they would fubmit their conduct
" the judgement of Cato, and depofit four th
" fand pounds a piece in his hands, to be for
" feited by thofe, whom he fhould condemn
" any irregular practice If the election pro
" free, *fays Cato*, as it is thought it will, Ca
' alone can do more than all the Laws and
" the Judges [*n*] "

A great part of this year was taken up in pub
lic trials Sufenas and C Cato, who had bee
Tribuns two years before, were tried in the b
ginning of July, *for violence and breach of pe*
in their Magiftracy, and both acquitted b
Procilus, one of their Colegues, " was co
" demned for killing a Citizen in his own hou
" whence we are to collect, *fays Cato*, that o
" Areopagites value neither bribery nor el
" tions, nor interregrams, nor attempts aga
" the State, nor the whole Republic, a rufh

[*m*] Comitiorum quotidie
fingulos continuari obnunti-
ationibus, negata voluntate
bonorum—Ad Quin 3 3
Obnuncio totis per Scae-
volam interpofita fingulis
diebus—Ad Att 4 16
[*n*] Tribuni Candidati
juraruntſe communem Catonis
petituros apud eum H
quingena depofuerunt,
qui a Catone damnatus e
id perderet, & compet tor
tot teredan— Si comitia
peterentur, gratuita futur
plus una Cato potuerit, qua
omnes eidem judices
15 Ad Quin 2 15

" mul

A Urb 699
Cic 53
Coff
L Domitius
Aheno-
barbus,
A. Claudius
Pulcher.

" muft not murder a man indeed in his own
" houfe, though that perhaps might be done
" moderately, fince twenty-two acquitted Pro-
" cilius, when twenty-eight condemned him [o] "
Clodius was the accufer in thefe impeachments:
which made Cato, as foon as he was acquitted,
feek a reconciliation with Cicero and Milo [p]   It
was not Cicero's bufinefs to reject the friendſhip
of an active and popular Senator, and Milo had
occafion for his fervice in his approaching fuit for
the Confulfhip   But though Cicero had no concern in thefe trials, he was continually employed
in others, through the reft of the fummer. " I
" was never, *fays he,* more bufy in trials than
" now, in the worft feafon of the year, and the
" greateft heats, that we have ever known;
" there fcarce paffes a day in which I do not de-
" fend fome [q]."   Befides his Clients in the
City, he had feveral towns and colonies under
his patronage, which fometimes wanted his help
abroad, as the Corporation of *Reate* did now, to
plead for them before *the Conful Appius, and ten
Commiffioners,* in a controverfy with their neighbours of *Interamna, about draining the lake* Veli-
nus *into the River* Nar, *to the damage of their*

[o] III Non Quint Suf-
fenas & Cato abfoluti   Pro-
cilius condemnatus   Ex quo
intellectum eft, τρισαρειο πα-
γ ras, ambitum comitia interregnum, majeftatem, totam deinque Remp hocci
non facere   Debemus patrem
familias domi fuæ occidere
nolle, neqve tamen id ipfum
abunde   Nam abfolverint
22, condemnarunt 28——— -
Ad Att 4 15

[p] Is tamen & mecum &
cum Milone in gratiam rediit
Ib 16
[q] Sic enim habeto nun
cuam me a caufis & judicis
aftrictiorem fuiffe, atque id
arni tempore graviffimo, &
caloribus maximis   Ad Quint.
2 16

Diem fcio effe nullum,
quo non dico pro reo   Ib
3

A Urb 699
Cic 53
Coff
L Domitius
Aheno-
barbus,
A Claudius
Pulcher.

grounds He returned from this caufe in the midft of *the Apollinarian fhews*, and, to relieve himfelf from the fatigue of his journey, went directly *to the Theater, where he was received by an univerfal clap* in the account of which to Atticus, he adds, *but this you are not to take notice of, and I am a fool indeed myfelf for mentioning it* [r]

He now alfo defended Meffius, one of Cæfar's Lieutenants, *who came from Gaul on purpofe to take his trial* then Drufus, accufed *of prevaricating or betraying a caufe, which he had undertaken to defend, of which he was acquitted by a majority orely of four voices* After that Vatinius, the laft year's *Prætor*, and Æmilius Scaurus, one of the Confular Candidates, *accufed of plundering the Province of* Sardinia [s], and about the fame time likewife his old friend, Cn Plancius, who had entertained him fo generoufly in his exil, and being now chofen *Ædile*, was accufed by a difappointed Competitor, M Laterenfis, *of bribery and corruption* All thefe were acquitted, but the Orations for them are loft, except that for Plancius, which remains a perpetual monument of Cicero's gratitude. for Plancius having obtained the Tribunate from the people, as the re

---

[r] Reatini me ad fua ———— duxerunt ut agerem caufam contra Interamnates —Redii Romam — Veni in fpectaculum, primum magno & æquabili plaufu, fed hoc ne cures, ego ineptus qui fcripferim,——— Ad Att 4 15

[s] Meffu defend ba———— nobis, e legatione re——— —— Defend me ex——— Drufum inde ad——— ———Ibid ———

Drufus erat de prævarica tione— abfolutus, in fumma quatuor fententiis— Fodem die poft meridiem Vatinium aderam defenfurus, ea re † ulis —— Scauri judicium ——— ———— bitur, cui no non de——— Ad Quin 2 16

——— beneficio defen ——— valde obligavi ——— Ib ——— 5

ward of his fidelity to Cicero, did not behave
himself in that post, with the same affection to
him as before, but seems studiously to have slighted him, while several of his Collegues, and especially Racilius, *were exerting all their power in*
the defence of his person and dignity [t] Yet Cicero freely undertook his cause, and as if no
coldness had intervened, displayed the merit of
his services in the most pathetic and affecting
manner, and rescued him from the hands of a
powerfull accuser, and his own particular friend.
" Drusus's trial was held in the morning, from
" which, after going home to write a few Let-
" ters, he was obliged to return to Vatinius's in
" the afternoon." which gives us a specimen of
the hurry in which he generally lived, and of
the little time which he had to spend upon his
private affairs, or his studies and though he
was now carrying on several great works of the
learned kind, " yet he had no other leisure, *he*
" *tells us*, for meditating and composing but
" when he was taking a few turns in h r-
" dens, for the exercise of his body, and re-
" freshment of his voice [u]." Vatinius had
been one of his fiercest enemies, was in a perpetual opposition to him in politics and, like
Bestia mentioned above, a seditious, profligate,
abandoned Libertine so that the defence of him
gave a plausible handle for some censure upon
Cicero but his engagements with Pompey, and
especially his new friendship with Cæsar, made it
necessary to embrace all *Cæsar's friends*, among

A Urb 699.
Cic 53
Coss
L Domitius
Aheno-
barbus,
A Claudius
Pulcher.

---

[t] Negas Tribunatum
Planci quicquam attulisse ad-
jurenti dignitati meæ At-
que hoc loco quod verissime
cere potes L Racili—
cina in me m cumu-

moras, &c Pro Plancio 32
[u] Ita quicquid conficio
aut cogito in ambulationis
fere tempus confero Ad
Quint

I whom

A Urb 699
Cic 53.
Coss
L Domitius
Aheno-
barbus,
A Claudius
Pulcher

whom Vatinius was most warmly recommended to him

GABINIUS being recalled, as has been said, from his government, returned to *Rome* about the end of September he bragged every where on his journey, that he was going *to the demand of a triumph*, and to carry on that farce, continued a while without the gates, till perceiving how odious he was to all within, *he stole privately into the City by night, to avoid the disgrace of being insulted by the populace* [x] There were *three different impeachments* provided against him the first, *for treasonable practices against the state*, the second, *for the plunder of his province*; the third, *for bribery and corruption*, and so many persons offered themselves to be prosecutors, *that there was a contest among them before the Prætor, how to adjust their several claims* [y] The first indictment fell to L Lentulus, who accused him the day after he entered the city, " that, " in defiance of religion and the decree of the " Senate, he had restored the King of *Ægypt* " with an army, leaving his own Province naked, " and open to the incursion of enemies, who " had made great devastations in it " Cicero, who had received from Gabinius all the provocation, which one man could receive from another, had the pleasure to see his insolent adver

[x] Ad urbem accessit A D xii Kal Oct nihil turpius, nec desertius Ad Q Fr 3 1 § 5
Cum Gabinius quacunque veniebat, triumphum se postulare dictitabat sub idque corpus Imperator noctu in urbem, hostium plane invasisset——Ib 2

[.] Gabinium tres adhuc factiones postulant &c I. 1 y 5
Cum hæc scribebam ante lucem, apud Catonem erat divinatio in Gabinium futura, inter Memmium, & Ti Neronem, & C & L Antonios Ib 2

A Urb 699
Cic 53
Coff
L Domitius
Aheno-
barbus,
A Claudius
Pulcher

fary at his feet, and was prepared to give him such a reception, as he deferved but Gabinius durft not venture to fhew his head for the firft ten days, till he was obliged to come to the Senate, in order to give them an account, according to cuftom, *of the ftate of his Province, and the troops which he had left in it.* as foon as he had told his ftory, he was going to retire, but the Confuls detained him, to anfwer to a complaint brought againft him *by the Publicans, or Farmers of the revenues,* who were attending at the door to make it good This drew on a debate, in which Gabinius was fo urged and teized on all fides, but efpecially by Cicero, *that, trembling with paffion, and unable to contain himfelf, he called Cicero, a banifhed man* upon which, fays Cicero, in a Letter to his Brother, " nothing " ever happened more honorable to me. the " whole Senate left their feats to a man, and " with a general clamor ran up to his very face; " while the Publicans alfo were equally fierce " and clamorous againft him, and the whole " company behaved juft as you yourfelf would " have done [z] "

Cicero had been deliberating for fome time, *whether he fhould not excufe Gabinius himfelf,* but *out of regard to Pompey* was content to appear

---

[z] Interim ipfo decimo die, quo ipfum oportebat ho—[…] numerum & militum renunciare, in re hafit, fumma in fequentia cum vellet exire, a Confulibus retentus eft, introducti publicani Homo undique actus, cum a me maxime vulnerare [..], non tulit, & me tremenda voce etiam appellavit Hic, O Di, nihil unquam honorificentius nobis accidit Confurrexit Senatus cum clamore ad unum, fic ut ad corpus ejus accederet Pari clamore atque impetu publicani Quid quæris? Omnes, tanquam fi tu efles, ita fuerunt.—Ib.

onely

A Urb 699
Cic 53
Cof
L Do 'tius
Aheno-
barbls,
A Claudius
Pulcher

onely *as a witness* againſt him [a]; and when
the trial was over, gives the following account
of it *to his Brother*

" Gabinius is acquitted nothing was ever
" ſo ſtupid, as his accuſer Lentulus , nothing ſo
" ſordid as the bench yet, if Pompey had not
" taken incredible pains, and the rumor of a
" Dictatorſhip had not infuſed ſome apprehen-
" ſions, he could not have held up his head
" even againſt Lentulus . ſince with ſuch an ac-
" cuſer, and ſuch Judges , of the ſeventy-two,
" who ſat upon him, thirty-two condemned
" him The ſentence is ſo infamous, that he
" ſeems likely to fall in the other trials ; eſpe-
" cially that of plunder , but there's no repub-
" lic, no Senate, no Juſtice, no dignity in any
" of us . what can I ſay more of the Judges ?
" There were but two of them of Prætorian
" rank, Domitius Calvinus, who acquitted him
" ſo forwardly, that all the world might ſee it,
" and Cato, who, as ſoon as the votes were de-
" clared, ran officiouſly from the Bench, to car
" ry the firſt news to Pompey Some ſay, and
" particu'ar'y Salluſt, that I ought to have ac-
" cuſed him but ſhould I riſk my credit with
" ſuch Judges ? What a figure ſhould I have
" made, if he had eſcaped from me But there
" were other things, which influenced me
" Pompey would have conſidered it as a ſtrug-
" gle, not about Gabinius's ſafety, but his own
" dignity it muſt have made a breach between
" us we ſhould have been matched like a pair
" of Gladiators , as Pacidianus, with Æſerninus

[a] Ego tamen me teneo nolo cum Pompeio pugnare,
ac accuſando vi mehercule. ſatis eſt quod inſtat de Milo
ſed tamen teneo, et quod ne —— Ib 3 2

" the

" the *Samnite*, he would probably have bitt off
" one of my ears, or been reconciled at leaft
" with Clodius — for after all the pains, which
" I had taken to ferve him, when I owed no-
" thing to him, he every thing to me, yet he
" would not bear my differing from him in pub-
" lic affairs, to fay no worfe of it, and when
" he was lefs powerfull than he is at prefent,
" fhewed what power he had againft me, in my
" florifhing condition; why fhould I now,
" when I have loft even all defire of power,
" when the Republic certainly has none, when
' he alone has all, chufe him of all men to
" contend with? for that muft have been the
" cafe I cannot think that you would have
" advifed me to it Salluft fays, that I ought
" to have done either the one or the other,
" and in compliment to Pompey have defended
" him, who begged it of me indeed very ear-
" neftly — A fpecial friend this Salluft! to wifh
" me to involve myfelf either in a dangerous
" enmity, or perpetual infamy I am delight-
" ed with my middle way, and when I had
" given my teftimony faithfully and religioufly,
" was pleafed to hear Gabinius fay, that if it
" fhould be permitted to him to continue in the
" City, he would make it his bufinefs to give
" me fatisfaction, nor did he fo much as interro-
" gate me————[*b*] " He gives the fame account of this trial to his other friends, " how
" Lentulus acted his part fo ill, that people
" were perfuaded that he prevaricated——— and
" that Gabinius's efcape was owing to the inde-
" fatigable induftry of Pompey, and the corrup-
" tion of the Bench [*c*] "

I 4   ABOUT

A Urb 699.
Cic 53
Coff
L Domitius
Aheno-
barbus,
A Claudius
Pulcher.

[*b*] Ad Quint 3 4   [*c*] Quodmodo ergo abfo-
                                                lutus?

A. Urb. 699.
Cic. 53.
Coss.
L. Domitius
Ahenobarbus,
A. Claudius
Pulcher.

About the time of this trial there happened *a terrible inundation of the Tiber*, which did much damage at *Rome*. many houses and shops were carried away by it, and *the fine gardens of Cicero's son-in-law, Crassipes, demolished*. It was all charged to the absolution of Gabinius, after his daring violation of Religion, and contempt of *the Sibyl's books*. Cicero applies to it the following passage of Homer [*d*].

As when in autumn Jove *his fury pours,*
And earth is loaden with incessant showers,
When guilty mortals break th' internal laws,
And Judges brib'd betray the righteous cause,
From their deep beds he bids the Rivers rise,
And opens all the flood-gates of the skies.
Mr. Pope, Il. 16. v. 466.

But Gabinius's danger was not yet over: he was to be tried a second time, *for the plunder of his Province*, where C. Memmius, one of the Tribuns, was his Accuser, and M. Cato his Judge, with whom he was not likely to find any favor. Pompey pressed Cicero *to defend him*, and would not admit of any excuse, and Gabinius's humble behaviour in the late trial was intended to make way for Pompey's sollicitation. Cicero stood him for a long time. *Pompey*, says he, *labors hard with me, but has yet made no im-*

lurus —— Accusatorum incredibilis infantia, id est L. Lentuli, quem fremunt omnes prævaricatum, deinde Pompeii mira contentio, Judicum sordes. Ad Att. 4. 16.

[*d*] Romæ, & maxime Appia ad Martis, mira proluvies. Crassipedis ambulatio ablata, horti, tabernæ plurimæ. Magna vis aquæ usque ad piscinam publicam. Viget illud Homeri— Cadit enim in absolutionem Gabinii. —Ad Quint. 3. 7.

pression

A. Urb. 699.
Cic 53.
Coſſ.
L Domitius
Aheno-
barbus,
A Claudius
Pulcher.

preſſion, nor, if I retain a grain of liberty, ever will [*e*] ,

Oh ! e'er that dire diſgrace ſhall blaſt my fame,
O'erwhelm me earth——   *Il.* 4. 218.

but Pompey's inceſſant importunity, backed by Cæſar's earneſt requeſt, made it vain to ſtruggle any longer; and forced him againſt his judgement, his reſolution, and his dignity, to defend Gabinius, at a time when his defence at laſt proved of no ſervice to him, for he was found guilty by Cato, and condemned of courſe to a perpetual baniſhment. It is probable, that Cicero's Oration was never publiſhed, but as it was his cuſtom to keep the minutes or rough draught of all his pleadings, in what he called *his Commentaries*, which were extant many ages after his death [*f*], ſo St Jerom has preſerved from them a ſmall fragment of this ſpeech, which ſeems to be a part of the apology, that he found himſelf obliged to make for it, wherein he obſerves, " that when Pompey's authority had " once reconciled him to Gabinius, it was no " longer in his power to avoid defending him; " for it was ever my perſuaſion, *ſays he*, that " all friendſhips ſhould be maintained with a re- " ligious exactneſs, but eſpecially thoſe, which " happen to be renewed from a quarrel · for in " friendſhips, that have ſuffered no interruption, " a failure of duty is eaſily excuſed by a plea of

[*e*] Pompeius a me valde contendit de reditu in gratiam, ſed adhuc nihil profecit nec ſullam partem libertatis tenuo, profec t —— Ad Quin ɔ 1 § 5

De Gabinio nihil fuit faciendum iſtorum, &c τοτε μοι χαιοι Il 4 218
[*f*] Quod feciſſe M Tullium Commentariis ipſius apparet Quintil l x c 7

" inadvertency,

A Urb 699
Cic 53.
Coff
L Domitius
Aheno-
barbus,
A Claudius
Pulcher

" inadvertency, or, at the worst, of negligence,
" whereas, if after a reconciliation any new of-
" fence be given, it never passes for negligent
" but wilfull, and is not imputed to impiudence,
" *but to perfidy* [g] "

THE Proconsul, Lentulus, who resided still
in Cilicia, having had an account from *Rome, of
Cicero's change of conduct, and his defence of Vati
rius,* wrote a sort of expostulatory Letter to him,
to know the reasons of it, telling him, *that he
had heard of his reconciliation with Cæsar and Appius, for which he did not blame him, but was at
a loss how to account for his new friendship with
Crassus; and above all, what it was that induced
him to defend Vatinius* This gave occasion to
that long and elaborate answer from Cicero, already referred to, written before Gabinius's trial;
which would otherwise have made his apology
more difficult, in which he lays open the motives
and progress of his whole behaviour from the
time of his exil——" As to the case of Vatinius,
" *he says,* as soon as he was chosen Prætor,
" where I warmly opposed him, in favor of Ca-
" to, Pompey prevailed with me to be recon-
" ciled to him, and Cæsar afterwards took sur-
" prizing pains with me to defend him, to
" which I consented, for the sake of doing what,
" as I told the court at the trial, *the Parasite,* in
" *the Eunuch,* advised the Patron to do
      " *Wherever she talks of Phadria do you pre
   sently praise Pamphila, &c. so I begged of
" the Judges, that since certain persons of di-
" stinguished rank, to whom I was much
" obliged, were so fond of my enemy, and affect-
" ed to caress him in the Senate before my face,
" with all the marks of familiarity, and since

[g] *Id Fragment Orat. on m* —

                                    " then

" they had their Publius to give me jealoufy, I
" might be allowed to have my Publius alfo, to
" teize them with in my turn——" Then as to
his general conduct, he makes this general defence, " that the union and firmnefs of the
" honeft, which fubfifted when Lentulus left
" *Rome*, confirmed, *fays he*, by my Confulfhip,
" and revived by yours, is now quite broken
" and deferted by thofe, who ought to have
" fupported it, and were looked upon as Pa-
" triots; for which reafon, the maxims and
" meafures of all wife Citizens, in which clafs I
" always wifh to be ranked, ought to be changed
" too   for it is a precept of Plato, whofe au-
" thority has the greateft weight with me, to
" contend in public affairs, as far as we can per-
" fuade our Citizens, but not to offer violence,
" either to our Parent or our Country————If I
" was quite free from all engagements, I fhould
" act therefore as I now do , fhould not think it
" prudent to contend with fo great a power ,
" noi if it could be effected, to extinguifh it in
" our prefent circumftances , nor continue al-
" ways in one mind, when the things themfelves
" and the fentiments of the honeft are altered ,
" fince a perpetual adherence to the fame meafuies
" has never been approved by thofe, who know
" beft how to govern eftates   but, as in failing, it
" is the bufinefs of art to be directed by the
" weather, and foolifh to peifevere with danger in
" the courfe, in which we fet out, rather than by
" changing it, to arrive with fafety, though later,
" where we intended ; fo to us, who manage
' public affairs, the chief end propofed being
" dignity with public quiet, our bufinefs is not
" to be always faying, but always aiming at the
" fame thing   Wherefore if all things, as I
                                        " faid,

A Urb 699.
Cic 53
Coff
L Domitius
Aheno-
barbus,
A Claudius
Pulcher.

A. Urb 699
Cic 53
Coff
L Domitius
Afeno-
barbus,
A Claudius
Pulcher

" faid, were wholly free to me, I fhould be the
" fame man that I now am   but when I am in-
" vited to this conduct on the one fide by kind
" neffes, and driven to it on the other by injuries,
' I eafily fuffer myfelf to vote and act what I
" take to be ufefull both to myfelf and the Re
" public, and I do it the more freely, as well
" on the account of my Brother's being Cæfar's
" Lieutenant, as that there is not the leaft thing,
" which I have ever faid or done for Cæfar, but
" what he has repaid with fuch eminent grati
" tude, as perfuades me, that he takes himfelt
" to be obliged to me, fo that I have as much
" ufe of all his power and intereft, which you
" know to be the greateft, as if they were my
" own   nor could I otherwife have defeated the
" defigns of my defperate enemies, if to thofe
" forces which I have always been mafter of, I
" had not joined the favor of the men of power
" Had you been here to advife me, I am per
" fuaded, that I fhould have followed the fame
" meafures. for I know your good nature and
" moderation, I know your heart, not onely
" the moft friendly to me, but void of all ma
" levolence to others, great and noble, open
" and fincere, &c. [*b*]." He often defends him
felf on other occafions by the fame allufion *to the*
art of failing   " I cannot reckon it inconftancy,
" *fays he,* to change and moderate our opinion,
" like the courfe of a fhip, by the weather of
" the Republic, this is what I have learnt, have
" obferved, have read, what the records of
" former ages have delivered, of the wifeft and
" moft eminent Citizens, both in this and all
" other Cities, that the fame maxims are not al-
" ways to be purfued by the fame men; but

" fuch,

A Urb. 699.
Cic 53.
Coff
L Domitius
Aheno-
barbus,
A Claudius
Pulcher.

" such, whatever they be, which the ſtate of the
" Republic, the inclination of the times, the
" occaſions of public peace require. this is what
" I am now doing, and ſhall always do——[1] "

The trial of C. Rabirius Poſtumus, *a perſon
of Equeſtrian rank*, was an appendix to that of
Gabinius. It was one of the articles againſt
Gabinius, *that he had received about two millions
for reſtoring King Ptolemy*, yet all his eſtate,
which was to be found, was not ſufficient to anſwer the damages in which he was condemned,
nor could he give any ſecurity for the reſt in
this caſe, the method was to demand the deficiency from thoſe through whoſe hands the management of his money affairs had paſſed, and
who were ſuppoſed to have been ſharers in the
ſpoil this was charged upon Rabirius *and that
he had adviſed Gabinius to undertake the reſtoration
of the king, and accompanied him in it, and was
employed to ſollicit the payment of the money, and
lived at* Alexandria *for that purpoſe, in the King's
ſervice, as the public Receiver of his taxes, and
wearing the Pallum or habit of the country.*

Cicero urged in defence of Rabirius, " that
" he had born no part in that tranſaction, but
" that his whole crime, or rather folly, was, that
" he had lent the King great ſumms of money
" for his ſupport at *Rome*, and ventured to truſt
" a Prince, who, as all the world then thought,

---

[1] Neque enim inconſtan-
tis puto, ſententiam tanquam
aliquod navigium atque cur-
ſum ex Reip tempeſtate
moderari Ego vero hæc
didici, hæc vidi, hæc ſcrip-
ta legi hæc de ſapienti-
ſimis & clariſſimis viris, &
hac Repub & in ali. ...
tatibus maxime tribus &
literæ prodiderint non ſem
per eaſdem tenendas ab iiſ-
dem, ſed quaſcunque Reip
ſtatus inclinatio temporum,
ratio concordia poſtularet, ei-
te defendendas Quod ego
& feci, & ſemper faciam
——! o ...

" Wa

" was going to be reftored by the authority of
" the *Roman* people   that the neceffity of going
" to *Ægypt* for the recovery of that debt, was
" the fource of all his mifery   where he was
" forced to take whatever the King would give or
" impofe. that it was his misfortune to be ob
" liged to commit himfelf to the power of an ar
" bitrary Monarch : that nothing could be more
" mad than for a Roman Knight, and Citizen
" of a Republic of all others the moft free, to
" go to any place, where he muft needs be a
" flave to the will of another, that all who ever
" did fo, as Plato and the wifeft had fometime
" done too haftily, always fuffered for it, this
" was the cafe of Rabirius. neceffity carried
" him to *Alexandria*; his whole fortunes were
" at ftake [*k*]; which he was fo far from im
" proving by his traffic with that King, that he
" was ill treated by him, imprifoned, threatened
" with death, and glad to run away at laft with
" the lofs of all   and at that very time, it was
" wholly owing to Cæfar's generofity, and re
" gard to the merit and misfortunes of an old
" friend, that he was enabled to fupport his for-
" mer rank and Equeftrian dignity—[*l*] "   Ga
binius's *trial* had fo near a relation to this, and
was fo often referred to in it, that the Profecu
tors could not omit fo fair an opportunity of *tal*
king Cicero, for the part which he had acted in
it   Memmius obferved, *that the Deputies of* Alexandria *had the fame reafon for appearing for* Gab
, which Cicero *had for defending him, the*
command of a Mafter—No, Mem*mius,* replied C-
cero, *my reafon for defending him, was a recomme n-*
c o t with him, for I am not offraid to own, tho'
my quarrels are mortal, my friendfhips immortal

and

A Urb 699
Cic 53
Coff
L Domitius
Aheno-
barbus,
A Claudius
Pulcher.

and if you imagine, that I undertook that cause for fear of Pompey, you neither krow Pompey, nor me, for Pompey would neither defire it of me against my will, nor would I, after I had preferved the liberty of my Citizens, ever give up my own [m]

VALERIUS MAXIMUS reckons Cicero's defence *of Gabinius and Vatinius,* among the great and laudable examples of humanity, which the *Roman* Hiftory furnifhed, *as it is nobler,* he fays, *to conquer injuries with benefits, than to repay them in kind, with an obftinacy of hatred* [n]. This turn is agreeable to the defign of that writer, whofe view it feems to be, in the collection of his ftories, to give us rather what is ftrange, than true, and to drefs up facts as it were into fables, for the fake of drawing a moral from them. for whatever Cicero himfelf might fay for it, in the florifhing ftile of an oration, it is certain, that he knew and felt it to be, what it really was, an indignity and difhonour to him, which he was forced to fubmit to by the iniquity of the times, and his engagements with Pompey and Cæfar, as he often laments to his friends in a very paffionate ftrain · *I am afflicted,* fays he, *my deareft Brother, I am afflicted, that there is no Republic, no Juftice in trials; that this feafon of my life, which ought to flo-*

---

[m] Ait etiam meus familiaris, eandem caufam Alexandrinis fuiffe, cur laudarent Gabinium, quæ mihi fuit, cur eundem defenderem Mihi, C Memmi, caufa defendendi Gabinii fuit reconciliatio gratiæ Neque vero me pœnitet, *mortales inimicitias femp ternas amicitias habere* Nam fi me invitum putas ne Cn Pompeii animum offenderem, defendiffe caufam &

illum & me vehementer ignoias Neque enim Pompei · me fua caufa quidquam facere voluiffet invitum; ne que ego, cu omnium civium libertas, ca mme fuiffet, meam projeciffem—Pro C Ra bir Poft 12

[n] Sed hujufce generis humanitas ea m in M Cic rone præcipua apparuit, &c Val. Max 4 2

A Urb 699
Cic 53
Coſſ
L. Dovitius
Aɾeɴo-
barbus,
A Claudius
Pulcher

...ſh in the authority of the Senatorian character,
either waſted in the drudgery of the Bar, or relieu
only by domeſtic ſtudies, that what I have ever be
fond of from a boy,

In every virtuous act and glorious ſtrife
To ſhare the firſt and beſt————

is wholly loſt and gone, that my enemies are part,
not oppoſed, partly even defended by me, and m
ther what I love, nor what I hate, left free
me [o]

WHILE Cæſar was engaged in *the Britiſh* ex
pedition, his Daughter Julia, *Pompey's wife,* di
in *child-bed at Rome,* after ſhe was delivered of
ſon, which died alſo ſoon after her. Her lo
was not more lamented by the Huſband a
Father, who both of them tenderly loved he
than by all their common friends, and well-wiſher
to the public peace, who conſidered it as a ſourc
of freſh diſturbance to the ſtate, from the ambi
tious views and claſhing intereſts of the Tw
Chiefs, whom the life of one ſo dear, and th
relation of Son and Father ſeemed hitherto
have united by the ties both of duty and affecti
on [p]. Cæſar is ſaid *to have born the news*

[ ] Angor, mi ſuaviſſime
frater, angor, nullam eſſe
Remp niha pɾaec a, noſtrum-
que noc tempus ætatis quod
in ila Senate a auctoritate
forere deuebat, aut forenſi
rbore jactar aut comeſti-
us litteris ſuſtentui Illud
vero quod a puero adama-
iam
Ni laucel in vɾai ſ-iɾ-jːɣɔι
τυυιɑ αλɾ/α,
H 7 208
reum occaſie, inimicos a

me partım non oppugnato
partım etiam eſſe defenſo
meum non modo animur
ſed ne odium quidem eſſe
berum—Ad Quin 3 5
[p] Cum medium jam
ex invidia potentiæ male c
hærentis inter Cn Pomp
um & C Cæſarem, conco
d æ p gnus, Julia uxor M
ri occeſit——Filius quoqu
parvus, Julia natus, int
breve ſpatium obiit Vel
Pat 2 47 Val M 4 6

her death with an uncommon firmness [q]   it is certain, that fhe had lived long enough to ferve all
the ends, which he propofed from that alliance,
and to procure for him every thing that Pompey's power could give   for while Pompey, for-
getfull of his honour and intereft, was fpending
his time inglorioufly at home, in the carefles of
a young wife, and the delights of *Italy*, and, as
if he had been onely Cæfar's agent, was continually decreeing frefh honors, troops, and money
to him,   Cæfar was purfuing the direct road to
Empire, training his Legions in all the toils and
difcipline of a bloody war,   himfelf always at
their head, animating them by his courage, and
rewarding them by his bounty, till from a great
and wealthy Province, having raifed money
enough to corrupt, and an army able to conquer
all who could oppofe him, he feemed to want
nothing for the vaft execution of his defigns, but
a pretext to break with Pompey, which, as all
wife men forefaw, could not long be wanted,
when Julia, the cement of their union, was removed   For though the power of the Triumvirate had given a dangerous blow to the liberty
of *Rome*, yet the jealoufies and feparate interefts
of the Chiefs obliged them to manage it with
fome decency, and to extend it but rarely, beyond the forms of the conftitution, but whe-
ever that league fhould happen to be diffolved,
which had made them already too great for private fubjects, the next conteft of courf muft be
for dominion, and the fingle maftery of the Empire

A Urb 6
Cic 53
Coff
L Domiti
Ahĕno-
barbu ,
A Claudii
Pulcher

[q] Cæfar — cum audivit   munera   Sueæ Confol ad
deceffie filam — inter teu-   Helv p 11
tee diem Imperatoria obit

A. U. b 699
Ce 55
Coff
L. DOMITIUS
AHENO-
BARBUS,
A. CLAUDIUS
PULCHER

ON the second of November, C. Pontinius triumphed over the Allobroges he had been *Prætor*, when Cicero *was Consul*, and at the end of his Magistracy obtained the government of that part of *Gaul*, which having been tampering with Catiline in his conspiracy, broke out soon afterwards into open Rebellion, but was reduced by the vigor of this General. For this service, he demanded *a Triumph*, but met with great opposition, which he surmounted with incredible patience: for he persevered in his suit *for five years successively*, residing all that while, according to custom, in the suburbs of the City, till he gained his point at last by a kind of violence. Cicero was his friend, and continued in *Rome* on purpose to assist him, and *the Consul* Appius *served him with all his power*, *but Cato protested, that Pon—— should never triumph while he lived, though this*, says Cicero, *like many of his other threats, will end at last in nothing* But *the Prætor Galba*, who had been his Lieutenant, having procured by stratagem *an act of the people in his favor*, he entered the City in his Triumphal Chariot, where he was so rudely received and opposed in his passage through the streets, *that he was forced to make his way with his sword, and the slaughter of many of his adversaries* [r]

IN the end of the year, Cicero consented *to be one of Pompey's Lieutenants in* Spain, *which he*

---

[r] Ea re non longius, —— velit —— quod Pontinio Triumphum volebant adire: etenim erat eo quid negotii &c. Ad Quin. 3. 5.
Pontinus —— A. D. IV Non. Nov. eum triumphare —— cum Cato & Servi-

lius Prætores aperte, & Q. Mucius Tribunus—— Sed erit cum Pontinio Appius Consul Cato tamen affirmat, se vivo illum non triumphare, id ego puto, ut multa ejusdem, ad nihil recasurum—— Ad Att. 4. 16. It. Dio l. 39. p. 120.

A Urb 699
Cic 53
Coff
L Domitius
Aheno-
barbus,
A Claudius
Pulcher.

began to think convenient to the present state of his affairs, and resolved to set forward for that Province, about the middle of January [s] but this seemed to give some umbrage to Cæfar, who, by the help of Quintus, hoped to disengage him gradually from Pompey, and to attach him to himself, and with that view had begged of him, in his Letters, to continue at *Rome* [t], for the sake of serving himself with his authority, in all affairs which he had occasion to transact there, so that, out of regard probably to Cæsar's uneasiness, Cicero soon changed his mind, and resigned *his lieutenancy* to which he seems to allude in a Letter to his Brother, where he says, *that he had no second thoughts in whatever concerned Cæsar, that he would make good his engagements to him, and being entered into his friendship with judgement, was now attached to him by affection* [u]

He was employed at Cæsar's desire along with Oppius, in settling the plan of a most expensive and magnificent work, which Cæsar was going to execute at *Rome, out of the spoils of* Gaul, *a new Forum*, with many grand buildings annexed to it; for the area of which alone, they had contracted to pay to the several owners, *about five hundred thousand pounds*, or, as Suetonius computes, *near double that* summ [x] Cicero calls it *a glorious*

---

[s] Sed heus tu, scripse-
ram e tibi me esse legatum
Pompeio & extra urbem
quidem fore, ex Id Jan vi-
sum est hoc mihi ad multa
quadrare—Ad Att 4 18

[t] Quod mihi tempus,
Romæ præsertim, ut iste me
rogat, manenti, vacuum of-
ficitur? Ad Quin 2 15

[u] Ego vero nullas deur-

pas esse] has, haber possum
in Cæsaris rebus— Videor id
judicio facere Jam enim
debeo sed tamen amore
sum incensus — Ad Quin 3
1 § 5

[x] Forum de manubiis
inchoavit, cujus area super
H S milies constitit Suet.
J Cæf 20

piece

pere of work, and fays, *that the partitions, or en-
closures of the Campus Martius, in which the Tribes
used to vote, were all to be made new of marble,
with a roof likewise of the fame, and a ſtately Portico carried round the whole, of a mile in Circui,
to which a public Hall or Town houſe was to be
joined* [y] While this building was going forward, L. Æmilius Paullus was employed in raising another, not much inferior to it, at his own
expence. for he repaired and beautified *en enc*
Baſilica in the old Forum, and built at the fame
time *a new one with Phrygian columns*, which was
called after *his own name*, and is frequently mentioned by the later writers, as a Fabric of wonderfull magnificence, computed to have coſt him
three hundred thouſand pounds [z]

THE new tribuns purſued the meaſures of
their Predeceſſors, and would not ſuffer an election of Conſuls, ſo that when the new year
came on, the Republic wanted its proper head:
in this caſe the adminiſtration fell into the hands
of *a Interré*, a proviſional Magiſtrate, who
muſt neceſſarily *be a Patrician, and choſen by the
body of Patricians*, called together for that pur-

[y] Itaque Cæſaris amici-
ſime dico & Oppium dirum-
pas licet in monumentum
illud, quod tu tollere laudibus
ſolebas, ut Forum laxaremus,
& uſque ad atrium
cxterremus conſumemus
HS Seſce... cum pri-
... non poteſt minoris
nore pecunia Efficiemus
rem glorioſiſſimam nam in
Campo Martio ſepta Tribu-
tis conſiſtiendis ... facimus,

& tecta facturi, eaque cinge-
mus excelſa porticu, ut mille
paſſuum conficiatur. Si-
adjungetur huic operi, ...
etiam publica — Ad Att. ..
16
[z] Paullus in medio Fo-
ro baſilicam jam pane tex-
uidem antiquis columnis illam autem quam locavit
fecit magnificentiſſimam. Nihil gradus illo monumento
nihil glorioſius—Ibid —

poſe by the Senate [*a*]. His power however was
but ſhort-lived, being transferred, *every five days,*
from one Inter rex to another, till an election of
Conſuls could be obtained, but the Tribuns,
whoſe authority was abſolute, while there were
no Conſuls to controul them, continued fierce
againſt any election at all ſome were for reviving *the ancient dignity of military Tribuns*, but
that being unpopular, a more plauſible Scheme
was taken up and openly avowed, *of declaring*
Pompey Dictator This gave great apprehenſions
to the City, for the memory of *Sylla's Dictator-*
ſhip, and was vigorouſly oppoſed by all the
Chiefs of the Senate, and eſpecially by Cato.
Pompey choſe to keep himſelf out of ſight, and
retired into the country, to avoid the ſuſpicion
of affecting it " The rumor of a Dictatorſhip,
" *ſays Cicero*, is diſagreeable to the honeſt, but
" the other things, which they talk of, are
" more ſo to me, the whole affair is dreaded,
' but flags Pompey flatly diſclaims it, though he
' never denied it to me before the Tribun Hir-
" rus will probably be the promoter good Gods!
" how ſilly and fond of himſelf without a rival?
" At Pompey's requeſt, I have deterred Craſſus
" Junianus, who pays great regard to me, from
" meddling with it It is hard to know whe-
" ther Pompey really deſires it or not, but if
" Hirrus ſtir in it, he will not convince us, that
" he is averſe to it [*b*]." In another Letter;
" Nothing

[*a*] Vid Aſcon argument in Milon —

[*b*] Rumor Dictatoris in-jucundus bonis mihi etiam magis quæ loquuntur Sed res & timetur & refri-geſcit Pompeius plane ſe negat velle antea ipſe mihi non negabat Hirrus auctor fore videtur O Dii, quam ineptus, & quam ſe amans ſine rivali ! Craſſum Junianum, hominem mihi deditum, per me deterruit Velit, nolit, ſcire

" Nothing is yet done as to the Dictatorship;
" Pompey is still absent, Appius in a great bu-
' tle, Hirrus preparing to oppose it, but seve-
" ral are named as ready to interpose their nega-
" tive the people do not trouble their heads
" about it, the Chiefs are against it I keep my-
" self quiet [c] " Cicero's friend, Milo, was irresolute how to act on this occasion, he was
for *acting an interest for the Consulship*, and if he
declared against *a Dictatorship, was of aid of making Pompey his enemy, or if he should not help the
opponents, that it would be carried by force*, in
both which cases, his own pretensions were sure
to be disappointed he was inclined therefore to
join in the opposition, but so far onely as to re-
pel any violence [d]

THE Tribunes in the mean time were growing
every day more and more insolent, and engrossing
all power to themselves, till Q Pompeius Rufus,
*the Grandson of Sylla, and the most factious espouser
of a Dictator, was, by a resolute decree of the Senate committed to prison* and Pompey himself, upon his return to the City, finding the greater and
better part utterly averse to his Dictatorship, yielded at last, after *an Interregnum of six months, that Cn
Domitius Calvinus, and M Messala, should be declared Consuls* [e]   These were agreeable likewise
to Cæsar. Cicero had particularly recommended

---

sere difficile est Hirro tamen agente nolle se non
probabit—Ad Quint 3 8
[c] De Dictatore tamen
actum nihil est Pompeius
abest Appius in scet Hirrus parat multi intercesso-
res numerantur populus non
curat principes nolunt ego
quiesco—Ib 9

[d] Hoc horret Milo—&
si ille Dictator factus sit, pæne
diffidit   Intercessorem dic-
tatura si juverit manu & præ-
sidio suo Pompeium met inimicum, si non juverit, timet, ne per vim perferatur—
Ib 8

[ ] Vid Dio l 40 f
141

Meſſala to him, of whom, he ſays in a Letter to his Brother, *As to your reckoning Meſſala and Calvinus ſure Conſuls, you agree with what we think here, for I will be anſwerable to Cæſar for Meſſala* [ſ]

A Urb 700
Cic 54
Coſſ
Cn Domiti-
us Calvi-
nus,
M Valerius
Messala

But after all this Buſtle about *a Dictator*, there ſeems to have been no great reaſon for being much afraid of it at this time for the Republic was in ſo great a diſorder, that nothing leſs than *the Dictatorial* power could reduce it to a tolerable ſtate ſome good of that kind might reaſonably be expected from Pompey, without the fear of any great harm, while there was ſo ſure a check upon him as Cæſar, who, upon any exorbitant uſe of that power, would have had the Senate and all the better ſort on his ſide, by the ſpecious pretence of aſſerting the public liberty : Cicero therefore judged rightly, in thinking, that there were other things, which might be apprehended, and ſeemed likely to happen, that, in their preſent ſituation, were of more dangerous conſequence than *a Dictatorſhip*

There had ſcarce been ſo *long an Interregnum in Rome*, ſince the expulſion of their Kings, during which, all public buſineſs, and eſpecially all judicial proceedings, were wholly interrupted which explanes a jocoſe paſſage in *one of Cicero's Letters to Trebatius*, *if you had not already*, ſays he, *been abſent from* Rome, *you would certainly have run away now for what buſineſs is there for a Lawyer in ſo many interregnums? I adviſe all my Clients, if ſued in any action, to move every In-*

[ſ] Meſſalam quod certum Conſulem cum Domitio numera is, nihil a noſtra opinione diſſentitis Ego Meſſalam Cæſari preſtabo — Ad Quint 3 8

terrex

tter a truce for more time   do not you think, th
I have learnt the law of you to good purpose [g]?

HE now began a correspondence of Letter,
with Curio, a young Senator of distinguished
birth and parts, who upon his first entrance into
the Forum had been committed to his care, and
was at this time *Quæstor in Asa*   He was pos
sessed of a large and splendid fortune, by the
late death of his Father, so that Cicero, who
knew his high spirit and ambition, and that he
was formed to do much good or hurt to his
country was desirous to engage him early in the
interests of the Republic, and by instilling great
and generous sentiments, to inflame him with a
love of true glory.   Curio had sent orders to his
agents at Rome, to provide a shew of gladiators
. . . of his deceased Father   but Cicero stopt the
declaration of it for a while, in hopes to dissuade
him from so great and fruitless an expence [h]
He foresaw, that nothing was more likely to
corrupt his virtue than the ruin of his fortunes,
or to make him a dangerous Citizen, than pro
digality   to which he was naturally inclined, and
which Cicero, for that reason, was the more de
sirous to check at his first setting out   but all his
endeavours were to no purpose, Curio resolved
to give *the shew of Gladiators*, and by a continual
profusion of his money, answerable to this be
ginning, after he had acted the Patriot for some

[g] Nisi ante Roma pro-
fectus esses, nunc eam certe
relinquere.   Quid enim tot
interregnis Jurisconfultum defi-
dera? Ego omnibus, unde
petitur, hoc consilii dederim,
ut à fingulis Interregibus bi-
nas . . . ations no luerint
Satisne tibi videor abs te jus
civile didicisse? Ep Fam 7 i

[h] Rupæ Studium non de
fuit declarandorum munerum
tuo nomine   sed nec mihi
placuit, nec cuiquam tuorum,
quidquam te absente fi
quod is, cum venisses, totum integrum, &c   Ep Fam
2 3

time with credit and applause, was reduced at last
to the neceſſity of ſelling himſelf to Cæſar.

There is but little of politics in theſe Letters, beſides ſome general complaints, *of the loſt and deſperate ſtate of the Republic* in one of them, after reckoning up the various ſubjects of Epiſtolary writing, *ſhall I joke with you then,* ſays he, *in my Letters? On my conſcience, there is not a Citizen, I believe, who can laugh in theſe times or ſhall I write ſomething ſerious? But what can Cicero write ſeriouſly to Curio, unleſs it be on the Republic? where my caſe at preſent is ſuch, that I have no inclination to write, what I do not think—*[i]. In another, after putting him in mind of the incredible expectation which was entertained of him at *Rome,* " not that I am afraid, *ſays he,*
' that your virtue ſhould not come up to the
" opinion of the public, but rather, that you
" find nothing worth caring for at your return,
" all things are ſo ruined and oppreſſed but I
" queſtion whether it be prudent to ſay ſo much
' —It is your part however, whether you retain
" any hopes, or quite deſpair, to adorn yourſelf
" with all thoſe accompliſhments, which can
" qualify a Citizen, in wretched times and pro-
" fligate morals, to reſtore the Republic to its
" ancient dignity [k] "

The firſt news from abroad after the inauguration of the Conſuls, was of the miſerable *death*

[i] Jocerne tecum per litteras? civem mehercule non puto eſſe, qui temporibus his ridere poſſit An grav us ali quid ſcribam? Quid eſt quod poſſit graviter a Cicerone ſcribi ad Curionem, niſi de Rep? Atque in hoc genere hæc mea cauſa eſt, ut neque ea, quæ non ſentio, velim ſcribere——ib 4

[k] Non quo verear ne tua virtus opinioni hominum non reſpondeat ſed mehercule, ne cum veneris, non habeas jam quod cures ita ſunt omnia debilitata jam prope & exſtincta &c ib 5

of

A Urb co
Cc 54
Coſſ
C. Domiti-
ts Calvi-
t,
M Valerius
Meſſala

of *Craſſus and his ſon Publius, with the total defeat of his army by the Parthians* This was one of the greateſt blows that *Rome* had ever received from a foreign enemy, and for which it was ever after meditating revenge the *Roman* writers generally imputed it to Craſſus's *contempt of the Auſpices*, as ſome *Chriſtians* have ſince charged it, *to his ſacrilegious violation of the Temple of* Jeruſalem, which he is ſaid to have plundered of two millions, both of them with equal Superſtition pretending to unfold the counſils of heaven, and to fathom thoſe depths, which are declared to be *unſearchable* [*l*] The chief and immediate concern, which the City felt on this occaſion, was for the detriment that the Republic had ſuffered, and the danger to which it was expoſed, by the loſs of ſo great an army, yet the principal miſchief lay in what they did not at firſt regard, and ſeemed rather to rejoice at, *the loſs of Craſſus himſelf* For after the death of Julia, Craſſus's authority was the onely means left of curbing the power of Pompey, and the ambition of Caſar, being ready always to ſupport the weaker, againſt the encroachments of the ſtronger, and keep them both within the bounds of a decent reſpect to the laws but this check being now taken away, and the power of the Empire thrown, as a kind of prize, between Two, it gave a new turn to their ſeveral pretenſions, and created a freſh competition for the larger ſhare, which, as the event afterwards ſhewed, muſt neceſſarily end in the ſubverſion of the whole

[*l*] M Craſſo quid acciderit videmus dirarum obnunciatione neglecta [De Dio, 1 16]

Being for his impious ſacrilege at Jeruſalem, which

deſtined to deſtruction, God did caſt infatuations into all his councils, for the leading him thereto ——— Prideaux Connect Par 2 p 36.

PUBLIUS

PUBLIUS CRASSUS, who perifhed with his Fathei in this fatal expedition, was a youth of an
amiable character, educated with the ftricteft
care, and peifectly inftructed in all the liberal
ftudies, he had a ready wit and eafy language;
was grave without arrogance, modeft without
negligence, adorned with all the accomplifhments
proper to form a principal Citizen and Leader of
the Republic by the force of his own judgement
he had devoted himfelf very early to the obfervance and imitation of Ciceio, whom he perpetually attended, and ieverenced with a kind of
filial piety Cicero conceived a mutual affection
foi him, and obferving his eagei thiift of glory,
was conftantly inftilling into him the true notion
oi it, and exhorting him to purfue that fuie path
to it, which his anceftois had left beaten and
traced out to him, through the gradual afcent of
civil honours But, by feiving undei Cæfai in the
Gallic wars, he had learnt, as he fancied, a
fhorter way to fame and powei, than what Cicero had been inculcating, and having fignalized
himfelf in a campaign or two as a foldier, was in
too much hafte to be a General, when Cæfar fent
him at the head of a thoufand horfe, to the affiftance of his Fathei in the *Parthian* war Here
the vigour of his youth and courage carried him
on fo far, in the purfuit of an enemy, whofe
chief art of conqueft confifted in flying, that
he had no way left to efcape, but what his high
fpirit difdained, by the defertion of his troops,
and a precipitate flight, fo that finding himfelf
oppofed with numbers, cruelly wounded, and
in danger of falling alive into the hands of the
Parthians, he chofe to die by the fword of his
Armour-beaiei Thus while he afpired, as Cicero fays, to the fame of another Cyius or Alexander,

A Urb 700
Cic ct
Coff
Cn Domiti-
us Calvi-
nis,
M Valerius
Messala

A. Urb. 702.
Coss.
Cn. Domiti-
us Calvi-
nus,
M. Valerius
Messala

ender, *he fell short of that glory, which many of his Predecessors had reaped, from a succession of honors, conferred by their country, as the reward of their services* [*m*]

By the death of *Young Crassus*, a place became vacant *in the College of Augurs*, for which Cicero declared himself a Candidate: nor was any one so hardy as to appear against him, except Hirrus, *the Tribun*, who trusting to the popularity of his office and Pompey's favor, had the vanity to pretend to it: but a Competition so unequal furnished matter of raillery onely to Cicero, who was chosen without any difficulty or struggle, *with the unanimous approbation of the whole body* [*n*]. This College, from the last regulation of it by Sylla, consisted *of fifteen*, who were all persons of the first distinction in *Rome*: it was a priesthood for life, of a character indelible, which no crime or forfeiture could efface: the Priests of all kinds were originally chosen by their Colleges, till Domitius, a Tribun, about fifty years before, transferred the choice of them to the people, whose authority was held to be supreme in sacred,

---

[*m*] Hoc magis sum Pub-
lo dolitus, quod re qua-
quam a scientia super a-
mus hoc tempore maxime,
sicut eteram o e rem &
observandi g [*Ep. Fam.*
5. 8.]

P. Crassum e omni robi-
s are ad ecc tem d luxi plu-
rimim, &c [*ib. 13. 10.*]

Cum P. Crasso, cum into
ætatis ad amiciam se me-
am consu itu, sæpe egi se
ad aug roi, cum e ni ve
rem unanime ion arem ut a-
ea laxds iam recuraem

esse diceret, quam majorem
ejus ei tritam reliquissent.
Erat enim cum instructus optime, tum plane perfecteque
eruditus. Incritque & ingenium satis cre, & oratio-
ion inelegans copia: præter-
eaque sine arrogantia gra-
e videbatur, & sine legi-
tia vereconnus, &c. Vid
B. ut p 407. It plut in
Crass

[*n*] Quomodo Hirrum pu-
tas Auguratus tui competito-
rem—*Ep Fam 8. 3*

as well as civil affairs [o] This act was reversed
by Sylla, and the ancient right restored to the
Colleges, but Labienus, when Tribun, in Cicero's Consulship, recalled the law of Domitius,
to facilitate Cæsar's advancement to the High-
Priesthood it was necessary however, *that every
Candidate should be nominated to the people by two
Augurs, who gave a solemn testimony upon oath of
his dignity and fitness for the office* this was done
in Cicero's case by Pompey and Hortensius, the
two most eminent members of the College, and
after the election, he was installed with all the
usual formalities by Hortensius [p]

As in the last year, so in this, the factions of
the City prevented the choice of Consuls. the
Candidates, T Annius Milo, Q Metellus Scipio,
and P Plautius Hypsæus, pushed on their several
interests with such open violence and bribery, as
t the Consulship was to be carried onely by *money or arms* [q]. Clodius was putting in at the
same time for the Prætorship, and employing all
his credit and interest to disappoint Milo, by
whose obtaining the Consulship, *he was sure to be
eclipsed and controuled, in the exercise of his subor-
dinate magistracy* [r] Pompey was wholly averse
to Milo, who did not pay him that court, which

A Urb 700
Cic 54
Coss
Cn Domiti-
us Calvi-
nus,
M Valerius
Messala.

[o] *Itque hoc idem de ca-
teris Sacerdotis Cn Domi-
us Tribunus Pl tulit, C c De
Leg Ag 2 7*

[p] *Quo etiam tempore me
Augurem a toto Collegio e-
petitum Cn Pompeius & Q
Hortensius nominaverunt, neque enim licebat a pluribus
nominari——Phlip 2 ?*

*Cooptat m ne b eo in
collegium recordaba, in quo*

*juratus judicum dignitatis
n cæ fecera. & in igur-
tum ib e cum, ex quo au-
gurum institutis in p rentis
cum loco colere debebam
Brut in t——*

[q] *Plutar in Cato——*
[r] *Occurrebat ei, man-
cam ac debilem Præturam
suam futuram Consule M. o-
ne- Pro Milon 9*

he

A Urb 700
Cic 54
Coss
Cn Domiti-
us Calvi
nus,
M Valerius
Messala

he expected, but seemed to affect an independency, and to trust to his own strength, while the other two competitors were wholly at his devotion Hypsæus had been *his Quæstor*, and always his Creature, and he designed to make Scipio *his Father-in law*, by marrying his daughter Cornelia, a Lady of celebrated accomplishments, the widow of *young Crassus*

CICERO, on the other hand, served Milo to the utmost of his power, and ardently wished his success this he owed to Milo's constant attachment to him, which at all hazards he now resolved to repay the affair however was likely to give him much trouble. as well from the difficulty of the opposition, as from Milo's own conduct, and unbounded prodigality, which threatened the ruin of all his fortunes, in a Letter to his Brother, who was still with Cæsar, he says, " Nothing " can be more wretched than these men and " these times wherefore since no pleasure can " now be had from the Republic, I know not " why I should make myself uneasy books, " study. quiet, my country houses, and above " all, my children are my sole delight Milo is " my onely trouble I wish his Consulship may " put an end to it, in which I will not take less " pains, than I did in my own, and you will " assist us there also, as you now do all things " stand well with him, unless some violence de- " feat us. I am afraid onely, how his money " will hold out for he is mad beyond all bounds " in the magnificence of his shews, which he is " now preparing at the expence of 250000*l* " but it shall be my care to check his inconside- ' ratenefs in this one article, as far as I am able, " &c [s] '   In

---

[s] Itaque ex Rep quoniam nihil jam voluptatis ca

P

IN the heat of this competition, Curio was coming home from *Asia*, and expected shortly at *Rome*, whence Cicero sent an express to meet him on the road, or at his landing in *Italy*, with a most earnest and pressing Letter to engage him to Milo's interest.

M T Cicero, to C Curio.

"BEFORE we had yet heard of your coming A Urb 701.
"towards *Italy*, I sent away S Villius, Milo's   Cic 55
"friend, with this Letter to you   but when
"your arrival was supposed to be near, and it
"was known for certain, that you had left *Asia*,
"and were upon the road to *Rome*, the impor-
"tance of the subject left no room to fear, that
"we should be thought to send too hastily
"when we were desirous to have it delivered to
"you as soon as possible   If my services to you,
"Curio, were really so great, as they are pro-
"claimed to be by you, rather than considered
"by me, I should be more reserved in asking,
"if I had any great favor to beg of you   for it

pi potest, cur stomacher, nescio Litteræ me & studia nostra, & otium, Villæque delectant, maximeque pueri nostri Angit unus Milo Sed velim finem afferat Consulatus in quo enitar non minus quam sum enisus in nostro tuque istinc, quod facis, adjuvabis De quo cætera (nisi plane vis eripuerit) recte sunt de re fam liari timeo

Od. *μαίνεται ἀκ ἔτ' ἀνεκῶς* --

Qu. ludos H S CCC com-

paret Cujus in hoc uno inconsiderantiam & ego sustinebo, ut potero—Ad Quint 3 9

Cicero had great reason for the apprehensions, which he expresses on account of Milo's extravagance for Milo had already wasted three estates in giving plays and shews to the people, and when he went soon after into exil was found to owe still above half a million of our money Plin l 36 15 Ascon Argum in Milon

"goes

"goes hard with a modeſt man, to aſk an
"thing conſiderable of one, whom he takes to
"be obliged to him, leſt he be thought to de
"mand, rather than to aſk and to look upon
"it as a debt, not as a kindneſs But ſince you
"ſervices to me, ſo eminently diſplayed in my
"late troubles, are known to all to be the greateſt,
"and it is the part of an ingenuous mind, to
"wiſh to be more obliged to thoſe, to whom
"we are already much obliged, I made no
"ſcruple to beg of you by Letter, what of all
"things is the moſt important and neceſſary to
"me For I am not afraid leſt I ſhould not
"be able to ſuſtain the weight of all your fa
"vors, though ever ſo numerous, being con
"fident, that there is none ſo great, which m
"mind is not able, both fully to contain, and
"amply to requite and illuſtrate. I have placed
"all my ſtudies, pains, care, induſtry, though
"and in ſhort, my very ſoul, on Milo's Conſul
"ſhip, and have reſolved with myſelf, to ex
"pect from it, not only the common fruit of
"duty, but the praiſe even of piety nor wa
"any man, I believe, ever ſo ſollicitous for his
"own ſafety and fortunes, as I am for his ho
"nor, on which I have fixed all my views and
"hopes You, I perceive, can be of ſuch ſer
"vice to him, if you pleaſe, that we ſhall have
"no occaſion for any thing farther. We have
"already with us the good wiſhes of all the
"honeſt, engaged to him by his Tribunate,
"and, as you will imagine alſo, I hope, by his
"attachment to me or the populace and the
"multitude, by the magnificence of his ſhew,
"and the generoſity of his nature or the youth
"men of intereſt, by his own peculiar cre
"and diligence among that ſort he has al
                                              "my

A Urb 701.
Cic 55.

" my affiftance likewife, which though of little
" weight, yet being allowed by all to be juft and
' due to him, may perhaps be of fome influence.
" What we want, is a Captain and Leader, or
" a Pilot, as it were, of all thofe winds, and
" were we to chufe one out of the whole City,
" we could not find a man fo fit for the purpofe
" as you Wherefore, if from all the pains,
" which I am now taking for Milo, you can be-
" lieve me to be mindfull of benefits, if grate-
" full, if a good man, if worthy in fhort of
" your kindnefs, I beg of you to relieve my
" prefent follicitude, and lend your helping hand
" to my praife, or, to fpeak more truly, to my
" fafety. As to T Annius himfelf, I promife
" you, if you embrace him, that you will not
" find a man of a greater mind, gravity, con-
" ftancy, or of greater affection to you and as
" for myfelf, you will add fuch a lufter and frefh
" dignity to me, that I fhall readily own you,
" to have fhewn the fame zeal for my honor,
" which you exerted before for my prefervation.
" If I was not fure, from what I have already
" faid, that you would fee how much I take my
" duty to be interefted in this affair, and how
" much it concerns me, not only to ftruggle,
" but even to fight for Milo's fuccefs, I fhould
" prefs you ftill farther, but I now recommend
' and throw the whole caufe, and myfelf alfo
" with it, into your hands, and beg of you, to
" affure yourfelf of this one thing, that if I ob-
" tain this favor from you, I fhall be more in-
" debted almoft to you, than even to Milo
" himfelf, fince my fafety, in which I was prin-
" cipally affifted by him, was not fo dear, as
" the piety of fhewing my gratitude will be
" agreeable to me, which I am perfuaded, I

" shall be able to effect by your assistance
" Adieu [*t*] "

THE Senate and the better sort were general
ly in Milo s interest but *Three of the Tribuns*
were violent against him, Q Pompeius Rufus,
Munatius Plancus Bursa, and Salluft *the Historian*
the other seven were his fast friends, but above
all M Cælius, who, out of regard to Cicero,
served him with a particular zeal But while all
things were proceding very prosperously in his
favor, and nothing seemed wanting to crown his
success, but to bring on the election, which his ad
versaries, for that reason, were laboring to keep
back. all his hopes and fortunes were blasted at
once by an unhappy rencounter with his old ene
my Clodius, in which Clodius *was killed by his*
servants, and by his command

THEIR meeting was wholly accidental, on
the *Appian* road, not far from the City , Clodius
coming home from the country towards *Rome*,
Milo going out about three in the afternoon ; the
first on horseback, with three companions, and
thirty servants well armed , the latter in a Chariot
with his wife and one friend, but with a much
greater retinue, and among them some Gladia
tors The servants on both sides began present
ly to insult each other , when Clodius turning
briskly to some of Milo's men, who were nearest to him, and threatning them with his usual
fierceness, received a wound in his shoulder, from
one of the Gladiators , and after receiving several
more in the general fray, which instantly ensued,
finding his life in danger, was forced to fly for
shelter into a neighbouring Tavern. Milo heat
ed by this success, and the thoughts of revenge,

[*t*] Fp Fam 2 6

anc

and reflecting, that he had already done enough
to give his enemy a great advantage againft him,
if he was left alive to puifue it, iefolved, whatever was the confequence, to have the pleafure
of deftroying him, and fo ordered the houfe to
be ftormed, and Clodius to be dragged out and
murdered the mafter of the Tavern was likewife killed, with eleven of Clodius's feivants,
while the reft faved themfelves by flight fo that
Clodius's body was left in the road, where it fell,
till S Tedius, a Senatoi, happening to come by,
took it up into his Chaife, and biought it with
him to *Rome* , where it was expofed in that con-
dirion, all covered with blood and wounds, to
the view of the populace, who flocked about it in
crowds to lament the miferable fate of their
Leader The next day the mob, headed by S
Clodius, a kinfman of the deceafed, and one of
his chief Incendiaries, carried the body naked, fo
as all the wounds might be feen, into the Forum,
and placed it in the Roftra; wheie the Three
Tribuns, Milo's enemies, were piepared to ha-
rangue upon it in a ftile fuited to the lamentable
occafion, by which they inflamed their mercenaries to fuch a height of fury, that fnatching up the
body, they ran away with it into the Senate-houfe,
and tearing up the benches, tables, and every
thing combuftible, dreffed up a funeral pile upon
the fpot, and, together with the body, buint the
houfe itfelf, with a *Bafilica* alfo, or public Hall
adjoining, called the *Porcian* , and, in the fame
fit of madnefs, proceded to ftorm the houfe of
Milo, and of M Lepidus, the Interrex, but
were repulfed in both attacks, with fome lofs [*u*].

T.iefe

[ ] Quanquam re vera, fu-   l 6 c 5
 pugna fortuita Quintil   'b. ɪɜɑc——'ɔʏ ᴛᴋ ᴆ/ɪᴋ ᴛ..
                      ɪ, ɜ   λ ʹɪɑɑ/ɪɜ

A Up no†
Ce s†

THESE extravagancies raised great indignation in the City, and gave a turn in favor of Milo, who looking upon himself as undone, was meditating nothing before, but *a voluntary exile*; but now taking courage, he ventured to appear in public, and was introduced *into the Rostra, Court,* where he made his defence to the people, and, to mitigate their resentment, distributed through all the Tribes *above three pounds a man to every poor Citizen.* But all his pains and expence were to little purpose, for *the three Tribunes* employed all the arts of party and faction to keep up the ill humor of the populace, and what was more essential, Pompey would not be brought into any measures of accommodating the matter, so that the tumults still increasing, the Senate passed a decree, *that the Interrex, assisted by the Tribunes and Pompey, should take care, that the Republic received no detriment, and that Pompey, particularly, should raise a body of troops for that purpose;* which he presently drew together from all parts of *Italy.* In this confusion *the name of a Dictator was again industriously spread,* and gave a fresh alarm to the Senate, who to avoid the greater evil, resolved presently to create *Pompey the single Consul;* so that the Interrex, *Servius Sulpicius,* declared his election accordingly, *the ordinance him of near two months [*

---

ibidem effet, exturbari abs- // n m junt — Itâ Clodius // tus extractus est, multis // vulneribus confectus — // Vid Asconii Argum in // lon //   [x] Vid Dio ibid & // con Argum

---

POMPEY applied himself immediately to calm the public disorders, and published several *new Laws*, prepared by him for that purpose one of them was, to appoint *a special commission to inquire into Clodius's death, the burning of the Senate-house, and the attack on M Lepidus*, and to appoint *an extraordinary Judge, of Consular rank, to preside in it* a second was, *against bribery and corruption in elections, with the infliction of new and severer penalties* By these laws, the method of trials was altered, and the length of them limited *three days were allowed for the examination of witnesses, and the fourth for the sentence, on which the accuser was to have two hours only, to enforce the charge, the Criminal three, for his defence* [y] which regulation Tacitus seems to consider, as *the first step towards the ruin of the Roman eloquence by imposing reins, as it were, upon its free and ancient course* [z] Cælius opposed his negative to these Laws, *as being rather privileges than Laws, and provided particularly against Milo* but he was soon obliged to withdraw it, upon Pompey's declaring, *that he would support them by force of Arms* The *three Tribuns*, all the while, were perpetually haranguing, and terrifying the City with forged stories, of *magazines of arms prepared by Milo, for massacring his enemies, and burning the City*, and produced their creatures in *the Rostra, to vouch the truth of them to the people* they charged him particularly *with a design against Pompey's life*, and brought one Licinius, *a killer of the victims for sacrifice*, to declare that Milo's servants had confessed it to him in their cups, and then endeavoured to kill him, lest

---

|] Ibid

[z] Primus tertio Consulatu Cn Pompeius astrinxit,

imposuitque veluti frænos eloquentiæ—&c. Dialog de Oratori 38.

L 3

be

A Urb 701
Cic 55
Cn Pompei-
us Mag-
nus III
Sine Collega

he should discover it   and to make his story the more credible, shewed a slight wound in his side, made by himself, which he affirmed to have been given by the stroke *of a Gladiator* Pompey himself confirmed this fact, *and laid an account of it before the Senate*, and by doubling his guard affected to intimate a real apprehension of danger [a]   Nor were they less industrious to raise a clamor against Cicero, and, in order to deter him from pleading Milo's cause, threatened him also with trials and prosecutions, giving it out every where, *that Clodius was killed indeed by the hand of Milo, but by the advice and connivance of a greater man* [b]. Yet such was his constancy to his friend, says Asconius, that *neither the loss of popular favor, nor Pompey's suspicions, nor his own danger, nor the terror of arms, could divert him from the resolution of undertaking Milo's defence* [c].

BUT it was Pompey's *influence and authority, which ruined Milo* [d]   He was the onely man in *Rome* who had the power either to bring him to a trial, or to get him condemned. not that he was concerned for Clodius's death, or the manner of it, but pleased rather, that the

[a] Audiendus Popa Licinius, nescio qui de Circo maximo, servos Milonis apud se ebrios factos confessos esse, de interficiendo Cn Pompeio conjurasse--de amicorum sententia rem defert ad Senatum --Pro Milon 24

[b] Scitis, Judices, fuisse, qui in hac rogatione suadend. dicerent, Milonis manu cædem esse factam, consilio vero majoris alicujus videlicet me latronem & sicarium abjecti homines describebant

Ib 18
[c] Tanta tamen constantia ac fides fuit Ciceronis, ut non populi a se alienatione, non Cn Pompeii suspicionibus, non periculi futuri metu,--non arms, quæ palam in Milonem sumpta erant, deterreri potuerit a defensione ejus   Argum Milon

[d] Milonem reum non magis invidia facti, quam Pompeii damnavit voluntas Vell P 2. 47.

A Urb 701
Cic 55
Cn Pompei-
us Mag-
nus III
Sine Collega.

Republic was freed at any rate from so pestilent Demagogue, yet he resolved to take the benefit of the occasion, for getting rid of Milo too, from whose ambition and high spirit he had cause to apprehend no less trouble. He would not listen therefore to any overtures, which were made to him by Milo's Friends, and when Milo *offered to drop his suit for the Consulship,* if that would satisfy him, he answered, *that he would not concern himself with any man's suing or desisting, nor give any obstruction to the power and inclination of the Roman people* He attended the trial in person with a strong guard to preserve peace, and prevent any violence from either side there were many clear and positive proofs produced against Milo, though some of them were supposed to be forged among the rest, the *Vestal virgins deposed, that a woman unknown came to them, in Milo's name, to discharge a vow, said to be made by him, on the account of Clodius's death* [e]

WHEN the examination was over, Munatius Plancus called the people together, and exhorted them to appear in a full body the next day, when judgement was to be given, and to declare their sentiments in so public a manner, that the criminal might not be suffered to escape, which Cicero reflects upon in the defence, as an insult on the liberty of the Bench [f] Early in the morning, *on the eleventh of April,* the shops were all shut, and the whole City gathered into the Forum, where the avenues were possessed by Pompey's soldiers, and he himself seated in a conspicuous part, to overlook the whole proceding,

[e] Vid Ascoru argum in Milon.

[f] Ut intelligatis contra hesternam illam concionem licere vobis, quod sentiatis, licere judicare Pro Mil 26 Vid Ascon ibid.

and hinder all disturbance. The accusers were, *Young App—r, the Nephew of Clodius, M. Au-r.s,* and *P. Velerius,* who, according to the new law, employed *two hours,* in supporting their indictment. Cicero was the onely advocate on Milo's side; but as soon as he rose up to speak he was received with so rude a clamor *by the Clodians, that he was much discomposed and daunted at his first setting out, yet recovered spirit enough to go through his speech of three hours, which was taken down in writing, and published as it was delivered,* though the copy of it now extant is supposed to have been retouched and corrected by him afterwards, for a present to Milo in his exil [g]

In the council of Milo's friends, several were of opinion, that he should defend himself, *by acccou· g the death of Clodius to be an act of public benefit.* But Cicero thought that defence too desperate, as it would disgust the grave, by opening so great a door to licence, and offend the powerfull, lest the precedent should be extended to themselves. But *Young Brutus* was not so cautious, who, in an oration, which he composed and published afterwards in vindication of Milo, maintained *the killing of Clodius to be right and just,* and of great service to the Republic [h] It was notorious, that on both sides, they had often *threatened death to each other ·* Clodius especially had declared several times both to the

---

[g] Cicero, cum inciperet dicere, acceptus est acclamatore Clodianorum — itaque non ea, qua solitus erat, constantia dixit. Manet autem illa quoque excepta ejus Oratio — a scon Argum ——

[h] Cum quibusdam placuisset, ita defendi crimen, interfeci Clodium pro Repub fuisse, quam formam M. Brutus secutus est in ea oratione, quam pro Milone composuit, & edidit, quamvis non egisse, Ciceroni id non placuit —— ibid

Senate

Senate and the people, *that Milo ought to be killed,*
and that, if the Consulship could not be taken from
him, his life could and when Favonius asked him
once, what hopes he could have of playing his mad
pranks, while Milo was living, he replied, that in
three or four days at most, he should live no more
which was spoken just *three days* before the fatal
rencounter, and *attested by Favonius* [i] Since
Milo then was charged with being the contriver
of their meeting, and the aggressor in it, and several testimonies were produced to that purpose,
Cicero chose to risk the cause on that issue, in
hopes to persuade, what seemed to be the most
probable, *that Clodius actually lay in wait for*
Milo, and contrived the time and place, and that
Milo's part was but a necessary act of self defence
This appeared plausible, from the nature of their
equipage, and the circumstances in which they
met for though Milo's company was the more
numerous, yet it was much more encumbered,
and unfit for engagement, than his adversary's;
he himself being in a chariot with his wife, and all
her women along with him, while Clodius with his
followers were on horseback, as if prepared and
equipped for fighting [k] He did not preclude
himself

A Urb 701.
Cic 55
Cn Pompei-
us Mag-
nus III
Sine Collega.

---

[i] Etenim palam dictita-
bat, consulatum Miloni eripi
non posse, vitam voti Sig-
nificavit hoc sepe in Senatu,
dixit in concione Quin-
tum Favonio, quærenti ex
eo, qua spe rueret, Milone
vivo Respondit, triduo illum, ad summum quatriduo
periturum Pro Milo

Post diem tertium gesta res
est, quam dixerat Ib 16.

[k] Interim cum sciret
Clodius—Iter solenne — ne-
cessarium— Miloni esse La-
nuvium— Roma ipse profec-
tus pridie est, ut ante suum
fundum, quod re intellectum
est, insidias Miloni colloca-
ret— Milo autem cum in Senatu fuisset eo die, quoad Senatus dimissus est, domum
venit, calceos & vestimenta
mutavit paullisper, dum se
uxor,

A Urb 701.
Cc 55
Cn. Pompei-
us Mag-
nus III
Sine Collega.

himself however by this from the other plea, which he often takes occasion to insinuate, *that if Milo had really designed and contrived to kill Clodius, he would have deserved honors instead of punishment, for cutting off so desperate and dangerous an enemy to the peace and liberty of Rome* [*l*]

In this speech for Milo, after he had shewn the folly of paying such a regard to the idle rumors and forgeries of his enemies, as to give them the credit of an examination, he touches Pompey's conduct and *pretended fears*, with a fine and masterly raillery, and from a kind of prophetic foresight of what might one day happen, addresses himself to him in a very pathetic manner ——— " I could not but applaud, *says he*, " the wonderfull diligence of Pompey in these " inquiries but to tell you freely, what I think " those who are charged with the care of the " whole Republic, are forced to hear many " things, which they would contemn, if they " were at liberty to do it He could not refuse " an audience to that paultry fellow, Licinius, " who gave the information about Milo's ser " vants——— I was sent for among the first of

uxor, ut fit, comparat, commoratus est — obviam fit ei Clodius, expeditus in equo, nulla rheda, nullis impedimentis, nu'lis Græcis Comitibus, fine uxore, quod nunquam fere , cum hic Insidiator,— (Milo — cum uxore in rheda veheretur penulatus, magno impedimento, ac muliebri & delicato ancillarum & paerorum comitatu ——— Pro Mil 10 it 21

[*l*] Quamobrem fi cruen-

tum gladium tenens clamaret T Annius, adeste, quæso, atque audite cives, P Clodium interfeci ejus furori, quos nullis jam legibus, null. judiciis frænare poteramu hoc ferio, atque hac dextra a cervicibus veftris repuli &c ———Vos tanti fceleris ultorem non modo honoribus nullis afficietis, fed etiam ad fupplicium rapi patiemini'— Pro Mil 28—&c

" those

A Urb 701.
Cic 55.
Cn Pompei-
us Mag-
nus III
Sine Collega

" thofe friends, by whofe advice he laid it be-
" fore the Senate ; and was, I own, in no fmall
" confternation, to fee the Guardian both of me
" and my Country under fo great an apprehen-
" fion, yet I could not help wondering, that
" fuch credit was given to a Butcher, fuch re-
" gard to drunken flaves, and how the wound
" in the man's fide, which feemed to be the
' prick onely of a needle, could be taken for
" the ftroke of a Gladiator. But Pompey was
" fhewing his caution, rather than his fear and
" difpofed to be fufpicious of every thing, that
" you might have reafon to fear nothing. There
" was a rumor alfo, that Cæfar's houfe was at-
" tacked for feveral hours in the night the
" neighbours, though in fo public a place, heard
" nothing at all of it, yet the affair was thought
" fit to be enquired into I can never fufpect
" a man of Pompey's eminent courage, of be-
' ing timorous, nor yet think any caution too
' great in one who has taken upon himfelf the
" defence of the whole Republic A Senator
" likewife, in full houfe, affirmed lately in the
" Capitol, that Milo had a dagger under his
" gown at that very time Milo ftript himfelf
" prefently in that moft facred Temple, that,
" fince his life and manners would not give him
" credit, the thing itfelf might fpeak for him,
" which was found to be falfe, and bafely forged.
" But if, after all, Milo muft ftill be feared, it
" is no longer the affair of Clodius, but your
" fufpicions, Pompey, which we dread. your,
" your fufpicions, I fay, and fpeak it fo, that
" you may hear me — If thofe fufpicions ftick
" fo clofe, that they are never to be removed,
" if *Italy* muft never be free from new levies,
" nor the City from arms, without Milo's de-
                    " ftruction,

A Urb 701
Cic 55
Cʏ Pompei-
us Mac
ɴus III
Sine Collega

"ſtruction, he would not ſcruple, ſuch is his
"nature and his principles, to bid adieu to his
"Country, and ſubmit to a voluntary exil but
"at taking leave, he would call vpon Thee,
"O Thou Great One¹ as he now does, to con-
"ſider how uncertain and variable the condʲtion
"of life is how unſettled and inconſtant a
"thing fortune, what unfaithfullneſs there s
"in friends; what diſſimulation ſuited to times
"and circumſtances, what deſertion, wh.t
"cowardice in our dangers, even of thoſe, who
"are deareſt to us there will, there will, I
"ſay, be a time, and the day will certainly
"come, when you, with ſafety ſtill, I hope,
"to your fortunes, though changed perhaps by
"ſome turn of the common times, which, as
"experience ſhews, will often happen to us all,
"may want the affection of the friendlieſt, the
"fidelity of the worthieſt, the courage of the
"braveſt man living, &c [*m*]"

Of ore and fifty Judges, who ſat upon Milo
thirteen onely acquitted, and *thirty-eight* con
demned him, the votes were uſually given by
ballot, but Cato, who abſolved him, choſe to
give his vote openly, and "if he had done it
"earlier, *ſays Velleius*, would have drawn others
"after him, ſince all were convinced, that he,
"who was killed, was, of all who had ever
"lived, the moſt pernicious enemy to his
"Country, and to all good men [*n*]" Milo
went into exil at *Marſeiies*, a few days after his
condemnation his debts were ſo great, that he

[*m*] Pro Mil 24, 25, 26—
[*n*] M Cato palam lata
abſolvit ſententia, quam ſi
maturius tuliſſet, non cefuiſ-
ſent, q ſequerentur exem-

plum, probarentque eum ci
vem occiſum, quo nemo per
niciolior Reip neque bons
inimicior vixerat —— Vell
P 2 47.

A Urb 701.
Cic 55
Cn Pompei-
us Mag-
nus III
Sine Collega.

was glad to retire the sooner from the importunity of his creditors, for whose satisfaction his
whole estate was sold by public auction Here
Cicero still continued his care for him, and in
conceit with Milo's friends, ordered one of his
wife's freedmen, Philotimus, to assist at the sale,
and to purchase the greatest part of the effects,
in order to dispose of them afterwards to the
best advantage, for the benefit *of Milo and his
wife Fausta, if any thing could be saved for them.*
But his intended service was not so well relished
by Milo, as he expected, for Philotimus was
suspected of playing the knave, and secreting
part of the effects to his own use, which gave
Cicero great uneasiness, so that he pressed Atticus and Cælius to inquire into the matter very
narrowly, and oblige Philotimus " to give sa-
" tisfaction to Milo's friends, and to see espe-
" cially, that his own reputation did not suffer
" by the management of his servant [o]."
Through this whole struggle about Milo, Pompey treated Cicero with great humanity he assigned him a " guard at the trial, forgave all
" his labors for his friend, though in opposition

[o] Consilium meum hoc fuerat, primum ut in potestate nostra res esset, ne illum malus emptor & alienus mancipiis, quæ permulta secum habet, spoliaret deinde ut Faustæ, cui cautum ille voluisset, ratum esset Erat etiam illud, ut ipsi nos si quid servari posset, quam facillime servaremus Nunc rem totam perspicias velim— Si ille queritur —— Si idem Fausta vult, Philotimus, ut ego ei coram dixeram, mihique ille receperat, ne sit invito Milone in bonis—— Ad Att 5 8 it 6 4

Quod ad Philotimi liberti officium & bona Miloris attinet, dedimus operam ut & Philotimus quam honestissime Miloni absenti, ejusque necessariis satis faceret, & secundum ejus fidem & sedulitatem existimatio tua conservaretur ——Ep I am 8 3

3

" to

" to himself, and so far from resenting what he
" did, would not suffer other people's resent-
" ments to hurt him [*p*] "

THE next trial before the same Tribunal, and
for the same crime, was of M Saufeius, one of
Milo's confidents, charged with being the ring-
leader *in storming the house, and killing Clodius*
he was defended also by Cicero, and acquitted
onely *by one vote* but being accused a second
time on the same account, though for a different
fact, and again defended by Cicero, *he was ac-*
quitted by a great majority But Sex Clodius,
the Captain of the other side, had not the luck
to escape so well, but was condemned and ba-
nished, with several others of that faction, to the
great joy of the City, *for burning the Senate-house,*
and the other violences committed upon Clodius's
death [*q*]

POMPEY no sooner published his *new law*
against bribery, than the late Consular Candidates,
Scipio and Hypsæus, *were severally impeached up*
on it, and being both of them notoriously guilty, were in great danger of being condemned
but Pompey, calling the body of the Judges together, begged it of them as a favor, *that out*
of the great number of state Criminals, they would
remit Scipio to him whom, after he had rescued
from this prosecution, he declared *his Collegue in*
the Consulship, for the last five months of the year,
having first made him *his Father-in-law* by marrying his daughter. *Coincia* The other Can-

A Urb 701
Cic 55
Coss
Cn POMPEI-
us Mag-
nus III
Q CÆCILIUS
METELL-
us SCIPIO

[*p*] Qua tamen ate sunt
contionem meam pro Mi-
lore, adversante interdum
actionibus suis? Quo studio
pro eo, ne quis me illius
temporis in judicia urgeret

Cum me consilio, tum auctoritate, cum armis denique
tutatus is——Ib 3 10

[*q*] Ascon Argum pro
Milon——

A Urb 701
Cic 55
Cn Pompei-
us Mag-
nus III
Q Cæcilius
Metellus
Scipio

didate, Hypfæus, was left to the mercy of the law, and being likely to fare the worfe for Scipio's efcape, and to be made a facrifice to the popular odium, he watched an opportunity of accefs to Pompey, *as he was coming out of his both, and throwing himfelf at his feet, implored his protection* but though he had been his *Quæftor*, and ever obfequious to his will, yet Pompey is faid to have thruft him away with great haughtinefs and inhumanity, telling him coldly, *that he would onely fpoil his fupper by detaining him* [r].

BEFORE the end of the year, Cicero had fome amends for the lofs of his friend Milo, by the condemnation and banifhment of *Two of the Tribuns,* the common enemies of them both, Q Pompeius Rufus, and T Munatius Plancus Burfa, *for the violences of their Tribunate, and burning the Senate-houfe* As foon as their office expired, Cælius accufed the firft, and Cicero himfelf the fecond, the onely caufe, excepting that of Verres, in which he ever acted the part of *an Accufer* But Burfa had deferved it, both for his public behaviour in his office, and his perfonal injuries to Cicero, who had defended and preferved him in a former trial He depended on Pompey's faving him, and had no apprehenfion of danger, fince Pompey under-

---

[r] Cn autem Pompeius cuam infolenter Qui balneo egreffus, ante pedes fuos profratum Hypfæum ambitus reum & nobilem virum & fibi amicum, jacentem reliquit, contumeliofa voce proculcatum Nihil enim eum aliud agere, quam vt convivium fuum moraretur, refpondit— Ille vero P Scipionem, Socerum fuum, legibus noxium, quas ipfe tulerat, in maxima quidem reorum & illuftrium ruina, muneris loco a Judicibus depofcere——Val Max. 9. 5 it Plutar in Pomp

took

A Urb 701
Cic 55
Coss
C. Po pei-
us M. c
ius III
Q Cæcilius
Mete lus
Scipio

took to plead his caufe, before Judges of his
own appointing, yet by Cicero's vigor in ma
naging the profecution, he was condemned by a
unanimous vote of the whole bench [s] Cicero
was highly pleafed with this fuccefs, as he figni
fies in a Letter to his friend Marius, which will
explane the motives of his conduct in it.

"I know very well, *fays he*, that you rejoice
" at Buria's fate, but you congratulate me too
" coldly you imagine, you tell me, that for
" the foraidnefs of the man, I take the lefs
" pleafure in it but believe me, I have more
" joy from this fentence than from the death
" of my enemy for, in the firft place, I love
" to purfue, rather by a trial, than the fword,
" rather with the glory, than the ruin of a
" friend, and it pleafed me extremely, to fee
" fo great an inclination of all honeft men on
" my fide, againft the incredible pains of one,
" the moft eminent and powerful and laftly,
" what you will fcarce think poffible, I hated
" this fellow worfe than Clodius himfelf for I
" had attacked the one, but defended the other
" and Clodius, when the fafety of the Republic
" was rifked upon my head, had fomething
" great in view, not indeed from his own
" ftrength, but the help of thofe, who could
" not maintain their ground, whilft I ftood firm
" but this ill Ap., out of a gayety of heart,
" chofe me particularly for the object of his in
" vectives, and perfuaded thofe, who envied
" me, that he would be always at their fervice,
" to infult me at any warning Wherefore I
" charge you to rejoice in good earneft, for it

[s] Prcum qu omnibus fu condemnatus————
u m o tro au Philip 6 4.

"is

" is a great victory, which we have won   No A Urb 701
" Citizens were ever ſtouter than thoſe who   Cic 55
" condemned him, againſt ſo great a power of   Coſſ
" one, by whom themſelves were choſen Judges   Cn Pompei-
' which they would never have done, if they   us Mag-
" had not made my cauſe and grief their own   nus III
' We are ſo diſtracted here by a multitude of   Q Cæcilius
" trials and new laws, that our daily prayer is   Metellus
" againſt all Intercalations, that we may ſee you   Scipio
" as ſoon as poſſible [*t*] '

Soon after the death of Clodius, Cicero ſeems
to have written *his Treatiſe on laws* [*u*], after the
example of Plato, whom of all writers he moſt
loved to imitate   for as Plato, after he had
written on government in general, *drew up a bo-*
dy of laws, adapted to that particular form of it,
which he had been delineating, ſo Cicero choſe to
deliver his political ſentiments in the ſame method [*x*], not by tranſlating Plato, but imitating
his manner in the explication of them   This
work being deſigned then, as a ſupplement, or
ſecond volume, to his other upon *the Republic*,
was diſtributed probably, as that other was, into
ſix books   for we meet with ſome quotations
among the ancients, from *the fourth and fifth* ;
though there are but *three* now remaining, and
thoſe in ſome places imperfect   In the firſt of
theſe, he lays open *the origin of law, and the*
ſource of obligation, which he derives from *the*
univerſal nature of things, or, as he explanes it,
from *the conſummate reaſon or will of the ſupreme*

[*t*] Ep Fam 7 2   nium, qui princeps de Repub
[*u*] Vid de Legib 2 17   conſcripſit, idemque ſepara-
[*x*] Sed ut vir doctiſſimus   tim de legibus ejus, id in hi
fecit Plato, atque idem gra-   credo eſſe faciendum ——— De
viſſimus Philoſophorum om-   Legib 2 6

God [y] in the other two books, he gives a body of laws conformable to his own plan and idea of a well ordered City [z] first, those which relate *to religion and the worship of the Gods*, secondly, those which prescribe *the duty and power of the several Magistrates*, from which the peculiar form of each government is denominated These laws are generally taken *from the old conftitution or cuftom of Rome* [a], with some little variation and temperament, contrived to obviate the disorders, to which that Republic was liable, and to give it a ftronger turn towards *the ariftocratical fide* [b] in the other book which are loft, he had treated, as he tells us, of *the particular rights and privileges of the* Roman *people* [c]

POMPEY was preparing *an Infcription* this summer *for the front of the New Temple*, which he had lately built *to Venus the Conquerefs*, containing as ufual, *the recital of all his Titles* but in drawing it up, a queftion happened to be ftarted, *about the manner of expreffing his third*

---

[y] Hanc igitur video fapientiffimorum fuiffe fententiam legem neque hominum ingeniis excogitatam nec fcitum aliquod effe populorum fed æternum quiddam, quod univerfum mundum regeret imperandi prohibendique fapientia Ita principem legem illam & ultimam mentem effe dicebant, omnia ratione aut cogentis aut vetantis Dei — Quamobrem lex vera atque princeps —— ratio eft recta fummi Jovis Ib 2 4

[z] Non autem quorum

—quæ de optima Repub fentiremus, in fex libris ante diximus, accommodabimus hoc tempore leges ad illum, quem probamus, civitatis ftatum——Ib 3 2

[a] Et fi quæ forte a me hodie rogabuntur, quæ non fint in noftra Repub nec fuerint, tamen erunt fere in morum majorum, qui tum, ut lex valeat Ib 2 10

[b] Nihil habui, fane non multum, quod putarem novandum in legibus Ib 3

[c] Ib 3 20

Conful/hip

Confulfhip, whether it fhould be by *Conful Ter-*
tium or *Tertio.* This was referred to *the princi-*
pal Critics of Rome, who could not, it feems,
agree about it, fome of them contending for the
one, fome for the other, *fo that Pompey left it to*
Cicero, to decide the matter, and to infcribe what
he thought the beft. But Cicero being unwilling
to give judgement on either fide, when there were
great authorities on both, and Vario among
them, advifed Pompey *to abbreviate the word in*
queftion, and order TERT *onely to be infcribed*,
which fully declared the thing, without determining the difpute. From this fact we may obferve, how nicely exact they were in this age, in
preferving a propriety of language in their public monuments and infcriptions [*a*]

A M O N G the other acts of Pompey, in this
third Confulfhip, there was a new law againft bribery, contrived to ftrengthen the old ones, that
were already fubfifting againft it, " by difquali-
" fying all future Confuls and Prætors, from
" holding any province, till five years after the
" expiration of their Magiftracies " for this
was thought likely to give fome check to the
eagernefs of fuing and bribing for thofe great
offices, *when the chief fruit and benefit of them*
was removed to fuch a diftance [*e*]. But before
the law paffed, Pompey took care to provide an
exception for himfelf, " and to get the govern-
" ment of Spain continued to him for five years
" longer, with an appointment of money for
' the payment of his troops " and left this
fhould give offence to Cæfar, if fomething alfo

A Urb 701
Cic 55
Cof
CN POMPEI-
US MAG-
NUS III
Q CÆCILIUS
MTELIUS
SCIPIO.

[*a*] This ftory is told by
Tiro, a favorite flave and
freedman of Cicero, in a

Letter preferved by A Gel-
liu l 10 1
[*e*] Dio p 142

of an extraordinary kind was not provided for
him, he propoſed a law, *to diſpenſe with Cæſor's*
abſence in ſuing for the Conſulſhip, of which Cæſar at that time ſeemed very deſirous   Cælius
was the promoter of this law, engaged to it by
Cicero, *at the joint requeſt of Pompey and Cæ-*
ſar [g], and it was carried with the concurrence
of all the Tribuns, though not without difficulty
and obſtruction from the Senate   but *this un-*
lucky favour, inſtead of ſervng Cæſar, ſerved on-
ly, as Suetonius ſays, to raiſe his hopes and ad-
vance his ſchemes [g]

By *Pompey's law*, juſt mentioned, it was provided, that for a ſupply of Governors for the
interval "of five years, in which the Conſuls
" and Prætors were concerned, the Senators of
" Conſular and Prætorian rank, who had never
" held any more government, ſhould divide the
" vacant Provinces among themſelves by lot "
in conſequence of which Cicero, who was obliged to take his chance with the reſt, obtained
the Government of Cilicia, now in the hands of
Appius, the late Conſul   this Province included
alſo *Pſidia*, *Pamphilia*, *and three Dioceſes, as*
they were called, *or Diſtricts of Aſia, togethe*
with the *Iſland of Cyprus*, for the guard of all
which, " a ſtanding army was kept up of two
" Legions, or about twelve thouſand foot, with
" two thouſand ſix hundred horſe [*b*] "   and

---

[g] *Rogatus à Scipio Ro-*
gatur — *Quod ut adeptus es-*
venire de Cicero Tribunis — *cura jam meditaris &c.*
pleb. co—oautem I— *penus nullum largitio-*
a Cnæo—oſro — *Ad Att* *aut officiorum in quemquam*
I   *cero   publice privatimque*

[*g*] *Egi cum Tribunis* *Sueton. J Cæſ 26*
pleb. — utabierut &c.— [*b*] *Ad Att* 5 15
peius ſcurat Conſulatus &c.

thus one of those *Provincial Governments,* which were withheld from others by law, to correct their inordinate passion for them, *was, contrary to his will and expectation, obtain'd at last upon Cicero,* whose business it had been through life to avoid them [*i*]

THE City began now to feel the unhappy effects, both *of Julia's and Crassus's death,* from the mutual apprehensions and jealousies, which discovered themselves more and more every day between Pompey and Cæsar the Senate was generally in Pompey's interest, and trusting to the name and authority of so great a Leader, were determined to humble the pride and ambition of Cæsar, by recalling him from his Government, whilst Cæsar, on the other hand, trusting to the strength of his troops, resolved to keep possession of it in defiance of all their votes, and by drawing a part of his forces into *the Italic or Cisalpine Gaul,* so as to be ready at any warning to support his pretensions, began to alarm all *Italy* with the melancholy prospect of an approaching *civil war* and this was the situation of affairs, when Cicero set forward towards his Government of Cilicia.

A Urb 701
Cic 55
Coss
C. Pompeius Magnus III
Q Cæcilius Metellus Scipio

[*i*] Cum & contra voluntatem meam & præter opinionem accidisset, ut mihi cum imperio in Provinciam proficisci necesse esset Ep Fam 3 2

SECT. VII.

THIS year opens to us a new fcene in Cicero's life, and prefents him in a character, which he had never before fuftained, *of the Governor of a Province,* and *General of an army* Thefe preferments were, of all others, the moft ardently defired by the great, for the advantages which they afforded both of acquiring power, and amaffing wealth for their command, though accountable to the Roman people, was abfolute and uncontroulable in the Province, where they kept up the ftate and pride of foverein Princes, and had all the neighbouring Kings paying a court to them, and attending their orders If their genius was turned to arms, and fond of martial glory, they could never want a pretext for war, fince it was eafy to drive the fubjects into rebellion, or the adjoining nations to acts of hoftility by their oppreffions and injuries, till from the deftruction of a number of innocent people, they had acquired *the Title of Emperor,* and with it the pretenfion to a triumph, without which fcarce any Proconful was ever known to return from a remote and frontier Province [a] Their
opportunities

[a] While the ancient difcipline of the Republic fubfifted no general could pretend to a triumph who had not enlarged the bounds of the Empire, his conqueft, and flain at leaft in one fought field enemies in battle, with any confiderable lofs of his own foldiers This was expresfly enacted by an old law in fupport of which a fecond was afterwards provided, that made it peril for any of the triumphant Commanders to give a falfe account of the number of men either of their own army, or of the enemy's fide of

2

opportunities of raising money were as immense
as their power, and bounded only by their
own appetites the appointments from the treasury, for their equipage, plate, and necessary furniture, amounted, as appears from some instances, to near *a hundred and fifty thousand
pounds* [b] and, besides the revenues of kingdoms, and pay of armies, of which they had the
arbitrary management, they could exact what
contributions they pleased, not onely from the
Cities of their own jurisdiction, but from all the
states and Princes around them, who were under the protection of Rome But while their
primary care was to enrich themselves, they carried out with them always a band of hungry
friends and dependents, as their *Lieutenants, Tribunes, Præfects,* with a crew of freedmen and
favorite slaves, who were all likewise to be enriched by the spoils of the Province, and the
sale of their master's favors Hence flowed all
those accusations and trials for the plunder of
the subjects, of which we read so much in the
Roman writers for as few or none of the Procon-
suls behaved themselves with that exact justice,
as to leave no room for complaint, so the factions
of the City, and the quarrels of families, subsist-

A Urb 702
Cic 56
Cofl
SERV SULPI-
CIUS RUFUS,
M CLAU-
DIUS M. P
CELLUS

.

---

their own, and obliged them,
upon their entrance into the
City, to take an oath before
the Quæstors or public Trea-
surers, that the accounts,
which they had sent to the
Senate, of each number
were true [Val Max 2 8]
But these laws had long been
neglected and treated a ob-
solete, and the honor of a
Triumph usually granted, by
intrigue and faction, to every

General of any credit, who
had gained some little advantage against Pirates or fugi-
tives, or repelled the incur-
sions of the wild barbarians,
who bordered upon the di-
stant provinces

[b] Nonne H S centies &
octagies—quasi vasarii nomi-
ne-- ex ærario tibi attributum,
Romæ in quæstu reliquisti? in
Pison 35

ing

ing from former impeachments, generally excited some or other to revenge the affront in kind, by undertaking the cause of an injured Province, and dressing up an impeachment against their enemy.

But whatever benefit or glory this Government seemed to offer, it had no charms for Cicero: the thing itself *was disagreeable to his temper,* [*] nor worthy of those talents, which were formed to sit at the helm, and shine in the administration of the whole Republic: so that he considered it only, as an honourable exil, or a burthen imposed by his country, to which his duty obliged him to submit. His first care therefore was to provide, that this command might not be prolonged to him beyond the usual term of a year, which was frequently done, when the necessities of the Province, the character of the man, the intrigues of parties, or the hurry of other business at home left the Senate neither leisure nor inclination to think of changing the Governor: and this was the more likely to happen at present, through the scarcity of magistrates, who were now left capable by the late law of succeeding him. Before his departure therefore he solicited all his friends, not to suffer such a mortification to fall upon him, and after he was gone, scarce wrote a single letter to *Rome,* without urging the same request in the most pressing terms: in his first to Atticus, within three days from their parting, *do not imagine* says he, *that I*

[*] —orum negotium non —nte gentibus noftr. qui major onerat in Rep —re — — tis & fi leam —p f m

—rem r——me ap—m m.. . moribus, &c ad Att 5 10
  sed eft incredibile, quam me negoti. tœdeat, non hab —rs magnum campun ib tibi ncn ignotus curfus ani ne —ib 15

have any other consolation in this great trouble, than the hopes that it will not be continued beyond the year many, who judge of me by others, do not take me to be in earnest, but you, who know me, will use all your diligence, especially, when the affair is to come on [d]

A Urb 702
Cic 56.
Coss
Serv Sulpi-
cius Rufus,
M Clau-
dius Mar-
cellus.

HE left the City about the first of *May*, attended by his Brother and their two Sons for Quintus had quitted his commission under *Cæsar*, in order to accompany him into *Cilicia*, in the same capacity of *his Lieutenant*. *Atticus* had desired him, before he left *Italy*, to admonish his Brother, to shew more complaisance and affection to his wife *Pomponia*, who had been complaining to him of her husband's peevishness and churlish carriage, and left *Cicero* should forget it, he put him in mind again, by a letter to him on the road, that since all the family were to be together in the Country, on this occasion of his going abroad, he would persuade *Quintus* to leave his wife at least in good humor at their parting in relation to which, *Cicero* sends him the following account of what passed.

" When I arrived at *Arpinum*, and my Brother was come to me, our first and chief discourse
" was on you, which gave me an opportunity
" of falling upon the affair of your Sister, which
" you and I had talked over together at *Tuscu-*
" *lum* I never saw any thing so mild and mo-
" derate as my Brother was, without giving the
" least hint of his ever having had any real

---

[d] Noli putare mihi aliam consolationem esse hujus ingentis molestiæ, nisi quod spero non longiorem annia fore Hoc me ita velle multi non credunt ex consuetudine aliorum Tu, qui scis omnem diligentiam adhibebis, tum scilicet, cum id agi debebit Ib 2.

A. Urb 702,
C'c 56
Coſſ
Ser. Sulfi-
ciu. Rufus,
M Clau
dius Mar-
cellus.

" cauſe of offence from her　The next morn
" ing we left Arpinum, and that day being a
" feſtival, Quintus was obliged to ſpend it at Ar
" canum, where I dined with him, but went on
" afterwards to Aquinum　You know this Villa
" of his　as ſoon as we came thither, Quintus
" ſaid to his wife, in the civilleſt terms, do you,
" Pomponia, invite the women, and I will ſerd
" to the men　(nothing, as far as I ſaw, could
" be ſaid more obligingly, either in his words or
" manner) to which ſhe replied, ſo as we all
" might hear it, *I am but a ſtranger here myſelf*
" rererring, I gueſs, to my Brother's having ſen
" Statius before us to order the dinner　upon
" which, ſee, ſays my Brother to me, what I am
" forced to bear every day.　This, you will ſay,
" was no great matter　Yes, truly, great
" enough to give me much concern, to ſee
" her reply ſo abſurdly and fiercely both in her
" words and looks　but I diſſembled my unea
" ſineſs　When we ſat down to dinner, ſhe
" would not ſit down with us　and when Quin-
" tus ſent her ſeveral things from the table, ſhe
" ſent them all back　in ſhort, nothing could be
" milder than my Brother, or ruder than your
" Siſter　yet I omit many particulars, which gave
" more trouble to me than to Quintus himſelf
" I went away to Aquinum, he ſtaid at Arcanum
" but when he came to me early the next morn
" ing, he told me, that ſhe refuſed to lye with
" him that night, and at their parting continued
" in the ſame humor, in which I had ſeen her
" In a word, you may let her know from me,
" that, in my opinion, the fault was all on her
" ſide that day　I have been longer perhaps
" than was neceſſary, in my narrative, to let you

" ſee

" fee, that there is occafion alfo on your part for
" advice and admonition [e]."

A Urb 702.
Cic 56
Coff
Serv Sulpi-
cius Rufus,
M Clau-
dius Mar-
cellus

One cannot help obferving from this little incident, what is confirmed by innumerable inftances
in the Roman ftory, that *the freedom of a divorce,*
which was indulged without reftraint at Rome,
to the caprice of either party, gave no advantage
of comfort to the matrimonial ftate, but on the
contrary, feems to have encouraged rather a mutual perverfenefs and obftinacy, fince upon any
little difguft, or obftruction given to their follies,
the expedient of a change was ready always to
flatter them, with the hopes of better fuccefs in
another trial   for there never was an age or
Country, where there was fo profligate a contempt and violation of the nuptial bond, or fo
much lewdnefs and infidelity in the Great of both
fexes, as at this time in Rome.

Cicero fpent a few days as he paffed forward, at his *Cuman Villa,* near Baiæ, where there
was fuch a refort of Company to him, *that he
had,* he fays, *a kind of a little Rome about him:*
Hortenfius came among the reft, though much
out of health, to pay his compliments, and wifh
him a good voyage, and, at taking leave, when
he afked, *what commands he had for him in his
abfence,* Cicero begged of him onely, to ufe all
his authority, *to hinder his Government from being
prolonged to him* [f].   In fixteen days from
Rome, he arrived at Tarentum, where he had

[e] Ad Att 5 1
[f] In Cumano cum ef-
m, venit ad me, quod mi-
hi pergratum fuit, nofter
Hortenfius cui, depofcenti
mea mandata, cætera uni-
e mandavi, illud proprie,

ne pateretur quantum effet
in ipfo prorogari nobis provinciam — habuimus in Cu
mano quafi pufillam Romam
tanta erat in his locis multi
tudo — ib 2

promifed

A Urb 701
Cic 55
Coſ
Serv Sulpi
cius Rufus,
M C at
Dicdular
Cellus

promiſed to make a viſit to Pompey, who w. taking the benefit of that ſoft air, for the r. covert of his health, at one of his Villa's in th. parts and had invited and preſſed Cicero, ſpend ſome days with him upon his journe, they promiſed great ſatisfaction on both he from this interview, for the opportunity of co rering together with all freedom, on the preſer ſtate of the Republic, which was to be their ſub ject though Cicero expected alſo to get ſome k ſons of the military kind, from this renow Commander He promiſed Atticus an accou of this Conference, but the particulars being too delicate to be communicated by Letters, he ac quainted him onely in general, *that he found P pe, an excellent Citz, and provided for all even, which could poſſibly be apprehended* [g]

AFTER *three days ſtay with Pompey*, he pro ceded to Brundiſium, where he was detained ſ *twelve days by a ſlight indiſpoſition*, and the ex ec tation of his principal officers, particularly *of L. Pontius*, an experienced Leader, the ſame who had triumphed over *the Allobroges*, and on whoſe ſkill he chiefly depended in his milit affairs From Brundiſium, he ſailed to Actium *on the fifteenth of June*, whence partly by ſea

...] Nos Tarent, a o cum Pompeo 2 2, de Repub loqu us ad te perieroc in. — D, 5

...renam verſ a d w Kal Jun quod Pont ulun ſtracran expectare commo diſſimum duci eos cum Pompeo contulere coade magi quod e gra um ebe id videbam qui eti m a n petent, ut ſecum apul te c r quotide quod con

ceſſi libenter multos en jus prachros de Repub mones acc p ori i u tiam conſilis idoneis no fc noſt um negotium — ib 6

Igo, cum tridu m c Pompeio & apud Pon p fuiſſem, proficiſcebu r Bru cium — Civem illum egre gium relinquebam, & alia quæ timentur, propultare paratiſſimum —ib 7.

and partly by land, he arrived at *Athens on the twenty-fixth* [*h*] Here he lodged in the house of Ariftus, the principal profeffor of *the Academy*, and his Brother not far from him, with Xeno, another celebrated Philofopher of Epicurus's School they fpent their time here very agreeably, at home, in Philofophical difquifitions, abroad, in viewing the buildings and antiquities of the place, with which Cicero was much delighted there were feveral other men of learning, both Greeks and Romans, of the party, efpecially Gallus Caninius and Patro, an eminent Epicurean, and intimate friend of Atticus [*i*].

THERE lived at this time in exil at Athens, C. Memmius, banifhed upon a conviction of bribery, in his fuit for the confulfhip, who, the day before Cicero's arrival, happened to go away to Mitylene The figure, which he had born in Rome, gave him authority in Athens, and *the council of Areopagus* had granted him a piece of ground to build upon, where *Epicurus formerly lived, and where there ftill remained the ruins of his wall* But this grant had given great offence to the whole body of *the Epicureans*, to fee the remains of their mafter in danger of being deftroyed They had written to Cicero at Rome, to beg him to intercede with Memmius, to confent to a revocation of it, and now it Athens, Xeno and Patro renewed their inftances, and prevailed with him to write about it, in the moft effectual manner, for though Memmius had

A Urb 702.
Cic 56
Coff
SERV SULPI-
CIUS RUFUS,
M CLAU-
DIUS MAR-
CELLUS

[*b*] Ad Att 5 8 9

[*i*] Valde me Auctæ delectarunt urbs durtaxat tibs ornamenti in & hominum amores in te, & in nos reducta benevolentia, fed —

malorum & Philofophia — fi enim eft in Atino apud eum ejufmodi nam Xenonem tuum — Quæro concoeheram — ad Att 5 x Ep fam 2

laid

A Urb 702
Cic 56
Coss
SERV SULPI
CIUS RUFU,
M CLAU-
DIUS MAR-
CELLUS
laid afide his defign of building, *the Areopagites would not recall their decree without his leave* [*f*] Cicero's letter is drawn with much art and accuracy he laughs at the trifling zeal of thefe Philofophers, *for the old rubbifh and paultry ruins of their Founder, yet earneftly preffes Memmius, to indulge them in a prejudice, contracted through weaknefs, not wickednefs*, and though he profeffes an utter diflike of their Philofophy, yet he recommends them, *as honeft, agreeable, friendly men,* for whom he entertained the higheft efteem [*l*] From this letter one may obferve, that the greateft difference in Philofophy made no difference of friendfhip among the great of thefe times There was not a more declared enemy to Epicurus's doctrine, than Cicero he thought it deftructive of morality, and pernicious to Society, but he charged this confequence to the principles, not the Profeffors of them, with many of whom he held the ftricteft intimacy, and found them to be worthy, virtuous, generous friends, and lovers of their Country there is a jocofe Letter to Trebatius, when he was with Cæfar *in Gaul* upon his turning Epicurean, which will help to confirm this reflection.

CICERO *to* TREBATIUS.

" I was wondering, why you had given over
" writing to me, till Panfa informed me, that

[*f*] Vifum eft Xenon, & pot ipfi Patroni, ire ad Memmium fcribere, qui pridie quam ego Athenas veni, Mitylenas profectus erat, — non enim dubitabat Xeno, quin ab Areopagitis invito Memmio impetrari non poffet Memmius autem adificandi confilium abjeciffet, fed erat Patroni iratus, itaque fcripfi ad eum accurate— ad Att 5 11

[*l*] Ep fam. 13 1

" you

A. Urb. 702.
Cic. 56
Coss
Serv. Sulpi-
cius Rufus,
M. Clau-
dius Mar-
cellus

" you were turned Epicurean   O rare Camp!
" what would you have done if I had sent you
" to Tarentum, instead of Samerobriva? I began
" to think the worse of you, ever since you
" made my friend Seius your pattern   But with
" what face will you now pretend to practise the
" Law, when you are to do every thing for your
" own interest, and not for your Client's? and
" what will become of that old *aim*, and test of
' *fidelity, as true men ought to act truly, with
" one another?* what Law would you alledge for
" the distribution of common right, when no-
" thing can be common with those who mea-
" sure all things by their pleasure? with what
' face can you swear by Jupiter; when Jupiter,
" you know, can never be angry with any man?
" and what will become of your people of *Ulu-
" bræ*, since you do not allow a wise man to
' meddle with politics? wherefore if you are
" really gone off from us, I am sorry for it;
" but if it be convenient to pay this compliment
" to Pansa, I forgive you, on condition how-
" ever, that you write me word what you are
" doing, and what you would have me do for
" you here [*n*] "   The change of principles in
Trebatius, though equivalent in effect to a change
of Religion with us, made no alteration in Cicero's affection for him   This was the dictate of
reason to the best and wisest of the Heathens;
and may serve to expose the rashness of those
zealots, who, with the light of a most divine and
benevolent religion, are perpetually insulting and
persecuting their fellow Christians, for differences
of opinion, which, for the most part, are mere-
ly speculative, and without any influence on life,
or the good and happiness of civil Society

[*n*] Ep. Fam. 7. 12

After

A Urb 702
Cic 56
Coſſ
Sepr Sulpi-
cius Rufu,
M Clau-
dius Mar-
cellus

AFTER *ten days* spent at Athens, where Pomponius at laſt joined him, Cicero ſet ſail towards Aſia Upon leaving Italy, he had charged his friend Cælius with the taſk of ſending him the news of Rome, which Cælius performed very punctually, in a ſeries of Letters, which make a valuable part in the collection of his *familiar Epiſtles* they are polite and entertaining, full of wit and ſpirit, yet not flowing with that eaſy turn, and elegance of expreſſion, which we always find in Cicero's The firſt of them, with Cicero's anſwer, will give us a ſpecimen of the reſt

M. CÆLIUS *to* M CICERO

" ACCORDING to my promiſe at parting, to
" ſend you an account of all the news of the
" Town, I have provided one to collect it for
" you ſo punctually, that I am afraid, leſt you
" ſhould think my diligence at laſt too minute
" but I know how curious you are, and how
" agreeable it is to all, who are abroad, to be
" informed of every thing that paſſes at home,
" though ever ſo trifling I beg of you, however,
" not to condemn me of arrogance, for deputing
" another to this taſk ſince, as buſy as I now
" am, and as lazy, as you know me to be in
" writing, it would be the greateſt pleaſure to
" me, to be employed in any thing that revives
" the remembrance of you but the paquet it
" ſelf, which I have ſent, will, I imagine, rea
" dily excuſe me for what leiſure would it re
" quire, not only to tranſcribe, but to attend
" even to the contents of it? there are all the
" decrees of the Senate, Edicts, plays, rumors
" if the ſample does not pleaſe you, pray let me
" know it, that I may not give you trouble, a
                                                                        ' ni

" my coft   If any thing important happens in
" the republic, above the reach of thefe hack-
" ney writers, I will fend you an account of it
" myfelf, in what manner it was tranfacted,
' what fpeculations are raifed upon it ; what ef-
" fects apprehended   at prefent there is no
" great expectation of any thing · as to thofe ru-
" mors, which were fo warm at *Cumæ*, of af-
" fembling the Colonies beyond the *Po*, when I
" came to *Rome*, I heard not a fyllable about
" them   Marcellus too, becaufe he has not yet
" made any motion for a fucceffor to the two
" *Gauls*, but puts it off, as he told me himfelf,
" to the firft of *June*, has revived the fame talk
" concerning him, which was ftirring when we
" were at *Rome* together   If you faw Pompey,
" as you defigned to do, pray fend me word in
" what temper you found him , what converfa-
" tion he had with you , what inclination he
" fhewed , for he is apt to think one thing, and
" fay another, yet has not wit enough, to con-
" ceal what he really means   As for Cæfar,
" there are many ugly reports about him , but
" propagated onely in whifpers : fome fay, that
" he has loft all his horfe , which I take indeed
" to be true, others, that the feventh Legion
" has been beaten , and that he himfelf is be-
' fieged by the *Bellovaci* , and cut off from the
" reft of his army   There is nothing yet cer-
' tain; nor are thefe uncertain ftories publicly
" talked of , but among the few, whom you
" know, told openly, by way of fecrets · Do-
" mitius never mentions them, without clap-
" ping his hand to his mouth.   On the twenty-
" firft of *May*, the mob under the Roftra, fent
" about a report, (may it fall on their own heads)
" which was warmly propagated through the

A Urb 702.
Cic 56.
Coff.
Serv Sulpi-
cius Rufus,
M Clau-
dius Mar-
cellus.

A Urb 702
Cic 5t
Coss
Serv Sulpi-
cius Rufus,
M Clau-
dii Mar-
cellus

" Forum and the whole City, that you were
" killed upon the road by Q Pompeius but I,
" who knew him to be then at *Bauli*, and in such
" a starving condition, that I could not help pre-
" tving him, being forced to turn Pilot for his
" bread, was not concerned about it, and wished
" onely, that if any real dangers threatened you,
" we might be quit for this lie your friend
' Plancus Bursa is at Ravenna, where he has
" had a large donative from Cæsar, but is not
" yet easy, nor well provided Your books on
" government are applauded by all people [*n*]

M T CICERO, Proconsul, to M CÆLIUS

" How ! was it this, think you, that I charged
" you with, to send me the matches of Gladia
" tors, the adjournments of causes, and Chre-
" tus's news-letter, and what nobody dares men
" tion to me when at Rome? See, how much I
" ascribe to you in my judgement. nor indeed
' without reason, for I have never yet met with
" a better head for politics, I would not have
" you write what passes every day in public,
" though ever so important, unless it happen to
" affect myself others will write it, many bring
" accounts of it, and fame itself conveys a great
" part to me I expect from you, neither the
" past, nor the present, but as from one, who
" sees a great way before him, the future onely
" that when I have before me in your Letter
" the plan of the Republic, I may be able to
" judge what a sort of Edifice it will be No
" have I hitherto indeed any cause to complain
" of you, for nothing has yet happened, which

[*r*] Epist Fam 8 1

" so

A Urb 702.
Cic 56.
Coff
Serv Sulpi-
cius Rufus,
M Clau-
dius Mar-
cellus.

" you could forefee better than any of us efpe-
" cially myfelf, who fpent feveral days with
" Pompey, in converfing on nothing elfe, but
" the Republic, which is neither poffible nor
" proper for me to explane by Letter take this
' onely from me, that Pompey is an excellent
" Citizen, prepared both with courage and
" counfil for all events, which can be forefeen
' wherefore, give yourfelf up to the man, be-
" lieve me, he will embrace you, for he now
' holds the fame opinion with us, of good and
' bad Citizens After I had been ten days at
" Athens, where our friend Gallus Caninius was
" much with me, I left it on the fixth of July,
" when I fent away this Letter as I earneftly
" recommend all my affairs to you, fo nothing
" more particularly, than that the time of my
" Provincial Command be not prolonged this
" is every thing to me, which, when and how,
" and by whom it is to be managed, you will
" be the beft able to contrive Adieu [o].

He landed at *Ephefus* on *the twenty-fecond of
July*, after a flow but fafe paffage of *fifteen days*,
the tedioufnefs of which was agreeably relieved
by touching on the way at feveral of *the iflands of
the Ægean Sea*, of which he fends a kind of jour-
nal to Atticus [p] Many deputations from the
Cities of Afia, and a great concourfe of people
came to meet him as far as *Samos*, but a much
greater ftill was expecting his landing at Ephefus.
the Greeks flocked eagerly from all parts, to fee
a man fo celebrated through the empire, for the
fame of his learning and eloquence, fo *that all
his boaftings,* as he merrily fays, *of many years*

[o] Ep fam 2 8   d xi Kal Sext ——d Att 5
[p] Ephefum venimus a   13 vid ir ib 12.

N 2   *paft,*

A. Urb 702
Cic 56
Coſſ
SERV. SULPI-
CIUS RUFUS,
M. CLAU-
DIUS MAR-
CELLU

paſt, were now brought to the teſt [q] After re
poſing himſelf for *three days* at Epheſus, he march
ed forward towards his Province , and, on the laſt
of July, arrived at Laodicea, one of the Capital
Cities of his Juriſdiction From this moment
the date of his Government commenced , which
he bids Atticus take notice of, that he might
know how *to compute the preciſe extent of his annu*
al term [r]

IT was Cicero's reſolution, in this Provincial
Command, to practiſe thoſe admirable rules, which
he had drawn up formerly for his Brother , and
from an employment wholly tedious and diſagree
able to him to derive freſh glory upon his cha
racter, by leaving the innocence and integrity o
his adminiſtration, as a pattern of governing to
all ſucceeding Proconſuls It had always been
the cuſtom, when any Governors went abroad to
their Provinces, *that the Countries, through which*
they paſſed, ſhould defray all the charges of their
journey . but Cicero no ſooner ſet his foot on fo
reign ground, *than he forbad all expence whatſo*
ever, public or private, to be made either upon him
ſelf, or any of his company , which raiſed a great
admiration of him, *in all the cities of Greece* [s]

In

In *Afia* he did the fame, not fuffering his offi- cers to accept *what was due to them even by law, forage and wood for firing, nor any thing elfe, but mere houfe-room, with four beds*, which he remit- ted alfo, as oft as it was practicable, and obliged them *to lodge in their tents*, and by his example and conftant exhortations brought *his Lieutenants, Tribuns, and Præfects, fo fully into his meafures, that they all concurred with him*, he fays, *wonder- fully, in a jealous concern for his honor* [t]

A Urb 702.
Cic 56.
Coff
Serv Sulpi-
cius Rufus,
M Clau-
dius Mar-
cellus.

BEING defirous to put himfelf at the head of his army, before the Seafon of action was over, he fpent but little time in vifiting the Cities of his jurifdiction, referving *the winter months for fet- tling the civil affairs of the Province* [u]   He went therefore to the Camp, *at Iconium in Lycaonia, about the twenty-fourth of Auguft*, where he had no fooner reviewed the troops, than he received an account from *Antiochus, King of Comagene*, which was confirmed from the other Princes of thofe parts, *that the Parthians had paffed the Eu- phrates with a mighty force, in order to invade the Roman territory under the conduct of Pacorus, the*

Hoc animadverfum Græco- rum laude & multo fermone celebratur Ib 10

Nos adhuc iter per Græ- ciam fumma cum admiratione fecimus Ib 11

[t] Levantur miferæ civi- tates, quod nullus fit fump- tus in nos neque in Legatos neque in Quæftorem, necue in quemquam Scito, non modo nos fœnum, aut quod lege Julia dari folet non acci- pere, fed ne ligna quidem, nec præter quatuor lectos, & tectum, quemquam accipere

quidquam multis locis ne tectum quidem, & in taber- naculo manere plerumque — ad Att 5 16

Ut nullus teruncius infu- matur in quemquam, id fit etiam & Legatorum & Tri- bunorum & Præfectorum dili- gentia Nam omnes mirifice συμφιλοδοξουσιν gloria meæ —ib 17

[u] Erat mihi in animo recta proficifci ad exercitum, aftivos menfes reliquos rei militari dare, hibernos jurif- dictioni—ib 14

A Urb. 702
C.c 56
Coff
SERV SULPI-
CIUS RUFUS,
M CLAU-
DIUS MAR-
CELLUS

King's for Upon this news, he marched towards *Cilicia*, to secure his Province from the inroads of the enemy, or any commotions within, but as all access to it was difficult, except on the side of Cappadocia, an open country, and not well provided, he took his rout through that kingdom, and encamped in that part of it which *bordered upon Cilicia, near to the town of Cybistra, at the foot of mont Taurus.* His army, as it is said above, consisted of about *twelve thousand foot and two thousand six hundred horse,* besides the auxiliary troops of the neighbouring states, and especially of *Deiotarus, King of Galatia,* the most faithful *Ally of Rome,* and Cicero's particular friend, whose whole forces he could depend upon at any warning [x]

WHILE he lay in this Camp, he had an opportunity of executing a special commission, with which he was charged by the Senate, *to take Ariobarzenes, King of Cappadocia, under his particular protection,* and provide for the security of his person and government in honor of whom, the Senate had decreed, what they had never done before to any foreign Prince, that *his safety was of great concern to the Senate and people of*

[x] In caftra veni a d vii Kal Sept add in exercitum luftravit Ex his caftris cum graves de Parthis nuncii venerent, perrexi in Ciliciam, per Cappadocæ partem eam quæ Ciliciam attingit——

Regis Antiochi Comageni Legati primi mihi nunciarunt Parthorum magnas copias Euphratem tranfire cœpiffe —— Cum exercitum in

Ciliciam ducerem— mihi litteræ reddita funt a Tarcondimoto, qui fideliffimus focius trans Taurum Populi Rom exiftimatur Pacorum Orod Regis Parthorum filium, cum permagno equitatu tranfiff. Euphratem, &c Ep fam 15 1

Eodem die ab Jamblico, Phylarcho Arabum— littera de eifdem rebus, &c

Rome. His Father had been killed by the treachery of his subjects, and a conspiracy of the same kind was apprehended against the son Cicero therefore, in a council of his officers, gave the King an account of *the Decree of the Senate,* and that in consequence of it he was then ready to assist him with his troops and authority in any measures that should be concerted for the safety and quiet of his Kingdom—The King, after great professions of his thanks, and duty to the Senate for the honor of *their decree, and to Cicero himself* for his care in the execution of it, said, *that he knew no occasion for giving him any particular trouble at that time, nor had any suspicion of any design against his life or Crown* upon which Cicero, after congratulating him upon the tranquillity of his affairs, advised him however, *to remember his Father's fate, and, from the admonition of the Senate, to be particularly vigilant in the care of his person,* and so they parted. But the next morning the King returned early to the Camp, attended by his Brother and Counsellors, and with many tears implored the protection of Cicero, *and the benefit of the Senate's decree,* declaring, " that he had received undoubted intelligence of " a plot, which those, who were privy to it, " durst not venture to discover till Cicero's arri- " val in the Country, but trusting to his autho- ' rity, had now given full information of it, " and that his Brother, who was present, and " ready to confirm what he said, had been solli- " cited to enter into it by the offer of the crown " he begged therefore, that some of Cicero's " troops might be left with him for his better " guard and defence. Cicero told him, that un- " der the present alarm of the Parthian war, he " could not possibly lend him any part of his ar-

N 4 " my,

A Urb 702
Cic 56
Coss
Serv Sulpi
cius Rufus,
M Claudius Marcellus.

A Urb 702
Cic 56
Coff
SERV SULPI-
CIUS RUFUS,
M CLAU-
DIUS MAR
CELLUS

"my, that, since the conspiracy was detected
"his own forces would be sufficient for prevent
"ing the effects of it, that he should learn to
"act the King, by shewing a proper concern for
"his own life, and exert his legal power in pu
"nishing the authors of the plot, and pardoning
"all the rest, that he need not apprehend any
"farther danger, when his people were acquaint
"ed with the Senate's decree, and saw a *Roman*
"army so near to them, and ready to put it in
"execution" and having thus encouraged and
comforted the King, he marched towards *Cilicia*,
and gave an account of this accident, and of the
motions of the *Parthians*, in *two public Letters to
the Consuls and the Senate* he added a private
Letter also to Cato, who was a particular favorer,
and Patron of Ariobarzanes, in which he inform
ed him, "that he had not onely secured the King's
"person from any attempt, but had taken care,
"that he should reign for the future with honor
"and dignity, by restoring to his favor and ser
"vice his old Counsellors, whom Cato had re-
"commended, and who had been disgraced by
"the intrigues of his Court, and by obliging a
"turbulent young priest of *Bellona*, who was
"the head of the Malecontents, and the next
"in power to the King himself, to quit the coun-
"try [y]"

THIS King, Ariobarzanes, seems to have been
poor even to a proverb

Mancipiis locuples eget æris Cappadocum rex.
　　　　　　　　Hor Ep I 6

for he had been miserably squeezed and drained
by the *Roman* Generals and Governors, to whom

[y] Ep fam 15 2, 3, 4.

　　　　　　　　　　　　　　　　he

he owed vaft fumms, either actually borrowed,
or ftipulated to be paid for particular fervices. It
was a common practice with the Great of *Rome,*
to lend money at an exorbitant intereft, to the Princes
and Cities, dependent on the Empire, which was
thought an ufefull piece of policy to both fides;
to the Princes, for the opportunity of engaging
to their interefts the moft powerfull men of the
Republic, by a kind of honorable penfion, to
the *Romans,* for the convenience of placing their
money where it was fure to bring the greateft return of profit   The ordinary intereft of thefe
Provincial loans was, *one per Cent by the month,*
with intereft upon intereft . this was the loweft;
but, in extraordinary or hazardous cafes, it was
frequently four times as much. Pompey received
monthly from this very King, *above fix thoufand*
pounds fterling , which yet was fhort of his full
intereft   Brutus alfo had lent him a very large
fumm, and earneftly defired Cicero to procure the
payment of it, with the arrears of intereft · but
Pompey's agents were fo preffing, and the King
fo needy, that though Cicero follicited Brutus's
affair very heartily, he had little hopes of getting
any thing for him · when Ariobarzanes came
therefore to offer him the fame prefent of money,
which he had ufually made to every other Governor, he generoufly refufed it, and defired onely,
that inftead of giving it to him, it might be paid to
Brutus : but the poor Prince was fo diftreffed,
that he excufed himfelf, by the neceffity, which
he was under, of fatisfying fome other more preffing demands , fo that Cicero gives a fad account
of his negotiation, in a long letter to Atticus, who
had warmly recommended Brutus's interefts to
him.

3

" I come

A Urb 702
Cic 56
Coſſ
SERV SULPI-
CILS RUFL,
M CLAU
DILS MAR-
CELLUS

" I come now, ſays he, to Brutus, whom b
" your authority I embraced with inclination,
" and began even to love but———what am I
" going to ſay? I recall myſelf, left I offend
" you——— do not think, that I ever entered in
" to any thing more willingly, or took more
" pains, than in what he recommended to me
" He gave me a memorial of the particulars,
" which you had talked over with me before
" I purſued your inſtructions exactly in the firſt
" place, I preſſed Ariobarzanes to give that mo
" ney to Brutus, which he promiſed to me as
' long as the King continued with me, all things
" looked well, but he was afterwards ſeized by
" ſix hundred of Pompey's agents, and Pompey,
" for other reaſons, can do more with him than
" all the world beſides, but eſpecially, when it
" is imagined, that he is to be ſent to the Par
" thian war they now pay Pompey thirty-three
" Attic talents per month, out of the taxes, though
" this falls ſhort of a month's intereſt but our
" friend Cnæus takes it calmly, and is content
" to abate ſomething of the intereſt, without
" preſſing for the principal As for others, he
" neither does, nor can pay any man. for he
" has no treaſury, no revenues he raiſes taxes
" by Appius's method of capitation but theſe
' are ſcarce ſufficient for Pompey's monthly pay
" two or three of the King's friends are very
" rich, but they hold their own as cloſely, as
" either you or I--I do not forbear however to aſk,
" urge and chide him by Letters King Deiot-
" rus alſo told me, that he had ſent people to
" him on purpoſe, to ſollicit for Brutus, but
- they brought him word back, that he had real
" ly no money which I take indeed to be the
- caſe, that nothing is more drained than his
         " kingdom

" kingdom, nothing poorer than the King [z] " A Urb 702.

But Brutus had recommended another affair of the same nature to Cicero, which gave him much more trouble The City of *Salamis* in *Cy-prus* owed to two of his friends, as he pretended, Scaptius and Matinius, above *twenty thousand pounds sterling* upon bond, at a most extravagant interest, and he begged of Cicero to take their persons and concerns under his special protection Appius, who was Brutus's father-in-law, had granted every thing which was asked to Scaptius, *a Præfecture in Cyprus, with some troops of horse*, with which he miserably harassed the poor Sala-minians, in order to force them to comply with his unreasonable demands, for *he shut up their whole senate in the council-room, till five of them were starved to death with hunger* [a] Brutus labored to place him in the same degree of favor with Cicero. but Cicero being informed of this violence at Ephesus, *by a deputation from Salamis*, made it the first act of his government to recall the troops from Cyprus, and put an end to Scaptius's Præfecture, having laid it down for a rule, to grant no command to any man, *who was concerned in trade, or negotiating money* in the Province to give satisfaction however to Brutus, he injoined *the Salaminians to pay off Scaptius's bond*, which they were ready to do according to the tenor of his edict, by which he had ordered, *that no bonds in his province should carry above one per Cent by the month* Scaptius refused to take the money on those terms, insisting *on four per Cent.* as the condition of his bond expressed, which by

Cic 56.
Coss
Serv Sulpi-
cius Rufus,
M Clau-
dius Mar-
cellus

[z] Ad Att 6 1
[a] Fuerat enim Præfectus Appio, & quidem habuerat turmas Equitum, quibus in-
clusum in curia senatum Sa-lamine obsederet, ut fame se-natores quinque morerentur, ——ibid

computation

A Urb 702
Cic. 56.
Coſſ
SERV SULPI-
CIUS RUFUS,
M CLAU-
DIUS MAR-
CELLUS

computation almoſt doubled the principal ſumm,
while the Salaminians, as they proteſted to Cice
ro, *could not have paid the original debt, if they
had not been enabled to do it by his help, and out of
his own dues, that he had remitted to them, which
amounted to ſomewhat more than Scaptius's legal demand* [b]

THIS extortion raiſed Cicero's indignation, and
notwithſtanding the repeated inſtances of Brutus
and Atticus, he was determined to over-rule it,
though Brutus, in order to move him the more
effectually, thought proper to confeſs, *what he
had all along diſſembled, that the debt was really his
own, and Scaptius onely his agent in it* [c]. This
ſurpriſed Cicero ſtill more, and though he had a
warm inclination to oblige Brutus, yet he could
not conſent to ſo flagrant an injuſtice, but makes
frequent and heavy complaints of it in his letters
to Atticus——— " You have now, ſays he, in one
" of them, the ground of my conduct, if Bru-
" tus does not approve it, I ſee no reaſon
" why we ſhould love him, but I am ſure, it
" will be approved by his uncle, Cato [d]." In

---

[b] Itaque ego, quo die
tetigi provinciam, cum mihi
Cyprii Legati Epheſum obviam ven ſſent, litteras miſi ut
equites ex inſula ſtatim dece-
derent—ad Att 6 1 confe-
ceram, ut ſolverent centeſi-
mis — ad Scaptius quaternas
poſtulabat—ib homines non
modo non recuſare, ſed etiam
dicere, ſe a me ſolvere Quod
enim Præ ori dare conſueſ-
cent, quoniam ego non acce-
peram, ſe a me quodam mo-
do dare, atque etiam minus
eſe aliquanto in Scaptii no-

mine, quam in vectigali præ
torio—ib 5 21

[c] Atque hoc tempore ip
ſo impingit mihi epiſtolam
Scaptius Bruti, rem illam in
periculo eſſe quod nec mihi
unquam Brutus dixerat ne
tibi — ib nunquam ex ill
audivi illam pecuniam eſſ
ſuam—ib

[d] Habes meam cauſam
quæ ſi Bruto non probatu
neſcio cur illum amemus ſe
avunculo ejus certe probab
tur—ib. 5 21

another

another, "If Brutus thinks that I ought to al-
"low him four per Cent when by edict I have
"decreed but one through all the province, and
"that, to the satisfaction of the keenest usurers,
'if he complains, that I denied a Præfecture to
"one, concerned in trade, which I denied, for
"that reason, to your friend Lenius, and to Sex.
"Statius, though Torquatus sollicited for the
"one, and Pompey himself for the other, yet
"without disgusting either of them, if he takes
"it ill that I recalled the troops of horse out of
"Cyprus, I shall be sorry indeed, that he has
"any occasion to be angry with me; but much
"more, not to find him the man that I took
"him to be—I would have you to know how-
"ever, that I have not forgot what you intimat-
"ed to me in several of your Letters, that if I
"brought back nothing else from the province
"but Brutus's friendship, that would be enough·
"let it be so, since you will have it so, yet it
"must always be with this exception, as far as
"it can be done, without my committing any
"wrong——[*e*]." In a third, "How, my dear
"Atticus! you who applaud my integrity and
"good conduct, and are vexed sometimes, you

A Urb 702.
Cic 56
Coss
SERV. SULPI-
CIUS RUIUS,
M. CIAU-
DIUS MAR-
CELLUS.

[*e*] Si Brutus putabit me
quaternas centesimas oportu-
ise decernere, qui in tota
provincia singulas observa-
rem, itaque edixissem, idque
etiam acerbissimis fœneratori-
bus probaretur, si præfectu-
ram negotiatori denegatam
quereretur, quod ego Torquato
nostro in tuo Lenio, Pompeio
ipsi in S Statio negavi, & iis
probavi, si equites deductos
moleste feret, accipiam e
quidem dolorem, mini illum
irasci, sed multo majorem,
non esse eum talem, qualem
putassem——Sed plane te intelligere volui, mihi non ex-
cidisse illud quod tu ad me
quibusdam litteris scripsisses,
si nihil aliud de hac Provincia
nisi illius benevolentiam de-
portassem, mihi id satis esse
Sit sane, quoniam ita tu vis
sed tamen cum eo credo,
quod sine peccato meo fiat——
ibid

"say,

A Urb 702
Cic 55
Coss
Serv Sulpi-
cius Rufus,
M Cl u-
dius Mar-
cellus

"say, that you are not with me, how can such
"a thing, as Ennius says, come out of your
"mouth, to desire me to grant troops to Scap
"tius, for the sake of extorting money? could
"you, if you were with me, suffer me to do
"if I would?——if I really had done such
"thing, with what face could I ever read again,
"or touch those books of mine, with which you
"are so much pleased [*f*]?" He tells him like
wise in confidence, that all Brutus's Letters to
him, even when he was asking favors, *were in-*
solent, churlish, and arrogant, without regard
to either what, or to whom he was writing, and
if he continued in that humor; you may love him
more, says he, *if you please, you shall have no more*
of me, but he will come, I believe, to a better
mind [*g*] But to shew, after all, what a real in
clination he had to oblige him, he never left
urging *King Ariobarzanes, till he had squeezed from*
him a hundred talents, in part of Brutus's debt, or
about twenty thousand pounds, the same summ
probably, which had been destined to Cicero him
self [*h*]

WHILE

... Ad eundem Atice,
laudiorint grati elegan-
tia nostra aulus es hoc cure tuo, inquit Ennius, ut e-
unues Scapio ad pecuniam
cogendam darem, me rogare?
an tu, si mecum esse qui
scribo morderi te interdum
quod non similis, patereris
me ea facere si vellem——
& ego a idebo egere unquam,
aut atorgere eos libros, quos
tu d laudas? si ale quid fe-
cro— ad Attico c

... Ad me etiam cum ro-
gat aliquid, contumaciter, ar
roganter, ἀκοινωνήτως sole
scribere—ib 6 1

Omnino (soli enim sumus)
nullus unquam ad me literas
mittit Brutus— in quibus non
esset arrogans, ἀκοινώνητος ali
qui —in quo tamen ille mi
hi r tum magis quam stoma
cum im movere solet Sed pla
ne par im cogitat, quid scri
bat, aut ad quem—ib 6 3

[*h*] Bruti tui causa, ut sæ
pe ad te scripsi, feci omnia
—Ariobarzanes non in Pom
peium

A Urb 702
Cic 56
Coss
Serv Sulpi-
cius Rufus,
M Clau-
dius Mar-
cellus.

WHILE he lay encamped in Cappadocia, expecting what way the Parthians would move, he
received an account, that they had taken a different rout, and were advanced to Antioch in Syria, where they held C Caffius blocked up, and
that a detachment of them had actually penetrat-
ed into *Cilicia, but were routed, and cut off by
those troops, which were left to guard the Country*
Upon this he presently decamped, and by *great
journies over mount Taurus,* marched in all haste
to poffess himself *of the passes of Amanus* a great
and strong mountain, lying between Syria and
Cilicia, and the common boundary of them both
By this march, and the approach of his army to
the neighbourhood of Syria, the Parthians being
discouraged, retired from Antioch, which gave
Caffius an opportunity *of falling upon them in their
retreat, and gained a considerable advantage, in
which one of their principal commanders, Ofaces,
was mortally wounded* [2]

IN the suspence of the *Parthian* war, which
the late disgrace of Craffus had made terrible at
Rome, Cicero's friends, who had no great opinion of his military talents, were in some pain
for his safety and success but now that he
found himself engaged, and pushed to the neces-

reum prolixior per ipsum,
quam per me in Brutum——
pro ratione pecuniæ liberius
est Brutus tractatus, quam
Pompeius Bruto curata hoc
anno talenta circiter c Pompeio in tex menfibus promi-
fa ec —— ioid ——

[ ] Itaque confilium iter in
Ciliciam feci per Tauri py-
lis Tarfum veni a d iii
Non Oct inde ad Amanum
contendi qui Syriam a Cili

cia in aquarum divortio divi-
dit—rumore adventus noftri,
& Caffio, qui Antiochia tene-
batur, animu acceffit, & Parthis tiro injectus est Itaque eos cedentes ab oppido
Caffius infecutus rem bene
gessit Qua in fuga magna
auctoritate Ofaces dux Parthorum vulnus accepit, eo-
quen ex paucis post diebus
Ad Att , 20

A Urb 702
Cic 56
Coſſ
SERV SULPI-
CIUS RUFUS,
M CLAU-
DIUS MAR-
CELLUS

fity of acting the General, he feems to have wanted neither the courage nor conduct of an experienced Leader In a Letter to Atticus, dated
from his Camp, " We are in great fpirits, fays
" he, and as our counfils are good, have no
" diftruft of an engagement we are fecurely en-
" camped, with plenty of provifions, and in
" fight almoft of Cilicia, with a fmall army in-
" deed, but, as I have reafon to believe, intire-
" ly well affected to me, which I fhall double
" by the acceffion of Deiotarus, who is upon the
" road to join me I have the allies more firmly
" attached to me, than any Governor ever had
" they are wonderfully taken with my eafinefs
" and abftinence, we are making new levies of
" Citizens, and eftablifhing magazines it there
" be occafion for fighting, we fhall not decline
" it, if not, fhall defend ourfelves by the
" ftrength of our pofts wherefore be of good
" heart, for I fee as much as if you were with
" me. the fympathy of your love for me [*k*]"

BUT the danger of the Parthians being over for
this feafon, Cicero refolved, that his labor fhould
not be loft, and his army difmiffed, without attempting fomething of moment The inhabitant
of the mountains, clofe to which he now lay, were
a fierce, untamed race of Banditti or Freebooters,
who had never fubmitted to the Roman power,
but lived in perpetual defiance of it, trufting to
their forts and caftles, which were fuppofed to
be impregnable from the ftrength of their fituation He thought it therefore of no fmall importance to the Empire, to reduce them to a ftate of
fubjection and, in order to conceal his defign
and take them unprovided he drew off his forces

[*k*] Ib 5 3.

On

A Urb 702.
Cic 56
Coss
Serv Sulpi-
cius Rufus
M Clau-
dius Mar
cellus

on pretence of marching to the diftant parts of
Cilicia, but after a day's journey ftopt fhort,
and having refrefhed his army, and left his bag-
gage behind, turned back again in the night with
the utmoft celerity, and reached Amanus *before*
day on the thirtieth of October. He divided his
troops among his four Lieutenants, and himfelf,
accompanied by his Brother, led up one part of
them, and fo coming upon the natives by fur-
prize, they eafily killed or made them all pri-
foners they took *fix ftrong forts, and burned* many more, but the Capital of the mountain *Era-
na*, made a brave refiftance, and held out from
break of day, to four in the afternoon Upon
this fuccefs Cicero was faluted Emperor, and fat
down again at the foot of the hills, where he
fpent *five days* in demolifhing the other ftrong
holds, and wafting the lands of thefe Moun-
taineers In this place his troops were lodged in
the *fame Camp which Alexander the great had
formerly ufed, when he beat Darius at Iffus, and
where there remained thofe altars, as the monument
of his victory, which here his name to that day* a
circumftance, which furnifhed matter for fome
pleafantry, in his Letters to his friends at Rome [ ]

VOL. II.   O   FRO.

[ ] Qui mons erat hof-
tium plenus fanatis oram
Hos ad iii idus Octob
magnum numerum hoftium
occidimus Caftella nu-
..ra, nocturno Pontinu ad
vefa, noftio matutino cepimus, incend nd Imperia-
toresappellati fumus Caftra
fuos dies habuimus, ea ip-
fa Ce contra Darium ha-
b.. apud Iffum Alexander,
hic velior fa Impera......

or, quam aut tu aut ego Ib
die qu que horam i di epto
& caco Amano, inde dif-
ceffimus —Ad Att 5 20

Expedito exercitu noc-
tu iter feci, ut iii Id
Octob cum luchefceret, in A-
manum afcenderem d. ibu
tifque cohortibus & auxilii,
cum aliis Quintus frater Le-
gatus, mecum...ad aliis C
Pontinus Legatis, aliis
V... nereis & M Anneius
Ita...

A U... ...
Cic 56
Con...
Sess...
...R...,
...d...
...

... of ... Amanus, he led his army to another
p... of the High-lands, the most disaffected to
the Roman name, possessed by a stout and free
people, who had never been subject even to the
... of the Country. Their chief Town was
called a Pindenissum, situated on a steep and craggy
... the place, fortified by nature and art, and provided with every thing necessary for defence. It
was the common ... of all deserters, and the
harbour of ... ..., and at that very time
was expecting and prepared to receive the Parthians. Cicero, resolving therefore to check
their insolence, and bring them under the Roman
yoke, laid siege to it in form, and though he
pushed it on with all imaginable vigor, and a
continual battery of his Engines, yet it cost him
a ... ... to reduce it to the necessity *of
surrendering at discretion.* The inhabitants were
... ... *fierce*, and when Cicero was writing the
account ... on his Tribunal, he had already raised
*about a hundred thousand pounds by that sale; all
the other plunder, excepting the horses, was given
to the Soldiers.* In his letter upon it to Atticus
*the P... ..., says he, surrendered to me on the
Saturday, after a siege of seven-and-forty days
... ... left got, ..., are these Pin...
... ... of their name before——
Hort...* ... *I hope I could get I out Cilicia into Æ*

Leg... ...es... in eroso ... ... cepimus, castellaque
... opp... tes oppressi... —— ... capta compura incend...
Frename utem quis fu... ... ... His rebus ita gest...
... unter fit ... , ... radicibus Amani...
... ... cau... —— ... ... apud aras Alex...
... sep quis... L... into quo in ... & in reliqu...
... partum ... ... circum, in ... ...
... an eluceo tumore ... ... Rard—— ... uso ... com
... ... m, tum ... —— ...p fam 1, ...
... ...

3   to

A Urb 702
Cic 56
Coſſ
Serv Sulpi-
cius Rufus,
M Clau-
dius Mar-
cellus

tolia or *Macedonia?* take this however for certain, that no man could do more, than I have done, with such an army, &c [*m*]. After this action, another neighbouring nation, *of the same ſpirit and fierce-neſs, called Tiburani, terrified by the fate of Pinde-niſſum, voluntarily ſubmitted, and gave hoſtages,* ſo that Cicero ſent his army into winter quarters un-der the *command of his Brother, into theſe parts of the province, which were thought the moſt turbu-lent* [*n*]

WHILE he was engaged in this expedition, Papirius Pætus, an eminent wit and Epicurean, with whom he had a particular intimacy and cor-reſpondence of facetious Letters, ſent him ſome military inſtructions in the way of raillery, to which Cicero anſwered in the ſame jocoſe man-ner " Your Letter, ſays he, has made me a " complete commander I was wholly ignorant " before of your great ſkill in the art of war; but

[*m*] Confectis his rebus ad Oppidum Eleutherocilicum, Pindeniſſum, exercitum ad-duxi quod cum eſſet altiſſi-mo & munitiſſimo loco, ab ... incoleretur, qui ne Re-gibus quidem unquam paru-iſſent cum & fugitivos reci-perent, & Parthorum adven-tum acerrime expectarent ad exiſtimationem imperii pertinere arbitratus ſum com-primere eorum audaciam —— vallo & foſſa circum-deci ſex caſtellis, caſtriſque maximis ſepſi, aggere, vi-neis, turribus oppugnavi, u-tiuſque tormentis multis, mul-tis ſagittariis, magno labore meo—ſeptimo quadrageſimo die rem confeci — ... Pin ... 4

Qui (malum) iſti Pindeniſ-ſæ? qui ſunt? inquies no-men audivi nunquam Quid ego faciam? potui Ciliciam, Ætoliam, aut Macedoniam redderе? hoc jam ſic habeto, nec hoc exercitu hic tanta ne-gotiа geri potuiſſe — &c — ad Att 5 20

Mancipia vænibant Satur-nalibus tertiis, cum hæc ſcribe-bam in tribunali, res erat ad HS cxx lb —

[*n*] His erant finitimi pari ſcelere & audacia Tiburani ab his, Pindeniſſo capto, ob-ſides accepi, exercitum in hi-berna dimiſi Q Fratrem negotio præpoſui ut in vicis aut captis aut malo pacatis exercitus collocaretur Ep-iſtam 15 4

" perceive.

A U-b 702
Cic 56
Coſſ
Ser Sulpi
cius Rufus,
M Clau
D Mar
cellus

" perceive, that you have read Pyrrhus and C
" nes. Wherefore I intend to follow your pre
" cepts, and withal, to have some ships in rea
" diness on the coaſt, for they deny that there
' can be any better defence againſt the Parthian
" horſe. But raillery apart, you little think,
" what a General you have to deal with, for in
' this government I have reduced to practice,
" what I had worn out before with reading, the
" whole inſtitution of Cyrus, &c [*o*]" Theſe
martial exploits ſpread Cicero's fame into Syria,
where Bibulus was juſt arrived to take upon him
the Command, but kept himſelf cloſe within the
gates of Antioch, *till the Country was cleared of all
the Parthians* his envy of Cicero's ſucceſs, and
title of EMPEROR, made him impatient to pur
chaſe the ſame honor by the ſame ſervice, *or the
Syrian ſide of the mountain Amanus* but he had
the misfortune to be repulſed in his attempt, with
the intire loſs of *the firſt Cohort, and ſeveral offi
cers of diſtinction,* which Cicero *calls an ugly blow
both for the time and the effect of it* [*p*]

Though Cicero had obtained what he calls *a
juſt victory at Amanus,* and, in conſequence of it,
the appellation of Emperor, which he aſſumed from
this time, *yet he ſent no public account of it to
Rome, till after the affair of Pindeniſſum,* an ex
ploit of more eclat and importance, for which he
expected *the honor of a Thankſgiving,* and began to
entertain hopes even of a Triumph. His public
Letter is loſt, but that loſs is ſupplied by a par

[*o*] Ep fam
[*p*] Tacuis ſi mo tum
no uch in gra A
tum Book Cicero olet
ap d ſil ron cu in nob s
ſe r Inucon Amano

ccep t harcolam in muſt
quar re At ille cohorte
pri n m totim perdidit
ſa c plag m odioſam acce
rat tum ie tum tempore —
ad At 5 20

A. Urb 702
Cic 56
Coſſ
SERV SULPI-
CIUS RUFUS,
M CLAU-
DIUS MAR-
CELLUS

ticular narrative of the whole action in a private Letter to Cato the deſign of paying this compliment to Cato, was to engage his vote and concurrence to the *decree of the Supplication*, and by the pains, which he takes to obtain it, where he was ſure of gaining his point without it, ſhews the high opinion which he had of Cato's authority, and how deſirous he was to have the teſtimony of it on his ſide But Cato was not to be moved from his purpoſe by compliment, or motives of friendſhip he was an enemy by principle to all decrees of this kind, and thought them beſtowed too cheaply, and proſtituted to occaſions unworthy of them ſo that when Cicero's Letters came under deliberation, though he ſpoke with all imaginable honor and reſpect of Cicero, and highly extolled both his *civil and military adminiſtration, yet he voted againſt the Supplication*, which was decreed however without any other diſſenting voice, except that of Favonius, who loved always to mimic Cato, and of Hirrus, who had a perſonal quarrel with Cicero yet when the vote was over, *Cato himſelf aſſiſted in drawing up the decree, and had his name inſerted in it*, which was the uſual mark of a particular approbation of the thing, and friendſhip to the perſon in whoſe favor it paſſed [*q*] But Cato's anſwer to Cicero's Letter will ſhew the temper of the

[*q*] Nunc publice literas . . . ter . . . Hirrus . . .
Romam mittere pr . . . t . . . ſ . . . d . . . .
Locuti ſunt, quam . . . . Ve . . . ſi declarat illud
dra . . . iſſſem Had . . . hui honor . . . ſupplicat . . .
Deinde Triumpho, quer . . . . . . dum . . . te . . . .
meo . . . Reipub. ſempe . . . . ben . . . ſ . . . Hic . . .
. . . . at . . . . Sen . . . . ne . . . . .
Vi . . . ad . . . . mis . . . .
I . . po . . . aſſenſus eſt mus, hoc . . . . in . . .
. . . . meus Favonius, a' . . . . . .

O 3

man, and the grounds on which he acted on this occasion

M Cato to M T. Cicero, Emperor

"In compliance with what both the Repub-
"lic and our private friendship require of me, I
"rejoice that your virtue, innocence, diligence,
"approved in the greatest affairs, exerts itself
"every-where with equal vigor, at home in the
"gown, abroad in arms I did all therefore,
"that I could do, agreeably to my own judge-
"ment, when in my vote and speech, I ascrib-
"ed to your innocence and good conduct the
"defence of your province, the safety of the
"kingdom and person of Ariobarzanes, the re-
"covery of the allies to their duty and affection
"to our Empire I am glad however, that a
"Supplication is decreed, if, where chance had
"no part, but the whole was owing to your con-
"summate prudence and moderation, you are
"better pleased, that we should hold ourselves
"indebted to the Gods, than to you But if you
"think that a Supplication will pave the way
"to a Triumph, and for that reason chuse, that
"fortune should have the praise, rather than
"yourself. yet a Triumph does not always fol-
"low a Supplication, and it is much more ho
"norable than any Triumph, for the Senate to
"decree, that a Province is preserved to the
"Empire by the mildness and innocence of the
"General, rather than by the force of arms,
"and the favor of the Gods This was the pur
"pose of my vote, and I have now employed
"more words, than it is my custom to do, that
"you might perceive, what I chiefly wish to testi
"fy no desirous I am to convince you, that in
"regard to your glory I had a mind to do what

                         'I took

A Urb 702
Cic 56
Coſſ
SERV SULPI-
CIUS RUFUS,
M CLAU
DIUS MAR-
CELLU.

" I took to be the moſt honorable for you , yet
" rejoice to ſee that done which you are the
" moſt pleaſed with   Adieu, and ſtill love me ,
" and agreeably to the courſe, which you have
" begun, continue your integrity and diligence
" to the allies, and the Republic [r].

CÆSAR was delighted to hear of Cato's ſtiff-
neſs, in hopes that it would create a coldneſs between him and Cicero , and in *a congratulatory
letter to Cicero,* upon the ſucceſs of his arms,
and *the Supplication* decreed to him, took care to
aggravate *the rudeneſs and ingratitude of Cato* [s].
Cicero himſelf was highly diſguſted at it, eſpecially when Cato ſoon afterwards decreed a *Supplication* to his Son-in-law, *Bibulus, who had done much
leſs to deſerve it* Cato, ſays he, *was ſhamefully
malicious, he gave me what I did not aſk, a character of integrity, juſtice, clemency, but denied me
what I did— yet this ſame man voted a Supplication
of twenty days to Bibulus pardon me, if I cannot
bear this uſage—* [t] yet, as he had a good opinion
of Cato in the main, and a farther ſum to make
to the Senate, in the demand of a Triumph, he
choſe to diſſemble his reſentment, and returned
him a civil anſwer, to ſignify his ſatisfaction and
thanks for what he had thought fit to do [u].

CICERO's campaign ended juſt ſo, as Cælius
had wiſhed in one of his Letters to him, *with
fighting enough to give a claim to the Laurel, yet*

[r] Ep fam 15 5
[s] Itaque Cæſar his litteris, quibus mihi gratulatur,
& omnia pollicetur quo modo excitat Catonis in me in-
gratiſſimi injuria, ad Att 7
2

[t] Aveo ſcire—Cato quid
qui quidem in me tur-

pter fuit malevolus D   it
integritatis, juſtitiæ, clemen-
tiæ idei teſtimonium, quod
non quærebam, quod poſtu-
labam, negavit— it hic idem
Bibulo dierum viginti Ig-
noſce mihi , non poſſum hæc
ferre—ibid —
[u] Ep fam 15 6

without

... ... *of a war with the Parthians* [x]
During theſe months of action, he ſent away *th.*
the young Ciceros, the ſon and nephew, to King
Deiotarus's *court, under the conduct of the King,*
... who came on purpoſe to inure them they
were kept ſtrictly to their books and exerciſe,
and made great proficiency in both, *though the*
c.. of ..., as Cicero ſays, *wanted the bit, the*
... the ſpur, their Tutor Dionyſius attended
them, *a man of great learning and probity, but,* as
his young pupils complained, *horribly paſſio-*
nate [y] Deiotarus himſelf was ſetting forward
to join Cicero with all his forces, upon the firſt
news of the *Parthian irruption* he had with him
thirty cohorts, of four hundred men each, armed
and accoutred after the Roman manner, with two
thouſand horſe, but the Parthian alarm being over,
Cicero ſent Couriers to meet him on the road, in
order to prevent his marching to no purpoſe, ſo far
from ... deſired [z] the old King however ſeems to have brought the children back

---

[x] U on aſti, na eſſ, ve-
le en ... ... annodo
... ... eſet
... ...
... ...
... ... 8
5 ... ...
... ... De-
... ... a s
... ... m n
re... ... ... os
... ... locum
... ... Ad
... ...
... ...
... ...
d.. ... ...
... ...
... ...

autem ... urt cum furentes,
ra c ... Sed homo nec doc
tior nec ſanctior fieri poteſt
It. C n

[z] Mihi tamen cum D-
otaro convenit, ut ille in
meis caſtris eſſet cum omnibus
ſ... copiis habet autem co-
hortes quadringenariis jolin
armatura triginta, equit..
deorum in —ib

Deitorum confeſtim jam
ad me venientem cum magno
& firmo equitatu & peditatu
cum omnibus ſuis copiis
... rt orum teci ron videt
... ... cui ... eſſet a reg
... ... —Ep ...m I, 4

again

again in perfon, for the opportunity of paying his
compliments, and fpending fome time with his
friend, for, by what Cicero intimates, they appear to have had an interview [*a*]

A Urb 702
Cic 56.
Coff
Serv Sulpi-
cius Rufus,
M Clau-
dius Mar-
cellus

The remaining part of Cicero's Government
was employed in the civil affairs of the Province
where his whole care was to eafe the feveral cities and diftricts of that exceffive load of debts,
in which the avarice and rapacioufnefs of former
governors had involved them   He laid it down
for the fixt rule of his adminiftration, not to fuffer *any money to be expended either upon himfelf or
his officers*   and when one of his Lieutenants, L.
Tullius, in paffing through the country, *exacted
only the forage and firing, which was due by law;
and that but once a day, and not, as all others had
done before, from every Town and Village through
which they paffed*, he was much out of humor, and
could not help complaining of it, *as a ftain upon
his Government, fince none of his people befides had
taken even a fingle farthing*.   All the wealthier
Cities of the Province ufed to pay to all their
Proconfuls large contributions *for being exempted
from furnifhing winter quarters to the army*   Cyprus
alone paid yearly on this fingle account *two hundred talents, or about forty thoufand pounds*   but
Cicero remitted this whole tax to them, which
alone made a vaft revenue, and applied all the
cuftomary perquifites of his office to the relief of
the oppreffed Province   yet for all his fervices
and generofity, which amazed the poor people,
he would accept no honors, but what were mere-
ly verbal, prohibiting all expenfive monuments,
as Statues, Temples, brazen horfes, &c   which,

[*a*] Decotaru, mihi narravi, &c ad Att 6 1 5 21

by

A Urb 702
Cic 56
Coff
SERV SULPI
CIUS RUFU,
M CLAU
DIL-MAR-
CELLUS

by the flattery of Asia, used to be erected of
course to all Governors, though ever so corrupt
and oppressive　While he was upon his visita
tion of the Asiatic Districts, there happened to be
a kind of famine in the country, yet where ever
he came, he not only provided for his family at
his own expence, but prevailed with the Mer
chants and Dealers, who had any quantity of
corn in their store-houses, *to supply the people with
it on easy terms* [b]; living himself, all the while,
*splendidly and hospitably, and keeping an open table,
not onely for all the Roman officers, but the Genius
of the Province* [c]　In the following Letter to
Atticus, he gives him a summary view of his
manner of governing

" I see, says he, that you are much pleased
" with my moderation and abstinence; but you
" would be much so, if you were with me
" especially at Laodicea, where I did wonders at

---

[b] Cave putes quicquam
homines magis unquam esse
mirato　quam nullum terun-
cium, me ob nerte provin-
ciam, sumtu factum esse nec
in Reip nec in quemquam
meorum, praeterquam in L
Tu'um Legatum　Is caete
roqui abstinens (sed Jul ia lege
transitans, semel tamen in
diem, non ut alii solebant
omnibus vicis facit ut mihi
excipiendus sit, cum terun-
cium rogo sumtus factum
Praeter cum accipit nemo
Has sordes a nostro Q Tan
nio accep mat—ad At 5 21

Civitates locuple es re in
hiberna milites reciperent
magnas pecunias cabant
C talenta Attica cc Qua

ex insula (non υπερβολ ικως
verissime loquor) nummus nul
lum me obtinente erogabi ur
Ob haec beneficia, quibus ob
stupescunt, nullos honores
mihi, nisi verborum, dec mi
siro Statuas, fana, τεθριππ
prohibeo—ib

Fames, quae erat in hac
mea Asia, nihi optanda fue
rit Quacunque ne fec,
nulla vi,—auctoritate & c
hortatione perfeci, ut & Gr
ci & Cives Romani, qui fru
mentum compresserant, mag
num numerum populis poll
cerentur—ib

[c] Ita vivom, ut max
mos sumptus facio Mirit
delector hoc instituto A
At 5 15

A Urb. 702.
Cic 56.
Coſſ
Serv Sulpi-
cius Rufus,
M Clau-
dius Mar-
cellus.

" the ſeſſions, which I have juſt held, for the
" affairs of the Dioceſes, from the thirteenth of
" February to the firſt of May. Many cities are
" wholly freed from all their debts ; many great-
" ly eaſed ; and all, by being allowed to govern
" themſelves by their own laws, have recovered
" new life. There are two ways, by which I
" have put them into a capacity of freeing, or
" of eaſing themſelves at leaſt of their debts ;
" the one is by ſuffering no expence at all to be
" made on the account of my government
" When I ſay none at all, I ſpeak not hyperbo-
" lically ; there is not ſo much as a farthing it
" is incredible to think, what relief they have
" found from this ſingle article The other is
" this, their own Greek Magiſtrates had ſtrange-
" ly abuſed and plundered them. I examined
" every one of them, who had born any office
" for ten years paſt they all plainly confeſſed,
" and, without the ignominy of a public con-
" viction, made reſtitution of the money, which
" they had pillaged · ſo that the people, who
" had paid nothing to our farmers for the preſent
" Luſtrum, have now paid the arrears of the
" laſt, even without murmuring This has
" placed me in high favour with the Publicans,
" a grateful ſet of men, you'll ſay I have really
" found them ſuch—the reſt of my juriſdiction
" ſhall be managed with the ſame addreſs and
" create the ſame admiration of my clemency
" and eaſineſs. There is no difficulty of acceſs
" to me, as there is to all other Provincial Go-
" vernors, no introduction by my Chamber-
" lain · I am always up before day, and walking
" in my Hall, with my doors open, as I uſed
" to do, when a Candidate at Rome. this is
" great and gracious here, though not at all
" troubleſom

A Urb 702
Cc 56
Co1

Ser Sulpi-
cius Rufus,
M Clau-
dus Mar-
cellus

" troublesom to me, from my old habit and
" discipline—&c " [d]

THIS method of governing gave no small
umbrage to Appius, who considered it as a re
proach upon himself, and sent several querulous
Letters to Cicero, because he had reversed some
of his constitutions " And no wonder, says Cice
" ro, that he is displeased with my manner, for
" what can be more unlike, than his administra
" tion and mine? under him the Province wa
" drained by expences and exactions, under me,
" not a penny levied for public or private use
" what shall I say of his Præfects, attendants,
" Lieutenants? of their plunders, rapines, inju
" ries? whereas now, there is not a single fami
" ly governed with such order, discipline, and
" modesty, as my Province, This some of Ap
" pius's friends interpret ridiculously, as if I was
" taking pains to exalt my own character, in
" order to depress his, and doing all this, not
" for the sake of my own credit, but of his dis
" grace [e] ' But the truth was, that, from
the time of his reconciliation with Appius, he
had a sincere desire to live on good terms with
him, as well out of regard to the splendor
of his birth, and fortunes, as to his great al
liances, for one of his daughters was married to
Pompey's son, and another to Brutus [f] so
tha

[ ] Ita e
Quæ in perfode
quæ quam cum
pute, exceunariese
provinciam,
searcetne pun
regum
pri fe

[f] Lgo Appium ut e
cum ime locum sum valde
igo Neque ab codib
capium en, ut simulta
tem deposui, senti jam
Pompei eam efe su
Brutum me ama intelli
gis Quid est caise, cu
non ontet est com
pl

A Urb 702
Cic 56
Coss
SERV SULPI-
CIUS RUFUS,
M CLAU-
DIUS MAR-
CELLUS

that, though their principles and maxims were totally different, yet he took care to do every thing with the greatest professions of honor and respect towards Appius, even when he found it necessary to rescind his decrees, considering him-self onely, he says, *as a second Physician called in to a case of sickness, where he found it necessary to change the method of cure, and when the Patient had been brought low by evacuations, and blood-letting, to apply all kinds of lenitive and restoring medicines* [g]

As soon as the Government of Cilicia was al-lotted to him, he acquainted Appius with it by Letter, begging of him, *that, as no man could suc-cede to it with a more friendly disposition than him-self, so Appius would deliver up the Province to him, in such a condition, as one friend could expect to re-ceive it from another* [h] in answer to which, Appius, having intimated some desire of an in-terview, Cicero took occasion to press it with much earnestness, as a thing of great service to them both, and, that it might not be defeated, gave him an account of all his stages and mo-tions, and offered to regulate them *in such a manner, as to make the place of their meeting the*

plecti hominem, florentem
state, opibus, honoribus, in-
genio, liberis, propinquis af-
finibus, amicis ——— Ep far
2 13

[g] Ut si Medicus, cum
aegrotus alio medico tradidus
transierit ei se ico qui
succederit, si quid ipse in
curando constituere mutare
ad Sic Appius, cum
te σ as provinciam erranti
quirenti miserit, de ad

Att 6 1

[h] Cum contra volu
tem meam — accuisser it
n hi cum imperio i Prov
cum re necess esset t
te e solutio ocur iebit,
q neque tio a me or, qu
ego iam, quince in p
succedere, tam ego id ro
p de i sc ta
let c in h i p
ram syhe t g

A Urb 702
Cic 56.
Coff
Serv Sulpi-
cius Rufus,
M Clau-
dius Mar-
cellus

most agreeable to Appius's convenience· but Appius being disgusted by the first edicts which Cicero published, resolved for that reason to disappoint him, and *as Cicero advanced into the Province, retired still to the remoter parts of it,* and contrived to come upon him at last so suddenly, that Cicero had not warning enough given *to go out and meet him,* which Appius laid hold of, as a fresh ground of complaint against Cicero's pride, for refusing that common piece of respect to him [*i*]

THIS provoked Cicero to expostulate with him, with great spirit——" I was informed, says " he, by one of my Apparitors, that you com " plained of me for not coming out to meet you, " I despised you, it seems, so as nothing could " be prouder—— when your servant came to me " near midnight, and told me, that you would " be with me at *Iconium* before day, but could " not say, by which road, when there were " two, I sent out your friend Varro by the one, " and Q Lepta, the Commander of my Artil- " lery, by the other, with instructions to each " of them, to bring me timely notice of your " approach, that I might come out in person to " meet you. Lepta came running back presently " in all haste to acquaint me, that you had already " passed by the Camp, upon which I went di " rectly to *Iconium,* where you know the rest " Did I then refuse to come out to you? to Ap " pius Claudius, to an Emperor, then, ac " cording to ancient custom; and above all

[*i*] —— me liberte ad eam ... nofter, cum me ad par ... m provincie prim ... ... re videt, profec'us eſſe enitrum, quo te ma ... Tarium uſque Laod ... â——ad velle ... ... rarer 17

                                " to

"to my friend? I, who of all men am apt to
"do more in that way than becomes my digni-
"ty? but enough of this. The same man told
"me likewife, that you faid, What! Appius
"went out to meet Lentulus, Lentulus to Ap-
"pius, but Cicero would not come out to Ap-
"pius Can you then be guilty of fuch imper-
"tinence? a man, in my judgement, of the
"greateft prudence, learning, experience, and
"I may add politenefs too, which the Stoics
"rightly judge to be a virtue? do you imagine,
"that your Appius's and Lentulus's are of more
"weight with me than the ornaments of virtue?
"before I had obtained thofe honors, which, in
"the opinion of the world, are thought to be
"the greateft, I never fondly admired thofe
"names of yours I looked indeed upon thofe,
"who had left them to you, as great men, but
"after I had acquired, and born the higheft
"Commands, fo as to have nothing more to de-
"fire, either of honour or glory, I never indeed
"confidered myfelf as your fuperior, but hoped,
"that I was become your equal nor did Pom-
"pey, whom I prefer to all men, who ever
"lived, nor Lentulus, whom I prefer to my-
"felf, think otherwife if you however are of
"a different opinion, it will do you no harm to
"read with fome attention what Athenodorus
"fays on this fubject, that you may learn where-
"in true nobility confifts But to return to the
"point I defire you to look upon me, not one-
"ly as your friend, but a moft affectionate one ·
"it fhall be my care by all poffible fervices to con-
"vince you, that I am truly fo. but if you have
"a mind to let people fee, that you are lefs con-
"cerned for my intereft, in my abfence, than
                              " my

A Urb 702.
Cic 56
Coff
SERV SULPI-
CIUS RUFUS,
M CLAU-
DIUS MAR-
CELLUS.

A Urb oe
Cie 50
Coss

Serv Sulpi-
ciu Rufus,
M Clau
d u Mar-
cellus

" my pains for yours deserved, I free you from
" that trouble,

" *For I have friends enough to serve and love*
" *Both me and mine, and above all Great Jove*

Ib 1 174

" but if you are naturally querulous, you sha'l
" not still hinder my good offices and wishes for
' you · all that you will do, is to make me less
" sollicitous how you take them   I have writ
" ten this with more than my usual freedom,
" from the consciousness of my duty and affec
" tion, which being contracted by choice and
" judgement, it will be in your power to preserve,
" as long as you think proper   Adieu [k]"

CICERO's Letters to Appius make one book
of *his familiar Epistles*, the greatest part of which
are of the expostulatory kind, on the subject of
their mutual jealousies and complaints in this slip
pery state of their friendship, an accident happened
at Rome, which had like to have put an end to it
His daughter Tullia, after parting from her se
cond husband Crassipes, as it is probably though,
by a letter [l], was married in her father's absence
to a third, P Cornelius Dolabella   several partie
had been offered to her, and among them Ti
Claudius Nero, who afterwards married Livia,
whom Augustus took away from him   *Nero made
his proposals to Cicero in Cilicia*, who referred
him to the women, to whom he had left the

---

[k] Fam 3 [...]   him as the only Senato, o
[l] What concerns his [...] es Ih sus, to whom he d
re en is, hat Cic pro [...] not think it to wri [...]
[...] to have been alive t [...] t affair of his *sup* [...]
t [...] e, and under Cice o [...] at 7 1
c [...] we ch o s

managen [...]

management of that affair, but before those
overtures reached them, they had made up the
match with Dolabella, *being mightily taken with
his complaisant and obsequious address* [m] He
was a nobleman of *Patrician descent, and of great
parts and politeness*, but of a violent, daring,
ambitious temper, warmly attached to Cælar,
and by a life of pleasure and expence, which the
prudence of Tullia, it was hoped, would correct,
greatly diftreffed in his fortunes, which made
Cicero very uneafy, when he came afterwards to
know it [n]   Dolabella, at the time of his marriage, for which he made way also *by the divorce
of his wife* [o], gave a proof of his enterpri-
fing genius, by impeaching Appius Claudius, *of
practices against the state, in his government of C-
lia, and of bribery and corruption in his suit for
the Consulship*. This put a great difficulty upon
Cicero, and made it natural to fufpect, that he
privately favored the impeachment, where *the
Accufer was his son-in-law* but in clearing himfelf of it to Appius, though he diffembled a little

A Urb 702
Cic 56
Cofſ
Serv Sulpi-
cius Rufus,
M. Clau-
dius Mar-
cellus

[m] Ego dum in provincia
omnibus rebus App um orno,
fubito fum factus accufatoris
ejus focer — fed crede mihi
nihil minus putaram ego, qui
Ti Nerone, qui mecum
erant, certos homines ad
mulieres miferam, qui Ro-
mam venerunt factis fponfa-
libus Sed hoc fpero melius
Mores quidem valde intel-
ligo delectari obfequio & co-
mitate adolefcentis —ad Att
6

[o] Gener eft fuavis——
fummum is vel ingenii, vel
humanitatis, fatis Reliqua

que noftra ferenda Ad Att
7 3
Dolabellam a te gaudeo
primum laudari, deinde e-
tiam amari Nam ea quæ
fperas Tulliæ mea prudentia
poffe temperari fcio cui tuæ
epiftolæ refpondeant I p
fam 2 15 it 8 13
Hæc oblectabit fpecula,
Dolabellim meum fore ab iis
moleftiis, quas libertate fua
contraxerit, liberum—ib 16
[o] Illud mihi occurrit quod
inter poftulationem, & nominis delationem uxor a Dolabella difceffit ——ib 8 6

A Urb 702
Cic 56
Coſſ
SERV SULPI
CIUS RUͨUs,
M CLAͧU-
DIͧUsMͧAR
CELLUS

perhaps in diſclaming any part or knowledge of that match, yet he was very ſincere, in pro-feſſing himſelf an utter ſtranger to the impeach ment, and was in truth greatly diſturbed at it But as from the circumſtance of his ſucceding to Appius in his Government, he was of all men the moſt capable of ſerving or hurting him at the trial . ſo Pompey, who took great pains to ſkreen Appius, was extremely deſirous to engage him on their ſide, *and had thoughts of ſending one of h s ſons to him for that purpoſe* but Cicero ſaved them that trouble, by declaring early and openly for Appius, and promiſing every thing from the Province that could poſſibly be of ſervice to him, which he thought himſelf obliged to do the more forwardly, *to prevent any ſuſpicion of trea-chery to his friend, on the account of his new alli ance* [p] ſo that Appius, inſtead of declining a trial, contrived to bring it on as ſoon as he could, and with that view, having dropt his pretenſions to a Triumph, entered the City, and offered himſelf to his Judges, before his Accuſer was prepared for him, and was acquitted without any difficulty of both the indictments.

In a little time after his trial he was choſen *Cenſor*, together with Piſo, *Cæſor's father-in-law*, the laſt who bore that office during the freedom of the Republic *Clodius's law*, mentioned a

[p] Pompeius dicitur valde pro App o laborare, ut eti-am patent alterutrum de filis ad te miſſurum Ib d ——
Poſt hoc nego um autem & temeritatem roſſi. Dola-bellæ deprecatorum me pro il us periculo propeo—ib 2 13
Tamen hæc mihi affinitate

nunciata non majore eſ dem ſtudio, ſed ac us, apu tius, ſignificantius dignitatem tuam defendiſſ m — nam t vetus noſtra ſmultas ai ſt mulabat me, ut caveren ne cui ſuſpicionem ſ te r conciliata gratiæ darem i affinitas novam curiam affo cavendi Ib 3 12

bow

bove, which had greatly reftrained the power of thefe Magiftrates, was repealed the laft year by Scipio, the Conful, and their ancient authority reftored to them [q], which was now exercifed with great rigor by Appius who though really a libertin, and remarkable for indulging himfelf in all the luxury of life, yet by an affectation of feverity, hoped to retrieve his character, and pafs for an admirer of that ancient difcipline, for which many of his anceftors had been celebrated. Cælius gives a pleafant account of him to Cicero, "Do you know, fays he, that the Cenfor Ap-"pius is doing wonders amongft us, about fta-"tues and pictures, the number of our acres, "and the payment of debts? he takes the Cen-"forfhip for foap or nitre, and thinks to fcour "himfelf clean with it, but he is miftaken, for ' while he is laboring to wafh out his ftains, he "opens his very veins and bowels, and lets us "fee him the more intimately run away to us "by all the Gods, to laugh at thefe things. ' Drufus fits Judge upon Adultery, by the ' Scantinian law · Appius on ftatues and pic-"tures [r]" But this vain and unfeafonable attempt of reformation, inftead of doing any good, ferved onely *to alienate people from Pompey's caufe*, with whom Appius was ftrictly allied · whilft his colleague Pifo, who forefaw that ef-fect, chofe to fit ftill, and fuffer him to *difgrace*

A Urb 702.
Cic 56
Coff
Serv Sulpi-
cius Ruius,
M Clau-
dius Mar-
cellus.

[q] Dio, p 147.
[r] Scis Appium Cenfo-rem hic oftenta facere? de fignis & tabulis, de agri mo-do, & ære alieno accerrime a-gere? perfuafum eft ei, Cen-furam lomentum aut nitrum effe Errare mihi videtur

Nam fordes eluere vult, ve-nas fibi omnes & vifcera a-perit Curre per Deos, & quam primum hæc rifum ve-ni Legis Scantiniæ judici-um apud Drufum fieri Ap-pium de tabulis & fignis age-re —Ep fam 8 14

the

A Urb 702
Cic 56
Coff
SEPT SULPI
CIUS RUFUS,
M CLAU-
DIUS MAR-
CELLUS

the Knights and Senators at pleasure, which he did with great freedom, and among others, turned Salluft, *the Hiftorian, out of the Senate*, and was hardly reftrained from putting the fame affront upon Curio, which added ftill more friends and ftrength to Cæfar [s]

As to the public news of the year, the grand affair, that engaged all people's thoughts, was the expectation of a breach between Cæfar and Pompey, which feemed now unavoidable, and in which all men were beginning to take part, and ranging themfelves on the one fide or the other On Pompey's, there was *a great majority of the Senate and the Magiftrates, with the better fort of all ranks on Cæfar's, all the criminal and obnoxious, all who had fuffered punifhment, or deferved it, the greateft part of the youth, and the City mob, fome of the popular Tribunes, and all who were oppreffed with debts, who had a Leader fit for their purpofe, daring, and well provided, and wanting nothing but a caufe.* This is Cicero's account, and Cælius's is much the fame *I fee*, fays he, *that Pompey will have the Senate, and all who judge of things, Cæfar, all who live in fear and uneafinefs, but there is no comparifon between their armies* [t] Cæfar had put an end to the *Gallic war*, and reduced the whole Province to the *Roman* yoke. bu

---

[s] Dio l 40 p 150

[t] Hoc vidco, cum homine audacifumo, paratifumoque negotium efle omnes damnatos, omnes igno-minia affecto, omnes damna-tione ignominiaque dignos hæc facere Omnem fere juventutcm omnem illam urbanam ac perditam plebem, Tribunos valentes — omnes, qui ære alieno premantur—

caufam folam illa caufa non habet, cæteris rebus abund ————ad Att 7 3

In hac difcordia video Cn Pompcium fenatum, qui-que res judicant, fecum ha-buturum ad Cæfarem omnes qui cum timore aut mala vivant ad Cæfarem acced 10s Exercitum confe-dum non effe Ep fam 8 14

thoug'

A Urb 702
Cic 56
Coſſ
SERV SULPI-
CIUS RUFUS,
M CLAU-
DIUS MAR-
CELIUS

though his commiſſion was near expiring, he ſeemed to have no thoughts of giving it up, and returning to the condition of a private ſubject he pretended, *that he could not poſſibly be ſafe, if he parted with his army,* eſpecially, while *Pompey held the Province of Spain, prolonged to him for five years* [u] The Senate, in the mean while, in order to make him eaſy, had conſented *to let him take the Conſulſhip, without coming to ſue for it in perſon ·* but when that did not ſatisfy him, the Conſul, M Marcellus, one of his fierceſt ene-mies, moved them *to abrogate his Command di-rectly, and appoint him a ſucceſſor ; and ſince the war was at an end, to oblige him to disband his troops, and to come likewiſe in perſon to ſue for the Conſulſhip, nor to allow the freedom of the City to his Colonies beyond the Po* this related particular-ly to *a favorite Colony, which Cæſar,* when Con-ſul, had ſettled *at Comum, at the foot of the Alps, with the freedom of the City granted to it by the Va-tinian law* [x] All the other Colonies on that ſide of the Po had before obtained from Pom-pey's father *the rights of Latium,* that is, the free-dom of Rome to thoſe who had born *an annual Magiſtracy* in them but M Marcellus, out of a ſingular enmity to Cæſar, would allow no ſuch right to *his Colony of Comum,* and having caught *a certain Comenſian Magiſtrate,* who was acting *the Citizen at Rome,* he ordered him to be ſeized, and *publicly whipt,* an indignity, from which all Citizens were exempted by law, *bidding the man go and ſhew theſe marks of his Citizenſhip to Cæ-*

---

[u] Cæſari autem perſua-ſum eſt, ſe ſalvum eſſe non poſſe, ſi ab exercitu receſſe-rit Fert illam tamen con-

ditionem, ut ambo exercitus tradant Ibid

[x] Sueton J Cæſ c 28. Strabo, l 5 326

ſar.

A U D 702
Cc 56.
Coſſ
SER. SULPI-
CIUS RUFUS,
M CLAU-
DIUS MAR
CELLUS

ſay [y] Cicero condemns this act as violent and unjuſt, Marcellus, ſays he, *behaved ſhamefully in the caſe of the Comenſes for if the man had never been a Magiſtrate, he was yet of a colony beyond the Po, ſo that Pompey will not be leſs ſhock'd at it then Cæſar himſelf* [z]

THE other Conſul, Serv Sulpicius, was of a more candid and moderate temper, and being unwilling to give ſuch a handle for a civil war, oppoſed and over-ruled the motions of his Colleague, by the help of ſome of the Tribuns nor was Pompey himſelf diſpoſed to procede ſo violently, or to break with Cæſar on that foot, but thought it more plauſible to let his term run out, and his command expire of itſelf, and ſo throw upon him the odium of turning his arms againſt his Country, if he ſhould reſolve to act againſt the Senate and the laws This counſil prevailed after many warm conteſtations, in which the ſummer was chiefly ſpent, and a decree was offered on the laſt of September, " That the Conſuls ' elect, L Paullus and C Marcellus ſhould " move the Senate on the firſt of march, to ſet " tle the Conſular Provinces, and if any Ma " giſtrate ſhould interpoſe, to hinder the effect " of their decrees, that he ſhould be deemed an " enemy to the Republic, and if any one actu " ally interpoſed, that this vote and reſolution " ſhould be entered into the journals, to be con " ſidered ſome other time by the Senate, and " laid alſo before the people " But four of the Tribuns gave their joint negative to this decree, C. Cælius, L. Vinicius, P Cornelius, and C V.

[y] Appian 2 443

[z] Marcellus fœde de Comenſi etſi ille Magiſtratum non geſſerit, erat tamen tranſ padanus Ita mihi videtur non minus ſtomachi noſtro, ac Cæſari moviſſe Ad At 5 11

bius

bius Panſa In the courſe of theſe debates, Pompey, who affected great moderation in whatever
he ſaid of Cæſar, was teized and urged on all
ſides to make an explicit declaration of his ſentiments When he called it unjuſt to determine
any thing about Cæſar's Government, *before the*
firſt of march, the term preſcribed to it by law,
being aſked, " What, if any one ſhould then
" put a negative upon them, *he ſaid,* there was
" no difference whether Cæſar refuſed to obey
" the decrees of the Senate, or provided men
" to obſtruct them What, *ſays another,* if he
" ſhould inſiſt on being Conſul, and holding his
" Province too ? What, *replied Pompey,* if my
" ſon ſhould take a ſtick and cudgel me [a] ?" intimating the one to be as incredible, and as impious alſo as the other

Cicero's friend Cælius obtained *the Ædileſhip* this Summer from his Competitor Hirrus,
the ſame who had oppoſed Cicero in the Augu-
rate, and whoſe diſappointment gave occaſion to
many jokes between them in their Letters [b] In
this magiſtracy, it being cuſtomary to procure
wild beaſts of all kinds from different parts of the
Empire for the entertainment of the City, *Cælius
begged of Cicero to ſupply him with Panthers from
Cilicia, and to employ the Cibarites,* a people of
his Province famed for hunting, *to catch them :
for it would be a reflection upon you,* ſays he, *when
Curio had ten Panthers from that Country, not to*

[a] Cum interrogaretur, quit alius, & Conſul eſſe &
ſi qui tum intercederent dix- exercitum habere volit, at
it hoc nihil intereſſe, utrum ille quam clementer Quid
C Cæſar Senatui dicto audi- ſi filius meus fuſtem mihi im-
ens futurus non eſſet, an pa- pingere volet ? Ep fam 8 8
raret, qui Senatum decernere [b] Lp fam 2 9, 10 11.
non pateretur Quid ſi in- 8 2, 3, 9

let

A Urb 702
C 56
Coſſ
Serv Sul pi-
cius Ru us,
M Cl l-
r Mar-
cellus

let me have many more. He recommends to him at the fame time M Feridius, *a Roman Knight,* who had an Eftate in Cilicia, charged with fome fervices or quit-rent to the neighbouring Cities, which he begs of him *to get difcharged fo as to make the lands free* [c] he feems alfo to have defired Cicero's confent to his levying certain contributions upon the Cities of his Province, *towards defraying the expence of his fhews at Rome,* a prerogative, which the Ædiles always claimed, and fometimes practifed, though it was denied to them by fome Governors, and particularly by Quintus Cicero in Afia, upon the advice of his Brother [d] in anfwer to all which, Cicero replied, " that he was forry to find that his actions " were fo much in the dark, that it was not yet " known at Rome, that not a farthing had been " exacted in his Province, except for the pay " ment of juft debts that it was neither fit for " him to extort money, nor for Cælius to take " it, if it were defigned for himfelf and admo- " nifhed him who had undertaken the part of " accufing others, to live himfelf with more cau- " tion — and as to Panthers, that it was not con " fiftent with his character to impofe the charge " of hunting them upon the poor people [e]."

[ ] Fere litteris omnibus t ce Patreris fcripfi Turpe   eur Paticum Curiori decem Pantheras mittie, te ron multi pa tibus plures, &c Ep fam 8, 9

M Feridum — tibi commendo Agros quos t uctu aio habent civitates vult tio offic o, cuod tibi facile & rei uin factu eft, immures effe——ib

[d] Ad Quint Irat 1 1 § 9

[e] Refcripfi, me molefte ferre, fi ego in tenebris litrem, nec audiretur Romæ, null min mea provinci i num mum nifi in as alienum erogari, docuique nec mihi conciliare pecuniam licere, re i li capere, monuique can, Sc ad Att 1

But though he would not break his rules for the
ſake of his friend, yet he took care to provide
Panthers for him at his own expence, and ſays
pleaſantly upon it, *that the Beaſts made a ſad com-*
plaint againſt him, and reſolved to quit the country,
ſince no ſnares were laid in his Province for any other
Creature but themſelves [f]

A Urb 702
Cic 56
Coſſ
SERV SULPI
CIUS RUFUS,
M CLAU-
DIUS MAR-
CELLUS

CURIO likewiſe obtained the *Tribunate* this
Summer, which he fought with no other deſign,
as many imagined, than for the opportunity of
mortifying Cæſar, againſt whom he had hitherto
acted with great fierceneſs [g]   But Cicero, who
knew from the temper and views of them both,
how eaſy it would be to make up matters between
them, took occaſion to write a congratulatory
Letter to him upon this advancement, in which
he exhorts him with great gravity, " to conſider
" into what a dangerous criſis his Tribunate had
" fallen, not by chance, but his own choice,
" what violence of the times, what variety of
" dangers hung over the Republic, how uncer-
" tain the events of things were, how change-
" able mens minds, how much treachery and
" falſhood in human life—he begs of him there-
" fore to beware of entering into any new coun-
" fils, but to purſue and defend, what he him-
" ſelf thought right, and not ſuffer himſelf to be
" drawn away by the advice of others"—referring
without doubt to M Antony, the chief companion and corrupter of his youth   in the conclu-
ſion, he conjures him, to " employ his preſent

---

[f] De Pantheris, per eos,
qui venari ſolent, igitur man-
dato meo diligenter ſed mira paucitas eſt & eas, quæ
ſunt, valde aiunt queri quod
nihil cuiquam inſidiarum in
mea provincia niſi ſibi fiat

——Ep fam 2 11

[g] Sed ut ſpero & volo,
& ut ſe fert ipſe Curio, bonos & ſenatum malit To-
tus ut nunc eſt, hoc ſcaturit
——Ib 8 4

" power

" power to hinder his Provincial trouble from
" being prolonged by any new act of the S-
" nate —[h] Cicero's suspicions were soon con
firmed by Letters from Rome, whence Cæ[?]
sent h[?]m word of *Curio's changing sides, and de
claring himself for Cæsar* in answer to wh[?]ch,
Cicero says, *the last page of your Letter in your
own hand really touched me* What do you say [?]
*Curio turned advocate for Cæsar? who would have
thought it besides my self? for let me die, if I'd
not a put [?]! Good Gods, how much do I long to [?]
laughing with you at Rome* [i]?

A Urb -o3. THE new Consuls being Cicero's particular
Cic 57 friends he wrote congratulatory Letters to them
Coff both upon their election, in which he begged t[?]
L Æ ILIUS *concurrence of their authority to the decree of b[?]
PAULLUS, *supplication*, and what he had more at heart, *the
C CLAUDIUS *they would not suffer any prolongation of his amial
MARCELLUS *term* in which they readily obliged him, and
received his thanks also by letter for that favor [k].
It was expected, that something decisive would
now be done in relation to *the Two Gauls*, and
the appointment *of a successor to Cæsar*, since
both the Consuls were supposed to be his enemies
but all attempts of that kind were still frustrated
by the intrigues of Cæsar, for when C Marcellus
began to renew the same motion, which his kins
man had made the year before, he was obstruct
ed by *his Colleague Paulus, and the Tribun Curio,
whom Cæsar had privately gained by immense bribes,
to suffer nothing prejudicial to his interest to pass
during their Magistracy* [l] He is said to have

[i] Ep fam 2 7

[?] Extrem pagella [?]
git me tuo chirographo
Quid ai Cæsarem [?] de-
[?] Curio quisnoc pla-

ret præter me? nam ita [?]
vam putavi—ib 13

[k] Ep fam 15 7, 1[?]
11, 12, 13

[l] Sueton J Cæs 20
g[?]

given Paullus *about three hundred thousand pounds,* and to *Curio much more* [*m*] The firſt wanted it to defray the charges of *thoſe ſplendid buildings,* which he had undertaken to raiſe at his own coſt the ſecond, to clear himſelf *of the load of his debts, which amounted to about half a million* [*n*] for he had waſted his great fortunes ſo effectually in a few years, *that he had no other revenue left,* as Pliny ſays, *but in the hopes of a civil war* [*o*] Theſe facts are mentioned by all the Roman writers,

A Urb 703.
Cic 57
Coſſ
L ÆMILIUS PAULIUS,
C CLAUDIUS MARCELIUS.

> *Momentumque fuit mutatus Curio rerum,*
> *Gallorum captus ſpoliis & Cæſaris auro—*
>
> Lucan 4 819
>
> *Caught by the ſpoils of Gaul, and Cæſar's gold,*
> *Curio turn'd traitor, and his country ſold*

and Servius applies that paſſage of Virgil, *Vendidit hic auro patriam,* to the caſe of Curio's *ſelling Rome to Cæſar.*

CICERO in the mean time was expecting with impatience the expiration of his annual term, but before he could quit the Province, he was obliged to ſee the account of all the money, which had paſſed through his own or his officers hands, ſtated and balanced, *and three fair copies provided, two to be depoſited in two of the principal Cities of his Juriſdiction, and a third in the Treaſury at Rome* That his whole adminiſtration therefore might be of a piece, he was very exact and punctual in acquitting himſelf of this duty, *and would not indulge his officers in the uſe of any*

[*m*] Appian l ii p 442
[*n*] Sexcenties Seſtertium * æris alieni* Val Max 9 1
[*o*] Qui nihil in cenſu ha-

buerit, præter diſcordiam principum Plin Hiſt l 36. 15

public

A Uro reg
Cic 5-
Coff
L Æ i ius
Paulius,
C Claudius
Marcellus

pil money beyond the legal time, or above the form prescribed by law, as appears from his Letters to some of them who desired it [*p*] Out of the annual revenue, which was decreed to him for the use of the Province, *he remitted to the Treasury all that he had not expended, to the amount of above eight hundred thousand pounds*

" This, says he, makes my whole company
" groan, they imagine that it should have
" been divided among themselves, as if I ough
" to have been a better manager for the treasu
" ries of Phrygia and Cilicia, than for our own
" But they did not move me, for my own ho
" nor weighed with me the most yet I have
" not been wanting to do every thing in my
" power that is honorable and generous to them
" all [*q*] "

His last concern was, to what hands he should commit the Government of his Province upon his leaving it, since there was no successor appointed by the Senate on account of the heats among them about the case of Cæsar, which disturbed all their debates, and interrupted all other

[*p*] Iam certe me pro[m]is acceptarum rerum omnis præceptum —— id est quod in hoc genere cujusun po[s]m commodare ad Id sum 2 1[5]

Illud omen certe iam est quod reti[n]ebat, ut a pud cives civitatis inducen iem, & Anati alism quæ nobis maxim[e] de[be]ntur —— rationes confectas & consu datas deponerimus, &c ib 5 20

[*q*] Cum enim rectum & glorio[s]um putarem e[ss]e no

sumptu, qui mihi decretu est Me C Cælio Quæst[o] i relinquere annuum, refecit in æ arium ad H S cro, in gemuit nostra cohors, omne illud putans distribui sibi o por[t]ere ut ego amicior in ven[t]er Phrygum aut Ci c[i]m ararim, quam nost[r]o Sed me non moverunt, na[m] n[o]a laus apud me plurimum ralut Nec tamen quicquam ho[no]rifice in quemquam he potu[i]t, quod prætermiserim ad Ait 7 1

busineſs   He had no opinion of his Quæſtor, A Urb 703.
C Cælius, a young man of noble birth, but of   Cic 57
no great virtue or prudence, and was afraid af- Coſſ
ter his glorious adminiſtration, that by placing ſo   L ÆMILIUS
great a truſt in one of his character, he ſhould C CLAUDIUS
expoſe himſelf to ſome cenſure   But he had no   MARCELLUS
body about him *of ſuperior rank*, who was willing
to accept it, and did not care to force it upon his
Brother, left that might give a handle *to ſuſpect
him of ſome intereſt or partiality in the choice* [*r*]
He dropt the province therefore, after ſome deliberation, into Cælius's hands, and ſet forward
immediately upon his journey towards Italy

But before he quitted Aſia, he begged of Atticus by Letter to ſend him a particular detail of all
the news of the City— " There are odious re-
" ports, ſays he, about Curio and Paullus, not
" that I ſee any danger, while Pompey ſtands,
" or I may ſay indeed, while he ſits, if he has
" but his health, but in truth, I am ſorry for
" my friends Curio and Paullus If you are now
" therefore at Rome, or as ſoon as you come
' thither, I would have you ſend me a plan of
' the whole Republic, which may meet me on
" the road, that I may form myſelf upon it, and
' reſolve what temper to aſſume on my coming
" to the City for it is ſome advantage not to
" come thither a mere ſtranger [*s*] " We ſee
                                    what

[*r*] Ego de provincia decedens Quæſterem Cælium
reponi pro ciæ Parem?
quem at Quæſtorem, at
nobilem adoleſcentem, at
omnium fere exemplo Ne-
que erat ſuperiore honore u-
ſus quem præficerem Pon-
tius multo ante diſceſſerat

A Quinto fratre impetrari
non poterat quem tamen ſi
reliquiſſem, dicerent iniqui,
non me placit poſt annum, ut
Senatus voluiſſet, de provin
cia deceſſiſſe,quoniam alteram
me reliquiſſem Ep fam 2
15 vit it ad Att o 5,6
[*s*] Huc odioſa afferaban-
                        tur

A Urb 703
Cic 57
Coſ
L Æmilius
Paullus
C Claudius
Marcellus

what a confidence he placed in Pompey, on whom indeed their whole proſpect either of peace with Cæſar, or of ſucceſs againſt him, depended as to the intimation about his health, it is expreſſed more ſtrongly in another Letter, *All our hopes, ſays he, hang upon the life of one man, who is attacked every year by a dangerous fit of ſickneſs* [t]. His conſtitution ſeems to have been peculiarly ſubject to fevers, the frequent returns of which, in the preſent ſituation of affairs, gave great apprehenſion to all his party in one of thoſe fevers, which threatened his life for many days ſucceſſively, *all the Towns of Italy put up public prayers for his ſafety*, an honor, which had never been paid before to any man, while Rome was free [u].

UPON taking leave of Cilicia, Cicero paid a viſit to Rhodes, *for the ſake*, he ſays, *of the children* [x]. His deſign was to give them a view of that floriſhing Iſle, and a little exerciſe perhaps in that celebrated School of eloquence, where he himſelf had ſtudied with ſo much ſucceſs under Molo Here he received *the news of Hortenſius's death* [y], which greatly affected him,

---

tur de Carcere, de Paullo ronque totum periculum videerim in e Pompeio, vel etam federie, valeat modo Sed mehercule Curionis & Antoni meum tam ſumonium recemuole Forſan igitur in totæ Rep. summe Roma aut certe veſt modo ſum ni civis is. ne Incumbe ſ igerepoſ fes, &c ad Att 6 3 . . . Hic . . . omnes quoteum . . . regi . . . . ſpes habemus——— ibid 8 2

[u] Quo quidem tempore univerſa Italia vota pro ſalute ejus, primo omnium civium ſuſcepit ——— Vell Pat 2 48 Dio, p 155

[x] Rhodum volo puerorum cauſa Ad Att 6 ·

[y] Cum e Cilicia deceden Rhodum veniſſen & communi de Q Hortenſii morte ehet allatum, opinione omnium majorem animo cepi . . . . . . ——— Brut init

by

by recalling to his mind the many glorious struggles that they had fustained together at the Bar,
in their competition for the prize of eloquence
Hortenfius reigned abfolute in the Forum, when
Cicero firft entered it, and as his fuperior fame
was the chief fpur to Cicero's induftry, fo the
fhining fpecimen, which Cicero foon gave of himfelf, made Hortenfius likewife the brighter for it,
by obliging him to exert all the force of his genius to maintain his ground againft his young Rival   They paffed a great part of their lives in a
kind of equal conteft and emulation of each
other's merit   but Hortenfius, by the fuperiority
of his years, having firft paffed through the ufual
gradation of public honors, and fatisfied his ambition by obtaining the higheft, *began to relax
fomewhat of his old contention. and give way to the
claims of eafe and luxury*, to which his nature ftrongly inclined him [z], till he was forced at laft, by
the general voice of the City, to yield the poft of
honor to Cicero, who never loft fight of the
true point of glory, nor was ever diverted by
any temptation of pleafure from his fteady courfe
and laborious purfuit of virtue   Hortenfius publifhed feveral orations which were extant long
after his death, and it were much to be wifhed,
that they had remained to this day, to enable us
to form a judgment of the different talents of
thefe two great men   but they are faid to have
owed a great part of their credit to the advantage of his action, which yet was thought *to have
more of art than was neceffary to an Orator*, fo that
his compofitions *were not admired fo much by the*

[z] Nam is poft Confula-
tum—fummum illud fuum
ftudium remifit, quo a puero
fuera incenfius, atque in omnium rerum abundantia vo-
luit beatius, ut ipfe putabat,
remiffius certe vivere   Brut
p 443

Reader

Reader as they had been by the Hearer [a]; while Cicero's more valued productions made all others of that kind leſs ſought for, and conſequently the leſs carefully preſerved   Hortenſius however was generally allowed by the Ancients, and by Cicero himſelf, to have poſſeſſed every accom pliſhment, which could adorn an Orator, *the grace of ſtile, art of compoſition, fertility of inven tion, ſweetneſs of elocution, gracefulneſs of acti on.* [b]   Theſe two Rivals lived however always with great civility and reſpect towards each other, and were uſually in the ſame way of thinking and acting in the affairs of the Republic, till Cicero, in the caſe of his exil, diſcovered the plain marks of a lurking envy and infidelity in Hortenſius yet his reſentment carried him no farther than to ſome free complaints of it to their common friend Atticus, who made it his buſineſs to mitigate this diſguſt, and hinder it from proceding to an open breach, ſo that Cicero, being naturally placable, lived again with him after his return on the ſame eaſy terms as before, and lamented his death at this time with great tenderneſs, not onely as the private loſs of a friend, but a public misfortune to his Country, in being deprived of the ſervice and authority of *ſo experienced a ſtateſman* at ſo critical a conjuncture [c].

FROM

---

[a] Motus & geſtus etiam us artis habebit, quam erat Oratoria is   Brut 425 di cebat melius quam ſcripſit Hortenſius Orator p 261

Eas ſer p antum intra ſamil ſunt, quod a princeps Orator n——e ſi natu eſt, nova re quod viſu, ſecur a, ac app reat diſcuſſe a e o e conis, quod le

gentes non invenimus —— Quint l 3

[c] Lrat in verborum ſplen dore elegans, compoſitione aptus, facultate cop oſus —— nec prætermittebat fere qui quam, quod erat in cauſa vox canora & ſuavis —— Brut 425

[c] Nam & am co amici cum conſuetudine jucun

tu 1

FROM Rhodes he paffed on to Ephefus, whence he fet fail on the firft of *October*, and after a tedious paffage landed at Athens on the fourteenth [*d*] Here he lodged again in his old quarters, at the houfe of his friend Ariftus His Predeceffor, Appius, who paffed alfo through Athens on his return, had ordered a *new Portico or Veftibule to be built at his coft to the Temple of the Eleufinian Ceres*, which fuggefted a thought likewife to Cicero of adding fome ornament of the fame kind *to the Academy*, as a public monument of his name, as well as of his affection for the place *for he hated*, he fays, *thofe falfe infcriptions of other people's ftatues* [*e*], with which the Greeks ufed to flatter their new Mafters, by effacing the old titles, and infcribing them anew to the great men of Rome He acquainted Atticus with his defign, and defired his opinion upon it but in all probability, it was never executed, fince his ftay at Athens was now very fhort, and his thoughts wholly bent on Italy. for as all his Letters confirmed to him *the certainty of a war*, in which he muft neceffarily bear a part, fo he was impatient to be at home, that he might have the clearer view of the ftate of affairs, and take

A Urb 703
Cic 57
Coff
L ÆMILIUS
PAULUS,
C CLAUDIUS
MARCELLUS

[*d*] m multorum officiorum conjunctione me privatum v--- — augebat etiam mo--- quod magna fapien--- vium bonorumque pecunia, vir egregius, conjunctif-que mecum confilio--- omnium focietate theri--- Reipab tempore ex--- Brut in t — Pridie Id October Athenas veni-mus, cum fane ad---

verfis ventis ufi effemus — Lp tum 14 5

[*e*] Audio Appium --- ---, Eleufine facere Num incepti fuerimus, fi nos quo-que Academiæ facerimus? — equidem valde iplas A-thenas amo Volo efie ali-quod monumentum Doleo — --- indicio --- Sat ita Sed ubi pac-cb — Ad ---

his measures with the greater deliberation [ ] yet not was not still without hopes of peace, and that he should be able to make up the quarrel between the parties; for he was, of all men, the best qualified to effect it, on account not only of his authority, but of his intimate friendship with them both, who severally paid great court to him at this time, and depended upon him as their only arbiter, in virtue of his own declaration to each [ ]

In his voyage from Athens towards Italy, Tiro, one of his slaves, whom he soon after made free, happened to fall sick, and was left behind at P— there to the care of friends and a Physician. The mention of such an accident will seem trifling to those who are not acquainted with the character and excellent qualities of Tiro, and how much we are indebted to him for preserving and transmitting to posterity the precious collection of Cicero's Letters, of which a great part still remain, and one intire book of them written to Tiro himself, several of which relate to the subject of *this a j a'efe*. Tiro was trained up in Cicero's family, among the rest of his young slaves, in every

---

[ ] Cogno re—mu' orum
amico un ver — ac arma
tem spectare. Ut m i cum
Cicero, a mnare on Les
2, que tenetur. Sed qua i
Adeunte fortuna on eo cit
u—deb tu operam it vem
m cum facius de ded e
deliberem —— Ep la—
1

ore en m rd concer m
ris neduci notel, five ac bo
rorum ictorum, tanusve
re re ad nd orem de c—
— l cicero a re p um

—Ad Att — 3

[ ] Ipsum tamen Pom
um temet m ad concor
hortar er. Ib

Ac auten uterque rum
re suem. Nisi forte sim
al er. Nam Pompeis
dubitat ere eum jud
ea, qua de Repub nunc a
tia whit valde proban l
trial co nutem accent he
e, imod —— it neu er que
quem o antum p ns t
qua mas delett. Ib

1

A Urb 703
Cu 7
Co
L A I us
I AUIUS,
C Cicuris
Marullus

kind of usefull and polite learning, and being a ,outh of singular parts and industry, soon became n eminent Scholar, and extremely serviceable to his master in all his affairs both civil and domestic "As for Tiro, says he to Atticus, I see you "have a Concern for him though he is won- "derfully usefull to me, when he is well, in "every kind both of my business and studies, "yet I wish his health more for his own huma- "nity and modesty, than for any service which I "reap from him [*l*]" But his Letter to Tiro himself will best shew what an affectionate master he was for from the time of leaving him, he never failed writing to him by every messenger or ship which passed that way, though it were twice or thrice a day, and often sent one of his servants express to bring an account of his health the first of these Letters will give us a notion of the rest.

M T Cicero to Tiro

"I thought that I should have been able to 'bear the want of you more easily, but in truth "I cannot bear it, and though it is of great im- "portance to my expected honor, to be at Rome "as soon as possible, yet I seem to have commit- "ted a sin when I left you But since you were 'utterly against proceeding in the voyage till "your health was confirmed, I approved your "resolution, nor do I now think otherwise, if ', ou continue in the same mind But after you have begun to take meat again, if you think

---

[*l*] De Tirone ... vel studiorum meorum ta- ... Quem ... men propter human ... rem & ... & si mirabiles utilitate. modium ... od il u ..., sum ... probes, cum ... a prop ... ... Ad nit ... g ne ...

A. Urb. 703
C... ..
Con.
L. Æmil. ..
P. ....
C. Claudius
Marcellus

" That you shall be able to overtake me, that is
" left to your consideration. I have sent Mario
" to you with instructions, either to come with
" you to me as soon as you can, or if you should
" stay longer, to return instantly without you.
" Assure yourself however of this, that, as far
" as it can be convenient to your health, I wish
" nothing more than to have you with me, but
" if it be necessary for the perfecting your reco-
" very, to stay a while longer at Patræ, that I
" wish nothing more than to have you well. If
" you sail immediately, you will overtake me at
" Leucas: but if you stay to establish your health,
" take care to have good company, good wea-
" ther, and a good vessel. Observe this one
" thing, my Tiro, if you love me, that neither
" Mario's coming, nor this Letter hurry you.
" By doing what is most conducive to your health,
" you will do what is most agreeable to me. weigh
" all these things by your own discretion. I want
" you, yet so as to love you; my love makes
" me wish to see you well, my want of you,
" to see you as soon as possible: the first is the
" better, take care therefore, above all things,
" to get well again. of all your innumerable ser-
" vices to me, that will be the most acceptable.
" ——the third of November [1] "

By the honor, that he mentions in the Letter,
he means *the honor of a Triumph*, which his friends
encouraged him to demand for his success at A-
manus and Pindenissum. in writing upon it to
Atticus, he says, " consider what you would ad-
" vise me with regard to a Triumph to which
" my friends invite me. for my part, if Bibulus
" who, while there was a Parthian in Syria, ne-

"

A Urb 703.
Cic 57
Coff
L Æmilius
Paullus,
C Claudius
Marcellus

" ver set a foot out of the gates of Antioch,
" any more than he did upon a certain occasion
" out of his own house, had not follicited a
' Triumph, I should have been quiet, but now
' it is a shame to sit still [*k*] " Again, " as to a
' Triumph, I had no thoughts of it before Bi-
" bulus's most impudent Letters, by which he
' obtained an honorable supplication If he had
' really done all that he has written, I should
" rejoice at it, and wish well to his suit, but for
' him, who never stirred beyond the walls,
" while there was an enemy on this side the Eu-
" phrates, to have such an honor decreed, and
" for me, whose army inspired all their hopes
' and spirits into his, not to obtain the same,
" will be a disgrace to us, I say to us, joining
' you to myself wherefore I am determined to
" push it all, and hope to obtain all [*l*] "

After the contemptible account, which Cicero gives of Bibulus's conduct in Syria, it must
appear strange to see him honored with a supplication, and aspiring even to a Triumph but this
was not for any thing that he himself had done,
but for what his Lieutenant Cassius had performed in his absence against the Parthians; the success of the Lieutenants being ascribed always to
the auspices of the General, who reaped the reward and glory of it and as the Parthians were

---

[*k*] Ad Att 6 8

[*l*] De Triumpho, nulla
me cupidit as unquam tenuit
ante B buli impudentissimæ
litteræ quas amplissima su-
pplicatio consecuta est Nec
si ea gessisset, quæ scripsit,
gauderem & honori faverem
illorum, qui peditem pol-
quod hostis c i phra

tem fuit, non extulit ho-
nori augeri, me, in cujus e
cre p ipsum illius exercitu s
habuit, idem non esse qui, de-
cessu ex nostrum, nostrum
inquam, te conjungens Itaque omnia experiar, & ut
spero, assequar ——— Ad Att
2

the

... the most dangerous enemies of the Republic, and ... the more ... ly dreaded at this time for their ... so any advantage gained ... are to be well received at Rome, ... the honors that could reason ...

... proconsul returned from his ... with pretensions *to a Triumph, his Fasces ..., were wreathed ...* with this ... Cicero landed at Brundusium ... of November, where ... at the same moment to meet ..., *but the sufficiation was to ...* from Brundisium he ... by flow stages towards Rome, ... his business on the road to confer with ... of both parties, who came out to ... and to learn their sentiments on the present state of affairs, from which he soon perceived, what of all things he most dreaded, an universal disposition to war. But as he foresaw the consequences of it more coolly and clearly, then any of them, so his first resolution was to apply all his endeavours and authority to the mediation of a peace. He had not yet declared for either side, not that he was irresolute which of them to chuse, *his inclinations determined within him ... to Pompey*, but the difficulty was, how to ... in the mean time towards Cæsar, so as to ... the ... previous decrees, which ... conjuring his ... and his forces on ... here he wished to ... a while, that he might act the ... the better grace and effect [*m*]

Iv

In this difposition he had an interview with
Pompey on *the tenth of December*, of which he
gives the following Account " We were toge-
' ther, *fays he*, about two hours. He feemed
' to be extremely pleafed at my return, he ex
' horted me to demand a Triumph, promifed
" to do his part in it, advifed me not to appear
' in the Senate, before I had obtained it, left I
' fhould difguft any of the Tribuns by declaring
" my mind in a word, nothing could be more
" obliging than his whole difcourfe on this fub-
" ject But as to public affairs, he talked in
" fuch a ftrain as if a war was inevitable, with-
" out giving the leaft hopes of an accommoda-
" tion He faid, that he had long perceived
" Cæfar to be alienated from him, but had re-
' ceived a very late inftance of it, for that
" Hirtius came from Cæfar a few days before,
" and did not come to fee him, and when Bal-
" bus promifed to bring Scipio an account of
' his bufinefs, the next morning before day,
' Hirtius was gone back again to Cæfar in the
" night this he takes for a clear proof of Cæ-
" far's refolution to break with him   In fhort,
" I have no other comfort but in imagining,
" that he, to whom even his enemies have
" voted a fecond Confulfhip, and Fortune given
" the greateft power, will not be fo mad as to
' put all this to hazard yet if he begins to

A Urb 703.
Cic 57
Coff
L. Æmilius
Paulus,
C Claudius
Marcellus

vero, qui eadem eodem   Cn Pompeio faf nu—ib 3
t......ere ad portam Brundin-   Nunc inef fo in determinen
nam venit, quo ego in por-   ipfum —d durr ojeram, ut
con inifique obviam foro   eliciam ferufion meum —
fui Ibid——   tu autem de noftro ftatu co-
    Mora   in mente   gitabis jamum quo art fi-
...... a Pompeio quoerei i-   co fuenir benevolentiam
a — die M Julii of, ad   Cefaris——ib 1

" rush on, I see many more things to be apprehended then I dare venture to commit to writing: at present I propose to be at Rome on the third of January [*n*] "

THERE is one little circumstance frequently touched in Cicero's letters, which gave him a particular uneasiness in his present situation, *his owing a sum of mone, to Cæsar*, which he imagined might draw some reproach upon , since he thought it *dishonorable and indecent*, he says, *to be a debtor to one, against whom we were acting in public affairs: yet to pay it at that time would deprive him of a part of the money which he had raised for his Triumph* [*o*] He desires Atticus however very earnestly to see it paid, which was done without doubt accordingly, since we meet with no farther mention of it: it does not appear, nor is it easy to guess, for what occasion this debt was contracted, unless it was to supply the extraordinary expence of his buildings after his return from exil, when he complained of being in a particular want of money from that general dissipation of his fortunes.

POMPEY, finding Cicero wholly bent on peace, contrived to have a second conference with him before he reached the City, in hopes to allay his fears and beat him off from that vain project of an accommodation, which might help to cool the zeal of his friends in the senate. he over took him therefore at Lavernium, and came on

[*n*] Ad Att... ... de ... nomine rogare, ... sequitur Ib

... Latin ...

est, quod solvendi sunt nummi Cæsari, & instrumentum triumphi eo conferendum. Ef enim ... Ib -

with him to Formiæ, where they spent a whole
afternoon in a close conversation Pompey strongly discouraged all thoughts of a pacification, declaring, " that there could be none but what
" was treacherous and dangerous , and that if
" Cæfar should disband his army, and take the
" Confulship, he would throw the republic into
" confusion but he was of opinion, that when
" he understood their preparations against him,
" he would drop the Confulship, and hold fast
' his army . but if he was mad enough to come
" forward and act offensively, he held him in
' utter contempt from a confidence in his own
" troops, and those of the Republic. They
" had got with them the copy of a speech,
" which Antony, one of the new Tribuns,
' made to the people four days before it was
" a perpetual invective on Pompey's conduct
' from his first appearance in public, with great
" complaints against the violent and arbitrary
" condemnation of Citizens, and the terror of
' his arms After reading it over together,
" what think you, says Pompey, would Cæfar
" himfelf do, if in poffeffion of the Republic,
' when this paultry, beggarly fellow, his Quæ-
" ftor, dares to talk at this rate ? on the whole,
" Pompey feemed not onely not to defire, but
" even to dread a peace [*p*] '

CICERO however would not still be driven
from the hopes and pursuit of an accommodation , the more he obferved the difpofition of
both parties, the more he perceived the neceffity
of it the honest, as they were called, were dif-
united among themfelves · many of them diffatisfied with Pompey , all fierce and violent, and

[*t*] Ib 7, 8

denouncing

A Urb 703.
Cic 57
Coff
L ÆMILIUS
PAULIUS,
C CLAUDIUS
MARCELLUS

denouncing nothing but ruin to their adversaries, he clearly forefaw, what he declared without fcruple to his friends, " that which fide foever got " the better, the war muft neceffarily end in a " Tyranny, the onely difference was, that if " their enemies conquered, they fhould be pro " fcribed, if their friends, be flaves " Though he had an abhorrence therefore of Cæfar's caufe, yet his advice was, to grant him his own term, rather than try the experiment of arms, " and " prefer the moft unjuft conditions to the jufteft " war fince after they had been arming him " againft themfelves for ten years paft, it was too " late to think of fighting, when they had made " him too ftrong for them [*q*] "

A Urb 704
C.c 58
Cof
C Claudius
Marcellus,
L Corneli
us Lentu
lus Cruf

This was the fum of his thoughts and counfils, when he arrived at *Rome on the fourth of January*, where he found the two new Confuls intirely devoted to Pompey's interefts On his approach towards the City great multitudes came out to meet him with all poffible demonftrations of honor *his laft ftage was from Pompey's villa near Albe, becaufe his own at Tufculum lay out of the great road, and was not commodious for a public entry on his arrival,* as he fays, *he fell into the very flame of civil difcord,* and found the war in

[*q*] De Rep. quoad.e
eg tmeo Novembri Lo
n ut pareant, comendat
Quos ego Equites Romanos
oros Sermo civici, cu acerrime tum cavera tum hoc
uer Pompeii vituperarent
Pace civil of evictori cum
multa mala, tum certe Ty-
rannus exiftet ——Ib 7 5

L Civil of protcri-
bere vicen, tamen fer-

vias Ib 7 7

Ad pacem hortari non d
hiro, qua vel injufta uti
eft quam juftiffimum bellum
——Io 7 14

Mallem tantas ei vires non
dediffet quam nunc tam va
lenti refifterit Ib 7 3

Nifi forte hæc fumma ar
ma dedimus, ut nunc cum
bene parato pugnaremus lo
7 6

effect proclamed [r] for the Senate, at Scipio's
motion, had juft voted a decree, " that Cæfar
' fhould difmifs his army by a certain day, or
" be declared an enemy, and when M. Antony
" and Q. Caffius, two of the Tribuns, oppofed
" their negative to it," as they had done to
every decree propofed againft Cæfar, and could
not be perfuaded by the intreaties of their friends,
to give way to the authority of the Senate, they
proceded to that vote, which was the laft re
fort in cafes of extremity, " that the Confuls,
" Prætors, Tribuns, and all who were about the
" city with Proconfular power, fhould take care
" that the Republic received no detriment "
As this was fuppofed to arm the Magiftrates
with an abfolute power, to treat all men as they
pleafed, whom they judged to be enemies, fo
the *Two Tribuns*, together with Curio, immediately *withdrew themfelves upon it, and fled in dif-*
guft to Cæfar's camp, on pretence of danger and
violence to their perfons, though none was yet offered
c defigned to them [s]

M. ANTONY, who now began to make a
figure in the affairs of Rome, was of an ancient
and noble extraction, the Grandfon of that celebrated ftatefman and orator, who loft his life
in the maffacres of Marius and Cinna   his Fa-

A Urb 704.
Cic 58
Coff

C Claudius
Marcellus,
L Corneli-
us Lentu-
lus Crus.

---

[r] Igo ad urbem acceffi
pu' non Jan obviam mihi
c eft proditum, ut nihil pof-
t fi ii ornatius Sed incidi in
ipfam flammam civilis difcor-
diæ vel potius belli————
&, Fam 16 11

Ego in Tufculanum nihil
hoc tempore Devium eft
τὰς ἀτριβῆσι, &c ad Att

[s] Antonius quidem no-
fter & Q Caffius nulla vi ex-
pulfi, ad Cæfarem cum Curi-
one profecti erant, poftea
quum fenatus Confulibus,
Prætoribus, Tribunis plebis
& nobis, qui Proconfules fumus, negotium dederat, ut
curaremus, ne quid Refp
detrimenti caperet———— Ep
Fam 16 11

ther,

ther, as it is already related, had been honored
with one of the most important commissions of
the Republic, but after an inglorious discharge
of it, died with the character of a corrupt, oppressive, and rapacious Commander   The Son,
trained in the discipline of such a Parent, whom
he lost when he was very young, launched out
at once into all the excess of riot and debauchery, and *wasted his whole patrimony before he had
put on the manly gown*, shewing himself to be the
genuin Son of that Father, who was born, as
Salluft says, *to squander money, without ever employing a thought on business, till a present necessity
urged on*   His comely person, lively wit, in-
sinuating address, made young Curio infinitely
fond of him, so that, in spight of the commands of a severe Father, who had often turned
Antony out of doors, and forbidden him his
house, he could not be prevailed with to forsake
his company, but supplied him with money for
his frolics and amours, till he had involved himself on his account in a debt of *fifty thousand
pounds*   This greatly afflicted *old Curio, and
Cicero was called in to heal the distress of the family*, whom the Son entreated, with tears in his
eyes, to intercede for Antony, as well as for
himself, and not suffer them to be parted, but
Cicero having prevailed with the father to make
his son easy, by discharging his debts, advised
him to insist upon it as a condition, and to enforce it by his paternal power, that he should
have no farther commerce with Antony [*]

I his

[*] Tene'ne memoria Præ-
textatum te decoxisse? ——
——o urged a patrempts
——is could tam —— ——

——cor ni potestate, quam tu in
Curionis   Quoties te p e
——do no ——o cjecit ——
——e me de debus mihi ——
——bita ——

A Urb 704
Cic 58
Coff
C Cifudius
Marcellus,
L Cornelius Lentulus Crus.

This laid the foundation of an early aversion in Antony to Cicero, encreased still by the perpetual course of Antony's life, which fortune happened to throw among Cicero's inveterate enemies for, by the second marriage of his mother, he became *son in law to that Lentulus,* who was put to death for conspiring with Catiline, by whom he was initiated into all the cabals of a traiterous faction, and infected with principles pernicious to the liberty of Rome To revenge the death of this father, he attached himself to Clodius, and during his *Tribunet* , was one of the ministers of all his violences , yet was detected at the same time in some *crim rei mirigae* in his family, injurious *to the honor of his Patron* [*u*] From this education in the City, he went abroad to learn the art of war under Gabinius, the most profligate of all Generals , who gave him *the command of h s horfe in Syria,* where he signalized his courage in *the restoration of King Ptolemy,* and acquired the first taft of martial glory, in an expedition undertaken against *the laws and religion of his Country* [*x*] From *Egypt, instead*

of

---

tiffimisdicere secondaretempus illud cum Pater Curio marens jacebat in luto, filius te ad pedes meo prosternens, lacrymans te mihi commendabat, orabat, ut te contra patrem fuum, fi HS sex gies peteret defenderem tantum enim se pro te intercessie ipse autem amore ardens confirmabat quod desiderium tui ferre non posset ——— quo ego tempore mala forensium fama sedavi vel potia sisti

li patri persuasi, ut se alienum sun cistolie et, &c —— [Philip z 18 ——] M Antonius, p roande pecuniæ genitis vacuasque cui , nisi in antibus Sallust H or rægm I in

[*u*] Te do a P Lentuli educatia —— Phil z 7] Latinus ait in Tribunatu Clodio —— cius o mandinu c ad rusn fa —— cuius etiam d n quiddam contum mo- , &c ib o

ib inde

A Urb 704
Cic 58
Coss
C Claudius
Marcellus,
L Cornelius Lentulus Crus

of coming home, where his debts would not suffer him to be easy, *he went to Cæsar into Gaul,* the sure refuge of all the needy, the desperate, and the audacious and after some stay in that Province, being furnished with money and credit by Cæsar, he returned to Rome to sue for the Quæstorship [y] Cæsar recommended him in a pressing manner to Cicero, " entreating him to " accept Antony's submission, and pardon him " for what was past, and to assist him in his " present suit with which Cicero readily complied, and obliged Antony so highly by it, that he declared war presently against Clodius, " whom he attacked with great fierceness in the " Forum, and would certainly have killed, if " he had not found means to hide himself under some stairs " Antony openly gave out, " that he owed all this to Cicero's generosity, to " whom he could never make amends for for " mer injuries, but by the destruction of his ene " my Clodius [z] " Being chosen Quæstor, he went back immediately to Cæsar, without expecting *his lot, or a decree of the Senate,* to appoint him his Province where, though he had all imaginable opportunities of acquiring money, yet by squandering, as fast as he got it, he came

---

em contra senatus auctoritatem, contra Pompeio & reliquorum sed habebat ducem Gallorum, &c ib

[y] Primum ultimam Galliam ex Ægypto quam domum vivit e Gallia ad Quæsturam petendam — ib — ad Pharsal in Anton

[z] acceperim me ante Clodium Petens mini satisfacturum te — postea

cuftoditus fum a te, tu a me obfervatus in petitione Quæsturæ, quo quidem tempore P Clodium — in foro te conatus occidere — ita prædicabas te non existimare nisi illum interfecisses, unquam nihil pro tuis in me injuriis satis esse facturum — ib 20

Cum se ille fugiens in scalarum tenebras abdidisset, &c pro Mil 15

a second

second time *empty and beggarly to Rome, to put in for the Tribunate*; in which office, after the example of *his friend Cato,* having fold himfelf to Cæfar, he was, as Cicero fays, *as much the caufe of the enfuing war, as Helen was of that of Troy* [a]

It is certain at leaft, *that Antony's flight gave the immediate pretext to it,* as Cicero had foretold ' Cæfar, *fays he,* will betake himfelf to arms, " either for our want of preparation, or if no " regard be had to him at the election of Con- " fuls, but efpecially, if any Tribun, obftruct- " ing the deliberations of the Senate, or exciting " the people to fedition, fhould happen to be " cenfured or over-ruled, or taken off, or ex- " pelled, or pretending to be expelled, run " away to him——[b] " in the fame Letter he gives a fhort, but true ftate of the merit of his caufe · " What, *fays he,* can be more impudent ? " You have held your government ten years, " not granted to you by the Senate, but extort- " ed by violence and faction the full term is ' expired, not of the law but of your licentious " will but allow it to be a law, it is now de- " creed, that you muft have a fucceffor you " refufe, and fay, have fome regard to me do " you firft fhew your regard to us will you

A Urb 704
Cic 5
Coff
C Claudius Marcellu,
I Corneli-
us Lentu-
lus Crus

[a] Deinde fine fenatus confulto, fine forte, fine lege ad Cæfarem cucurriti Id enim unum in t his egefta us, æris alieni, nequitiæ, per- dias et rationibus perfu- gium efte ducebat —adiolata tiens ad Tribunatum, ut in eo Magiftratu ſi poffes, via te fini his eues— at Helenu Trojanis, ſic iſte hu c Reipub

[b] Aut audita caufa, ſi forte Tribunus pleb fenatum impediens, aut populum in- citans, notatus, aut fenatus confulto circumfcriptus aut fublatu aut expulſus ſit ci- cenſve ſe excuſum ad me confugeret —ad Att ~ 9

" pretend

A Urb 704
Cic 58
Coff
C Claudius
Marcellus,
L Corneli-
us Lentu-
lus Crus

" pretend to keep an army longer than the peo-
" ple o dered, and contrary to the will of the
" Senate [c]?" but *Cæsar's strength lay not in
the goodness of his cause, but of his troops [d]*, a
confiderable part of which he was now drawing
together towards the confines of Italy, to be
ready to enter into action at any warning *the
fight of the Tribuns* gave him a plaufible handle
to begin, and feemed to fanctify his attempt,
but " his real motive, *fays Plutarch*, was the
" fame that animated Cyrus and Alexander be-
" fore him to difturb the peace of mankind,
" the unquenchable thirft of Empire, and the
" wild ambition of being the greateft man in
" the world, which was not poffible, till Pom
" pey was firft deftroyed [e]" Laying hold
therefore of the occafion, he prefently paffed the
Rubicon, which was *the boundary of his Province*
on that fide of Italy, and marching forward in
an hoftile manner, poffeffed himfelf without re
fiftance of the next great Towns in his way, A
riminum, Pifaurum, Ancona, Aretium, &c [f].

In this confufed and difordered ftate of the
City, Cicero's friends were folliciting *the decree
of his Triumph*, to which the whole Senate figni
fied their ready confent but " the conful Len-
" tulus, to make the favor more particularly h

---

[c] Ibd it Ep fam 16
1.

[c] Aterius dicis caufa
me or videbatur alterus e-
rat firm or Hic omni a fpe-
ciofa, ilic valentia Pom-
peium fenatus auctoritas Cæfarem militum arma a fidu-
cia Vell Pat 2 40

[e] Plutar in Anton

] an ille ad rec a

quod paulo ante decretum
eft, ut exercitum citra Rubi
conem, qui finis eft Galliæ,
educeret —Philip 6 3

Itaque cum Cæfar ame
tia quadam raperetur, & —
Ariminum, Pifaurum, Anco
nam, Arretium occupuiff
Urbem reliquimas—Ep fam
16

                    " own

A Urb 704
Cic 58.
Cofl
C Claudius
Marcellus.
L Corneli-
us Leniu-
lus Crus

" own, defired that it might be deferred for a
" while, till the public affairs were better fettled,
" giving his word, that he would then be the
" mover of it himfelf [g]." But Cæfar's fudden march towards Rome put an end to all farther thoughts of it, and ftruck the Senate with
fuch a panic, that, as if he had been already at
the gates, they refolved prefently to quit the
City, and retreat towards the fouthern parts of
Italy All the principal Senators had particular
diftricts affigned to their care, to be provided
with troops, and all materials of defence againft
Cæfar *Cicero had Capua, with the infpection of
the Sea coaft from Formiæ. he would not accept any
greater charge for the fake of preferving his authority in the tafk of mediating a peace [h]*, and for
the fame reafon, when he perceived his new Province wholly unprovided againft an enemy, *and
that it was impoffible to hold Capua without a ftrong
Garrifon, he refigned his Employment, and chofe not
to act at all [i]*.

Vol II   R   Capua

---

[g] Nobis tamen inter h¹s
verbis Senatus frequens flagi
avit Triumphum fed Len-
tulus Conful, quo majus fuum
beneficium faceret, fimul at
que expediffet quæ effent ne-
ceff ria de Repub dixit fe
laturum Ep Fam 16 11

[i] Ego negotio præfum
ron turbulento, vult enim
me Pompeius effe, quem to
ta hæc Campana & mariti-
ma ora habeat ἀπιστο πω¹, ad
quem delectus & fumma ne-
gotii referentur Ad Att 7,

Ego adhuc oræ maritimæ

præfum a Formiis Nullum
majus negotium fufcipere volui, quo plus apud illum meæ
litteræ cohortationefque ad
pacem valerent Ep fam 16.
12

[i] Nam certe neque tum
peccavi, cum imparatam jam
Capuam, non folum ignaviæ
delectus, fed etiam peridæ
fufpicionem fugiens, accipere
nolui—ad At 8 12

Quod tibi oftenderam, cum
a me Capuam rejeciebam,
quod feci non vitandi one is
caufa, fed quod videbam te-
neri illam urbem fine exercitu

CAPUA had always been the common ſemina-
ry o place of educating Gladiators for the grea-
men of Rome, where Cæſar had a famous ſchool
of them at this time, which he had long maintained under the beſt maſters for the occaſions of
his public ſhews in the City, and as they were
very numerous and well furniſhed with arms,
there was reaſon to apprehend that they would
break out, and make ſome attempt in favor of
their maſter, which might have been of dangerous conſequence in the preſent circumſtances of
the Republic, ſo that Pompey thought it necef-
ſary to take them out of their ſchool, and diſtri-
bute them among the principal Inhabitants of
the place, *aſſigning two to each maſter of a family,*
by which he ſecured them from doing any miſchief [k]

WHILE the Pompeian party was under no
ſmall dejection on account of Pompey's quitting
the City, and retreating from the approach of
Cæſar, T. Labienus, one of the chief Commanders on the other ſide, *deſerted Cæſar,* and
came over to them, which added ſome new life
to their cauſe, and raiſed an expectation that

---

cta ror poſſe—Ep Cic ad
Pomp Ad Att 8 11

As Cicero, when Procon-
ſul of Cilicia, often men-
tons the *Dioceſes* that were
annexed to his government,
[Ep Fam 13 67] ſo in
this command of Capua he
calls himſelf the *Epiſcopus* of
the Campanian coaſt which
ſhews, that theſe names,
which were appropriated afterwards in the Chriſtian
Church to characters and

powers Eccleſiaſtical, carried
with them in their original
uſe, the notion of a real authority, and juriſdiction

[k] Gladiatores Cæſaris,
qui Capuæ ſunt—ſane com
mode Pompeius diſtribuit, bi
nos ſingulis patribus familia
rum Scutorum in ludo 100
fuerunt eruptionem factum
fuiſſe dicebantur—ſane mul
tum in eo Reip proviſum eſt
Ad Att 7 14

many

many more would follow his example Labienus had eminently diftinguifhed himfelf in the
Gallic war, where next to Cæfar himfelf, he had
born the principal part, and by Cæfar's favor,
had raifed an immenfe fortune fo that he was
much careffed, and carried about every where
by Pompey, who promifed himfelf great fervice
from his fame and experience, and efpecially
from his credit in Cæfar's army, and the knowledge of all his counfils but his account of
things, like that of all defertors, was accommo-
dated rather to pleafe, than to ferve his new
friends, reprefenting *the weaknefs of Cæfar's
troops, their averfion to his prefent defigns, the dif-
affection of the two Gauls, and difpofition to revolt,*
the contrary of all which was found to be true
in the experiment and as he came to them fingle, without bringing with him any of thofe
troops with which he had acquired his reputation, fo his defertion had no other effect, than
to ruin his own fortunes, without doing any
fervice to Pompey [*l*]

But what gave a much better profpect to all
honeft men, was the propofal of an accommodation, which came about this time from Cæfar,

A Urb 704.
Cic 58
Coff
C Claudius
Marcellus,
L Corneli-
us Lentul-
lus Crus.

[*l*] Maximam autem pla-
gam accepit, quod is, qui
fummam auctoritatem in illius exercitu habebat, T Labienus focius fceleris effe no-
luit reliquit illum, & no-
bifcum eft multique idem
facturi dicuntur Ep fam
iC 12

  Aliquantum animi videtur
ſtuliſſe nobis Labienus—ad
ſt 7 12

  Labienum fecum habet

(Pompeius) non dubia, tem
de imbecillitate C   copiarum ejus adverfa Cnæ-
us nofter multo animi plus
habet Ib 7 16

  Nam in Labieno primum eft
dignitatis Ib 8 2

——— , ſin cinis
Cæfaris Labienus erat nunc
par fuga—lis ———
         Lucan 5 345

A. U-b 704
C.c 58
Cof
C. CLAUDIUS
MARCELLU
L. CORNEL.
L. LENTU-
LUS CRUS

who while he was pushing on the war with in-credible vigor, talked of nothing but peace, and endeavoured particularly to persuade Cicero, " that he had no other view, than to secure him-" self from the insults of his enemies, and yield " the first rank in the state to Pompey [m] " The conditions were, " that Pompey should go ' to his government of Spain, that his new le-" vies should be dismissed, and his garrisons ' withdrawn, and that Cæsar should deliver up ' his Provinces, the farther Gaul to Domitius, " the hither to Considius, and sue for the Con-" sulship in person, without requiring the privi-" lege of absence " These terms were readily embraced in a grand council of the Chiefs at Capua, and young L. Cæsar, who brought them, was sent back with Letters from Pompey, and the addition onely of one præliminary article, " that " Cæsar in the mean while should recall his " troops from the Towns, which he had seized " beyond his own Jurisdiction, so that the Senate ' might return to Rome, and settle the whole ' affair with honor and freedom [n] " Cicero was present at this council, of which he gave an account to Atticus, " I came to Capua, *says he,* " yesterday the twenty-sixth of January, where

---

[m] Balbus major ad me scribit nihil malle Cæsarem, quam, principe Pompeio, si-ne metu vivere. Tu, puto, hæc credis. Ad Att 8, 9

[n] Feruntur omnino con-ditiones ab illo aut Pompeius eat in Hispaniam, dilectus qui sunt habiti, & præsidia nostra dimitantur se ulteri-orem Galliam Domitio, & te-riorem Considio Nomano —

t aditurum Ad Consulatus petitionem se venturum, ne que se jam velle, absente se, rationem sui haberi Ep fam 16 12 ad Att 7 14

Accepimus conditiones, sed ita ut removeat præsidia ex iis locis, quæ occupavit, ut sine metu de iis ipsis con ditionibus Romæ Senatus ha beri posset Ibid

" I mu

" I met the Confuls, and many of our order
" they all wifh that Cæfar would ftand to his
" conditions, and withdraw his troops Favo-
" nius alone was againft all conditions impofed
" by Cæfar, but was little regarded, by the
" Council for Cato himfelf would now rather
" live a Slave than fight, and declares that if
" Cæfar recall his garrifons, he will attend the
" Senate, when the conditions come to be fettled,
" and not go to Sicily, where his fervice is
" more neceffary, which I am afraid will be
" of ill confequence————there is a ftrange va-
" riety in our Sentiments, the greateft part are
" of opinion, that Cæfar will not ftand to his
' terms, and that thefe offers are made onely to
" hinder our preparations but I am apt to think
" that he will withdraw his troops, for he gets
" the better of us by being made Conful, and
" with lefs iniquity, than in the way, which he
" is now purfuing, and we cannot poffibly come
" off without fome lofs, for we are fcandaloufly
" unprovided both with foldiers, and with money,
" fince all that which was either private in the
" City, or public, in the treafury, is left a prey
" to him [o] "

DURING the fufpence of this treaty, and the
expectation of Cæfar's anfwer, Cicero began to
conceive fome hopes that both fides were relent-
ing, and difpofed to make up the quarrel, Cæfar from a reflection on his rafhnefs, and the
Senate on their want of preparation but he ftill
fufpected Cæfar, and the fending a meffage fo
important by a perfon fo infignificant, as *young
Lucius Cæfar, looked,* he fays, *as if he had done it
by way of contempt, or with a view to difclaime it,*

[o] Ad Att 7. 15.

R 3   efpecially

A Urb 704
Cic 58
Cofl
C Claudius
Marcellus,
L Corne
lius Le ru-
lius Crus

efpecially, when after offering conditions, which
were likely to be accepted, he would not fit ftill
to wait an anfwer, *but continued his march with
the fame ardour, and in the fame hoftile manner,
as before* [*p*] His fufpicions proved true, for
by letters, which came foon after from Furnius
and Curio, he perceived, *that they made a mere jeft
of the Exprefs* [*q*]

It feems very evident, that Cæfar had no
real thoughts of peace, by his paying no regard
to Pompey's anfwer, and the trifling reafons
which he gave for flighting it [*r*] but he had
a double view in offering thofe conditions, for
by Pompey's rejecting them, as there was reafon
to expect from his known averfion to any treaty,
he hoped to load him with the odium of the war
or by his embracing them, to flacken his preparations, and retard his defign of leaving Italy;
whilft he himfelf in the mean time, by following
him with a celerity that amazed every body [*s*,
might

[*p*] Spero nos præfentiam pacem — Nam & il-
lum furer — re noftrum
copiarum fuperaverit. Ib.

Tamen deorit his ipfi
(Cæfari contentent Num-
cia vita me data dedit. Tit. I.
Curio — d tum effe, ne illo
quæstor — d in refponfi ruer
re — . Ib.

Cui rem quidem, L. Cæ-
fare com — rebus de pace
nihil tum — agit occurra.
loca occupare — b 19.

L. Cæfarem — ad me in-
fim num le vid — ca —
c — fio — a re
rtus hic r — cent ad mit
— fone on cu — & hic

fermone aliquo arrepto pro
me dat abitus ef — ib 11

[*q*] Accepi litteris tu
Philotimi, Furnii Cu o
ad Furnium, quibus irid —
L. Cæfaris legatiorem ——
ib 19

[*r*] Cæf. Commen ce
Bel. Cv l 1

] O celeritatem ncred
b lem — ad itt q — Cæ-
ro call him a monftci of v
gil ace ond fcelertv ——
b 8 o] fer from his pal
iage of the Rubicon, thoug
new s forced to the in a
the great Tow n of his road
a d fpent feven days bc
Certarum, yet in lus no

might chance to come up with him before he could
embark, and give a decisive blow to the war;
from which he had nothing to apprehend, but
it's being drawn into length. " I now plainly
" see, says Cicero, though later indeed than I
" could have wished on account of the assurances
" given me by Balbus, that he aims at nothing
" else, nor has ever aimed at any thing from the
" beginning, but Pompey's life [t] "

A Urb 704
Cic 58.
Coss
C Claudius
Marcellus,
L Cornelius Lentulus Crus

If we consider this famous *passage of the Rubicon,* abstractedly from the event, it seems to
have been so hazardous and desperate, that
Pompey might reasonably contemn the thought
of it, as of an attempt too rash for any prudent
man to venture upon. If Cæsar's view indeed had been to possess himself onely of Italy,
there could have been no difficulty in it his army was undoubtedly the best which was then in
the world, flushed with victory, animated with
zeal for the person of their General, and an over-
match for any which could be brought against it
into the field but this single army was all that
he had to trust to, he had no resource the loss
of one battle was certain ruin to him, and yet he
must necessarily run the risk of many before he
could gain his end for the whole Empire was
armed against him, every Province offered a
fresh enemy, and a fresh field of action, where
he was like to be exposed to the same danger as
on the plains of Pharsalia. But above all, his e-

two months he marched
through the whole length of
Italy, and came before the
gates of Brundisium before
Pompey could embark on the
9th of March Ad Att 9
13

[t] Intelligo serius equidem quam vellem, propter
epistolas sermonesque Balbi,
sed video plane nihil aliud
agi, nihil actum ab initio,
quam ut hunc occideret Ad
Att 9 5

nemies

A Uro 704
Cic 58
Coss
C Claudius
Marcellus,
L Corneli-
us Lentu-
lus Crus

nemies were masters of the sea, so that he could not transport his forces abroad without the hazard of their being destroyed by a superior fleet, or of being starved at land by the difficulty of conveying supplies and provisions to them Pompey relied chiefly on this single circumstance, and was persuaded, *that it must necessarily determine the war in his favor* [r] so that it seems surprising, how such a superiority of advantage, in the hands of so great a Commander, could possibly fail of success, and we must admire rather the fortune, than the conduct of Cæsar, for carrying him safe through all these difficulties to the possession of the Empire.

CICERO seldom speaks of his attempt, but *as a kind of madness* [r], and seemed to retain some hopes to the last, that he would not persist in it the same imagination made Pompey and the Senate so resolute to defy, when they were in no condition to oppose him. Cæsar on the other hand might probably imagine, that their stiffness proceeded from a vain conceit of their strength, which would induce them to venture a battle with him in Italy, in which case he was sure enough to beat them so that both sides were drawn farther perhaps than they intended, by mistaking each other's view. Cæsar, I say, might well apprehend, that they designed to try their strength with him in Italy for that was the constant persuasion of the whole party, who thought it the best scheme which could be pursued Pompey humored them in it, and always talked big to keep up their spirits, and though he

[r] Existimat, (Pompei)
qui mare teneat, eum rece ?
rerum potiri— itaq e i avil?
ppara. u ei fer , ei En qui?

sima cura fuit Ib 10 8
[r] Cum Cæsar amentia
quadam raperetur—Ep tam
16 12

A Urb 704.
Cic 58
Coss
C Claudius
Marcellus
L Corneli-
us Lentu-
lus Crus

saw from the firft *the neceffity of quitting Italy,* yet he kept the fecret to himfelf, and wrote word at the fame time to Cicero, *that he fhould have a firm army in a few days, with which he would march againft Cæfar into Picenum, fo as to give them an opportunity of returning to the City* [y] The plan of the war, as it was commonly under- ftood, was to poffefs themfelves of the principal pofts of Italy, and act chiefly on the defenfive, in order to diftrefs Cæfar by their different armies, cut off his opportunities of forage, hinder his ac- cefs to Rome, and hold him continually employ- ed, till the veteran army from Spain, under Pompey's Lieutenants, Afranius, Petreius, and Varro, could come up to finifh his overthrow [z] This was the notion which the Senate entertained of the war; they never conceived it poffible that Pompey fhould fubmit to the difgrace of flying before Cæfar, and giving up Italy a prey to his enemy in this confidence Domitius, with a very confiderable force, and fome of the princi- pal Senators, threw himfelf into Corfinium, a ftrong town at the foot of the Apennine, on the

[y] Omnes nos ατροσρω-
νισι, expertes fui tanti &
am inufitati confilii relinque-
bat Ad Att 8 8

Pompeius— ad me fcribit,
paucis diebus fe firmum exer
citum habiturum, fpemque
affert, fi in Picenum agrum
ipfe venerit, nos Romam re-
dituros effe Ib 7 16

[z] Sufcepto autem bello,
aut tenenda fit urbs, aut ea
relicta, ille commeatu & re-
liquis copiis intercludendus—
ad Att 7 9

Sin autem ille fuis condi-
tionibus ftare noluerit, bellum paratum eft — tantum-
modo ut eum intercludamus,
ne ad urbem poffit accedere
quod fperabamus fieri poffe ·
dilectus enim magnos habebimus— ex Hifpaniaque fex
legiones & magna auxilia, A-
franio & Petreio ducibus, habet a tergo Videtur, fi in-
faniet, poffe opprimi, modo
ut urbe falva— Ep fam 16
12

Summa autem fpes Afra-
nium cum magnis copiis ad-
ventare—ad Att 8 3

Adriatic

A Urb 704
Cc 58
Co.
C Claudius
Marcell.
L Cornel.
us Lentu-
lus Crus

Adriatic fide, where he propofed to make a ftand
againſt Cæſar, and ftop the progreſs of his march,
but he loft all his troops in the attempt, to the
number of *three Legions*, for want of knowing
Pompey's fecret.　Pompey indeed, when he
faw what Domitius intended, preſſed him earneſt-
ly, by feveral Letters, to come away and join
with him, telling him, " that it was impoſſible
" to make any oppoſition to Cæſar, till their
" whole forces were united, and that as to him
" felf, he had with him onely the two Legions,
" which were recalled from Cæſar, and were not
" to be truſted againſt him, and if Domitius
" ſhould entangle himſelf in Corfinium, fo as to
" be precluded by Cæſar from a retreat, that he
" could not come to his relief with fo weak an
" army, and bad him therefore not to be fur-
" prized to hear of his retiring, if Cæſar ſhould
" perſiſt to march towards him [*a*] " yet Domitius, prepoſſeſſed with the opinion, that Italy
was to be the *feat of the war*, and that Pompey
would never ſuffer fo good a body of troops, and
fo many of his beſt friends to be loft, would not
quit the advantageous poſt of Corfinium, but depended ſtill on being relieved, and when he was
actuall, beſieged, ſent Pompey word, *how eaſy
Cæſar might be intercepted between their two armies* [*b*]

[*a*] Non directa manu na-
.. adverſarii iſte non poſ-
..tur ——

Quamobrem toto com-
move., ſi aut eris me regre-
.. to to Cæſar ad me ve-
.. —— etiam atque etiam te
.. ut cum omni copia
..mum ad me venias
—— .. Pomp ad Do-

m. .. Att 8 12.

[*b*] Domitius ad Pom-
um —— mittit, qui petant ..
que orent, ut ſibi ſubveni..
Cæſarem duobus exercitibu
& locorum anguſtiis interclu-
d poſſe, frumentoque prohi-
beri, &c

Cæf Comment de Be
civ l 1

CICER.

CICERO was as much difappointed as any of
the reft; he had never dreamt of their being
obliged to quit Italy, till by Pompey's motions
he perceived at laft his intentions, of which he
fpeaks, with great feverity, in feveral of his Letters, and begs Atticus's advice upon that new
face of their affairs, and to enable Atticus to
give it the more clearly, he explanes to him in
fhort what occurred to his own mind on the one
fide and the other. " The great obligations,
" fays he, which I am under to Pompey, and
' my particular friendfhip with him, as well as
" the caufe of the Republic itfelf, feem to per-
" fuade me, that I ought to join my counfils
" and fortunes with his Befides, if I ftay be-
" hind, and defert that band of the beft and
" moft eminent Citizens, I muft fall under the
" power of a fingle perfon, who gives me many
' proofs indeed of being my friend, and whom,
' as you know, I had long ago taken care to
' make fuch from a fufpicion of this very ftorm,
" which now hangs over us, yet it fhould be
  well confidered, both how far I may venture
' to truft him, and fuppofing it clear, that I
' may truft him, whether it be confiftent with
' the character of a firm and honeft Citizen to
' continue in that City, in which he has born
  the greateft honors, and performed the great-
" eft acts, and where he is now invefted with
  the moft honorable Priefthood, when it is to be
' attended with fome danger, and perhaps with
' fome difgrace, if Pompey fhould ever reftore
" the Republic Thefe are the difficulties on
" the one fide, let us fee what there are on the
" other · nothing has hitherto been done by our
' Pompey, either with prudence or courage,
' I may add alfo nothing but what was contra-
" ry

A Urb 704
Cic 58
Coff
C CLAUDIUS
MARCELLUS.
L CORNELI-
US LENTU-
LUS CRUS

A. Urb 704
Cic 58
Coſ
C. Claudius
Marcellus,
L Cornelius Lentulus Crus

"ry to my advice and authority. I will omit
"thoſe old ſtories how he firſt nurſed, raiſed
"and armed this man againſt the Republic,
"how he ſupported him in carrying his laws by
"violence, and without regard to the Auſpices,
"how he added the farther Gaul to his Govern-
"ment, made himſelf his ſon-in-law, aſſiſted as
"Augur in the Adoption of Clodius, was more
"zealous to reſtore me, than to prevent my
"being expelled, enlarged the term of Cæſar's
"command, ſerved him in all his affairs in his
"abſence, nay, in his third Conſulſhip, after
"he began to eſpouſe the intereſts of the Re
"public, how he inſiſted, that the ten Tribuns
"ſhould jointly propoſe a law to diſpenſe with
"his abſence in ſuing for the Conſulſhip, which
"he confirmed afterwards by a law of his own,
"and oppoſed the Conſul Marcellus, when he
"moved to put an end to his government on the
"firſt of March. but to omit, I ſay, all this,
"what can be more diſhonorable, or ſhew a
"greater want of conduct than this retreat, or
"rather ſhamefull flight from the City? what
"conditions were not preferable to the neceſſity
"of abandoning our country? the conditions, I
"confeſs, were bad, yet what can be worſe than
"this? but Pompey, you'll ſay, will recover
"the Republic, when? or what preparation is
"there for it? is not all Picenum loſt? is not
"the way left open to the City? is not all our
"treaſure both public and private given up to
"the enemy? in a word, there is no party, no
"forces, no place of rendezvous for the friends
"of the Republic to reſort to, Apulia is choſen
"for our retreat, the weakeſt and remoteſt
"part of Italy, which implies nothing but de-
"ſpair, and a deſign of flying by the opportu-

3　　　　　　　　　　　　　　"nity

" nity of the fea, &c [c] In another Lettei, A Urb 704.
" there is but one thing wanting, fays he, to Cic 58
" complete our friend's difgrace, his failing to Cosl
" fuccour Domitius. nobody doubts but that C Claudius Marcellus,
" he will come to his ielief, yet I am not of L Corneli-
" that mind Will he then defeit fuch a Citi- us Lentu-
" zen, and the reft, whom you know to be lus Crus
" with him? efpecially when he has thirty co-
" horts in the Town yes, unlefs all things de-
" ceive me, he will defeit him he is ftrangely
" frightened, means nothing but to fly, yet
' you, for I perceive what your opinion is,
" think, that I ought to follow this man. For
" my part, I eafily know, whom I ought to fly,
" not whom I ought to follow As to that
" faying of mine, which you extoll, and think
" worthy to be celebiated, *that I had rather be*
" *conquered with Pompey, than conquer with Cæ-*
" *fai*, 'tis true, I ftill fay fo, but with fuch a
" Pompey as he then was, or as I took him to
" be but as for this man, who runs away, be-
" fore he knows from whom, or whither, who
" has betrayed us and ours, given up his coun-
" try, and is now leaving Italy, if I had rather
" be conquered with him, the thing is over, I
" am conquered, &c. [d] "

THERE was a notion in the mean while, that
univerfally prevailed through Italy, of *Cæfer's*
cruel and revengeful tempei, fiom which horrible
effects were apprehended Cicero himfelf was
ftrongly poffeffed with it, as appears from many
of his Letters, where he feems to take it for
granted, that he would be *a fecond Phalaris, not*
a Pififtratus, a bloody, not a gentle Tyrant This
he inferred from the *violence of his paft life, the*

[c] Ad Att 8 3;   [d] Ad Att 8 ⁓

A Urb 704
Cic 58
Coſſ
C Claudiu.
Marcellus
L Cornelius Le tu-
lus Crus

nature of his preſent enterprize, and above all, from the character of his friends and followers; who were, generally ſpeaking, a needy, proflıgate, audacıous crew, prepared for every thing that was deſperate [e] It was affirmed likewıſe with great confidence, that he had openly declared, *that he was now coming to revenge the deaths of Cn Cerbo, M Brutus, and all the other Marian Chiefs,* whom Pompey, when acting under Sylla, had cruelly put to death for their oppoſition to the Syllan cauſe [f] But there was no real ground for any of theſe ſuſpicions for Cæſar, who thought Tyranny, as Cicero ſays *the greateſt of Goddeſſes,* and whoſe ſole vıew it had been through life to bring his affaırs to this crıſis, and to make a bold puſh for Empire, had, *from the obſervation of paſt times, and the fate of former Tyrants,* laid it down for a maxim, *that clemency in victory was the beſt means of ſecuring the ſtability of it* [g] Upon the ſurrender therefore of Corfinium, where he had the firſt opportunity of giving a public ſpecimen of himſelf, he

---

[e] Iſtum cujus ea ἀρίϭύϋν times, omnıa teterrıme facturum puto Ad Att 7 12

Incertum eſt Phalarim ne an Pıſiſtratum ſit imitaturus —ıb 20

Nam crede n ıdeo ſı ιcerıt —— & regnum ron modo Romano homini ſed ne Perſæ quıdem to'erabıle —— ıb 10 8

Quı hıc poteſt ſe gerere non perdıte ι vıta, mores ante facta, ratio ſuſceptı negoti, locı—ıb 9 2 ıt 9 19

[f] Atque eam loqui quidem aud.vıas narrabant, Cn Cırbon, M Bru ſe 9 7

pœnas perſequı, &c Al 1ı 9 14

[g] Τἠν θεὦν μεγίϭην ι εχειν τυραννίδα Ad Att 7 11

Tentemus hoc modo, ſi poſſumus, omnıum volun tes recuperare, & dıuturna vıctoria utı quonıam relıqui credulıtate odıum effugere non potuerunt, neq, victorıam dıutıus tenere, prætei uι um L Syllam, quem ımıtaturus non ſum Hæc nova ſit ratio vıncendı, ut miſerıcorda & liberalıtate nos munıamus —Ep Cæſaris ad Opp A

◦ſhewed

shewed a noble example of moderation, by the A Urb 704
generous difmiffion of Domitius, *and all the o-* Cic 58
ther Senators who fell into his hands, among whom Coff
was Lentulus Spinther, Cicero's particular C CLAUDIUS
friend [*b*] This made a great turn in his favor, MARCELLUS.
by eafing people of the terrors, which they had L CORNELI-
before conceived of him, and feemed to confirm US LENTU-
what he affected every where to give out, *that* LUS CRUS.
he fought nothing by the war but the security of his
perfon and dignity Pompey on the other hand
appeared every day more and more defpicable,
by flying before an enemy, whom his pride and
perverfenefs was faid to have driven to the neceffity of taking arms——" tell me, I beg of you,
' fays Cicero, what can be more wretched, than
" for the one to be gathering applaufe from the
" worft of caufes, the other giving offence in
" the beft ? the one to be reckoned the preferver
' of his enemies, the other the defertor of
" his friends ? and in truth, though I have all
' the affection which I ought to have for our
' friend Cnæus, yet I cannot excufe his not
" coming to the relief of fuch men; for if he
" was afraid to do it, what can be more paultry ?
" or if, as fome think, he thought to make
" his caufe the more popular, by their deftru-
" ction, what can be more unjuft ? *&c.* [*t*]."
from this firft experiment of Cæfar's clemency,

[*b*] Cæf Comment 1 1
Plutar in Cæf ——

[*t*] Sed obfecro te, quid
hoc miferius quam alterum
plaufus in fœdiffima caufa
quærere, alterum offenfiones
n optima ? alterum exifti-
mari confervatorem inimico-
rum, alterum defertorem a-
micorum ? & mehercule

quamvis amemus Cnæum no-
ftrum ut & facimus & debemus, tamen hoc, quod tali-
bus viris non fubvenit, laudare non poffum Nam five
timuit quid ignavius five,
ut quidam putant, meliorem
fuam caufam populum credi
fore putavit quid injuftius ?
——ad Att 8 9

A Urb 704
Cic 58
Coff
C Claudius
Marcellu,
L Corneli
us Lentu-
lus Cof
Cicero took occasion to send him a Letter of compliment, and to thank him particularly for his generous treatment of Lentulus, who when Consul, had been the chief author of his restoration, to which Cæsar returned the following answer.

Cæsar Emperor to Cicero Emperor

" You judge rightly of me, for I am tho
' roughly known to you, that nothing is farther
" removed from me than cruelty, and as I have
" a great pleasure from the thing itself, so I re
" joice and triumph to find my act approved by
" you nor does it at all move me, that those,
" who were difmiffed by me, are said to be gone
" away to renew the war against me for I de
" sire nothing more, than that I may always act
" like myself, they like themselves. I wish that
" you would meet me at the City, that I may
" use your counsil and affiftance as I have hither-
" to done in all things Nothing, I affure you,
' is dearer to me than Dolabella, I will owe
' this favor therefore to him nor is it possible
" for him indeed to behave otherwise, such is
" his humanity, his good sense, and his affec-
" tion to me Adieu [k] "

WHEN Pompey, after the unhappy affair of Corfinium, found himself obliged to retire to Brundifium, and to declare, what he had never before directly owned, *his design of quitting Italy, and carrying the war abroad* [l], he was very defirous to draw Cicero along with him, and wrote two Letters to him at Formiæ, to press him to come away directly, but Cicero, already

[k] Ad Att 9 16   denique me certiorem confili
[l] Qui amifo Confinio fui fecit ——ib 9 2

much

much out of humor with him, was difgufted ftill A Urb 704
the more by his fhort and negligent manner of Cic 58
writing, upon an occafion fo important [*m*] the Coff
fecond of Pompey's Letters, with Cicero's an- C Claudius
fwer, will explane the prefent ftate of their af- Marcellus
fairs, and Cicero's fentiments upon them L Cornelius Lentulus Crus

Cn Pompeius Magnus Proconful to M Cicero Emperor

"If you are in good health, I rejoice I read
"your Letter with pleafure for I perceived in
"it your ancient virtue by your concern for the
"common fafety The Confuls are come to
"the army, which I had in Apulia I earneftly
"exhort you, by your fingular and perpetual
"affection to the Republic, to come alfo to us,
"that by our joint advice we may give help and
"relief to the afflicted ftate I would have you
"make the Appian way your road, and come
"in all hafte to Brundifium. Take care of your
"health."

M Cicero Emperor to Cn. Magnus Proconful.

"When I fent that letter, which was deli-
"vered to you at Canufium, I had no fufpicion
"of your croffing the fea for the fervice of the
"Republic, and was in great hopes, that we
"fhould be able, either to bring about an ac
"commodation, which to me feemed the moft
"ufefull, or to defered the Republic with the great-
"eft dignity in Italy In the mean time, be-

[*m*] Epiftolarum Pompeii   fcribendo diligentiam volui
duarum, quas ad me mifit,   tibi totam cite carum ex-
negligentiam, meamque in   empli ad te m.fi Ib 8 11

A Urb. 704
Cc 58
Coſſ
C Claudius
Marcel.
L Corneli-
us Le tu
lus Crus

"fore my Letter reached you, being informed
"of your reſolution, by the inſtructions which
"you ſent to the Conſuls, I did not wait till I
"could have a Letter from you, but ſet out im-
"mediately towards you with my Brother and
"our children for Apulia. When we were come
"to Theanum, your friend C Meſſius, and ma-
"ny others told us, that Cæſar was on the road
"to Capua, and would lodge that very night at
"Æſernia I was much diſturbed at it, becauſe,
"if it was true, I not onely took my journey to
"be precluded but myſelf alſo to be certainly
"a priſoner I went on therefore to Cales with
"intent to ſtay there, till I could learn from
"Æſernia the certainty of my intelligence at
"Cales there was brought to me a copy of the
"Letter, which you wrote to the Conſul Lentu
"lus, with which you ſent the copy alſo of one
"that you had received from Domitius, dated
"the eighteenth of February, and ſignified
"that it was of great importance to the Repub
"lic, that all the troops ſhould be drawn toge
"ther, as ſoon as poſſible, to one place, ſo
"ſo as to leave a ſufficient Garriſon in Capua
"Upon reading theſe Letters, I was of the ſame
"opinion with all the reſt, that you were re
"ſolved to march to Corfinium with all your
"forces. whither, when Cæſar lay before the
"Town, I thought it impoſſible for me to come
"While this affair was in the utmoſt expectati
"on, we were informed at one and the ſame
"time both of what had happened at Corfinium,
"and that you were actually marching towards
"Brundiſium and when I and my Brother re
"ſolved without heſitation to follow you thither,
"we were advertiſed by many, who came from
"Samnium, and Apulia, to take care that we
                                                "did

" did not fall into Cæsar's hands, for that he was
" upon his march to the same places where our
" road lay, and would reach them sooner than
" we could possibly do   This being the case, it
" did not seem adviseable to me or my Brother,
" or any of our friends, to run the risk of hurt-
" ing, not onely ourselves, but the Republic, by
" our rashness   especially when we could not
" doubt, but that if the journey had been sure
" to us, we should not then be able to overtake
" you.   In the mean while I received your Let-
" ter, dated from Canusium the twenty-first of
" February, in which you exhort me to come in
" all haste to Brundisium   but as I did not receive
" it till the twenty-ninth, I made no question
" but that you were already arrived at Brundi-
" sium, and all that road seemed wholly shut
" up to us, and we ourselves are surely intercept-
" ed as those who were taken at Corfinium   for
' we did not reckon them onely to be prisoners,
" who were actually fallen into the enemy's hands,
" but those too not less so, who happen to be
" enclosed within the quarters and garrisons of
" their adversaries   Since this is our case, I
" heartily wish in the first place, that I had al-
" ways been with you, as I then told you when
" I relinquished the Command of Capua, which
" I did not do for the sake of avoiding trouble,
" but because I saw that the Town could not be
" held without an army, and was unwilling
" that the same accident should happen to me,
" which to my sorrow has happened to some of
" our bravest Citizens at Corfinium   but since it
" has not been my lot to be with you, I wish
" that I had been made privy to your counsils ·
" for I could not possibly suspect, and should
" sooner have believed any thing, than that for

A. Urb 701
Cic 58
Coss
C. Claudius
Marcellus
L. Cornelli-
us Lentul-
lus Crus

"the good of the Republic, under such a Lea
"der as you, we should not be able to stand our
"ground in Italy nor do I now blame your
"conduct, but lament the fate of the Republic,
"and though I cannot comprehend what it is
"which you have followed, yet I am not the
"less persuaded, that you have done nothing,
"but with the greatest reason You remember,
"I believe, what my opinion always was; first,
'to preserve peace even on bad conditions, then
"about leaving the City, for as to Italy, you
"never intimated a tittle to me about it but I
'do not take upon myself to think, that my
'advice ought to have been followed I follow
"ed yours, nor that for the sake of the Repub
"lic, of which I despaired, and which is now
"overturned, so as not to be raised up again
"without a civil and most pernicious war I
"sought you, desired to be with you; nor will I
"omit the first opportunity which offers of ef
"fecting it I easily perceived, through all the
"affair, that I did not satisfy those who are fond
"of fighting for I made no scruple to own,
'that I wished for nothing so much as peace
"not but that I had the same apprehension
"from it as they, but I thought them more to
"lerable than a civil war, then, after the war
"was begun, when I saw that conditions of
"peace were offered to you, and a full and ho
"norable answer given to them, I began to
"weigh and deliberate well upon my own con
"duct, which, considering your kindness to me,
"I fancied that I should easily explane to your
"satisfaction I recollected that I was the onely
"man, who, for the greatest services to the pub-
"lic, had suffered a most wretched and cruel pu
"nishment that I was the onely one, who, if I
"offended

" offended him, to whom at the very time when
' we were in arms against him, a second Con-
" fulship and most splendid Triumph was offer-
" ed, should be involved again in all the same
" struggles, so that my person seemed to stand
" always expofed as a public mark to the infults
' of profligate Citizens. nor did I fufpect any
' of these things till I was openly threatned with
" them, nor was I fo much afraid of them, if
" they were really to befall me, as I judged it
' prudent to decline them, if they could ho-
" neftly be avoided You fee in short the state
' of my conduct while we had any hopes of
" peace, what has fince happened deprived me
" of all power to do any thing but to thofe
" whom I do not pleafe I can eafily anfwer, that
" I never was more a friend to C Cæfar than
" they, nor they ever better friends to the Re-
" public than myfelf the onely difference be-
" tween me and them is, that as they are ex-
" cellent Citizens, and I not far removed from
" that character, it was my advice to procede
" by way of treaty, which I underftood to be
" approved alfo by you, theirs by way of arms,
" and fince this method has prevailed, it shall be
" my care to behave myfelf fo, that the Repub-
" lic may not want in me the fpirit of a true
" Citizen, nor you of a friend Adieu [*n*] "

THE difguft, which Pompey's management
had given him, and which he gently intimates
in this Letter, was the true reafon why he did
not join him at his time he had a mind to deliberate a while longer, before he took a ftep fo
decifive. this he owns to Atticus, where, after
recounting all the particulars of his own conduct,

[*n*] Ad Att 8 11

which

A. Urb 704
Cic 58
Coff
C CLAUDIUS
MARCELLUS.
L CORNELI-
US LENTU-
LUS CRUS.

A Urb. 70..
Ce..s
Co̅
C C..n..ts
M.. c..ll..
L ..m ..u..
t.. L.. ..t
ILS C. ts

which were the moft liable to exception, he adds,
I have neither done nor omitted to do any thing,
when he has not both a probable and prudent excuse—
and ... with a s ...d g to confider a little longer,
what were ..ght ... d fit for me to do [o] The
chief ground of his deliberation was, that he ftill
thought a peace poffible, in which cafe Pompey and Cæfar would be one again, and he had
no mind to give *Cæfar any cause to be an enemy to*
... ... was ... a friend to Pompey

WHILE things were in this fituation, Cæfar
fent young Balbus after the Conful Lentulus, to
endeavour to perfuade him *to ftay in Italy, and re-*
turn to the Ci..., by the offer of every thing that
could tempt him he called upon Cicero on his
way, who gives the following account of it to
Atticus ' Young Balbus came to me on the
" twenty-fourth in the evening, running in all
" hafte by private roads after Lentulus, with Let-
" ters and inftructions from Cæfar, and the offer
" of any Government, if he will return to Rome
' but it will have no effect unlefs they happen
" to meet he told me that Cæfar defired no-
" thing fo much as to overtake Pompey, which
" I believe, and to be friends with him again
" which I do not believe, and begin to fear,
" that all his clemency means nothing elfe at laft
" but to give that one cruel blow The elder
' Balbus writes me word, that Cæfar wifhes no-
" thing more than to live in fafety, and yield
' the nift rank to Pompey You take him I
" fuppofe to be in earneft [p] "
CICERO feems to think, *that Lentulus might*

[ ] Nihi praetermiffum eft
cafa ren inbe.. pieram
excufa..oren —a pl.. quid
ro.. m, & quid facere..n
    mihi effet, diutius cogitare
redui—ib 8 1..
    [p] Ad Att 8 9

have been perfuaded to ftay if Balbus and he had met together; for he had no opinion of the firmnefs of thefe Confuls, but fays of them both on another occafion, *that they were more eafily moved by every wind, than a feather or a leaf.* He received another Letter foon after from Balbus, of which he fent a copy to Atticus, *that he might pity him,* he fays, *to fee what a dupe they thought to make of him* [q].

A Urb 704.
Cic. 58
Coſſ
C Claudius
Marcellus.
L Cornelius Lentuius Crus.

Balbus to Cicero Emperor.

" I conjure you, Cicero, to think of fome
" method of making Cæfar and Pompey friends
" again, who by the perfidy of certain perfons
" are now divided it is a work highly worthy
" of your virtue take my word for it, Cæfar
" will not onely be in your power, but think him
" felf infinitely obliged to you if you would
" charge yourfelf with this affair I fhould be
" glad if Pompey would do fo too ; but in the
" prefent circumftances, it is what I wifh rather
" than hope, that he may be brought to any
" terms but whenever he gives over flying and
" fearing Cæfar, I fhall not defpair, that your
" authority may have its weight with him Cæ
" far takes it kindly, that you were for Lentu
" lus's ftaying in Italy, and it was the greateft
" obligation which you could confer upon me.
" for I love him as much as I do Cæfar himfelf.
" if he had fuffered me to talk to him as freely
" as we ufed to do, and not fo often fhunned
" the opportunities which I fought of conferring
" with him, I fhould have been lefs unhappy

[q] Nec me Confules movent, qui ipfi pluma aut folio
tacilius moventur— ut vicem meam doleres, cum me derideri videres Ib 8 15

S 4

" than

A Urb 702
Cic 58
Cof

C C n t
Marcell
I C n e
t L t
its C t

"than I now am for affure yourfelf that no
"man can be more afflicted than I, to fee one,
"who is dearer to me than myfelf, acting his
"part fo ill in his Confulfhip, that he feems to
"be any thing rather than a Conful; but fhould
"he be difpofed to follow your advice, and take
"your word for Cæfar's good intentions, and
"pafs the reft of his Confulfhip at Rome, I
"fhould begin to hope, that by your authority
"and at his motion, Pompey and Cæfar may
"be made one again with the approbation even
"of the Senate Whenever this can be brought
"about, I fhall think that I have lived long
"enough you will certainly approve, I am fure,
"what Cæfar did at Corfinium in an affair of
"that fort, nothing could fall out better, than
"that it fhould be tranfacted without blood I
"am extremely glad, that my Nephew's vifit
"was agreeable to you, as to what he faid
"on Cæfar's part, and what Cæfar himfelt
"wrote to you, I know Cæfar to be very fin-
"cere in it, whatever turn his affairs may
"take [r]. "

CÆSAR at the fame time was extremely follicitous not fo much to gain Cicero, for that was
not to be expected, as to prevail with him *to ftand
neuter* He wrote to him feveral times to that
effect, and employed all their common friends to
prefs him with Letters on that head [s]. who,
by his keeping fuch a diftance at this time from
Pompey, imagining that they had made fome
impreffion, began to attempt a fecond point with
him, viz *to perfuade him to come back to Rome*

[r] Ad Att 8 15

[s] od quæ s quid Cæ
far ad me fcripferit Quo
fape gratiffimam fibi effe

quod quietim oratque ut in
eo perfeverem Balbus n
nor hæc eadem mandata Io
8 11

end

and affift in the councils of the Senate, which Cæfar
defigned to fummon at his return from following
Pompey. with this view in the hurry of his march
towards Brundifium, Cæfar fent him the following Letter

A Urb 704.
Cic 58
Coff
C Claudius
Marcellus,
L Cornfli-
us Lentu-
lus Crus

Cæfar Emperor to Cicero Emperor.

" When I had but juft time to fee our friend
" Furnius, nor could conveniently fpeak with,
" or hear him, was in hafte, and on my march,
' having fent the Legions before me, yet I could
" not pafs by without writing, and fending him
" to you with my thanks, though I have often
" paid this duty before, and feem likely to pay
" it oftner, you deferve it fo well of me. I de-
" fire of you in a fpecial manner, that, as I hope
" to be in the City fhortly, I may fee you there,
" and have the benefit of your advice, your in-
" tereft, your authority, your affiftance in all
" things. But to return to the point. you will
" pardon the hafte and brevity of my Letter, and
" learn the reft from Furnius." To which Cicero anfwered.

Cicero Emperor to Cæfar Emperor.

" Upon reading your Letter, delivered to me
" by Furnius, in which you preffed me to come
" to the City, I did not fo much wonder at what
" you there intimated of your defire to ufe my
" advice and authority, but was at a lofs to find
" out what you meant by my intereft, and affift-
" ance yet I flattered myfelf into a perfua-
" fion, that out of your admirable and fingular
" wifdom, you were defirous to enter into fome
" meafures for eftablifhing the peace and con-
" cord

" cord of the City ; and in that cafe I looked
" upon my temper and character as fit enough to
" be employed in fuch a deliberation If the
" cafe be fo, and you have any concern for the
" fafety of our friend Pompey, and of recon-
" ciling him to yourfelf, and to the Republic,
" you will certainly find no man more proper for
" fuch a work than I am, who from the very
" firft have always been the advifer of peace
" both to him and the Senate , and fince this
" recourfe to arms have not meddled with any
" part of the war, but thought you to be really
" injured by it, while your enemies and enviers
" were attempting to deprive you of thofe ho-
" nors, which the Roman people had granted
" you   But as at that time I was not onely a fa-
" vorer of your dignity, but an encourager alfo
" of others to affift you in it , fo now the dig-
" nity of Pompey greatly affects me   for many
" years ago I made choice of you two, with
" whom to cultivate a particular friendfhip, and
" to be, as I now am, moft ftrictly united.
" Wherefore I defire of you, or rather beg and
" implore with all my prayers, that in the hurry
" of your cares you would indulge a moment to
" this thought, how by your generofity I may be
" permitted to fhew myfelf an honeft, gratefull,
" pious man, in remembering an act of the
" greateft kindnefs to me. If this related onely
" to myfelf, I fhould hope ftill to obtain it from
" you   but it concerns, I think, both your honor
" and the Republic, that by your means I fhould
" be allowed to continue in a fituation the beft
" adapted to promote the peace of you two, as
" well as the general concord of all the Citizens.
" After I had fent my thanks to you before on
" the account of Lentulus , for giving fafety

" t

" to him who had given it to me , yet upon
" reading his Letter, in which he expresses the
" most gratefull Sense of your liberality, I took
" myself to have received the same grace from
' you, which he had done towards whom, if
" by this you perceive me to be gratefull, let it
" be your care, I beseech you, that I may be so
" too towards Pompey [*t*] "

CICERO was censured for some passages of this
Letter, which Cæsar took care to make public,
viz the compliment on *Cæsar's admirable wisdom*;
and above all, the acknowlegement *of his being*
inspired by his adversaries in the present war in excuse of which, he says, " that he was not sorry
" for the publication of it, for he himself had
" given several copies of it, and considering
" what had since happened, was pleased to have
" it known to the world how much he had al-
" was been inclined to peace . and that in urg-
' ing Cæsar to save his Country, he thought it
" his business to use such expressions as were the
" most likely to gain authority with him, with-
" out fearing to be thought guilty of flattery,
" in urging him to an act, for which he would
" gladly have thrown himself even at his
" feet [*u*]."

HE received another Letter on the same subject, and about the same time, written jointly by

A Urb 704.
Cic 58
Coss
C CLAUDIUS
MARCELIUS,
L CORNELI-
US LENTU-
LUS CRUS

[*t*] Ad Att 9 6 11

[*u*] Epistolam meam quod pervulgatam scribis esse non fero moleste Quin etiam ipse mul is dedi describendam F. enim & accidetunt j m & impendent, ut testatum esse vlim de pace quid sentiam Cum autem eum hortarer, im prater im hominem, non videbar ullo modo facilius moturus, quam si id, quod eum hortarer, convenire ejus sapientiæ dicerem Eam si admirabilem dixi, cum eum ad salutem patriæ hortarer, non sum veritus, ne viderer assentiri, cui tali in re lubenter me ad pedes abjecissem, &c Ib 8 9

Balbus

A Urb 704
Cic 58
Co.

C Claudius
Marcellus,
L Cornel-
us Lentu-
lus Crus

Balbus and Oppius, two of Cæsar's chief confidents

Balbus and Oppius to M Cicero

" THE advice, not onely of little men, such
" as we are, but even of the greatest, is gene-
" rally weighed, not by the intention of the
" giver, but the event, yet relying on your hu-
" manity, we will give you what we take to be
" the best in the case about which you wrote to
" us, which, though it should not be found pru-
" dent, yet certainly flows from the utmost fide-
" lity and affection to you. If we did not know
" from Cæsar himself, that, as soon as he comes
" to Rome, he will do what in our judgement
" we think he ought to do, treat about a recon-
" ciliation between him and Pompey, we should
" give over exhorting you to come and take
" part in those deliberations, that by your help,
" who have a strict friendship with them both,
" the whole affair may be settled with ease and
" dignity or, if on the contrary, we believed
" that Cæsar would not do it, and knew that he
" was resolved upon a war with Pompey, we
" should never try to persuade you, to take arms
" against a man to whom you have the greatest
" obligations. in the same manner as we have al-
" ways entreated you, not to fight against Cæsar.
" But since at present we can onely guess rather
" than know what Cæsar will do, we have no
" thing to offer but this, that it does not seem
" agreeable to your dignity, or your fidelity, so
" well known to all, when you are intimate with
" them both, to take arms against either . and
" this we do not doubt but Cæsar, according to
" his humanity, will highly approve yet if you
" judge

"judge proper, we will write to him, to let us
"know what he will really do about it, and if
"he returns us an answer, will prefently fend
"you notice, what we think of it, and give
"you our word, that we will advife onely, what
"we take to be moft fuitable to your honor, not
"to Cæfar's views, and are perfuaded, that Cæ-
"far, out of his indulgence to his friends, will
"be pleafed with it [x]." This joint Letter
was followed by a feparate one from Balbus.

A Urb 704.
Cic 58.
Coff
C Claudius
Marcellus
L Corneli-
us Lentu-
lus Crus

Balbus to Cicero Emperor.

"IMMEDIATELY after I had fent the com-
"mon Letter from Oppius and myfelf, I re-
"ceived one from Cæfar, of which I have fent
"you a copy; whence you will perceive how
"defirous he is of peace, and to be reconciled
'with Pompey, and how far removed from all
"thoughts of cruelty It gives me an extreme
"joy, as it certainly ought to do, to fee him in
"thefe fentiments As to yourfelf, your fide-
'lity, and your piety, I am intirely of the fame
mind, my dear Cicero, with you, that you
"cannot, confiftently with your character and
"duty, bear arms againft a man to whom you
"declare yourfelf fo greatly obliged that Cæfar
"will approve this refolution, I certainly know
"from his fingular humanity, and that you
'will perfectly fatisfy him, by taking no part
"in the war againft him, nor joining yourfelf
"to his adverfaries this he will think fufficient,
"not onely from you, a perfon of fuch dignity
"and fplendor, but has allowed it even to me,
"not to be found in that camp, which is likely

[x] Ad Att 9 8.

"to

A Urb 701
C.c 58
Coss
C Claudius
Marcellus,
L Corneli-
us Lentu-
lus Crus

" to be formed againft Lentulus and Pompey, from
" whom I have received the greateft obligations
" it was enough, he faid, if I performed my
" part to him in the City and the gown, which
" I might perform alfo to them if I thought fit
" wherefore I now manage all Lentulus's affairs
" at Rome, and difcharge my duty, my fidelity
" my piety to them both yet in truth I do not take
" the hopes of an accommodation, though now
" fo low, to be quite defperate, fince Cæfar is in
" that mind in which we ought to wifh him
" one thing would pleafe me, if you think it
" proper, that you would write to him, and de
" fire a guard from him, as you did from Pom
" pey, at the time of Milo's trial, with my ap
" probation I will undertake for him, if I right
" ly know Cæfar, that he will fooner pay a re
" gard to your dignity, than to his own intereft
" How prudently I write thefe things, I know
" ot but this I certainly know, that whatever
" I write, I write out of a fingular love and af
" fection to you for (let me die, fo as Cæfar
" may but live) if I have not fo great an efteem
" for you, that few are equally dear to me
" When you have taken any refolution in this
" affair, I wifh that you would let me know it
" for I am exceedingly follicitous that you fhould
" difcharge your duty to them both, which in
" truth I am confident you will difcharge. Take
' care of your health [*y*]."

THE offer of a guard was artfully infinuated
for while it carried an appearance of honor and
refpect to Cicero's perfon, it muft neceffarily have
made him Cæfar's prifoner, and deprived him of
the liberty of retiring, when he found it proper,

out of Italy   but he was too wife to be caught by it, or to be moved in any manner by the Letters themfelves, to entertain the leaft thought of going to Rome, fince to affift in the Senate, when Pompey and the Confuls were driven out of it, was in reality to take part againft them. What gave him a more immediate uneafinefs, was the daily expectation of an interview with Cæfar himfelf, who was now returning from Brundifium by the road of Formiæ, where he then refided   for though he would gladly h e avoided him, if he could have contrived to do it decently, yet to leave the place juft when Cæfar was coming to it, could not fail of being interpreted as a particular affront   he refolved therefore *to wait for him, and to act on the occafion with e firmnefs and gravity, which became his rank and character*

THEY met as he expected, and he fent Atticus the following account of what paffed between them . " My difcourfe with him, fays he, " was fuch, as would rather make him think " well of me than thank me   I ftood firm in " refufing to go to Rome, but was deceived in " expecting to find him eafy, for I never faw " any one lefs fo   he was condemned, he faid, " by my judgement; and, if I did not come, " others would be the more backward   I told " him that their cafe was very different from " mine   After many things faid on both fides, " he bad me come however, and try to make " peace: fhall I do it, fays I, in my own way? " do you imagine, replied he, that I will pre- " fcribe to you? I will move the Senate, then, " fays I, for a decree againft your going to Spain, " or tranfporting your troops into Greece, and " fay a great deal befides in bewailing the cafe of
                                        " Pompey:

A Urb 704
Cic 53
Coſſ
C CLAUDIUS
MARCELLUS,
L CORNELI
US LENTU-
LUS CRUS

" Pompey: I will not allow, replied he, ſuch
" things to be ſaid ſo I thought, ſays I, and
" for that reaſon will not come, becauſe I muſt
" either ſay them, and many more, which I
" cannot help ſaying, if I am there, or not come
" at all　The reſult was, that to ſhift off the
" diſcourſe, he wiſhed me to conſider of it,
" which I could not refuſe to do, and ſo we
" parted I am perſuaded, that he is not pleaſed
" with me, but I am pleaſed with myſelf, which
" I have not been before of a long time. As
" for the reſt, good Gods, what a crew he has
" with him！ what a helliſh band, as you call
" them！—— what a deplorable affair！ what de-
" ſperate troops！ what a lamentable thing, to ſee
" Servius's ſon, and Titinius's, with many more
" of their rank in that camp, which beſieged
" Pompey！ he has ſix legions, wakes at all
" hours, fears nothing, I ſee no end of this ca-
" lamity　His declaration at the laſt, which I
" had almoſt forgot, was odious ; that if he was
" not permitted to uſe my advice, he would uſe
" ſuch as he could get from others, and purſue
" all meaſures which were for his ſervice [z]"
From this conference, Cicero went directly to
Arpinum, and there inveſted his ſon, *at the age
of ſixteen, with the manly gown* he reſolved to
carry him along with him to Pompey's camp,
and thought it proper to give him an air of man-
hood before he enliſted him into the war . and
ſince he could not perform that ceremony at
Rome, choſe to oblige his Countrymen, by celebrating this Feſtival in his native City [a]

[z] Ad At 9 18
[a] Ego meo Ciceroni,
quoniam Roma caremus, Ar-
pini potiſſimum togam puram
dedi, idque municipibus noſtris fuit gratum—ib 19

WHILE

WHILE Cæsar was on the road towards Rome, young Quintus Cicero, the nephew, a fiery giddy youth, privately wrote to him to offer his service, with a promise of some information concerning his uncle, upon which, being sent for and admitted to an audience, he assured Cæsar, *that his Uncle was utterly disaffected to all his measures, and determined to leave Italy and go to Pompey* The boy was tempted to this rashness *by the hopes of a considerable present,* and gave much uneasiness by it both to the Father and the Uncle, *who had reason to fear some ill consequence from it* [b]: but Cæsar desiring still to divert Cicero from declaring against him, and to quiet the apprehensions which he might entertain for what was past, took occasion to signify to him in a kind Letter from Rome, that he retained *no resentment of his refusal to come to the City, though Tullus and Servius complained, that he had not shewn the same indulgence to them——ridiculous men,* says Cicero, *who, after sending their sons to besiege Pompey at Brundisium, pretend to be scrupulous about going to the Senate* [c]

CICERO's behaviour however, and residence *in those villa's* of his, which were nearest to the sea,

A Urb 704
Cic 58
Cost
C CLAUDIUS
MARCELLUS,
L CORNE
LIUS LENTU
LUS CRUS

[b] Litteras ejus ad Cæsarem missas ita graviter tulimus, ut te quidem celaremus ——tantum scito post Hirtium conventum, arcessitum, ab Cæsare, cum eo de meo animo ab suis consiliis alienissimo, & consilio relinquendae Italiam——ib 10 4, 5, &c
Quintum puerum accepi vehementer Avaritiam vitio fuisse, & spem magni congiarii Magnum hoc mal a est ——ib 10 7

[c] Cæsar mihi ignoscit per litteras, quod non Romam venerim, se sequi in optimam partem id accipere dicit Facile patior, quod scribit, secum Tullum & Servium questos esse, quia non idem sibi, quod mihi remisisset Homines ridiculos, qui cum suos misissent ad Cn Pompeium circumsidendum, ipsi in senatum venire dubitarent Ib 10 3.

A Urb 704
Cic 58
Coff
C Claudius
Marcelli.
L Corneli-
us Lentu
lus Crus

gave rife to a general report, that he was waiting
onely for a wind to carry him over to Pompey,
upon which Cæfar fent him another preffing Let
ter, to try, if poffible, to diffuade him from that
ftep.

Cæfar Emperor, to Cicero Emperor.

" Though I never imagined that you would do
" any thing rafhly or imprudently, yet moved by
" common report, I thought proper to write to
" you, and beg of you by our mutual affection,
" that you would not run to a declining caufe,
" whither you did not think fit to go while it
" ftood firm   For you will do the greateft inju-
" ry to our friendfhip, and confult but ill for
" yourfelf, if you do not follow, where fortune
" calls   for all things feem to have fucceded moft
" profperoufly for us, moft unfortunately for
" them   nor will you be thought to have follow-
" ed the caufe, (fince that was the fame, when
" you chofe to withdraw yourfelf from their coun
" cils) but to have condemned fome act of mine
" than which you can do nothing that could
" affect me more fenfibly, and what I beg by
" the rights of our friendfhip, that you would
" not do.   Laftly, what is more agreeable to
" the character of an honeft, quiet man, and
" good Citizen, than to retire from civil broils?
" from which fome, who would gladly have
" done it, have been deterred by an apprehen-
" fion or danger   but you, after a full teftimony
" of my life, and trial of my friendfhip, will
" find nothing more fafe or more reputable, than
" to keep yourfelf clear from all this contention.
" the 16th of April on the road [d] "

Ad Att x 8

ANTONY

A Urb 701
Cic 58
Cofl
C CLAUDIUS
MARCELLUS
L CORNELI-
US LENTU-
LUS CRUS

ANTONY alfo, whom Cæfar left to guard Italy in his abfence, wrote to him to the fame purpofe, and on the fame day.

Antonius Tribun of the people and Proprætor, to Cicero Emperor

"If I had not a great efteem for you, and
"much greater indeed than you imagine, I
"fhould not be concerned at the report which
"is fpread of you, efpecially when I take it to
"be but falfe. But out of the excefs of my af-
"fection, I cannot diffemble, that even a report,
"though falfe, makes fome impreffion on me.
"I cannot believe that you are preparing to crofs
"the fea, when you have fuch a value for Dola-
"bella, and your daughter Tullia, that excel-
"lent woman, and are fo much valued by us all,
"to whom in truth your dignity and honor are
"almoft dearer than to yourfelf. yet I did not
"think it the part of a friend not to be moved
"by the difcourfe even of ill-defigning men,
"and wrote this with the greater inclination, as
"I take my part to be the more difficult on the
"account of our late coldnefs, occafioned rather
"by my jealoufy, than any injury from you.
"For I defire you to affure yourfelf, that nobo-
"dy is dearer to me than you, excepting my
"Cæfar, and that I know alfo that Cæfar
"reckons M Cicero in the firft clafs of his
"friends Wherefore I beg of you, my Ci-
"cero, that you will keep yourfelf free and un-
"determined, and defpife the fidelity of that
"man who firft did you an injury, that he might
"afterwards do you a kindnefs, nor fly from
"him, who, though he fhould not love you,
"which is impoffible, yet will always defire to
"fee you in fafety and fplendor. I have fent

T 2 "Calpurnius

"Calpurnius to you with this, the moſt inti-
"mate of my friends, that you might perceive
"the great concern which I have for your life
"and dignity [e]"

Cælius alſo wrote to him on the ſame ſub-
ject, but finding by ſome hints in Cicero's an-
ſwer, that he was actually preparing to run away
to Pompey, he ſent him a ſecond Letter, in a
moſt pathetic, or, as Cicero calls it, *lamentable*
from [f], in hopes to work upon him by alarm-
ing all his fears

Caelius to Cicero

"Being in a conſternation at your Letter,
"by which you ſhew that you are meditating
"nothing but what is diſmal, yet neither tell
"me directly what it is, nor wholly hide it from
"me, I preſently wrote this to you. By all
"your fortunes, Cicero, by your children, I
"beg and beſeech you, not to take any ſtep in-
"jurious to your ſafety for I call the gods and
"men, and our friendſhip to witneſs, that what
"I have told, and forewarned you of, was not
"any vain conceit of my own, but after I had
"talked with Cæſar, and underſtood from him,
"how he reſolved to act after his victory, I in-
"formed you of what I had learnt If you
"imagine that his conduct will always be the
"ſame, in diſmiſſing his enemies and offering
"conditions, you are miſtaken he thinks and
"even talks of nothing but what is fierce and
"ſevere, and is gone away much out of humor
"with the Senate, and thoroughly provoked by
"the oppoſition which he has met with, nor will

[e] Ibid   ſcriptam miſerabiliter — ib
[f] M Cæli ep

"there

" there be any room for mercy Wherefore, if you
" yourfelf, your onely fon, your houfe, your
' remaining hopes be dear to you if I, if
" the worthy man, your fon-in-law, have any
" weight with you, you fhould not defire to
' overturn our fortunes, and force us to hate or
" to relinquifh that caufe in which our fafety
" confifts, or to entertain an impious wifh againft
' yours Laftly, reflect on this, that you have
" already given all the offence which you can
" give, by ftaying fo long behind, and now to
declare againft a Conqueror, whom you would
' not offend, while his caufe was doubtful, and
to fly after thofe who run away, with whom
" you would not join, while they were in condition to refift, is the utmoft folly Take
" care, that while you are afhamed not to ap-
" prove yourfelf, one of the beft Citizens, you
" be not too hafty in determining what is the
" beft. But if I cannot wholly prevail with
" you, yet wait at leaft till you know how we
" fuccede in Spain, which, I now tell you, will
" be ours as foon as Cæfar comes thither What
' hopes they may have when Spain is loft, I
' know not, and what your view can be in ac-
" ceding to a defperate caufe, by my faith I
' cannot find out As to the thing, which you
" difcover to me by your filence about it, Cæfar
" has been informed of it, and after the firft fa-
" lutation, told me prefently what he had heard
" of you I denied that I knew any thing of
' the matter, but begged of him to write to
" you in a manner the moft effectual, to make
" you ftay. He carries me with him into Spain;
" if he did not, I would run away to you where-
" ever you are, before I came to Rome, to dif-
" pute this point with you in perfon, and hold

A Urb 704.
Cic 58
Cofl
C Claudius
Marcellus.
L Corneli-
us Lentu-
lus Crus.

T 3   " you

"you faft even by force. Confider, Cicero,
" again and again, that you do not utterly ruin
" both you and yours, that you do not know-
" ingly and willingly throw yourfelf into diffi-
" culties, whence you fee no way to extricate
" yourfelf   But if either the reproaches of the
" better fort touch you, or you cannot bear the
" infolence and haughtinefs of a certain fet of
" men, I would advife you to chufe fome place
" remote from the war, till thefe contefts be
' over, which will foon be decided   if you do
" this, I fhall think that you have done wifely,
" and you will not offend Cæfar [g].

C ELIUS's advice, as well as his practice, was
grounded upon a maxim, which he had before
advanced in a Letter to Cicero, *that in a public*
diffenfion, as long as it was carried on by civil me-
thods, one ought to take the honefter fide, but when
it came to arms, the ftronger, and to judge that the
beft which was the fafeft [h].   Cicero was not of
his opinion, but governed himfelf in this, as he
generally did, in all other cafes, by a contrary
rule, *that where our duty and our fafety interfere,*
we fhould adhere always to what is right, whatever
danger we incur by it

CURIO paid Cicero *a friendly vifit of two days*
about this time on his way towards Sicily, the
command of which Cæfar had committed to
him.   Their converfation turned on the unhappy condition of the times, and the impending
miferies of the war, in which Curio was open,
and without any referve, in talking of Cæfar's

[g] Ep fam 8. 16
[h] Illud te non arbitror
fugere, quin homines in dif-
fenfione domeftica debeant
quamdiu civiliter fine armis
cernetur, honeftiorem fequi
partem   ubi ad bellum &
caftra ventum fit, firmiorem
& id melius ftatuere, quæ
tutius fit   Ep fam. 8 14

views : " He exhorted Cicero to chuse some
" neutral place for his retreat, assured him, that
" Cæsar would be pleased with it, offered him
" all kind of accommodation and safe passage
" through Sicily, made not the least doubt, but
" that Cæsar would soon be master of Spain,
" and then follow Pompey with his whole force,
" and that Pompey's death would be the end of
" the war : but confessed withal, that he saw
" no prospect or glimmering of hope for the
" Republic. said, that Cæsar was so provoked
" by the Tribun Metellus at Rome, that he
" had a mind to have killed him, as many of
' his friends advised, that if he had done it,
" a great slaughter would have ensued, that
" his clemency flowed, not from his natural
" disposition, but because he thought it po-
' pular, and if he once lost the affections of
" the people, he would be cruel that he was
" disturbed to see the people so disgusted by his
" seizing the public treasure, and though he
" had resolved to speak to them before he left
" Rome, yet he durst not venture upon it for
" fear of some affront, and went away at last
" much discomposed [*i*]."

THE leaving *the public treasure at Rome a prey
to Cæsar*, is censured more than once by Cicero,
as one of the blunders of his friends [*k*] but it
is a common case in civil dissensions, for the
honester side, through the fear of discrediting
their cause by any irregular act, to ruin it by an
unseasonable moderation The public money
was kept *in the temple of Saturn*, and the Consuls contented themselves with *carrying away the
keys*, fancying, that the sanctity of the place

A Urb 704.
Cic 58
Coss
C Claudius
Marcellus
L Cornel-
us Lentu-
lus Crus

[*i*] Ad Att x 4   [*k*] Ib. 7 12 15

T 4   would

A U⸱o 70⸱
Cic 58
Co⸱
C CLAUDUS
MARCELLS
L COR EII-
US LENTU
LUS CRUS

wou'd fecure it from violence , efpecially when the greateſt part of it was a *fund of a facred kind,* *fet apart by the laws for occafions* onely of the laſt exigency, *or the terror of a Gallic invafion* [*l*] Pompey was fenfible of the miſtake, when it was too late, and fent inſtructions to the Con- fuls to go back and fetch away *this facred trea-* *fure* but Cæfar was then fo far advanced, that they durſt not venture upon it , and Lentulus coldly fent him word, *that he himfelf fhould firſt* *march againſt Cæfar : to Picenum, that they might* *i⸱a e to do it with fafety* [*m*]　Cæfar had none of thefe fcruples, but as foon as he came to Rome, ordered " the door of the Temple to " be broken open, and the money to be feized " for his own ufe, and had like to have killed " the Tribun Metellus," who truſting to the authority of his office, was filly enough to at- tempt to hinder him　He found there an im- menfe treafure, " both in coin and wedges of " folid gold, referved from the fpoils of con " quered nations from the time even of the " Punic war for the Republic, *as Pliny fays,* " had never been richer than it was at this " day [*n*] "

CICERO was now impatient to be gone, and the more fo, on account of the inconvenient pomp of *his Laurel, and Lictors and ſtile of* *Emperor*, which in a time of that jealoufy and diſtraction expofed him too much to the eyes of the public, as well as to *the taunts and raillery*

<hr>

[*l*] Dio p 161

[*m*] C Caſus—— attulit mandata ad Confules, ut Ro- mam ve⸱rent, pecuniam de fanctiore ærario au erent—— Conful refcripfit, ut prius

ipfe in Picenum— ad Att 21

[*n*] Nec fuit alus tempo- r bus Refpub locupletior Plin Hiſt 33 3

of his enemies [*o*]. He resolved to cross the sea
to Pompey, yet knowing all his motions to be
narrowly watched, took pains to conceal his intention, especially from Antony, who resided at
this time in his neighbourhood, and kept a strict
eye upon him. He sent him word therefore by
Letter, that he had " no design against Cæsar;
" that he remembered his friendship, and his
" son-in-law Dolabella, that if he had other
" thoughts, he could easily have been with
' Pompey, that his chief reason for retiring
' was to avoid the uneasiness of appearing in
' public with the formality of his Lictors [*p*] "
But Antony wrote him a surly answer, which
Cicero calls *a Laconic Mandate*, and sent a copy
of it to Atticus, *to let him see*, he says, *how ty-
rannically it was drawn*

" How sincere is your way of acting? for
" he, who has a mind to stand neuter, stays at
" home, he, who goes abroad seems to pass a
" judgment on the one side or the other. But
" it does not belong to me to determine, whe-
" ther a man may go abroad or not. Cæsar has
" imposed this task upon me, not to suffer any
" man to go out of Italy. Wherefore it signi-
" fies nothing for me to approve your resoluti-
" on, if I have no power to indulge you in it.
" I would have you write to Cæsar, and ask
" that favor of him. I do not doubt but you

A Urb 704.
Cic 58
Coss
C Claudius
Marcellus,
L Corneli-
us Lentu-
ius Crus.

[*o*] Accedit etiam molesta hæc pompa lictorum meorum nomenque imperii quo appellor — sed incurrit hæc molera laus non solum in oculos sed jam etiam in vocuis malevolorum —— Ep fam 2 16
[*p*] Cum ego sæpissime

scripsissem, nihil me contra Cæsaris rationes cogitare, meminisse me generi mei, meminisse amicitiæ, potuisse si aliter sentirem, esse cum Pompeio, me autem, quia cum lictoribus invitus cursarem, abesse velle — ad Att. x 10

" will

A Urb 704
Cic 58
Coff
C CLAUDIUS
MARCELLUS,
L CORNELI-
US LENTU-
LUS CRUS

" will obtain it, efpecially fince you promife to
" retain a regard for our friendfhip [q]."

AFTER this Letter, Antony never came to fee
him, but fent an excufe, *that he was afhamed to
do it, becaufe he took him to be angry with him,*
giving him to underftand at the fame time by
Trebatius, *that he had fpecial orders to obferve his
motions* [r].

THESE Letters give us the moft fenfible
proof of the high efteem and credit in which
Cicero florifhed at this Time in Rome when
in a conteft for Empire, which force alone was
to decide, we fee the Chiefs on both fides fo
follicitous to gain a man to their party, who
had no peculiar fkill in arms or talents for war
but his name and authority was the acquifition
which they fought, fince whatever was the fate
of their arms, the world, they knew, would
judge better of the caufe which Cicero efpoufed
The fame Letters will confute likewife in a great
meafure the common opinion of his want of
refolution in all cafes of difficulty, fince no man
could fhew a greater than he did on the prefent
occafion, when againft the importunities of his
friends, and all the invitations of a fuccefsfull
power, he chofe to follow that caufe which he
thought the beft, though he knew it to be the
weakeft.

DURING Cæfar's abfence in Spain, Antony,
who had nobody to controul him at home,
gave a free courfe to his natural difpofition, and
indulged himfelf without referve in all the ex-

[q] Ad Att x 10
[r] Nominatim de me fibi
imperatum dicit Antonius,
nec me tamen ipfe adhuc vi-
derat, fed hoc Trebatio nar-
ravit Ib x 12,
Antonius— ad me mifit fe
pudore deterritum ad me non
venifle, quod me fibi fuccenfere putaret—ib x 15

cefs of lewdnefs and luxury.   Cicero defcribing
his ufual equipage in travelling about Italy, fays,
" he carries with him in an open Chaife the
" famed Actrefs Cytheris; his wife follows in a
" fecond, with feven other clofe Litters, full of
" his whores and boys. See by what bafe hands
" we fall, and doubt, if you can, whether Cæ-
" far, let him come vanquifhed or victorious,
" will not make cruel work amongft us at his
" return   For my part, if I cannot get a fhip,
" I will take a boat to tranfport myfelf out of
" their reach; but I fhall tell you more after I
" have had a conference with Antony [s]."   A-
mong Antony's other extravagances, he had the
infolence to appear fometimes in public, *with his
miftrefs Cytheris in a Chariot drawn by Lions.* Cicero alluding to this, in a Letter to Atticus, tells
him jocofely, *that he need not be afraid of Antony's
Lions* [t], for though the beafts were fo fierce,
the mafter himfelf was very tame.

PLINY fpeaks of this fact, *as a defigned infult
on the Roman people,* as if *by the emblem of the
Lions, Antony intended to give them to underftand,
that the fierceft fpirits of them would be forced to
fubmit to the yoke* [u]   Plutarch alfo mentions it;
                                            but

A Urb 704
Cic 58
Coff
C CLAUDIUS
MARCELLUS.
L CORNELI-
US LENTU-
LUS CRUS.

---

[s] Hic tamen Cytheridem
fecum lectica aperta portat,
alterea uxorem feptem præ-
teria conjunctæ lecticæ funt
amicarum, an amicorum?
vide quam turpi leto perea-
mus & dubita, fi potes, quin
ille feu victus, feu victor re-
dierit, cædem facturus fit.
Ego vero vel lintriculo, fi
navis non erit, eripiam me ex
iftorum parricidio Sed plura

fcribam cum illum convenero
—ib x 10
   [t] Tu Antonii leones per-
timefcas, cave Nihil eft illo
homine jucundius   Ib x.
13
   [u] Jugo fubdidit eos,
primufque Romæ ad currum
junxit Antonius, & quidem
civili bello cum dimicatum
effet in Pharfalicis campis,
non fine oftento quodam tem-
                          porum

A Urb 704
Cic 58
Coſſ
C CLAUDIUS
MARCELLUS
L COR ELI-
US LENTU-
LL CRUS

but both of them place it *after the battle of Pharſalia*, though it is evident from this hint of it given by Cicero, that it happened long before

WHILST Cicero continued at Formiæ, deliberating on the meaſures of his conduct, he formed ſeveral *political theſes's*, adapted to the circumſtances of the times, for the amuſement of his ſolitary hours " Whether a man ought " to ſtay in his Country, when it was poſſeſſed " by a Tyrant whether one ought not by all " means to attempt the diſſolution of the Ty- " ranny, though the City on that account was " expoſed to the utmoſt hazard . whether there " was not cauſe to be afraid of the man who " ſhould diſſolve it, left he ſhould advance him- " ſelf into the other's place whether we ſhould " not help our country by the methods of peace, " rather than war whether it be the part of a " Citizen to ſit ſtill in a neutral place, while " his country is oppreſſed, or to run all hazards " for the ſake of the common liberty whe- " ther one ought to bring a war upon his city, " and beſiege it, when in the hands of a Ty- " rant whether a man, not approving the diſ- " ſolution of a Tyranny by war, ought not to " join himſelf however to the beſt Citizens " whether one ought to act with his benefactors " and friends, though they do not in his opi- " nion take right meaſures for the public inte- " reſt whether a man, who has done great " ſervices for his country, and for that reaſon

porum, generoſo ſpiritus ju-   ſupra monſtra etiam illarum
gum ſubire illo prodigio ſig-   calamitatum fuit. —— Plin
nificante nam quod ita vec-   Hiſt 8 16.
tus eſt cum mima Cytheride

4   " has

" has been envied and cruelly treated, is still
' bound to expose himself to fresh dangers for
" it, or may not be permitted at last to take
" care of himself and his family, and give up
" all political matters to the men of power——
' by exercising myself, *says he*, in these questions,
" and examining them on the one side and the
" other, I relieve my mind from its present an-
" xiety, and draw out something which may be
" of use to me [*x*] "

A Urb 704.
Cic 58.
Coss
C. Claudius
Marcellus,
L Corneli-
us Lentu-
lus Crus.

FROM the time of his leaving the City, together with Pompey and the Senate, there passed
not a single day in which he did not write *one or
more Letters to Atticus* [*y*], the onely friend whom
he trusted with the secret of his thoughts. From
these letters it appears, that the summ of Atticus's advice to him agreed intirely with his
own sentiments, *that if Pompey remained in Italy,
he ought to join with him, if not, should stay behind,
and expect what fresh accidents might produce* [*z*].
This was what Cicero had hitherto followed;
and as to his future conduct, though he seems
sometimes to be a little wavering and irresolute,
yet the result of his deliberations constantly turned in favor of Pompey. His personal affection
for the man, preference of his cause, the re-

[*x*] In his ego me consul-
tationibus exercens, differens
in utramque partem, tum
græce tum latine, abduco pa-
umper animum a molestus
& ε πϛεϛγε τι dul beio Ad
Att 9 4

[*y*] Hujus autem epistolæ
non solu n ea causa est, ut ne
quis a me dies intermittetur,
quin dem ad te literas, sed
—ib 8 12

Alteram tibi eodem die
hanc epistolam dictavi, &
pridie dederam mea manu
longiorem—ib x 3

[*z*] Ego quidem tibi non
sim auctor, si Pompeius Italiam relinquit, te quoque
profugere, summo enim periculo facies, nec Reipub pro-
deris, cui quidem posterius
poteris prodesse, si manseris
—ib 9 10

proaches

A Urb. 704.
Cic. 58
Coff.
C CLAUDIUS
MARCELLUS,
L CORNELI-
US LENTU-
LUS CRUS.

proaches of the better fort, who began to cenfure his tardinefs, and above all, *his gratitude for fa-vors received,* which had ever the greateft weight with him, made him refolve at all adventures to run after him; and though he was difpleafed with his management of the war, *and without any hopes of his fuccefs* [a]; though he knew him before *to be no politician, and now perceived him,* he fays, *to be no general,* yet with all his faults, he could not endure the thought of deferting him, nor hardly forgive himfelt for ftaying fo long behind him, " For as in love, fays he, any thing dirty " and indecent in a miftrefs will ftifle it for the " prefent, fo the deformity of Pompey's con- " duct put me out of humor with him, but " now that he is gone, my love revives, and " I cannot bear his abfence, &c [b] "

WHAT held him ftill a while longer was *the tears of his family, and the remonftrances of his daughter Tullia,* who entreated him *to wait oney the iffue of the Spanifh war,* and urged it as the *advice of Atticus* [c] He was paffionately fond of this daughter, and with great reafon, for fhe was a woman of fingular accomplifhments, with

[a] Ingrati animi crimen horreo—ib 9 2, 5, 7 —

Nec mehercule hoc facio Reip b caufa, quam fundi-tus celeram puto, fed nequis me putet ingratum in eum, qui me levavit iis incommo-dis quibus ipfe affecerat—b 9 19

Fortunæ funt committenda omnia Sine fpe conanur ulla Si mel us quid acc r.r.rab mur—ib x 2

/ Sicut ... τοις .. .. alterat ... munda ... ...

indecoræ fic me illius fugæ negligentiæque deformitas a vertit ab amore — nunc e mergit amor, nunc defide rium ferre non poffum Ib 9 10

[c] Sed cum ad me mea Tu lia fcribat, orans, ut quid in Hifpania geratur expectem, & femper adfcribat idem vi deri tibi—ib x 8

Lacrymæ meorum me in terdum molliunt, precantium ut de Hifpanis expectemus— ib. x. 9

the

the utmoft affection and piety to him : fpeaking
of her to Atticus, " how admirable, fays he, is
" her virtue ? how does fhe bear the public ca-
" lamity ? how her domeftic difgufts ? what a
" greatnefs of mind did fhe fhew at my parting
" from them ? in fpight of the tendernefs of her
" love, fhe wifhes me to do nothing but what
" is right, and for my honor [d] " But as to
the affair of Spain, he anfwered, " that what-
" ever was the fate of it, it could not alter the
" cafe with regard to himfelf for if Cæfar fhould
" be driven out of it, his journey to Pompey
" would be lefs welcome and reputable, fince
' Curio himfelf would run over to him · or if the
" war was drawn into length, there would be no
" end of waiting or laftly, if Pompey's army
" fhould be beaten, inftead of fitting ftill, as they
" advifed, he thought juft the contrary, and fhould
" chufe the rather to run away from the violence
" of fuch a victory He refolved therefore, *he*
" *fays*, to act nothing craftily but whatever be-
" came of Spain, to find out Pompey as foon as
" he could, in conformity to Solon's law, who
" made it capital for a Citizen not to take part
" in a civil diffenfion [e] "

A Urb 704.
Cic 58.
Coff
C Claudius
Marcellus,
L Corneli-
us Lentu-
lus Crus

[d] Cujus quidem virtus
mirifica Quomodo illa fert
publicam cladem ? quomodo
comefticas tricas ? quantus
autem animus in difceffu noftio ? fit ϛοφϡ, fit fummᵒ
εὐνοῖς, tamen nos recte face e & bene audire vult Ib
x 8

[e] Si pelletur, quam gra-
us aut quam honeftus tum erit
ad Pompeium nofter adventus,
cum ipfum Curionem ad ip-
fum tranfiturum putem ? fi

trahitur bellum, quid expectem, aut quamdiu ? relin-
quitur, ut fi vincimur in Hifpania, quiefcamus Id ego
contra puto iftum enim vic-
torem relinquendum magis
puto, quam victum—ibid —

Aftute nihil fum acturus,
fiat in Hifpania quidlibet. Ib.
x 6

Ego vero Solonis— legem
negligam, qui capite fanxit,
fi qui in feditione non alter-
utrius partis fuiffet—ib x 1.

BEFORE his going off, Servius Sulpicius ſent him word from Rome, that *he had a great deſire to have a conference with him, to conſult in common what meaſures they ought to take* Cicero conſented to it, in hopes to find Servius in the ſame mind with himſelf, and to have his company to Pompey's camp for in anſwer to his meſſage, he intimated his own intention *of leaving Italy* , and if Servius was not in the ſame reſolution, adviſed him *to ſave himſelf the trouble of the journey, though if he had any thing of moment to communicate, he would wait for his coming* [f] But at their meeting he found him ſo timorous and deſponding, and ſo full of ſcruples upon every thing which was propoſed, that inſtead of preſſing him to the ſame conduct with himſelf, he found it neceſſary to conceal his own deſign from him " of all the men, ſays he, whom I have met " with, he is alone a greater Coward than C " Marcellus, who laments his having been " Conſul , and urges Antony to hinder my " going, that he himſelf may ſtay with a better " grace [g] "

CATO, whom Pompey had ſent to poſſeſs himſelf of Sicily, thought fit to quit that poſt,

[f] Sin autem tibi homini prudentiſſimo videtur utile eſſe, nos colloqui, quanquam long us etiam cogitabam ab urbe diſcedere, cujus jam etiam no nen invitus audio, tamen propius accedam——— Ep fam 4 1

Reſtat ut diſcedendum putem , in quo reliqua videtur eſſe deliberatio, quod conſilium in diſceſſu, quæ loca ſequamur— ſi habes jam ita utum que tibi agendum pu-

tes, in quo non ſit conjunctum conſilium tuum cum meo, ſuperſedeas hoc labore itineris—ib 4 2

[g] Servii conſilio nihil expeditur Omnes captiones in omni ſententia occurrunt Unum C Marcello cognovi timidiorem, quem Conſulem fuiſſe pœnitet — qui etiam Antonium confirmaſſe dicitur, ut me impediret, qui ipſe, credo honeſtius — Ad Att x 15

and yield up the Island to Curio, who came like- A Urb 704.
wise to seize it on Cæsar's part with a superior Cic 58
force Cicero was much scandalized at Cato's   Coss
conduct, being persuaded that he might have Marcellus,
held his possession without difficulty, and that L Corne-
all honest men would have flocked to him espe- lius Lentu-
cially *when Pompey's fleet was so near to support* lus Crus.
him for if that had but once appeared on the
coast, and begun to act, Curio himself as he
confessed, *would have run away the first. I wish,*
says Cicero, that Cotta may hold out Sardinia as it
is said he will for if so, how base will Cato's act
appear [b]

In these Circumstances, while he was preparing all things for his voyage, and waiting
onely for a fair wind, he removed from his *Cu-*
man to his Pompeian Villa beyond Naples, which,
not being so commodious for an embarkment,
would help *to lessen the suspicion of his intended*
flight [i] Here he received a private message
from the Officers of three Cohorts, which were
in garrison at Pompeii, to beg leave to wait upon
him the day following, in order to deliver up
their troops and the town into his hands; but
instead of listening to the overture, he slipt away
the next morning before day to avoid seeing them;
since such a force or a greater could be of no ser-

[b] Curio mecum vixit—
Siciliæ diffidens, si Pompeius
navigare cœpisset—ib x 7
Curio—Pompeii classem ti-
mebat quæ si esset, se de Si-
cilia arbiturum Ib x 4
Cato qui Siciliam tenere
nullo negotio potuit & si te-
nuisset omnes boni ad eum
contulissent, Syracusis profectus est a d 8 Kal. Maii

—utinam, quod aiunt, Cotta
Sardiniam teneat Est enim
rumor O, si id fuerit, tur-
pem Catonem !——ib x 16
[i] Ego ut minuerim sus-
picionem profectionis,—profectus sum in Pompeianum
a d iiii Id Ut ibi essem,
dum quæ ad navigandum o-
pus esset, pararentur Ib.

A Urb ꝛol
Cic 58
Coff
C Claudius
Marcellu
L Cornell
us Lentu
lus Crus

vice there, and he was apprehensive that it was designed onely as a trap for him [*k*]

THUS pursuing at last the result of all his deliberations, and preferring the consideration of duty to that of his safety, he embarked to follow Pompey, and though from the nature of the war, he plainly saw and declared, " that it " was a contention onely for rule, yet he " thought *Pompey the modester, honester and* " *juster King of the two*, and if he did not con- " quer, that the very name of the Roman peo- " ple would be extinguished, or if he did, that " it would still be after the manner and pattern " of Sylla, with much cruelty and blood [*l*]." With these melancholy reflections he set sail *on the eleventh of June* [*m*], " rushing, as he tells " us

---

[*k*] Cum ad villam venis sem venturus est ad me, Cen turiones trium Cohortium, quæ Pompeus sunt, me velle postridie, hæc mecum Nin nius noster, velle eos mihi se, & oppidum tradere At ego tio postridie a villa ante lu cem, ut me omnino illi non viderunt Quid enim erat in tribus cohortibus quid si plures, quo apparatu ?—& si mul feri poterat, ut tentare mur Omnem igitur suspi cionem sustuli—ibid

[*l*] Dominatio quæsita ab utroque est Id 8 11

Regnandi contentio est, in qua pulsus est modestior Rex & probior & integrior, & is qui nisi vincit, nomen po puli Romani deleatur necesse est Sin autem vincit, Sylla-

no more, exemploque vince —ib x 7

[*m*] a d iii Id Jun Ep fam 14 7 It is remark able, that among the reasons, which detained Cicero in Ita ly longer than he intended, he mentions the *tempestuous weather of the Equinox, and the calms that succeeded it*, yet this was about the end of May [ad Att x 17. 18] which shews what a strange confusion there was at this time in the Roman Kalendar, and what necessity for that reformation of it, which Cæ sar soon after effected, in or der to reduce the computation of their months to the regular course of the seasons from which they had so widely va ried Some of the commen

tator

A. Urb 704.
Cic 58.
Coss
C. Claudius
Marcellus
L Corneli-
us Lentu-
lus Crus.

" us, knowingly and willingly into voluntary
" destruction, and doing just what cattel do
" when driven by any force, running after those
" of his own kind, for as the ox, *says he,* fol-
" lows the herd, so I follow the honest, or
" those at least, who are called so, though it be
" to certain ruin [*n*] " As to his brother Quintus, he was so far from desiring his company in
this flight, that *he pressed him to stay in Italy* on
account of his personal obligations to Cæsar, and
the relation he had born to him yet Quintus
would not be left behind, but declared, *that he
would follow his Brother, whithersoever he should
lead, and think that party right which he should
chuse for him* [*o*].

WHAT gave Cicero a more particular abhorrence of the war, into which he was entering, was,
to see Pompey on all occasions affecting to imitate Sylla, and to hear him often say with a superior air, *could Sylla do such a thing, and cannot
I do it?* as if determined to make Sylla's victory
the pattern of his own He was now in much
the same circumstances in which that Conqueror

---

tators, for want of attending
to this cause, are strangely
puzzled to account for the
difficulty ; and one of them
ridiculously imagines, that
by the *Equinox,* Cicero co-
vertly means Antony, who
used to make *his days and
nights equal,* by sleeping as
much as he waked —

[*n*] Ego prudens ac sciens
ad pestem ante oculos posi-
tam tum profectus [Ep fam.
6 6]

Prudens & sciens tanquam
ad interitum ruerem volunta-

rium [pro M Marcel 5]
quid ergo acturus es ? idem,
quod pecudes, quæ dispulsæ
sui generis sequuntur greges.
Ut bos armenta, sic ego bonos viros, aut eos, quicunque
dicentur boni, sequar, etiam
si ruent—ad Att 7 7

[*o*] Fratrem—socium hu-
jus fortunæ esse non erat æ-
quum cui magis etiam Cæ-
sar irascetur Sed impetrare
non possum, ut maneat [ib.
9 1] frater, quicquid mihi
placeret, id rectum se putare
aiebat Ib 9 6

had

A Urb 701
Cic 58
Coſſ
C Claudie
Marcelus
L Corel
us Lent
lus C us

had once been, ſuſtaining the cauſe of the Senate by his arms, and treated as an enemy by
thoſe who poſſeſſed Italy, and as he flattered
himſelf with the ſame good fortune, ſo he was
meditating the ſame kind of return, and threaten-
ing ruin and proſcription to all his enemies. This
frequently ſhocked Cicero, as we find from many
of his Letters, to conſider with what cruelty and
effuſion of civil blood the ſucceſs even of his own
friends would certainly be attended [p]

We have no account of the manner and circumſtances of his voyage, or by what courſe he
ſteered towards Dyrrachium, for after his leaving Italy, all his correſpondence with it was in
great meaſure cut off, ſo that from June, in
which he ſailed, we find an intermiſſion of about
nine months in the ſeries of his Letters, and not
more than four or them written to Atticus during
the continuance of the war [q] He arrived
however ſafely in Pompey's camp with *his ſon,
his brother, and nephew,* committing the fortunes of the whole family to the iſſue of that
cauſe. and that he might make ſome amends for
coming ſo late, and gain the greater authority
with his party, *he furniſhed Pompey, who was
in great want of money, with a large ſumm out of
his own ſtock for the public ſervice* [r]

---

[p] Quam crebro illud
Sylla potuit ego non potero —
Ita Sylla erit animus ejus,
& proſcriptio diu [Att 9
5] Cneus noſter Syllani regni
ſimilitudinem concupivit, ει-
δως ται λεγω [ib 7] ut non
nominatim ſed generatim
proſcriptio eſſet informata
ib 10

[q] Vid Ad Att xi 1, 2,
4

[r] Etſi egeo rebus omni-
bus, quod is quoque in anguſtiis eſt, quicum ſumus, cui
magnam dedimus pecuniam
mutuam, opinantes nobis,
conſtitutis rebus, eam rem e-
tiam honore fore [ib xi 3]
ſi quas habuimus facultates,
eas Pompeio tum, cum id vi-
debamur ſapienter facere,
detulimus Ib 13

A Urb 704.
Cic 58
Coff
C Claudius
Marcellus
L Cornlli
us Lentu-
lus Crus.

But as he entered into the war with reluctance, so he found nothing in it but what increased his disgust. he disliked every thing *which they had done, or designed to 'do, saw nothing good amongst them but their cause*, and that their own counsels would ruin them · for all the chiefs of the party trusting to the superior fame and authority of Pompey, and dazzled with the splendor of the troops, which the Princes of the East had sent to their assistance, assured themselves of victory; and, without reflecting on the different character of the two armies, would hear of nothing but fighting It was Cicero's business therefore to discourage this wild spirit, and to represent the hazard of the war, the force of Cæsar, and the probability of his beating them, if ever they ventured a battel with him but all his remonstrances were slighted, and *he himself reproach-ed as timorous and cowardly by the other Leaders: though nothing afterwards happened to them, but what he had often foretold* [s] This soon made him *repent of embarking in a cause so imprudently conducted*, and it added to his discontent, to find himself even *blamed by Cato for coming to them at all*, and deserting that neutral post, which might have given him the better opportunity of bringing about an accommodation [t]

In this disagreeable situation he declined all employment, and finding his counsils wholly

[s] Quippe mihi nec quæ accidunt, nec quæ aguntur, ullo modo probantur [ib vi 4] nihil boni præter causam [Ep fam 7 3] itaque ego, quem tum fortes illi viri, Domitii & Lentuli, timidum esse dicebant, &c [ib 6 ·1] quo quidem in bello, ni-

hil adversi accidit non prædicente me Ib 6

[t Cujus me mei facti pœnituit, non tam propter periculum meum, quam propter vitia multa, quæ ibi ostendi, quo veneram Ib 7 3 — Pluti in Cic

nighted

A Urb 704
Cic 58
Coss
C Claudius
Marcellus
L Cornelius Lentulus Crus

flighted, refumed his ufual way of raillery, and what he could not diffuade by his authority, endeavoured to make ridiculous by his *jests* This gave occafion afterwards to Antony, in a fpeech to the Senate, to cenfure the levity of his behaviour in the calamity of a civil war, and to reflect not onely upon his fears, but the unfeafonablenefs alfo of his *jokes*, to which Cicero anfwered, " that " though their camp indeed was full of care " and anxiety, yet in circumftances the moft " turbulent, there were certain moments of re- " laxation, which all men, who had any huma- " nity in them, were glad to lay hold on but " while Antony reproached him both with de- " jection and joking at the fame time, it was a " fure proof that he had obferved a proper tem- " per and moderation in them both [*u*].

[*u*] Ipfe fugi adhuc omne munus eo magis, quod ita mihi potuit agi, ut mihi & meis rebus aptum effet [Att xi 4] Quod autem idem mœftitiam meam reprehendit idem jocum, magno argumento eft me in utroque fuiffe moderatum Phil z 16

Some of Cicero's fayings on this occafion are preferved by different writers When Pompey put him in mind of his coming fo late to them how can I come too late, faid he, when I find nothing ready among you? and upon Pompey's afking him farcaftically where he had left his fon Dolabella etc, he is with your Father-in-law, replied he To a perfon new-

ly arrived from Italy, and informing them of a ftrong report at Rome, that Pompey was blocked up by Cæfar, and ou failed hither therefore, faid he, that you might fee with your own eyes And even after their defeat, when Nonnius was exhorting them to courage, becaufe there were feven eagles ftill left in Pompey's camp, you encourage us well, faid he, if we were to fight with Jackdaws By the frequency of thefe fplenetic jokes, he is faid to have provoked Pompey fo far as to tell him, I wifh that you would go over to the other fide, that you may learn to fear us Vid Macrob Saturn 2 3 Plutar in Cicer

YOUNG Brutus was alſo in Pompey's camp, where he diſtinguiſhed himſelf by a peculiar zeal which Cicero mentions as the more re-markable, becauſe he had always profeſſed *an ir-reconcileable hatred to Pompey, as to the murderer of his Father* [x] But he followed the cauſe, not the man, ſacrificing all his reſentments to the ſervice of his country, and looking now upon Pompey *as the General of the Republic,* and the defender of their common liberty

DURING the courſe of this war Cicero never ſpeaks of Pompey's conduct but *as a perpetual ſuc-ceſſion of blunders* His firſt ſtep *of leaving Italy* was condemned indeed by all, *but particularly by Atticus,* yet to us at this diſtance, it ſeems not onely to have been prudent, but neceſſary [y]. What ſhocked people ſo much at it was the diſ-covery that it made of his weakneſs and want of preparation; and after the ſecurity which he had all along affected, and the defiance ſo oft declared againſt his adverſary, it made him appear con-temptible to run away at laſt on the firſt approach of Cæſar " Did you ever ſee, ſays Cælius, a " more ſilly creature than this Pompey of yours, " who, after raiſing all this buſtle, is found to " be ſuch a trifler ? or did you ever read or hear " of a man more vigourous in action, more tem-" perate in victory, than our Cæſar [z] ?"

U 4　　　　　　　POMPEY

A Urb 704
Cic 56
Coſſ
C CLAUDIUS MARCELLUS
L CORNELI-US LENTU-IUS CRUS.

[x] Brutus amicus in cauſa verſatur acriter Ad Att xi 4
　Vid Plutar. in Brut & Pomp.
　[y] Quorum dux quam αϛραϊηϒιϊος, tu quoque ani-madvertis, cui ne Picena qui-dem nota ſunt quam autem ſine concilio, res teſtis. Ad

Att ˜ 13
　Si iſte Italiam relinquet, faciet omnino male, & ut ego exiſtimo αλογίϛως, &c ib 9. 10
　[z] Ecquando tu hominem ineptiorem quam tuum Cn Pompeium vidiſti ? qui tan tas turbas, qui tam nugax eſ-ſet commorit ? ecquem au-tem

A Urb 704
Cic 58
Coss
C Claudius
Marcellus
L Corneli-
us Lentu
lus Coss

POMPEY had left Italy about a year before Cæsar found it convenient to go after him; during which time he had gathered a vast fleet from all the *maritime States and Cities dependent on the Empire*, without making any use of it to distress an enemy who had no fleet at all   he suffered Sicily and Sardinia to fall into Cæsar's hands, without a blow, and the important town of Marseilles, after having endured a long seige for its affection to his cause   but his capital error was the giving up Spain, and neglecting to put himself at the head of the best army that he had, in a country devoted to his interests, and commodious for the operations of his naval force   when Cicero first heard of this resolution, he thought it *monstrous* [a], and in truth, the committing that war to his Lieutenants against the superior genius and ascendant of Cæsar, was the ruin of his best troops and hopes at once.

SOME have been apt to wonder, why Cæsar, after forcing Pompey out of Italy, instead of crossing the sea after him, when he was in no condition to resist, should leave him for the space of a year to gather armies and fleets at his leisure, and strengthen himself, with all the forces of the East   But Cæsar had good reasons for what he did   he knew that all the troops, which could be drawn together from those countries, were no match for his, that if he had pursued him directly to Greece, and driven him out of it, as he

---

tem Cæsare nostro acriorem in rebus agendis, eodem in victoria temperatiorem, aut legisti aut audisti Ep fam 8 15

[a] Omnis hæc classis Alexandria, Colchis, Tyro, Sidone, Cypro, Pamph, in Ly-

ca, Rhodo, &c ad intercludendos Italiæ commeatus —comparatur—ad Att 9 9

Nunciat Ægyptum—cogitare, Hispaniam abjecisse Monstra narrant——ad Att 9 11

2   had

had done out of Italy, he fhould have driven him probably into Spain, where of all places he defired the leaft to meet him; and where in all events Pompey had a fure refource, as long as it was poffeffed by a firm and veteran army, which t was Cæfar's bufinefs therefore to deftroy in the firft place, or he could expect no fuccefs from the war, and there was no opportunity of deftroying it fo favorably, as when Pompey himfelf was at fuch a diftance from it This was the reafon of his marching back with fo much expedition to find, as he faid, *an army without a General, and return to a General without an army* [b] The event fhewed, that he judged right, for within *forty days* from the firft fight of his enemy in Spain, he made himfelf mafter of the whole Province [c].

AFTER the reduction of Spain, he was cre-a'ed *Dictator* by *M. Lepidus*, then *Prætor at Rome*, and by his *Dictatorial* power declared himfelf Conful, with P Servilius Ifauricus, but he was no fooner invefted with this office, than he marched to Brundifium, and embarked on the fourth of January, in order to find out Pompey. The carrying about in his perfon the fupreme dignity of the Empire, added no fmall authority to his caufe, by making the Cities and States abroad the more cautious of acting againft him, or giving them a better pretence at leaft *for opening their gates to the Conful of Rome*———[d]. Cicero all this while defpairing of any good from

A Urb 705
Cic 59
Coff
C Julius
Cæsar II
P Servilius
Vatia Isau-
ricus

---

[b] Ire fe ad exercitum une duce, & inde reverfurum ad ducem fine exercitu Sueton J Cæf 34
[c] Cæf. Comment 1 2

[d] Illi fe daturos negare, neque portas Confuli præclufuro. Cæf Comm 1 3 590.

the

A Urb 705
Cic 59
Coff
C Julius
Cæsar II
P Servilius
Vatia Isau-
ricus.

the war, had been ufing all his endeavours to
difpofe his friends to peace, till Pompey forbad
any farther mention of it in council, declaring,
that he valued neither life nor country, for which
he muft be indebted to Cæfar, as the world muft take
the cafe to be, fhould he accept any conditions in his
prefent circumftances [e]　　He was fenfible that he
had hitherto been acting a contemptible part, and
done nothing equal to the great name which he
had acquired in the world, and was determined
therefore, to retrieve his honour before he laid
down his arms, by the deftruction of his adverfary, or to perifh in the attempt.

During the blockade of Dyrrhachium, it
was a current notion in Cæfar's army, *that Pom-*
pey would draw off his troops into his fhips, and
remove the war to fome diftant place.　Upon this
Dolabella, who was with Cæfar, fent a Letter to
Cicero into Pompey's Camp, exhorting him,
" that if Pompey fhould be driven from thefe
" quarters, to feek fome other country, he would
" fit down quietly at Athens, or any City remote
" from the war · that it was time to think of his
" own fafety, and be a friend to himfelf, rather
" than to others　that he had now fully fatisfied
" his duty, his friendfhip, and his engagements to
" that party. which he had efpoufed in the Re
" public . that there was nothing left, but to be,
" where the Republic itfelf now was, rather than

[e] Defperans victoriam,
primum cœpi fuadere pacem,
cujus fueram femper auctor,
deinde cum ab ea fententia
Pompeius valde abhorreret
Ep fam 7 3
　Vibullius —— de Cæfaris
mandatis agere inftituit, eum

ingreffum in fermonem Pom
peius interpellavit, & loqui
plura prohibuit　Quid mihi,
inquit, aut vita aut civitate
opus eft, quam beneficio Cæ
faris habere videbor ? Cæf
Comm 3 596 .

" by

" by following that ancient one to be in none at
" all—— and that Cæfar would readily approve
" this conduct [*f*]." but the war took a quite
different turn, and inftead of *Pompey's running
away from Dyrrhachium*, Cæfar, by an unexpected defeat before it, was forced to retire the firft,
and leave to Pompey the credit of purfuing him,
as in a kind of flight towards Macedonia.

A. Urb 705
Cic 59.
Coff.
C Julius
Cæsar II
P Servilius
Vatia Isau-
ricus.

WHILE the two armies were thus employed,
Cælius, now Prætor at Rome, trufting to his
power, and the fuccefs of his party, began to
publifh feveral violent and odious laws, efpecially
one *for the cancelling of all debts* [*g*] This raifed
a great flame in the City, till he was over-ruled
and depofed from his magiftracy by the Conful
Servilius, and the Senate but being made defperate by this affront, he recalled Milo from his
exil at Marfeilles, whom Cæfar had refufed to
reftore, and in concert with him, refolved to
raife fome public commotion in favor of Pompey.
In this difpofition he wrote his laft Letter to Cicero, in which, after an account of his conver-
fion, and the fervice which he was projecting,
" You are afleep, fays he, and do not know how
" open and weak we are here what are you do-
" ing? are you waiting for a battel, which is
" fure to be againft you? I am not acquainted
" with your troops, but ours have been long ufed
" to fight hard, and to bear cold and hunger with

[*f*] Illud autem a te peto,
ut, fi jam ille evitaverit hoc
periculum, & fe abdiderit in
claffem, tu tuis rebus confu-
las & aliquando tibi potius
quam cuivis, fis amicus Satis factum eft jam a te vel
officio, vel familiaritati, fa-
tisfactum etiam partibus, &

ei Re:pub quam tu probabas
Reliquum eft, ubi nunc eft
Refpub ibi fimus potius,
quam dum veterem illam fe-
quamur, fimus in nulla Ep.
fam 9 9
[*g*] Cæf Comment 3
600.

" eafe,

A Urb 705
Cic 59
Coss
C Julius
Cæsar II
P Servilius
Vatia Isau-
ricus.

" eafe [*h*]." But this difturbance, which began to alarm all Italy, was foon ended by the death of the Authors of it, Milo and Cælius, who perifhed in their rafh attempt, being deftroyed by the foldiers, whom they were endeavouring to debauch. They had both attached themfelves very early to the interefts and the authority of Cicero, and were qualified by their parts and fortunes to have made a principal figure in the Republic, if they had continued in thofe fentiments, and adhered to his advice, but their paffions, pleafures, and ambition got the afcendant, and through a factious and turbulent life hurried them on to this wretched fate.

ALL thoughts of peace being now laid afide, Cicero's next advice to Pompey was, to draw the war into length, nor ever to give Cæfar the opportunity of a battel. Pompey approved this counfil, and purfued it for fome time, till he gained the advantage above-mentioned before Dyrrhachium, which gave him fuch a confidence in his own troops, and fuch a contempt of Cæfar's, " that from this moment, fays Cicero, " this great man ceafed to be a General, op- " pofed a raw, new-raifed army, to the moft ro- " buft and veteran Legions; was fhamefully " beaten, and, with the lofs of his Camp, forced " to fly away alone [*i*] "

HAD Cicero's advice been followed, Cæsar must inevitably have been ruined for Pompey's fleet would have cut off all supplies from him by sea, and it was not possible for him to subsist long at land ; while an enemy, superior in number of troops, was perpetually harassing him, and wasting the country and the report every where spread of his flying from Dyrrhachium before a victorious army, which was pursuing him, made his march every way the more difficult, and the people of the country more shy of assisting him : till the despicable figure, that he seemed to make, raised such an impatience for fighting, and assurance of victory in the Pompeian chiefs, as drew them to the fatal resolution of giving him battel at Pharsalia.   There was another motive likewise suggested to us by Cicero, which seems to have had no small influence in determining Pompey to this unhappy step , his superstitious regard to *omens, and the admonitions of Diviners* ; to which *his nature was strongly addicted* The Haruspices were all on his side, and flattered him with every thing that was prosperous and besides those in his own camp, the whole fraternity of them at Rome were sending him perpetual accounts of the *fortunate and auspicious significations which they had observed in the entrails* of their victims [k].

BUT after all, it must needs be owned, that Pompey had a very difficult part to act, and much less liberty of executing what he himself approved, than in all the other wars, in which he had been engaged. In his wars against foreign

---

[k] Hoc civili bello, Dii immortales ! ——— quæ nobis in Græciam Româ responsa Haruspicum missa sunt quæ dicta Pompeio ?——— etenim ille admodum extis & ostentis movebatur. De Div 2 24.

enemies

A Urb 705.
Cic 59
Coff.
C Julius
Cæsar II
P Servilius
Vatia Isau-
ricus.

enemies, his power was absolute, and all his motions depended on his own will, but in this, besides several Kings and Princes of the East, who attended him in person, he had with him in his Camp almost all the chief Magistrates and Senators of Rome; men of equal dignity with himself, who had commanded armies, and obtained triumphs, and expected a share in all his counsils, and that in their common danger, no step should be taken, but by their common advice   and as they were under no engagement to his cause, but what was voluntary, so they were necessarily to be humored, lest through disgust they should desert it.   Now these were all uneasy in their present situation, and longed to be at home in the enjoyment of their estates and honors, and having a confidence of victory from the number of their troops, and the reputation of their Leader, were perpetually teizing Pompey to the resolution of a battel, charging him with a design to protract the war, for the sake of perpetuating his authority, and calling him another Agamemnon, *who was proud of holding so many Kings and Generals under his command* [l], till, being unable to withstand their reproaches any longer, he was driven by a kind of shame, and against his judgement, to the experiment of a decisive action.

Cæsar was sensible of Pompey's difficulty, and persuaded, that he could not support the indignity of shewing himself afraid of fighting, and

[l] Καὶ ἐπὶ τῶδε αὐτὸν βα-
σιλέα καὶ Ἀγαμεμνονα ἀπὲ-
τα", ὅτι ρακειὰ Βασιλέων
διὰ τὸν πολέμο ἦρχεν, ἐξεσι
τῶν οἰκειαν λογισμοῖς, καὶ ἐνε-
δανει αὐτοῖς. App ρ 470

Milites otium, focii moram, Principes ambitum ducis increpabant Flor l 4
2 Dio p 185. Plut in Pomp

from that affurance expofed himfelf often more
rafhly than prudence would otherwife juftify for
his befieging Pompey at Dyrhachium, who was
mafter of the fea, which fupplied every thing to
him that was wanted, while his own army was
ftarving at land; and the attempt to block up
entrenchments fo widely extended, with much
fmaller numbers than were employed to defend
them, muft needs be thought rafh and extravagant, were it not for the expectation of drawing
Pompey by it to a general engagement for when
he could not gain that end, his perfeverance in
the fiege had like to have ruined him, and would
inevitably have done fo, if he had not quitted it,
as he himfelf afterwards owned [*m*].

A. Urb 705.
Cic 59.
Coff.

C Julius
Cæsar II
P Servilius
Vatia Isau-
ricus.

It muft be obferved likewife, that, while Pompey had any walls or entrenchments between him
and Cæfar, not all Cæfar's vigor, nor the courage
of his veterans, could gain the leaft advantage
againft him ⋅ but on the contrary, that Cæfar was
baffled and difappointed in every attempt. Thus
at Brundifium he could make no impreffion upon
the Town, till Pompey at full leifure had fecured his retreat, and embarked his troops. and at
Dyrrhachium, the onely confiderable action, which
happened between them, was not onely difadvan-
tageous, but almoft fatal to him. Thus far Pompey
certainly fhewed himfelf the greater Captain, in
not fuffering a force, which he could not refift in

[*m*] Cæfar pro natura fe-
rox, & conficiendæ rei cupi-
dus, oftentare aciem, provo-
care, laceffere, nunc obfidi-
one caftrorum, quæ fedecim
millium vallo obduxerat, (fed
quid his obeffet obfid.o qui
patente mari omnibus copiis
abundarent ⋅) nunc expugna-
tione Dyrrhachii irrita, &c.
Flor l 4 c 2
ὡμολόγει τε μεταγινώσκειν
πρὸς Δυρράχιω ϛρατοπεδεύ-
σας, &c. App p 468.

the

A Urb 705
Cic 59.
Coss
C Julius
Cæsar II.
P Servilius
Vatia Isau-
ricus

the field. to do him any hurt, or carry any point
against him; since that depended on the skill of
the General By the help of entrenchments he
knew how to make his new raised soldiers a
match for Cæsar's Veterans, but when he was
drawn to encounter him on the open plain, he
fought against insuperable odds, by deserting *his
proper arms, as Cicero says, of caution, counsil,
and authority, in which he was superior, and committing his fate to swords and spears, and bodily strength,
in which his enemies far excelled him* [n].

CICERO was not present at the battel of Pharsalia, but was left behind at Dyrrhachium much
out of humor, as well as out of order: his discontent to see all things going wrong on that side,
and contrary to his advice, had brought upon him
an ill habit of body, and weak state of health;
which made him decline all public command, but
he promised Pompey to follow, and continue with
him as soon as his health permitted [o], and as
a pledge of his sincerity, sent his son in the mean
while along with him, who, though very young,
behaved himself gallantly, and acquired *great applause by his dexterity of riding and throwing the ja-
velin*, and performing every other part of military discipline at the head *of one of the wings of*

---

[n] Non iis rebus pugna-
bamus, quibus valere potera-
mus, consilo auctoritate,
causa, quæ erant in nobis su-
periora, sed lacertis & viri-
bus, quibus pares non fuimus
Ep fam 4 7
Dolebamque pilis & gla-
diis, non consiliis neque auc-
toritatibus nostris de jure pub-
lico disceptari—Ep fam 6 1.

[o] Ipse fugi adhuc omne
munus, eo magis, quod ni-
hil ita poterat agi, ut mihi in
meis rebus aptum esse — me
conficit sollicitudo, ex qua
etiam summa infirmitas corporis, qua levata, ero cum
eo, qui negotium gerit, est
que in magna spe — ad Att
xi 4.

Horse, of which Pompey had given him the com- A Urb 705
mand [p]. Cato staid behind also in the Camp Cic 59
at Dyrrhachium, which he commanded with *fif-* Coß
teen Cohorts, when Labienus brought them the C Julius
news of Pompey's defeat, upon which Cato of- Cæsar II
fered the command to Cicero as the superior in P Servilius
dignity, and upon his refusal of it, as Plutarch Vatia Isau-
tells us, *young* Pompey was so enraged, *that he* ricus
drew his sword, and would have killed him upon the
spot, if Cato had not prevented it This fact is
not mentioned by Cicero, yet seems to be referred to in his speech for Marcellus, where he says,
that in the very war, he had been a perpetual asser-
tor of peace, to the hazard even of his life [q].
But the wretched news from Pharsalia threw them
all into such a consternation, that they presently
took shipping, and dispersed themselves severally,
as their hopes or inclinations led them into the different provinces of the Empire [r] The greatest part who were determined to renew the war,
went directly into Afric, the general rendezvous
of their scattered forces, whilst others, who
were disposed to expect the farther issue of things,
and take such measures as fortune offered, retired to Achaia · but Cicero was resolved to make
this *the end of the war to himself,* and recommended the same conduct to his friends. declar-

---

[p] Quo tamen in bello
cum te Pompeius alæ alteri
præfecisset, magnam laudem
& a summo viro & ab exer-
citu consequebare, equitando,
jaculando, omni militari labore tolerando atque ea
quidem tua laus pariter cum
Repub cecidit De Offic 2
13

[q] Multa de pace dixi, &
in ipso bello eadem etiam
cum capitis mei periculo sensi.
Pro Marcell 5
[r] Paucis sane post die-
bus ex Pharsalica fuga venisse
Labienum qui cum interi-
tum exercitus nunciavisset—
naves subito perterriti con-
scendistis De Divin 1 32.

Urb 705
Cic 59
  Coss
C Julius
Cæsar II
P Servilius
Vatia Isau-
ricus.

ing, *that as they had been no match for Cæsar, when
intire, they could not hope to beat him, when shat-
tered and broken* [s]: and so after a miserable
campaign of about eighteen months, he committed himself without hesitation to the mercy of
the Conqueror, and landed again at Brundisium
about the end of October.

[s] Hunc ego belli mihi
finem feci, nec putavi, cum
integri pares non fuissemus,
fractos superiores fore
fam 7 3

SECT.

SECT. VIII

CICERO no fooner returned to Italy, than he began to reflect, that he had been too hafty in coming home, before the war was determined, and without any invitation from the Conqueror, and in a time of that general licence, had reafon to apprehend fome infult from the foldiers, if he ventured to appear in public with *his Fafces and Laurel*, and yet to drop them, would be a diminution of that honor, which he had received from the Roman people, and the acknowledgement of a power fuperior to the laws *he condemned himfelf therefore for not continuing abroad, in fome convenient place of retirement, till he had been fent for*, or things were better fettled [t] What gave him the greater reafon to repent of this ftep was, *a meffage that he received from Antony*, who governed all in Cæfar's abfence, and with the fame churlifh fpirit, with which he would have held him before in Italy againft his will, feemed now difpofed *to drive him out of it* for he fent him *the copy of a Letter from Cæfar*, in which Cæfar fignified, "that he "had heard, that Cato and Metellus were at 'Rome, and appeared openly there, which "might occafion fome difturbance wherefore

A Urb 706
Cic 60
Coß
C Julius
Cæsar Dictator II
M Anto-
nius Mag
Equit

[t] Ego vero & incaute, ut fcribis, & celerius quam oportuit, feci, &c Ad Att xi 9

Quare voluntatis me mea nunquam pænitebit, confilii pænitet In oppido aliquo mallem refediffe, quoad arceffierer Minus fermonis fubiiffem minus accepiffem doloris ipfum hoc non me angeret Brundifii jacere in omnes partes eft moleftum. Propius accedere, ut fuades, quomodo fine lictoribus, quos populus dedit, poffum? qui mihi incolumi adimi non poffunt Ad Att xi 6

X 2   " he

A. Urb. 706
Coss.
C. Jul.
Cæsar Dic-
tator II
M. Anto
nius Mag.
Equit.

" he strictly injoined, that none should be suf-
" fered to come to Italy without a special licence
" from himself. Antony therefore desired Ci-
" cero to excuse him, since he could not help
" obeying Cæsar's commands. but Cicero sent
" L. Lamia to assure him, that Cæsar had order-
" ed Dolabella to write to him to come to Italy
" as soon as he pleased, and that he came upon
" the authority of Dolabella's Letter." so that
Antony in the Edict, which he published to exclude *the Pompeians from Italy*, excepted *Cicero by
name*; which added still to his mortification,
since all his desire was to be connived at onely,
or tacitly permitted, *without being personally distinguished from the rest of his party* [u]

But he had several other grievances of a domestic kind, which concurred also to make him
unhappy. his Brother Quintus, with his Son, after
their escape from Pharsalia, followed Cæsar into
Asia, to obtain their pardon from him in person.
Quintus had particular reason to be afraid of his
resentment, on account of the relation which he
had born to him, as one of his Lieutenants
in Gaul, where he had been treated by him with
great generosity, so that Cicero *himself would
have dissuaded him from going over to Pompey, but
could not prevail.* yet in this common calamity,
Quintus in order to make his own peace the
more easily, resolved to throw all the blame
upon his Brother, and for that purpose made i.

[u] Sed quid ego de histo-
ribus, qui prius e Italia de-
cedere ... nam qua me
... Antonius exemplum
Cæsaris ad se literarum in
... audisse, Ca-
... Roma ut esset
palam, &c. Tum ille edi-
xit ita, ut me exciperet & La-
lium nominatim. Quod sane
nollem. Poterat enim sine
nomine, re ipsa excipi. O
multas graves offensiones!—
...

the subject of *all his Letters and Speeches to Cæsar's* A Urb 7)
friends, to rail at him in a manner the most inhu- Cic 6)
man. Coss

CICERO was informed of this from all quarters, C Julius
and that young Quintus, who was sent before to- C sar De
wards Cæsar, *had read an oration to his friends,* tator II
which he had prepared to speak to him against his M Anto
Uncle Nothing, as Cicero says, *ever happened* nius Mag
more shocking to him, and though he had no small Equit.
diffidence of Cæsar's inclination, and many enemies labouring to do him ill offices, yet his greatest concern was, left his Brother and Nephew
should hurt themselves rather than him, by their
perfidy [x] for under all the sense of this provocation his behaviour was just the reverse of
theirs and having been informed, *that Cæsar in*
a certain conversation, had charged his Brother with
being the author of their going away to Pompey, he
took occasion to write to him in the following
terms

" As for my Brother, I am not less solicitous
" for his safety, than my own. but in my pre-
" sent situation dare not venture to recommend
" him to you all that I can pretend to, is, to
" beg that you will not believe him to have ever
" done any thing towards obstructing my good
" offices and affection to you, but rather, that

[x] Quintus misit filium —ipsi enim illi putavi per-
non solum sui deprecatorem, niciosum fore si ejus hoc
sed etiam accusatorem me— tantum scelus percrebuisset—
neque vero desistet, ubicun- ib 9
que est omnia in me male- Quintum filium—volumen
dicta conferre Nihil mihi sibi ostend sse orationis, quam
unquam tam incredibile ac- apud Cæsarem contra me es-
cidit, nihil in his malis tam set hact rus — multi postea
acerbum —ibid 8 Patris, con im h scelere Pa-
Epistolas mihi legerunt ple- trem esset locutum is is.
ras omnium in me probrorum

" he was always the adviſer of our union, and
" the companion, not the leader of my voyage
" wherefore in all other reſpects, I leave it to
" you to treat him, as your own humanity, and
" his friendſhip with you require, but I entreat
" you, in the moſt preſſing manner, that I may
" not be the cauſe of hurting him with you on any
" account whatſoever [y] "

HE found himſelf likewiſe at this time in ſome
diſtreſs for want of money, which in that ſeaſon
of public diſtraction, it was very difficult to procure, either by borrowing or ſelling · the ſumm,
which he advanced to Pompey had drained him
and his wife, by her indulgence to ſtewards, and
favorite ſervants, had made great waſte of what
was left at home . and inſtead of ſaving any
thing from their rents, had plunged him deeply
into debt, ſo that Atticus's purſe was the chief
fund which he had to truſt to for his preſent ſupport [z]

THE conduct of Dolabella was a farther mortification to him, who by the fiction of an adoption into a plebeian family, had obtained the tribunate this year, and was raiſing great tumults
and diſorders in Rome, by a law, which he publiſhed, *to expunge all debts.* Laws of that kind
had been often attempted by deſperate or ambitious magiſtrates, but were always deteſted by the
better ſort, and particularly by Cicero, who treats
them as pernicious *to the peace and proſperity of*

[y] Cum mihi litera a
Balbo m ore minute eſſent
Cæſarem exiſtimare Qui
— Fratrem / in te pro-
fu o ita de eum in ſcrip-
j —d A⁰ 12

[z] Vem conſidera t
ſit ui de nobis ſuppeditentur
ſimus neceſſarii Si quas
habu mus facultates, eas Pom
peio, tum, cum id videba
mur ſapienter facere, detulimus Ib 13, 2, 22, &c

states, *and fapping the very foundations of civil So-*
ciety, by deftroying all faith and credit among men [a].
No wonder therefore that we find him taking this
affair fo much to heart, and complaining fo heavily, in many of his Letters to Atticus, *of the*
famed acts of his Son-in-law as an additional fource
of affliction and difgrace to him [b]. Dolabella was
greatly embarraffed in his fortunes, and while he
was with Cæfar abroad, feems to have left his
wife deftitute of neceffaries at home, and forced
to recur to her Father for her fubfiftence Cicero
likewife, either through the difficulty of the times,
or for want of a fufficient fettlement on Dolabella's part, had not yet paid all her fortune, which
it was ufual to do *at three different payments,* within a time limited by law he had difcharged *the*
two firft, and was now preparing to make *the third*
payment, which he frequently and preffingly recommends to the care of Atticus [c] But Dolabella's whole life and character were fo entirely
contrary to the manners and temper both of Cicero and Tullia, that a divorce enfued between
them not long after, though the account of it is
delivered fo darkly, that it is hard to fay at what
time, or from what fide it firft arofe.

[a] Nec enim ulla res ve-
hementius Rempub continet,
quam fides, quæ effe nulla
poteft, nifi erit neceffaria fo-
lutio rerum creditarum, &c
de Offic 2 24

[b] Quod me audis fracti-
orem effe animo , quid putas,
cum videas acceffiffe ad fuperiores ægritudines præclaras
generi actiones ?—ad Att xi
12

Etfi omnium confpectum

horreo, præfertim hoc genero
—ib 14, 15, &c

[c] De dote, quod fcribis,
per omnes Deos te obteftor,
ut totam rem fufcipias, & illam miferam mea culpa——
tueare meis opibus, fi quæ
funt, tuis, quibus tibi non
moleftum erit facultatibus.
Ib xi 2

De penfione altera, oro te,
omni cura confidera quid faciendum fit —ib xi 4

In

A U⹁o 706
Cr 60
CoĨ
C JvL vs
C Æs-R D c-
ta cr II
M Axro-
ʌɪƖ Vlag
Equit.

In thefe circumftances Tullia paid her Father a vifit *at Brundifium on the thirteenth of June* but his great love for her made their meeting onely the more afflicting to him in that abject ftate of their fortunes, " I was fo far, fays he, " from taking that pleafure which I ought to " have done from the virtue, humanity, and pi- " ety of an excellent daughter, that I was ex- " ceedingly grieved to fee fo deferving a Crea- " ture in fuch an unhappy condition, not by her " own, but wholly by my fault I faw no rea- " fon therefore for keeping her longer here, in " this our common affliction but was willing to " fend her back to her mother as foon as fhe " would confent to it [*d*]."

AT Brundifium he received the news of Pompey's death, which did not fuprife him, as we find from the fhort reflection that he makes upon it " As to Pompey s end, fays he, I never had " any doubt about it . for the loft and defperate " ftate of his affairs had fo poffeffed the minds " of all the Kings and ftates abroad, that whi- " therfoever he went, I took it for granted that " this would be his fate I cannot however help " grieving at it , for I knew him to be an honeft, " grave, and worthy man [*e*] "

THIS was the fhort and true character of the

[*d*] Tullia mea ad me ve- nit prid Id Jun —Ego au- tem c ipfius virtute huma- ritate, pietate non modo eam voluptatem non cepi, quam capere ex fingularitic deb u, fed etiam incredib li fum do- lere affectu, tale ingenium in tam mifera fortuna verfari —ib ʋi i— Ep fam 14 11

[*e*] De Pompeii exitu mihi dubium nunquam fuit tanta enim defperatio rerum ejus, omnium Regum & populo rum animos occuparat, ut quocunque veniffet, hoc pu tarem futurum Non poffum ejus cafum non dolere ho minem enim integrum & caf tum & gravem cognovi Ad Att xi 6

man from one who perfectly knew him, not heigh-
tened, as we sometimes find it, by the shining co-
lors of his eloquence , nor depressed by the darker
strokes of his resentment Pompey had early acquired *the surname of the Great*, by that sort of merit, which, from the constitution of the Republic,
necessarily made him GREAT , a fame and success
in war, superior to what Rome had ever known
in the most celebrated of her Generals He had
triumphed at three several times over the three
different parts of the known world, Europe,
Asia, Africa , and by his victories had almost
doubled the extent, as well as the revenues of
the Roman dominion , for as he declared to the
people on his return from the Mithridatic war,
he had found the lesser Asia the boundary, but left
it the middle of their Empire He was about six
years older than Cæsar, and while Cæsar immersed
in pleasures, oppressed with debts, and suspected
by all honest men, was hardly able to shew his
head ; Pompey was florishing in the height of
power and glory, and by the consent of all parties placed at the head of the Republic. This
was the post that his ambition seemed to aim at,
to be the first man in Rome , *the Leader*, *not the*
Tyrant of his Country : for he more than once had
it in his power to have made himself the master
of it without any risk , if his virtue, or his phlegm
at least had not restrained him but he lived in a
perpetual expectation of receiving from the gift
of the people, what he did not care to seize by
force; and by fomenting the disorders of the
City, hoped to drive them to the necessity of
creating him Dictator It is an observation of all
the historians, that while Cæsar made no difference of power, *whether it was conferred or*
usurped whether over those who loved, or those who
feared

A Urb 706.
Cic 60.
Coss
C Julius
Cæsar Dic-
tator II
M Anto-
nius Mag.
Equit.

A Urb 705
Cic 60
Coſſ
C Julius
Cæsar Dic-
ta or II
M Anto-
nius Mag.
Equit.

feared him, Pompey ſeemed to value none but what was *offered*, *nor to have any deſire to govern, but with the good will of the governed* What leiſure he found from his wars, he employed in the ſtudy of polite Letters, and eſpecially of eloquence, *in which he would have acquired great fame, if his genius had not drawn him to the more dazzling glory of arms* yet he pleaded ſeveral cauſes with applauſe, in the defence of his friends and clients, and ſome of them in conjunction with Cicero. His language was copious and elevated, his ſentiments juſt, his voice ſweet, his action noble, and full of dignity. But his talents were better formed for arms, than the gown: for though in both he obſerved the ſame diſcipline, a perpetual modeſty, temperance, and gravity of outward behaviour, yet in the licence of camps, the example was more rare and ſtriking His perſon was extremely gracefull, and imprinting reſpect, yet with an air of reſerve and haughtineſs, which became the General better than the Citizen His parts were plauſible, rather than great ſpecious rather than penetrating; and his view of politics but narrow, for his chief inſtrument of governing was, *diſſimulation*, yet he had not always the art to conceal his real ſentiments. As he was a better ſoldier than a ſtateſman, ſo what he gained in the Camp he uſually loſt in the City; and though adored, when abroad, was often affronted and mortified at home; till the imprudent oppoſition of the Senate drove him to that alliance with Craſſus and Cæſar, which proved fatal both to himſelf and the Republic He took in theſe two, not as the partners, but the miniſters rather of his power, that by giving them ſome ſhare with him, he might make his own authority uncontroulable. he had no reaſon

to

to apprehend, that they could ever prove his Ri- A. Urb 706.
vals, fince neither of them had any credit or Cic 60
chara&ter of that kind, which alone could raife Coff
them above the laws; a fuperior fame and expe- C Julius
rience in war, *with the militia of the empire at* Cæsar Dic-
their devotion all this was purely his own, till tator II.
by cherifhing Cæfar, and throwing into his hands M Anto-
the onely thing which he wanted, *arms and mili-* nius Mag.
tary command, he made him at laft too ftrong Equit.
for himfelf, and never began to fear him, till it
was too late Cicero warmly diffuaded both *his*
union, and his breach with Cæfar, and after the
rupture, as warmly ftill, the thought *of giving*
him battel: if any of thefe counfils had been followed, Pompey had preferved his life and honor,
and the Republic its liberty But he was urged
to his fate by a natural fuperftition, and attention to thofe vain auguries, with which he was
flattered by all the Harufpices, he had feen the
fame temper in Marius and Sylla, and obferved
the happy effe&ts of it ' but they affumed it onely out of policy, he out of principle They
ufed it to animate their foldiers, when they had
found a probable opportunity of fighting, but
he againft all prudence and probability, was encouraged by it to fight to his own ruin. He faw
all his miftakes at laft, when it was out of his
power to corre&t them, and in his wretched
flight from Pharfalia was forced to confefs, *that*
he had trufted too much to his hopes, and that Ci-
cero had judged better, and feen further into things
than he The refolution of feeking refuge in
Egypt, finifhed the fad Cataftrophe of this great
man the Father of the reigning Prince had been
highly obliged to him for his prote&tion at Rome,
and reftoration to his kingdom and the Son had
fent a confiderable fleet to his affiftance in the
prefent

I

A Urb 705
Cic 60
Coss
C JULIUS
CÆSAR Dic-
tator II
M ANTO-
NIUS Mag.
Equit.

piesent war   but in this ruin of his fortunes, what gratitude was there to be expected from a Court, governed by *Eunuchs and meicenaiy Greeks?* all whose politics turned, not on the honor of the King, but the establishment of their own power; which was likely to be eclipsed by the admission of Pompey   How happy had it been for him to have died in that sickness, *when all Italy was putting up vows and prayers for his safe ty?* or if he had fallen by the chance of war on the plains of Pharsalia, in the defence of his Country's liberty, he had died still glorious, though unfortunate · but, as if he had been re-served for an example of the instability of human Greatness, he, who a few days before command-ed *Kings and Coifuls, and all the noblest of Rome,* was sentenced to die by *a council of slaves*; mur-thered by a *base desertoi*, cast out naked and head-less on the Egyptian strand, and when *the whole earth,* as Velleius says, *had scarce been sufficient for his victories, could not find a spot upon it at last for a grave*   His Body was burnt on the shoar by one of his freedmen, with the planks of an old fishing-boat, and his ashes being conveyed to Rome, were deposited privately *by his wife Cor-nelia in a Vault of his Alban Villa*   The Egyp-tians however raised a *monument* to him on the place, and adorned it with *figures of brass,* which being defaced afterwards by time, and *buried al-most in sand and rubbish,* was sought out and re-stored by the Emperor Hadrian [*f*]

[*f*] Hujus viri fastigium tantis auctibus fortuna extu-lit, ut primum ex Africa, ite-rum ex Europa, tertio ex A-sia triumpharet & quot par-tes terrarum Orbis sunt, to-dem faceret monumenta vic-toriæ, [Vell P 2 40] Ut ipse in concione dixit,— Asi-am ultimam provinciarum accepisse, mediam patriæ red-didisse Plin H 7 26 Flor

On the news of Pompey's death, *Cæfar was* A. Urb 706
declared Dictator the second time in his abfence, Cic 60
                               Coff
                         and C Julius
                            Cæsar Dic-

5] Potentiæ quæ honoris causa ad eum deferretur, non ut ab eo occuparetur, cupidiffimus, [Vell P 2 29 Dio p 178] Meus autem æqualis Cn Pompeius, vir ad omnia fumma natus, majorem dicendi gloriam habuiffet, nifi eum majoris gloriæ cupiditas ad bellicas laudes abftraxiffet Erat oratione fatis amplus rem prudenter videbat actio vero ejus habebat & in voce magnum fplendorem, & in motu fummam dignitatem [Brut 354 vid it pro Balbo 1, 2] Forma excellens, non ea, qua flos commendatur ætatis, fed ex dignitate conftanti [Vell P 2 29] Illud os probum, ipfumque honorem ex imæ frontis [Plin Hift 7 12] Solet enim aliud fentire & loqui, neque tantum valere ingenio, ut non appareat quid cupiat [Ep fam 8 1] Ille aluit, auxit, armavit—ille Galliæ ulterioris adjutor—ille provinciæ propagator, ille abfentis in omnibus adjutor [ad Att 8 3] aluerat Cæfarem, eundem repente timere cœperat [ib 8] Ego nihil prætermifi, quantum facere, nitique po ni, quin Pompeium a Cæfaris conjunctione avocarem——idem ego, cum jam omnes opes & fuas & populi Romani Pompeius ad Cæfarem detuliffet, feroque ea fentire cœ-

pifet, quæ ego ante multo providerim— pacis, concordiæ, compofitionis auctor effe non deftiti meaque illa vox ex noto multis Utinam, Pompei, cum Cæfare focietatem aut nunquam coiffes, aut nunquam diremiffes !—hæc mea, Antoni, & de Pompeio & de Repub confilia fuerunt quæ fi valuiffent, Refpub ftaret [Phil 2 10] Multi teftes, me & initio ne conjungeret fe cum Cæfare, monuiffe Pompeium, & poftea, ne fejungeret, &c [Ep fam. 6 6] Quid vero fingularis ille vir ac pene divinus de me fenferit, fciunt, qui eum de Pharfalica fuga Paphum profecuti funt, nunquam ab eo mentio de me nifi honorifica —cum me vidiffe plus fateretur, fe fperaviffe meliora. [ib. 15] Qui, fi mortem tum obiiffet, in ampliffimis fortunis occidiffet, is propagatione vitæ quot, quantas, quam incredibiles haufit calamitates ! [Tufc difp 1 35] In Pelufiaco littore, imperio vi-liffimi Regis, confiliis fpado-num, & ne quid malis defit, Septimii defertoris fui gladio trucidatur [Flor 4 2 52] Ægyptum petere propofuit, memor beneficiorum quæ in Patrem ejus Ptolemæi,— qui tum regnabat, contulerat—Princeps Romani nominis, imperio, arbitrioque Ægypti mancipii jugulatus eft——

Tator II
M Antonius Mag-
fe Equit.

A Urb 706
Cic 60
Coff
C Julius
Cæsar Dic-
tator II
M Anto-
nius Mag
Equit

and M *Antony his Master of the Horse,* who by virtue of that post governed all things absolutely in Italy. Cicero continued all the while at Brundisium, in a situation wholly disagreeable, and *worse to him,* he says, *than any punishment for the air of the place began to affect his health, and to the uneasiness of mind added an ill state of body* [g]: yet to move nearer towards Rome without leave from his new Masters, was not thought adviseable, nor did Antony encourage it, being pleased rather, we may believe, to see him well mortified so that he had no hopes of any ease or comfort, but in the expectation of Cæsar's return, which made his stay in that place the more necessary for the opportunity of paying his early compliments to him at landing

BUT what gave him the greatest uneasiness was, to be held still in suspence, in what touched him the most nearly, the case of his own safety, and of Cæsar's disposition towards him for though all Cæsar's friends assured him, *not onely of pardon, but of all kind of favor,* yet he had received no intimation of kindness from Cæsar himself, who was so embarrassed in Egypt, that he had no leisure to think of Italy, and did not so much as *write a Letter thither from December to June* for as he had rashly, and out of gaiety,

---

in tantum in illo viro a sediscordante fortuna, ut cui moco ad victoriam terra defuerat deefiet ad sepulturam Vel Pat 2 51 vid Dio p 186 it Appian 2 481

Provida Pompeio dederat Campania febres
Optandas Sed multæ urbes, & publica vota

Vicerunt Igitur fortuna ipsius & Urbis
Servatum victo caput abstulit
     Juv x 283
[g] Quodvis enim supplicium levius est hac permissone —Ad Att xi 18

Jam enim corpore vix sustineo gravitatem hujus cœli, qui mihi laborem affert, in dolore —ibid 22

as it were, involved himfelf there in a moft de- A Urb 706.
fperate war, to the hazard of all his fortunes, *he* Cic 60.
was afhamed, *as* Cicero fays [*b*], *to write any thing* Coſ
about it, till he had extricated himfelf out of that C Julius
difficulty. Cæsar Dic-

His enemies in the mean time had greatly M Anto-
ftrengthened themfelves in Africa, wheie P Varus, nius Mag.
who firft feized it on the part of the Republic, Equit
was fupported by all the force of *King Juba*,
Pompey's faft friend, and had reduced the whole
Province to his obedience, for Curio, after he
had driven Cato *out of Sicily*, being ambitious to
drive Varus *also out of Afric*, and having tranf-
ported thither the beft part *of four legions*, which
Cæfar had committed to him, was, after fome little fuccefs upon his landing, intirely defeated and
deftroyed with his whole army in an engagement
with Sabura, *King Juba's General*

Curio was a young nobleman of fhining parts,
admirably foimed by nature to adorn that character, in which *his Father and Grandfather* had
florifhed before him, of one of the principal
Orators of Rome. Upon his entrance into the Forum, he was committed to the caie of Cicero.
but a natural propenfion to pleafuie, ftimulated
by the example and counfils of his perpetual companion Antony, hurried him into all the extravagance of expence and debauchery. for Antony,
who always wanted money, with which Curio
abounded, was ever obfequious to his will, and
miniftring to his Lufts, for the opportunity of
gratifying his own · fo that, *no boy purchafed for
the ufe of lewdnefs, was more in a Mafter's power,*

[*b*] Ille enim ita videtur   Nec poft idus Decemb ab
Alexandriam tenere, ut eum   illo datas ullas litteras   Ib.
fcribere etiam pudeat de illis   17
rebus   Ib xi. 15

than

A Urb 706
Cic 60
Coff
C Julius
Cæsar Dic
tator II
M Anto-
nius Mag
Equit

than Antony in Curio's. He was equally prodigal of his money, and his modesty; and not onely of his own, but of other people's: so that Cicero alluding to the infamous effeminacy of his life, calls him in one of his Letters, *Miss* Curio. But when the Father, by Cicero's advice, had obliged him by his paternal authority *to quit the familiarity of Antony,* he reformed his conduct, and adhering to the instructions and maxims of Cicero, became the favorite of the City, the Leader of the young nobility and a warm assertor of the authority of the Senate, against the power of the *Triumvirate* After his Father's death, upon his first taste of public honors, and admission into the Senate, his ambition and thirst of popularity engaged him in so immense a prodigality, that to supply the magnificence *of his shews, and plays,* with which he entertained the City, he was soon driven to the necessity of selling himself to Cæsar, having *no revenue left, as* Pliny says, *but from the discord of his Citizens* For this he is considered commonly by the old writers, as *the chief instrument, and the Trumpet, as it were, of the civil war,* in which he justly fell the first victim, yet after all his luxury and debauch, fought and died with a courage truly Roman, which would have merited a better fate, if it had been employed in a better cause for upon the loss of the battel, and his best troops, being admonished by his friends to save himself by flight, he answered, *that after losing an army, which had been committed to him by Cæsar, he could never shew his face to him again,* and so continued fighting, till he was killed among the last of his soldiers [1]

CURIO'S

[1] *Hac d a ... tarta ... m tulit ... lle Poma* Lucan 4
El   Una

CURIO's death happened before the battel of Pharsalia, while Cæsar was engaged in Spain [k] by which means Afric fell intirely into the hands of the Pompeians, and became the general rendezvous of all that party hither Scipio, Cato, and Labienus, conveyed the remains of their scattered troops from Greece, as Afranius and Petreius likewise did from Spain, till on the whole they had brought together again a more numerous army than Cæsar's, and were in such high spirits, as to talk of coming over with it into Italy, before Cæsar could return from Alexandria [l] This was confidently given out, and expected at Rome, and in that case, Cicero was

A Urb 7
Cic. 63
Coss
C JULIUS
CÆSAR Dictaor II
M ANTONIUS Mag
Equit.

Una familia Curionem, in qua tres continua serie Oratores extiterunt Plin H 7 41

Naturam habuit admirabilem ad dicendum Brut 406

Nemo unquam puer, emptus libidinis causa, tam fuit in domini potestate, quam tu in Curionis [Philip 2 18] duce filiola Curionis [ad Att. 1 14]

Vir nobilis, eloquens, audax, suæ alienæque & fortunæ & pudicitiæ prodigus—cujus animo, voluptatibus vel libidinibus, neque opes ullæ neque cupiditates sufficere possent [Vell P 248]

Nisi meis puer olim fidelissimis atque amantissimis consiliis paruisses [Ep fam 2 1]

Bello autem civili — non alius majorem quam C Curio

subjecit facem— [Vell P 248]

Quid nunc Rома tibi prosit turbata, forumque
Unde Tribunitia plebeius signifer arce
Arma dabis populis, &c
			Lucan 4 800

At Curio, nunquam amisso exercitu, quem a Cæsare fidei suæ commissum acceperat, se in ejus conspectum reversurum, confirmat, atque ita prælians interficitur Cæf Comm de Bell Civ 2

[k] Ante jacet dira dira aces Pharsalia cesset,
Spectandumque tibi bellum civile negatum est
			Lucan ib

[l] In tres ex Africa jam affuturi videntur Ad Att 11 15

sure to be treated as a desertor, for while *Cæsar* used *upon all men as friends, who did not act against him,* and pardoned even enemies, who submitted to his power, it was declared law on the other side, *to consider all as enemies, who were not actually* ——— *their Camp [n]* so that Cicero had nothing now to wish, either for himself, or the Republic, but in the first place, *peace, of which he had still some hopes [n],* or else, that Cæs. might conquer, whose victory was like to prove the more temperate of the two. which makes him often lament the unhappy situation to which he was reduced, where *nothing could be of any service to him, but what he had always abhorred [o]*

UNDER this anxiety of mind, it was an additional vexation to him to hear, *that his reputation was arraigned at Rome,* for submitting so hastily to the Conqueror, or putting himself rather at all into his power. Some condemned him *for not following Pompey,* some more severely *for not going to him,* as the greatest part had done, others, *for not staying with many of his party to ————,* till they could see the farther progress of the war. as he was always extremely sensible of what was said of him by honest men, so he begs of Atticus to be his advocate, and gives

---

[n] ———————————————
———————————————————
———————————————————
———————————————————
———————————————————
———— Epiphorum,
———————————————
———————————————
———————————————
———————————————

significas, cogis me sperare
quod operandum vix ——— ad
Att. 11. 19. it 12 ———

[o] Mihi cum omnia sunt
intolerabilia ad dolorem, tum
maxime, quod in eam causam venisse me video, ut ea
sola utilia mihi esse videantur, quæ semper nolui. Ad
1. 13.

h n

him fome hints, which might be urged in his
defence As to the firft charge, *for not follow-*
ing Pompey, he fays, " that Pompey's fate
" would extenuate the omiffion of that ftep
" of the fecond, that though he knew many
" brave men to be in Afric, yet it was his opinion,
" that the Republic neither could, nor ought to
" be defended by the help of fo barbarous and
" treacherous a nation as to the land, he wifhes
" indeed that he had joined himfelf to thofe in
" Achaia, and owns them to be in a better con-
" dition than himfelf, becaufe they were many
" of them together, and whenever they return-
" ed to Italy, would be reftored to their own
" at once " whereas he was confined like a prifoner of war to *Brundifium,* without the liberty
of ftirring from it till Cæfar arrived [p]

WHILE he continued in this uneafy ftate,
fome of his friends at Rome contrived to fend
him a Letter *in Cæfar's name, dated the ninth of*
January from Alexandria, encouraging him *to lay*
afide all gloomy apprehenfions, and expect every
thing that was kind and friendly from him but it
was drawn *in terms fo flight and general,* that inftead of giving him any fatisfaction, it made him
onely fufpect, what he perceived afterwards to
be true, *that it was forged by Balbus or Oppius,*
on purpofe to raife his fpirits, and adminifter

[p] Dicebar debuiffe cum
Pompeio proficifci Extus
illius minuit ejus officii præ-
termiffi reprehenfionem ——
Sed ex omnibus nihil magis
defideratur, quam quod in
Africam non ierim Judicio
hoc fum ufus, non effe bar-
baris auxiliis fallacifffimæ gen-
tis Rempub defendendam——
extremum eft eorum, qui in
Achaia funt Ii tamen ipfi
fe hoc melius habent, quam
nos, quod & multi funt uno
in loco, & cum in Italiam
venerint, domum ftatim venerint Hæc tu perge, ut
facis, mitigare & probare
quam plurimis Ad Att xi

Y 2   fome

A Urb 706
Cic 60
Coss
C Julius
Cæsar Dic-
tator II
M Anto-
nius Mg
Equit

some little comfort to him [q]   All his accounts
however confirmed to him the report of Cæsar's
clemency and moderation, and his granting pardon without exception to all who asked it, and
with regard to himself, *Cæsar sent Quintus's vi-*
rulent Letters to Balbus, with orders to shew them
to him, as a proof of his kindness and dislike of
Quintus's perfidy   But Cicero's present despon
dency, which interpreted every thing by his fears,
made him *suspect Cæsar the more, for refusing*
grace to none, as if such a clemency must needs
be affected, *and his revenge deferred onely to a*
season more convenient   and as to his *Brother's*
Letters, he fancied, *that Cæsar did not send them*
to Italy, because he condemned them, but to make his
present misery and object condition the more notorious
and despicable to every body [s]

BUT after a long series of perpetual mortifications, he was refreshed at last by a very obliging
Letter from Cæsar, who confirmed to him the
full enjoyment *of his former state and dignity, and*
bad him resume his Fasces and stile of Emperor as
before [t]   Cæsar's mind was too great to listen

to

---

[q] Ut me ista epistola nihil consoletur, nam & exi-
gue scripta est et magnas sus-
piciones habet non esse ab
illo— ad Att xi 16

Ex quo intelligis illud de
literis a d v Id Feb datis
quod inane esset, etiam si
verum esset, non verum esse
Ib 17

[r] Omnino dicitur nemi-
ni negare quod ipsum est
suspectum, notionem ejus dif-
ferri Ib 20

Diligenter mihi fascicu-

lum reddidit Balbi tabellarius
—quod ne Cæsar quidem ad
istos videtur misisse, qua
quo illius improbitate offen
deretur, sed credo, uti no
tiora nostra mala essent,—ib
22.

[s] Redditæ mihi tandem
sunt a Cæsare litteræ satis li
berales Ep Fam 14 23

Qui ad me ex Ægypto lit
teris misit, ut essem idem,
qui fuissem qui cum ipse
Imperator in toto imperio
populi Romani unus esse
ess

to the tales of *the Brot'r and Nephew*, and in- A Urb 706
stead of approving their treachery, seems to have   Cic 60
granted them their pardon on Cicero's account,   Coss
rather than their own, so that Quintus, upon the   C Julius
trial of Cæsar's inclination, began presently to   Cæsar Dic
change his note, and *to congratulate with his Bro-*   tator II
ther on Cæsar's affection and esteem for him [*t*].   M Antonius Mag
Equit

CICERO was now preparing *to send his Son to
wait upon Cæsar, who was supposed to be upon his
journey towards home*, but the uncertain accounts
of his coming diverted him a while from that
thought [*u*], till Cæsar himself prevented it,
and relieved him very agreeably from his tedious
residence at Brundisium, by his sudden and unexpected arrival in Italy, where he landed at
Tarentum in the month of September, and on
the first notice of his coming forward towards
Rome, *Cicero set out on foot to meet him*

WE may easily imagine, what we find indeed
from his Letters, that he was not a little discomposed at the thoughts of this interview, and the
indignity of offering himself to a Conqueror,
against whom he had been in arms, in the midst
of a licentious and insolent rabble. for though
he had reason to expect a kind reception from
Cæsar, yet he hardly *thought his life*, he says,
*worth begging; since what was given by a Master,
might always be taken away again at pleasure* [*x*].

Y 3   But

---

esse me alterum passu est a   cogitabam Ib 17
quo—concessos fasces, laurea-   De illius Alexandria dis-
tos tenui, quoad tenendos pu-   cessu nihil adhuc rumoris,
tavi. Pro Ligar 3   contraque opinio—itaque nec
  [*t*] Sed mihi valde Quin-   mitto, ut constituam, Ci-
tus gratulatur Ad Att xi   ceronem— ib 18
23   [*x*] Sed non adducor,
  [*u*] Ego cum Sallustio Ci-   quemquam bonum ullam sa-
ceronem ad Cæsarem mittere   lutem mihi tanti fuisse pu-
                                   tare

But at the r meeting, he had no occasion to say
or do any thing that was below his dignity for
Cæsar received him, *he ch clighted and ran to*
embrace him, and walked with him alone, conversi-
ng together for nearly for several furlongs [y]

FROM this interview, Cicero followed Cæsar
towards Rome he proposed to be at *Tusculum on*
the jecond or third of October, and wrote to his
wife to provide for his reception there, *with a*
large company of friends, who desig ed to make some
stay with him. [z] From Tusculum he came afterwards to the City with a resolution to spend his
time in study and retreat, till the Republic should
be restored to some tolerable state, " having
" made his peace again, as he writes to Varro
" with his old friends, his books, who had been
" out of humour with him for not obeying their
" precepts but instead of living quietly with
" them, as Varro had done, committing himself
" to the turbulent counsils and hazards of war,
" with factious companions [a] "

On Cæsar's return to Rome, he appointed *P.*
V s and Q Fufius Calenus, Consuls for the
three left months of the year this was a very un
popular use of his new power, which he continued however to practise through the rest of his
reign creating these first Magistrates of the State,
without any regard to the ancient forms, or re-
course to the people, and at any time of the

t re ut eam peterem ab illo qu m in urbem venerim, re-
—ad it   diffe cum veteribus ami ,
S   no noc so que id est, cum libris nost i n
ca   ut a Domn rarsus gra iam—ignofcunt mihi, v
in eju uc n fi nr poti tat. Ib vocant in confuetud rem pri
20 ftin m, teque, qu d in ea
[ ] lu er in Cc permane r, fapien iorem,
[z] no fam ro quam me dicunt faule, ac
[a] Scio um me poter- Lp fam 9

year, which gave a sensible disgust to the City, and an early specimen of the arbitrary manner, in which he designed to govern them

ABOUT the end of the year, Cæsar embarked for Afric, to pursue the war against Scipio, and the other Pompeian Generals, who, assisted by King Juba, held the possession of that Province with a vast army   As he was sacrificing for the success of this voyage, *the victim happened to break loose and ran away from the Altar*, which being looked upon as an unlucky Omen, *the Aruspex admonished him not to sail before the winter solstice*   but he took ship directly in contempt of the admonition, and by that means, as Cicero says, *came upon his enemies unprepared, and before they had drawn together all their forces* [b]   Upon his leaving the City, he declared

Y 4

[b] Quid? ipse Cæsar, cum a Summo haruspice moveretur, ne in Africam ante brumam transmitteret, nonne transmisit? quod ni fecisset, uno in lobo omnes adversariorum copæ convenissent—— de Divin 2 24

Cum immolanti aufugisset hostia profectionem adversus Scipion &] eam non attulit—— Sueton J Cæf 59

Hirtius, in his account of his war, says that Cæsar embarked at Lilybæum for Afric on the 6th of the Kalends of Jan [de Bell Afric init] That is, *on the 27th of our December* whereas Cicero, in the passage just cited, declares him to have passed

over before the Solstice, or the shortest day   But this seeming contradiction is entirely owing to a cause already intimated, the great confusion that was introduced at this time into the Roman Kalendar, by which the months were all transposed from their stated seasons, so that *the 27th of December*, on which, according to their computation, Cæsar embarked was in reality coincident, or the same with our *8th of October*, and consequently above two months before the Solstice, or shortest day   All which is clearly and accurately explained in a learned dissertation, published by a person of eminent merit in the University

A Urb 706
Cic 60
Coss
C Julius
Cæsar Dictator II
M Antonius Mag Equit

A Urb 707
Cic 61
Coff
C Julius
Cæsar III
M Æmilius
Lepidus

clared himself Conful, together with M Lepidus for the year enfuing, and gave the government of *the Hither Goul to M Brutus, of Greece, to Servius Sulpicius*, the firft of whom had been in arms againft him at Pharfalia ; and the fecond was a favorer likewife of the *Pompeian coufe*, and a great friend of Cicero, yet feems to have taken no part in the war [c]

THE African war now held the whole Empire in fufpenfe, Scipio's name was thought ominous and invincible on that ground but while the general attention was employed on the expectation of fome decifive blow, Cicero, defpairing of any good from either fide, chofe to live retired, and out of fight, and whether in the City or the Country fhut himfelf up with his books, which, as he often fays, *had hitherto been the diverfion only, but were now become the fupport of his* [d] In this humor of ftudy he entered into a clofe friendfhip and correfpondence of Letters with M Terentius Varro, a friendfhip equally valued on both fides, and at Varro's defire, immortalized by the mutual dedication of their learned works to each other , *of Cicero's Academic Queftions to Varro, of Varro's treatife on the Latin Tongue to Cicero* Varro was a Senator of the firft diftinction, both for birth and merit, efteemed *the* of Rome , and though now above fourfcore years old, *yet continued ftill writing books to his eighty-eighth year* [e].

University of Cambridge, who chofe to conceal his name see Richee Literer Nº VIII Lond 1724 40

[ ] Brutum Galliæ præfecit, Sulpicium Graciæ Ep fam 5 6

[d] A quibus antea delectionem modo petebamus, nunc vero etiam falutem Ip fam 9 2

[e] Nifi M Varronem forem octogefimo octavo vitæ anno prodidiffe, &c Plin H 5 6 6

He

He was Pompey's *Lieutenant in Spain*, in the beginning of the war, but after the defeat of A-
franius and Petreius quitted his arms, and retired
to his studies; so that his present circumstances
were not very different from those of Cicero;
who in all his Letters to him, bewails with great
freedom the utter ruin of the state, and proposes,
" that they should live together in a strict com-
" munication of studies, and avoid at least the
" sight, if not the tongues of men, yet so, that
" if their new Masters should call for their help
" towards settling the Republic, they should run
" with pleasure, and assist, not onely as archi-
" tects, but even as masons to build it up again;
" or if nobody would employ them, should
" write and read the best forms of government;
" and, as the learned ancients had done before
" them, serve their Country, if not in the Se-
" nate and Forum, yet by their books and
" studies, and by composing treatises of morals
" and laws [f]"

In this retreat he wrote his book of *Oratorial
Partitions*, or the art of ordering and distributing
the parts of an Oration so, as to adapt them in
the best manner to their proper end, of moving
and persuading an audience. It was written for
the instruction of his son, now about eighteen
years old, but seems to have been the rude
draught only of what he intended, or not to have
been finished at least to his satisfaction, since we

---

[f] Non deesse si quis adhibere volet, non modo ut
Architectos, verum etiam ut
fabros, ad aedificandam Rempub. & potius libenter accur-
rere si nemo utetur opera
tamen & scribere & legere
τ Ἀθείας, & si minus in curia atque in foro, at in litteris & libris, ut doctissimi
veteres fecerunt, navare
Rempub. & de moribus &
legibus quaerere. Mihi haec
videntur. *L p fam 9 2*

find

find no mention of it in any of his Letters, as of all his other pieces which were prepared for the public.

ANOTHER fruit of this leisure was his Dialogue *on famous Orators*, called BRUTUS . in which he gives a short character of all, who had ever flourished either *in Greece or Rome*, with any reputation of eloquence, down to his own times and as he generally touches the principal points of each man's life, so an attentive reader may find in it an *Epitome*, as it were, *of the Roman History*. The conference is supposed to be held with *Brutus and Atticus in Cicero's garden at Rome, under the Statue of Plato* [g], whom he always admired, and usually imitated in the manner of his Dialogues, and in this seems to have copied from him the very form of his double title, *Brutus, or of famous Orators*, taken from the speaker and the subject, as in Plato's piece, called *Phædon, or of the Soul*. This work was intended as a *supplement, or a fourth book to the three*, which he had before published on *the compleat Orator*. But though it was prepared and finished at this time, while *Cato was living*, as it is intimated in some parts of it, yet, as it appears from the preface, it was not made public till the year following, after the death of his daughter Tulia.

As at the opening of the war we found Cicero in *debt to Cæsar*, so we now meet with several hints in his Letters of Cæsar's being indebted to him. It arose probably from a mortgage that Cicero had upon the confiscated estate of some Pompeian, which Cæsar had seized but

[g] Cum idem placuisset Platonis Statuam confidimus illas, tum in pratulo propter. —Brut 28

I

of

of what kind foever it was, Cicero was in pain A Urb 707.
for his money " he faw but three ways, he fays, Cic 61
" of getting it , by purchafing the eftate at Cæ- Coff
" far's auction , or taking an affignment on the C Julius
" purchafer , or compounding for half with the Cæsar III
" Brokers or Money-jobbers of thofe times, M Æmilius
Lepidus
" who would advance the money on thofe terms.
" The firft he declares to be bafe, and that he
" would rather lofe his debt, than touch any
" thing confifcated   the fecond he thought ha-
" zardous , and that nobody would pay any thing
" in fuch uncertain times   the third he liked the
' beft but defires Atticus's advice upon it [*b*] "

He now at laft *parted with his wife Terentia*,
whofe humor and conduct had long been uneafy
to him   this drew upon him fome cenfure , for
putting away a wife, who had lived with him
above *thirty years*, the faithfull partner of his bed
and fortunes , and the mother of *two Children*,
extremely dear to him   But fhe was a woman
of an imperious and turbulent fpirit, expenfive
and negligent in her private affairs , bufy and in-
triguing in the public , and, in the height of her
hufband's power, feems to have had the chief hand
in the diftribution of all his favors   He had eafily born her perverfenefs in the vigor of health,
and the flourifhing ftate of his fortunes , but in a
declining life, foured by a continual fucceffion of
mortifications from abroad, the want of eafe and
quiet at home was no longer tolerable to him   the
divorce however was not likely to cure the difficulties, in which her management had involved

[*b*] Nomen illud, quod a   de (quis erit cui credam ?)
Cæfare res et auctio-   — aut Vecleri conditionem,
nes, ut contoneman-hera,   femifte ereda rigitur Ad
pedere malo —) aut dele-   Att 12 3
gationem a mancipi, aliqua

him :

A Urb 707
Cic 61
Coff
C Julius
Cæsar III
M Æmilius
Lepidus

him : for fhe had brought him a great fortune, which was all to be reftored to her at parting this made a fecond marriage neceffary, in order to repair the ill ftate of his affairs , and his friends of both fexes were bufy in providing a fit match for him feveral parties were propofed to him, and among others, *a daughter of Pompey the Great*. for whom he feems to have had an inclination but a prudential regard to the times, and the envy and ruin under which that family then lay, induced him probably to drop it [*i*] What gave his enemies the greater handle to rally him was, his marrying a handfom young woman, named Publilia, of an age difproportionate to his own, to whom he was Guardian but fhe was well allied, and rich, circumftances very convenient to him at this time, as he intimates in a Letter to a friend, who congratulated with him on his marriage

    " As to your giving me joy, fays he, for what
" I have done, I know you wifh it but I fhould
" not have taken any new ftep in fuch wretched
" times, if at my return I had not found my pri-
" vate affairs in no better condition than thofe of
" the Republic For when through the wick-
" ednefs of thofe, who, for my infinite kindnefs
" to them, ought to have had the greateft con-
" cern for my welfare, I found no fafety or eaf
" from their intrigues and perfidy within my
" own walls, I thought it neceffary to fecure my-
" felf by the fidelity of new alliances againft the
" treachery of the old [*k*] "

CÆSAR

[ ] De Pompeii Magni fi-
lia tibi refcripfi nihil me
hoc tempore cogitare Al-
teram vero illam quam tu

fcribis, puto nofti Nihil
vidi fœdius —ib 12 11
[*k*] Ep fam 4 14
In cafes of divorce, when
thcre

CÆSAR returned victorious from Afric about the end of July, by the way of Sardinia, where he spent some days· upon which Cicero says pleasantly in a Letter to Varro, *he had never seen that farm of his before, which though one of the worst that he has, he does not yet despise* [*l*] The uncertain event of the *African War* had kept the Senate under some reserve, but they now began to push their flattery beyond all the bounds of decency, and decreed more extravagant honors to Cæsar, than were ever given before to man, which Cicero oft rallies with great spirit; and being determined to bear no part in that servile adulation, was treating about the *purchase of a House at Naples*, for a pretence of retiring still farther and oftener from Rome But his friends who knew his impatience under their present subjection, and the free way of speaking, which he was apt to indulge, were in some pain, lest he should forfeit the good graces of Cæsar and his

A Urb 707.
Cic 61
Coss.
C Julius
Cæsar III.
M Æmilius
Lepidus

---

there where children, it was the custom for each party to make a settlement by will on their common offspring, proportionable to their several estates which is the meaning of Cicero's pressing Atticus so often in his Letters to put Terentia in mind of making her will, and depositing it in safe hands Ad Att xi 21, 22, 24 xii 18 —

Terentia is said to have lived to the age of *an hundred and three years* [Val M 8 13 Plin H 7, 48] and took, as St Jerom says, for her second husband, Cicero—— Sal-

lust, and Messala for her third Dio Cassius gives her a fourth, Vibius Rufus, who was Consul in the reign of Tiberius, and valued himself for the possession of two things, which had belonged to the two greatest men of the age before him, *Cicero's wife, and Cæsar's chair, in which he was killed* Dio p 612 Hieron Op To 4 par 2 p 190

[*l*] *Illud enim adhuc prædium suum non inspexit neque illum habet deterius, sed tamen non contemnit* Ep fam 9 7

favorites,

A Urb 707
Cic 6.
Coſſ
C Julius
Cæſar III
M Emilius
Lepidus

favorites, and provoke them too far by the keenneſs of his raillery [m]   They preſſed him *to accommodate himſelf to the times*, and to uſe more caution in his diſcourſe, and to reſide more at Rome, eſpecial when Cæſar was there, who would interpret the diſtance and retreat which he affected, as a proof of his averſion to him

But his anſwers on this occaſion will ſhew the real ſtate of his ſentiments and conduct towards Cæſar, as well as of Cæſar's towards him, writing on this ſubject to Papirius Pætus, he ſays, " You are of opinion, I perceive, that it will " not be allowed to me, as I thought it might " be, to quit theſe affairs of the City. you tell " me of Catulus, and thoſe times, but what " ſimilitude have they to theſe? I myſelf was

[m] Some of his jeſts on Cæſar's adminiſtration are ſtill preſerved, which ſhew, that his friends had reaſon enough to admoniſh him to be more upon his guard Cæſar had advanced Labe rius a celebrated writer of farces, to the order of Knights but when he ſtept from the Stage into the Theater, to take his place on the Equeſtrian benches, none of the Knights would admit him to a ſeat among them As he was marching off therefore with diſgrace, happening to paſs near Cicero I would make room for you at my bench Cicero on our bench if we were not cloſe ſtowed already al luding to Cæſar's filling up the Senate and with the ſcumm of his creatures and

even with ſtrangers and bar barians At another time, being deſired by a friend, in a public company, to pro cure for his ſon *the rank of a Senator*, in one of the Cor porate towns of Italy, *he ſhall have it*, ſays he, *if you pleaſe, at Rome, but it will be difficult at Pompeii* An acquaintance likewiſe from Laodicea, coming to pay his reſpects to him, and being aſked, what buſineſs had brought him to Rome, ſaid, that he was ſent upon an em baſſy to Cæſar, *to intercede with him for the liberty of his country*, upon which Cicero replied, *if you ſucceed, you will be an Embaſſador alſo for* — Macrob Saturn 2 3 Sue on c 75

" unwilling

"unwilling at that time, to ftir from the guard
"of the ftate, for I then fat at the helm, and
"held the rudder; but am now fcarce thought
"worthy to work at the pump. would the Se-
"nate think you pafs fewer decrees, if I fhould
"live at Naples? while I am ftill at Rome, and
'attend the Forum, then decrees are all drawn
"at our friend's houfe, and whenever it comes
"into his head, my name is fet down, as if pre-
"fent at drawing them, fo that I hear from Ar-
"menia and Syria of decrees, faid to be made at
"my motion, of which I never heard a fyl-
"lable at home. Do not take me to be in jeft,
"for I affure you, that I have received Letters
"from kings, from the remoteft parts of the
"earth to thank me for giving them the title
"of King, when, fo far from knowing, that
'any fuch title had been decreed to them, I
"knew not even, that there were any fuch men
"in being. What is then to be done? why as
"long as our *mafter of manners* continues here,
"I will follow your advice, but as foon as he is
"gone, will run away to your mufhrooms, &c.
"[*n*]."

In another Letter, "Since you exprefs, fays
"he, fuch a concern for me in your laft, be af-
"fured, my dear Pætus, that whatever can be
"done by art, (for it is not enough to act with
"prudence, fome artifice alfo muft now be em-
"ployed) yet whatever, I fay, can be done by
"art, towards acquiring their good graces, I
"have already done it with the greateft care,
'nor as I believe without fuccefs, for I am
'fo much courted by all, who are in any de

[*n*] Ep. fam. 9. 15. *Pro* the *of Tus,* which the
us morum, or maj. the Senate had decreed to Cæ-
h

'gree

A Urb 707
Cic 61
Coss
C Julius
Cæsar III
M Æmilius
Lepidus

" gree of favor with Cæsar, that I begin to fan-
" cy that they love me and though real love is
" not easily distinguished from false, except in
" the case of danger, by which the sincerity of
" it may be tried, as of gold by fire, for all
" other marks are common to both, yet I have
" one argument to persuade me, that they real-
" ly love me, because both my condition and
" theirs is such, as puts them under no tempta-
" tion to dissemble and as for him, who has
" all power, I see no reason to fear any thing,
" unless that all things become of course uncer-
" tain, when justice and right are once deserted
" nor can we be sure of any thing, that depends
" on the will, not to say the passion of another
" Yet I have not in any instance particularly of-
" fended him, but behaved myself all along with
" the greatest moderation, for as once I took it
" to be my duty, to speak my mind freely in
" that City, which owed its freedom to me, so
" now, since that is lost, to speak nothing that
" may offend him, or his principal friends but
" if I would avoid all offence, of things said fa-
" cetiously or by way of raillery, I must give
" up all reputation of wit, which I would not
" refuse to do, if I could.   But as to Cæsar
" himself, he has a very piercing judgment,
" and as your brother Servius, whom I take to
" have been an excellent Critic, would readily
" say, *this verse is not Plautus's, that verse is,*
" having formed his ears by great use, to di-
" stinguish the peculiar stile and manner of dif-
" ferent Poets, so Cæsar, I hear, who has al-
" ready collected some volumes of Apophthegms,
" if any thing be brought to him for mine,
" which is not so, presently rejects it which he
" now does the more easily, because his friends
                                              " live

A Urb 707.
Cic 61
Coff
C Julius
Cæsar III.
M Æmilius
Lepidus.

" live almoſt continually with me, and in the
" variety of diſcourſe, when any thing drops
" from me, which they take to have ſome hu-
" mor or ſpirit in it, they carry it always to him,
" with the other news of the Town, for ſuch
' are his orders ſo that if he hears any thing
" beſides of mine from other perſons, he does not
" regard it, I have no occaſion therefore for your
" example of Ænomaus, though aptly applied
" from Accius for what is the envy, which
" you ſpeak of ? or what is there in me to be
' envied now ? but ſuppoſe there was every
" thing it has been the conſtant opinion of Phi-
' loſophers, the onely men in my judgement,
' who have a right notion of virtue, *that a wiſe*
' *man has nothing more to care for, then to keep*
" *himſelf free from guilt*, of which I take my-
' ſelf to be clear, on a double account, be-
" cauſe I both purſued thoſe meaſures, which
" were the juſteſt, and when I ſaw, that I had
" not ſtrength enough to carry them, did not
" think it my buſineſs to contend by force with
" thoſe, who were too ſtrong for me It is
' certain therefore, that I cannot be blamed, in
' what concerns the part of a good Citizen all
" that is now left, is not to ſay or do any thing
" fooliſhly and raſhly againſt the men in power,
' which I take alſo to be the part of a wiſe man
" As for the reſt, what people may report to be
' ſaid by me, or how he may take it, or with
" what ſincerity thoſe live with me, who now ſo
' aſſiduouſly court me, it is not in my power to
' anſwer I comfort myſelf therefore with the
' conſciouſneſs of my former conduct, and the
' moderation of my preſent; and ſhall apply
' your ſimilitude from Accius, not onely to the
" caſe of envy, but of fortune, which I conſider

A Urb 707
Cic 61
Coss
C Julius
Cæsar III
M Æmilius
Lepidus

" as light and weak, and what ought to be re-
" pelled by a firm and great mind, as waves by
" a rock For since the Greek History is full
" of examples, how the wisest men have en-
" dured Tyrannies at Athens or Syracuse, and
" when their Cities were enslaved, have lived
" themselves in some measure free ; why may
" not I think it possible to maintain my rank so,
" as neither to offend the mind of any, nor hurt
" my own dignity ?——&c [o]"

PÆTUS having heard, that Cæsar was *going
to divide some lands in his neighbourhood to the soldiers,* began to be afraid for his own estate, and
writes to Cicero, to know how far that distribution would extend to which Cicero answers,
" Are not you a pleasant fellow, who when
" Balbus has just been with you, ask me what
" will become of those towns and their lands?
" as if either I knew any thing, that Balbus
" does not, or if at any time I chance to know
" any thing, I do not know it from him: nay,
" it is your part rather, if you love me, to let
" me know what will become of me for you
" had it in your power to have learnt it from
" him, either sober, or at least when drunk
" But as for me, my dear Pætus, I have done
" enquiring about those things first, because
" we have already lived near four years, by
" clear gain, as it were if that can be called
" gain, or this, life, to outlive the Republic
" secondly, because I myself seem to know what
" will happen, for it will be, whatever pleases
" the strongest, which must always be decided
" by arms. it is our part therefore, to be con-
" tent with what is allowed to us he who cannot

[o] Ep fam 9 16.

" submit

" fubmit to this, ought to have chofen death. A Urb 707.
" They are now meafuring the fields of Veiæ Cic. 61.
" and Capenæ this is not far from Tufculum Coff
" yet I fear nothing I enjoy it whilft I may ; C Julius
" wifh that I always may, but if it fhould hap- Cæsar III.
" pen otherwife, yet fince, with all my courage M Æmilius
" and philofophy, I have thought it beft to live, Lepidus
" I cannot but have an affection for him, by
" whofe benefit I hold that life who, if he
" has an inclination to reftore the Republic, as
" he himfelf perhaps may defire, and we all
" ought to wifh, yet he has linked himfelf fo
" with others, that he has not the power to do
" what he would But I procede too far, for
" I am writing to you be iffured however of
" this, that not onely I, who have no part in their
" councils, but even the Chief himfelf does not
" know what will happen We are flaves to
" him, he to the times fo neither can he
" know, what the times will require, nor we,
" what he may intend, &c [p] "

THE Chiefs of the *Cæforian party*, who
courted Cicero fo much at this time, were Balbus, Oppius, Matius, Panfa, Hirtius, Dolabel-
la· they were all in the firft confidence with
Cæfar, yet profeffed the utmoft affection for Cicero, were every morning at his levee, and perpetually engaging him to fup with them, and
the two laft employed themfelves in a daily exercife *of declaiming at his houfe*, for the benefit
of his inftruction, of which he gives the following account in his familiar way to Pætus
" Hirtius and Dolabella are my fcholars in fpeak-
" ing; my mafters in eating for you have
" heard, I guefs, how they declame with me,

[p] Ep fam 9 17.

Z 2 " I fup

A Urb 707
Cic 07
Cos
C Julius
Cæsar III
M Æmilius
Lepidus

" I fup with them " In another Letter he tells
him, " that as King Dionyſius, when driven
" out of Syracuſe, turned ſchool-maſter at Co-
" rinth, ſo he, having loſt his kingdom of the
" Forum, had now opened a School— to which
" he merrily invites Pætus, with the offer of a
" ſeat and cuſhion next to himſelf, as his Uſh-
" er [*q*] " But to Varro more ſeriouſly, " I
" acquainted you, *ſays he*, before, that I am in-
" timate with them all, and aſſiſt at their coun-
" ſils I ſee no reaſon why I ſhould not— for
" it is not the ſame thing, *to bear what muſt be*
" *vorn, and to approve what ought not to be ap-*
" *proved* " And again, " I do not forbear to ſup
" with thoſe who now rule what can I do
" we muſt comply with the times [*r*] "

The onely uſe which he made of all this favor
was, to ſkreen himſelf from any particular calimity
in the general miſery of the times, and
to ſerve thoſe unhappy men, who were driven
from their country and their families, for their
adherence to that cauſe, which he himſelf had
eſpouſed Cæſar was deſirous indeed to engage
him in his meaſures, and attach him inſenſibly

[ ] Ut cum ego & Dol-
bella diceret diſcipulos habeo cœnandi magiſtros pu-
erum te aut ſe—illos a-
p t e declamitare me apud
c cœnitare Ib 16

Ut Dionyſus Tyrannus,
cum Syracuſis pulſus eſſet,
Corinthi dicitur ludum ape-
ruiſſe ſic ego— amiſſo regno
Forenſi, Ludim curſi ha-
bere cœperim— Bella tibi erit
in ludo ſi qua Hypodi-
didaſcalo proxima eam pul-

vinus ſequetur   Ib 18

[*r*] Oſtentavit tibi, me iſtis
eſſe familiarem, & conſiliis
eorum intereſſe Quod ego
cur nolim nihil video Non
enim eſt idem, ferre ſi quid
ferendum eſt, & probare ſi
quid probandum non eſt
Ib 6

Non deſino apud iſtos, qui
nunc dominantur, cœnitare
Quid faciam ? tempori ſer-
viendum eſt   Ib 7

A Urb 707.
Cic 61
Coſſ
C Julius
Cæſar III
M Æmilius
Lepidus

to his intereſts · but he would bear no part in an administration, eſtabliſhed on the ruins of his country, nor ever cared to be acquainted with their affairs, or to inquire what they were doing ſo that whenever he entered into their counſils, as he ſignifies above to Varro, it was onely when the caſe of ſome exiled friend required it, for whoſe ſervice he ſcrupled no pains of folliciting, and attending even Cæſar himſelf, though he was ſometimes ſhocked, as he complains, *by the difficulty of acceſs, and the indignity of waiting in an Antichamber*, not indeed through Cæſar's fault, who was always ready to give him audience, but from the multiplicity of his affairs, by whoſe hands *all the favors of the Empire were diſpenſed* [s] Thus in a Letter to Ampius, whoſe pardon he had procured,—" I have ſol-
" licited your cauſe, *ſays he*, more eagerly than
" my preſent ſituation would well juſtify for
" my deſire to ſee you, and my conſtant love
" for you, moſt aſſiduouſly cultivated on your
" part, over-ruled all regard to the preſent weak
" condition of my power and intereſt Every
" thing that relates to your return and ſafety is
' promiſed, confirmed, fixed, and ratified I
' ſaw, knew, was preſent at every ſtep for
" by good luck, I have all Cæſar's friends en-
" gaged to me by an old acquaintance and
" friendſhip ſo that next to him they pay the
" firſt regard to me Panſa, Hirtius, Balbus,
' Oppius, Matius, Poſtumius, take all occaſions
" to give me proof of their ſingular affection.
" If this had been ſought and procured by me,

[s] Quod ſi tardus fit quam volumus, magnis oc-cupationibus ejus, a quo om-nia petuntur, aditus ad eum difficiliores fuerunt —— Ep fam 6 13

" I ſhould

A Urb 707
Cic 61
Coff
C Julius
Cæsar III
M Æmilius
Lepidus.

" I fhould have no reafor, as things now ftand.
" to repent of my pains   but I have done no-
" thing with the view of ferving the times, I
" had an intimacy of long ftanding with them,
" all, and never gave over follicitng them on
" your behalf   I found Panfa however the
" readieft of them all to ferve you, and oblige
" me, who has not onely an intereft, but au
" thority with Cæfar, &c [*t*] "

BUT while he was thus careffed by Cæfar's
friends, he was not lefs followed, we may ima
gine, by the friends of the Republic   thefe had
always looked upon him as the chief Patron of
their liberty ; whofe counfils, if they had been
followed, would have preferved it, and whofe
authority gave them the only hopes that were
left, of recovering it   fo that his houfe was as
much frequented, and his levee as much crouded, as ever, fince *people now flocked*, he fays, *to*
fee a good Citizen, as a fort of rarity [*u*]. In
another Letter, giving a fhort account of his
way of life, he fays, " Early in the morning, I
" receive the compliments of many honeft men,
" but melancholy ones, as well as of thefe gay
" Conquerors, who fhew indeed a very offici-
" ous and affectionate regard to me   When
" thefe vifits are over, I fhut myfelf up in my
" Library, either to write or read . Here fome
" alfo come to hear me, as a man of learning,
" becaufe I am fomewhat more learned than
" they . the reft of my time I give to the care
" of my body : for I have now bewailed my

[*t*] Ib 6 12
[*u*] Cum falutationi nos
dedimus amicorum , quæ fit
hoc etiam frequentius, quam

folebat, quod quafi avem al-
bam, videntur bene fentien
tem civem videre, abdo me
in Bibliothecam Ib 7 28

" country

A Urb 707
Cc 61
Coff
C Julius
Cæsar III
M Æmilius
Lepidus

" country longer, and more heavily, than any
" mother ever bewailed her onely Son [x] "

It is certain, that there was not a man in the
Republic so particularly engaged, both by principle and intereft, to wifh well to it's liberty, or
who had fo much to lofe by the fubverfion of
it as he : for as long as it was governed by civil
methods, and ftood upon the foundation of it's
laws, he was undoubtedly the firft Citizen in it ;
had the chief influence in the Senate, the chief
authority with the people and as all his hopes
and fortunes were grounded on the peace of his
country, fo all his labors and ftudies were perpetually applied to the promotion of it it is no
wonder therefore, in the prefent fituation of the
City, oppreffed by arms, and a tyrannical power, to find him fo particularly impatient under
the common mifery, and expreffing fo keen a
fenfe of the diminution of his dignity, and the
difgrace of ferving, where he had been ufed to
govern.

Cæsar, on the other hand, though he
knew his temper and principles to be irreconcile-
able to his ufurped dominion, yet out of friendfhip to the man, and a reverence for his character, was determined to treat him with the greateft humanity. and by all the marks of perfonal
favor, to make his life not only tolerable, but

[x] Hæc igitur eft nunc vita noftra Mane faluta mus domi & bonos viros multos, fed triftes, & hos lætos victores, qui me quidem perofficiofe & peramanter obfervant Ubi falutatio defluxit, litteris me involvo, aut fcribo aut lego Veniunt etiam qui me audiunt, quifi doctam hominem, quia pauIlo fum, quam ipfi, doctior Inde corpori omne tempus datur Patriam eluxi jam gravius & diutius quam ulla mater unicum filium Ep fam 9 20

eafy

A Urb 707
Cic 6ı
Coſſ
C Jul. C
Cæſar VII
M Æ Lıd
Lepidus

eaſy to him yet all that he could do, had no other effect on Cicero, than to make him think and ſpeak ſometimes favorably of the *natural clemency of the victor*, and to entertain ſome hopes from it, that he would one day be perſuaded to reſtore the public liberty but excluſive of that hope, he never mentions his goverrment, but as a real *Tyranny*, or his perſon in any other ſtile, than as the oppreſſor of his Country

Bᴜᴛ he gave a remarkable proof at this time of his being no temporiſer, by writing a book *in praiſe of Cato*, which he publiſhed within a few months after Cato's death. He ſeems to have been left a *Guardian to Cato's Son*, as he was alſo to young *Lucullus*, Cato's *Nephew* [y] and this teſtimony of Cato s friendſhip and judgement of him, might induce him the more readily to pay this honor to his memory It was a matter however of no ſmall deliberation, in what manner he ought to treat the ſubject his friends adviſed him, not to be too explicit and particular in the detail of Cato's praiſes, but to content himſelf with a general encomium, for fear of irritating Cæſar, by puſhing the Argument too far In a Letter to Atticus, he calls this, " an " *Archimedean problem*, but I cannot hit upon " any thing, *ſays he*, that thoſe friends of yours " will read with pleaſure, or even with pa " tience, beſides, if I ſhould drop the account " of Cato s Votes and Speeches in the Senate, " and of his political conduct in the State, and " give a ſlight commendation onely of his con- " ſtancy and gravity, even this may be more, " than they will care to hear but the man can-

" no

" not be praifed, as he deferves, unlefs it be
" particularly explaned, how he foretold all that
" has happened to us, how he took arms to
" prevent its happening, and parted with life
" rather than fee it happen [z] " Thefe were
the topics, which he refolved to difplay with all
his force, and from the accounts given of the
work by antiquity, it appears, that he had fpared
no pains to adorn it, but *extolled Cato's virtue
and character to the fkies* [a]

THE book was foon fpread into all hands,
and Cæfar, inftead of expreffing any refentment,
affected to be much pleafed with it, yet declared, that he would anfwer it and Hirtius in the
mean while, drew up a little piece in the form
of a Letter to Cicero, filled with objections *to
Cato's character, but with high compliments to Cicero himfelf, which Cicero* took care to make
public, and calls *it a fpecimen of what Cæfar's
work was like to be* [b] Brutus alfo compofed
and publifhed a piece on the fame fubject, as
well as another friend of Cicero, Fabius Gal-

[z] Sed de Catone πρό-βλημα reχγραφικόν eft Non affequor ut fcribam, quod tui conviva non modo li-benter, fed etiam æquo ani-mo lege e poffint Quin e-tiam fi a fententiis ejus dic-tis fi ab omni voluntate, confiliifque quæ de Repub habuit, recedam, ψιλώcque velim gravitatem conftanti-amque ejus laudare, hoc ip-fum φ ευ-μα fit Sed vere laudari ille vir non poteft, nifi hæc ornata fint, quod ille ea, quæ nunc funt, & futura viderit, & ne fierent

contenderit, & facta ne vide-ret, vitam reliquerit Ad Att 12 4

[a] M Ciceronis libro, quo Catonem coelo æquavit, &c Tacit Ann 4 34

[b] Qualis futura fit Cæ-faris vituperatio contra lau-dationem meam perfpexi ex eo libro, quem Hirtius ad me mifit, in quo colligit vi-tia Catonis, fed cum maxi-mis laudibus meis Itaque mifi librum ad Mufcam, ut tuis librariis daret Volo eum divulgari, &c Ad Att. 12 40 it 41

Ius

A Urb 707
Cic 61
Coff
C Julius
Cæsar III
M Æmilius
Lepidus

lus [c] : but thefe were but little confidered in comparifon of Cicero's. and Brutus had made fome miftakes in his account of the transactions, in which Cato had been concerned; especially *in the debates on Catiline's plot* , in which he had given him *the first part and merit*, in derogation even of Cicero himfelf [d].

CÆSAR's anfwer was not publifhed till the next year, upon his return from Spain, after the defeat of Pompey's *Sons* It was a labored invective, anfwering Cicero's book paragraph by paragraph, and accufing *Cato with all the art and force of his Rhetoric, as if in a public trial before Judges* [e]; yet with expreffions of great refpect towards Cicero, whom, for his virtues and abilities, he compared *to Pericles and Thera- menes of Athens* [f]. and in a Letter upon it to Balbus, which was fhewn by his order to Cicero, he faid, *that by the frequent reading of Cice- ro's Cato, he was grown more copious; but af- ter he had read Brutus's, thought himfelf even eloquent* [g].

---

[c] Catonem tuum mihi mitte Cupio enim legere Ep fam 7 24

[d] Catonem primum fen- tentiam putat de animadver- fione dixiffe, quam omnes ante dixerant præter Cæfa- rem, &c ——— Ad Att 12. 21

From this and other par- ticulars, which are mention- ed in the fame Letter, we may obferve, that Salluft had probably taken his account of the debates upon *Cati- line's Accomplices*, from *Bru- tus's life of Cato*, and chofen

to copy even his miftakes, rather than do juftice to Ci- cero on that occafion

[e] Ciceronis libro— quid aliud Dictator Cæfar, quam refcripta oratione, velut apud Judices refpondit? Tacit Ann 4 34 it Quintil 3 7

[f] Plutar in Cic
[g] Legi epiftolam · mul ta de meo Catone, quo fæ piffime legendo fe dicit copi ofiorem factum; Bruti Ca- tone lecto, fe fibi vifum di fertum. Ad Att 13 46

THESE

THESE two rival pieces were much celebrated in Rome, and had their feveral admirers, as different parties and interefts difpofed men, to favor the fubject or the author of each and it is certain, that they were the principal caufe of eftablifhing and propagating that veneration, which pofterity has fince paid to the memory of Cato For his name being thrown into controverfy, in that critical period of the fate of Rome, by the Patron of liberty on the one fide, and the oppreffor of it on the other, became of courfe a kind of *Political teft* to all fucceding ages; and a perpetual argument of difpute between the friends of liberty, and the flatterers of power. But if we confider his character without prejudice, he was certainly a great and worthy man, a friend to truth, virtue, liberty yet falfely meafuring all duty by the abfurd rigor of the *Stoical* rule, he was generally difappointed of the end, which he fought by it, the happinefs both of his private and public life In his private conduct, he was fevere, morofe, inexorable, banifhing all the fofter affections, as natural enemies to juftice, and as fuggefting falfe motives of acting, from favor, clemency, and compaffion in public affairs he was the fame, had but one rule of policy, *to adhere to what was right*, without regard to times or circumftances, or even to a force that could controul him for inftead of managing the power of the Great, fo as to mitigate the ill, or extract any good from it, he was urging it always to acts of violence by a perpetual defiance, fo that, *with the beft intentions in the world, he often did great harm to the Republic* This was his general behaviour, yet from fome particular facts explained above, it appears, that his ftrength of mind was not always

ways

A Urb 707
Cic 61
Coſſ
C. Julius
Cæs - III
M Æ ...-
Lepidus

ways impregnable, but had its weak places of pride, ambition, and party zeal, which when managed and flattered to a certain point, would betray him sometimes into meaſures contrary to his ordinary rule of right and truth The laſt act of his life was agreeable to his nature and philoſophy *when he could no longer be, what he had been, or when the ills of life overbalanced the good,* which, by the principles of his ſect, was *lawful enough* [*b*], he put an end to his life, with a ſpirit and reſolution, which would make one imagine, *that he was glad to have found an occaſion of dying in his proper character.* On the whole, his life was rather admirable, than amiable, fit to be praiſed, rather than imitated [*i*]

As ſoon as Cicero had publiſhed his *Cato*, he wrote his piece called *the Orator*, at the requeſt of Brutus, containing the plan or delineation of what he himſelf eſteemed the moſt perfect eloquence or manner of ſpeaking He calls it *the fifth part or book*, deſigned to complete the argument of *his Brutus, and the other three, on the ſame ſubject* It was received with great approbation, and in a Letter to Lepta, who had complimented him upon it, he declares, *that what-*

[*h*] In quo enim plura ſunt, quæ ſecundum naturam ſunt, hujus officium eſt in vita manere in quo autem aut ſunt plura contraria, aut fore ʼmen hujus officium eſt e vita excedere De Fin 3 19

Verus eſt enim, ubi non ſit qui fuerit non eſſe cur velis vivere Ep fam 7 3

[*i*] Cato ſic abiit e vita,

ut cauſam moriundi nactum ſe eſſe gauderet — cum vero cauſam juſtam Deus ipſe dederit, ut tunc Socrati, nunc Catoni, &c Tuſc Quæſt 1 30

Catoni —moriundum potius, quam Tyranni vultus adſpiciendus fuit De Offic 1 31

Non immaturus deceſſit vixit enim, quantum debuit vivere Senec Conſol ad Marc 20

ever judgement he had in speaking, he had thrown A Urb 707
it all into that work, and was content to risk his Cic 61
reputation on the merit of it [k]   Coss

C Julius
Cæsar III

M Æmilius
Lepidus

He now likewise spoke that famous speech of
thanks to Cæsar, *for the pardon of M. Marcellus*,
which was granted upon the interceffion of the
Senate. Cicero had a particular friendship with
all the family of the Marcelli, but especially
with this Marcus, who from the defeat of Pompey at Pharfalia, retired to Mitylene in Lesbos,
where he lived with so much ease and satisfaction
to himself in a philosophical retreat, that Cicero, as it appears from his Letters, was forced
to use all his art and authority to persuade him
to return, and take the benefit of that grace,
which they had been laboring to obtain for him [l].
But how the affair was transacted, we may learn
from Cicero's account of it to Serv Sulpicius,
who was then Proconful of Greece ——— " Your
' condition, says he, is better than ours in this
" particular, that you dare venture to write your
" grievances, we cannot even do that with safe-
" ty · not through any fault of the Conqueror,
" than whom nothing can be more moderate,
" but of victory itself, which in civil wars is al-
" ways infolent we have had the advantage of
" you however in one thing, in being acquaint-
" ed a little sooner than you, with the pardon
" of your collegue Marcellus · or rather indeed
" in feeing how the whole affair pass for I
' would have you believe, that from the begin-

[k] Ita tres erunt de Oratore quartus Brutus quin-
tu, Orator De Div 2 1
    Oratorem meum tantopere
a te probari, vehementer gaudeo mihi quidem fic per-
fuadeo, me quicquid habu-
erim judicii in dicendo, in
illum librum contulisse. Ep
fam 6 18
    [l] Ep fam 4 7, 8, 9

A Urb 707
Cic 61
Coff
C Jɣ ɩs
Cɛsɑʀ ɪɪɪ
ʍ ɪ ɪɪ ɩs
Lɛᴘɪᴅɩ

" ning of thefe miferies, or ever fince the public
" right has been decided by arms, there has
" nothing been done befides this with any dig-
" nity For Cɛɩaɩ himfelr, after having com-
" plained of the morofenefs of Marcellus, for
" fo he called it, and praifed in the ftrongeft
' terms the equity and prudence of your con-
" duct, prefently declared beyond all our hopes,
" that whatever offence he had received from
" the man, he could refufe nothing to the inter-
" ceffion of the Senate What the Senate did
" was this upon the mention of Marcellus by
" Pifo, his Brother Caius having thrown him-
" felf at Cæfar's feet, they all rofe up, and went
" forward in a fupplicating manner towards Cæ-
" far in fhort, this day's work appeared to me
" fo decent, that I could not help fancying that
" I faw the image of the old republic reviving
" when all therefore, who were afked their opi-
" nions before me, had returned thanks to Cæ-
" far, excepting Volcatius, (for he declared,
" that he would not have done it, though he
" had been in Marcellus's place,) I, as foon as
" I was called upon, changed my mind, for I
" had refolved with myfelf to obferve an eternal
" filence, not through any lazinefs, but the lofs
" of my former dignity, but Cæfar's greatnefs
" of mind, and the laudable zeal of the Senate,
" got the better of my refolution I gave thanks
" therefore to Cæfar in a long fpeech, and have
" deprived myfelf by it, I fear, on other occa-
" fions, of that honeft quiet, which was my
" onely comfort in thefe unhappy times : but
" fince I have hitherto avoided giving him of-
" fence, and if I had always continued filent,
" he would have interpreted it perhaps, as a
' proof of my taking the Republic to be ruined,
" I fhall

" I fhall fpeak for the future not often, or rather
" very feldom, fo as to manage at the fame
" time both his favor, and my own leifure for
" ftudy [*m*] "

A Urb 707.
Cic 61
Coff
C Julius
Cæsar III
M Æmilius
Lepidus

CÆSAR, though he faw the Senate unanimous
in their petition for Marcellus, yet took the pains
to call for the particular opinion of every Senator
upon it · a method never practifed, except in
cafes of debate, and where the houfe was divided ·
but he wanted the ufual tribute of flattery upon
this act of grace, and had a mind probably to
make an experiment of Cicero's temper, and to
draw from him efpecially fome incenfe on the occafion, nor was he difappointed of his aim, for
Cicero, touched by his generofity, and greatly
pleafed with the act itfelf, on the account of his
friend, returned thanks to him in a fpeech, which,
though made upon the fpot, yet for elegance of
diction, vivacity of fentiment, and politenefs of
compliment, is fuperior to any thing extant of
the kind in all antiquity. The many fine things,
which are faid in it of Cæfar, have given fome
handle indeed for a charge of infincerity againft
Cicero: but it muft be remembered, that he was
delivering a fpeech of thanks, not onely for himfelf, but in the name and at the defire of the Senate, where his fubject naturally required the em-
bellifhments of Oratory, and that all his compliments are grounded on a fuppofition, *that Cæfar*
intended to reflore the Republic of which he enter-
tained no fmall hopes at this time, as he fignifies in
a letter to one of Cæfar's *principal friends* [*n*] This
therefore he recommends, enforces, and requires
from him in his fpeech, with the fpirit of an old

[*m*] Ep fam 4 4
[*n*] Sperare tamen videor,
Cæfari, collegæ noftro, fore

cure & effe, ut habeamus a-
liquam Rempublicam Ep
fam 13 68

Roman,

A Urb 707
Cic 6'
     Coſ
C Jul c.
C æſar III
M Æmil us
Lepidus

Roman, and no reaſonable man will think it
ſtrange, that ſo free an addreſs to a Conqueror,
in the height of all his power, ſhould want to be
tempered with ſome few ſtrokes of flattery. But
the following paſſage from the oration itſelf will
juſtify the truth of what I am ſaying

" IF this, ſays he, Cæſar, was to be the end
" of your immortal acts, that after conquering
" all your enemies, you ſhould leave the Repub-
" l c in the condition, in which it now is, con-
" ſider, I beſeech you, whether your divine vir-
" tue would not excite rather an admiration of
" you, than any real glory for glory is the il-
" luſtrious fame of many and great ſervices either
" to our friends, our country, or to the whole
" race of mankind This part therefore ſtill re
" mains, there is one act more to be perform'd
" by you, to eſtabliſh the Republic again, thar
" you may reap the benefit of it yourſelf in peace
" and proſperity When you have paid this
" debt to your country, and fulfilled the ends of
" your nature by a ſatiety of living, you may
" then tell us, if you pleaſe, that you have lived
" long enough yet what is it after all, that we
" can really call long, of which there is an end,
" for when that end is once come, all paſt plea-
" ſure is to be reckoned as nothing, ſince no
" more of it is to be expected Though your
" mind, I know, was never content with theſe
" narrow bounds of life, which nature has aſ-
" ſigned to us, but inflamed always with an ar-
" dent love of immortality nor is this in-
" deed to be conſidered as your life, which is
" compriſed in this body and breath, but that,
" that, I ſay, is your life, which is to flouriſh in
" the memory of all ages which poſterity will
" cheriſh, a d eternity itſelf propagate. It is to
                                    " this

" this that you muft attend, to this that you
" muft form yourfelt· which has many things
" already to admire, yet wants fomething ftill,
" that it may praife in you   Pofterity will be
" amazed to hear and read of your commands,
" provinces, the Rhine, the Ocean, the Nile,
" your innumerable battles, incredible victories,
" infinite monuments, fplendid triumphs   but
" unlefs this City be eftablifhed again by your
" wifdom and counfils, your name indeed will
" wander far and wide, yet will have no certain
" feat or place at laft, where to fix itfelf   There
" will be alfo amongft thofe, who are yet un-
   born, the fame controverfy, that has been
" amongft us, when fome will extoll your ac-
" tions to the fkies, others perhaps will find
" fomething defective in them, and that one
· thing above all, if you fhould not extinguifh
" this flame of civil war, by reftoring liberty to
" your country   for the one may be looked up-
" on as the effect of fate, but the other is the
" certain act of wifdom   Pay a reverence there-
" fore to thofe Judges, who will pafs judgement
" upon you in ages to come, and with lefs par-
" tiality perhaps than we, fince they will neither
" be biaffed by affection or party, nor prejudiced
" by hatred or envy to you   and though this, as
" fome falfely imagine, fhould then have no re-
" lation to you, yet it concerns you certainly at
   the prefent, to act in fuch a manner, that no
" oblivion may ever obfcure the lufter of your
" praifes   Various were the inclinations of the
" Citizens, and their opinions wholly divided
" nor did we differ onely in fentiments and wifhes,
" but in arms alfo and camps   the merits of the
" caufe were dubious, and the contention be-
" tween two celebrated Leaders   many doubted

A Urb 707.
Cic 61
Coff
C Julius
Casar III
M Æmilius
Lepidus.

A Urb 707
Cic 61
Coff
C Julius
Cæsar III
M Æmilius
Lepidus

" what was the beſt, many what was conveni-
" ent, many what was decent, ſome alſo what
" was lawful, &c [*o*]"

But though Cæſar took no ſtep towards reſtoring the Republic, he employed himſelf this
ſummer in another work of general benefit to
mankind, *the reformation of the Kalendar*; *by ac-*
commodating the courſe of the year, to the exact courſe
of the Sun, from which it had varied ſo widely,
as to occaſion a ſtrange confuſion in all their accounts of time

The Roman year, from the whole inſtitution
of Numa, was lunar, borrowed from the Greeks,
amongſt whom it conſiſted of *three hundred and*
fifty four days. Numa added one more to them
to make the whole number odd, which was
thought the more fortunate, and to fill up the
deficiency of his year to the meaſure of the ſolar
courſe, inſerted likewiſe or *intercalated,* after the
manner of the Greeks, an extraordinary month
of twenty two days, every ſecond year, and *twenty*
three every fourth, between *the twenty third and*
twenty fourth day of February [*p*]. he committed
the care of *intercalating* this month and the ſuper-
numerary day, to the College of Prieſts, who in
proceſs of time partly by a negligent, partly a
ſuperſtitious. but chiefly by an arbitrary abuſe of
their truſt, uſed either to drop or inſert them,
as it was found moſt convenient to themſelves or
their friends, to make the current year longer

[ ] Pro M Marcell 8, 9,
10

[*p*] This was uſually called
Intercalaris, though Plutarch
gives it the name of Merce-
donius, which none of the
Romans mention, ex-

cept that Feſtus ſpeaks of
ſome days under the title of
Mercedonia, becauſe the
Merces or wages of work-
men were commonly paid
upon them

or fhorter [*q*]. Thus Cicero, when haraffed by a perpetual courfe of pleading, prayed, *that there might be no intercalation* to lengthen his fatigue; and when Proconful of Cilicia, preffed Atticus to exert all his intereft, to prevent *any intercalation within the year*, that it might not protract his government, and retard his return to *Rome* [*r*]. Curio, on the contrary, when he could not perfuade the Priefts to prolong the year of his Tribunate by an *Intercalation*, made that a pretence for abandoning the Senate, and going over to Cæfar [*s*]

THIS licence of *intercalating* introduced the confufion above-mentioned, in the computation of their time fo that the order of all their months was tranfpofed from their ftated feafons, the winter months carried back into Autumn, the Autumnal into Summer till Cæfar refolved to put an end to this diforder by abolifhing the fource of it, the ufe of *intercalctions*, and inftead of the *Lunar* to eftablifh the *Solar* year, adjufted to the exact meafure of the Sun's revolution in the *Zodiac*, or to that period of time, in which it returns to the point, from which it fet out and as this, according to the Aftronomers of that age, was fuppofed to be *three hundred and fixty five days, and fix hours*, fo he divided the days into

A Urb 707.
Cic 61
Coff
C JULIUS
CÆSAR III
M ÆMILIUS
LÆPIDUS.

[*q*] Quod inftitutum perite a Numa, pofteriorum Pon fi cum negligentia diffolutum et De Leg 2 12 vid Cenforin de die Nat c 20. Macrob Sat 1 14

[*r*] Nos hic in mu titudine & celebritate judiciorum — ita deftinemur, ut quotidie vota faciamus ne intercaletur Ep fam 7 2

Per fortunas primum illud prærule. atque premiani quæ-io ut fimus annui, ne inter caleur quidem Ad Att 5 13 it 9

[*s*] Leviffime enim quia de in ercalando non obtrue-rat, transfugit ad populum & pro Cæfare loqui cœpit, Ep fam 8 6 Dio p 145

twelve

twelve artificial months, and to supply the deficiency of the six hours, by which they fell short of the Sun's complete course, he ordered a day *to be intercalated* after every four years, between *the twenty third and twenty fourth of February* [t].

But to make this new Year begin, and procede regularly, he was forced to insert into the current year, *two extraordinary months*, between November and December, the one of *thirty three*, the other of *thirty four days*, besides the ordinary *intercalary month of twenty three days*, which fell into it of course, which were all necessary to fill up the number of days, that were left to the old year, by the omission of *intercalations*, and to replace the months in their proper seasons [v] All this was effected by the care and skill of Sosigenes, a celebrated *Astronomer of Alexandria*, whom Cæsar had brought to Rome for that purpose [x] and a *new Kalendar* was formed upon it by Flavius *a Scribe*, digested according to the order of the Roman Festivals, and the old manner of computing their days by *Kalends, Ides, and Nones*, which was published and authorized by *the Dictator's Edict*, not long after his return from *Rome*. This year therefore was the longest, that Rome had ever known, consisting of *fifteen months*, or *four hundred and forty five days*, and is called *the last of the confusion* [y], because it introduced

[t] This day was called *Bissextile* from its being a repetition or a phrase of the Sixth of the Calend of March which fell always on the 24 and hence our Bissextile or Leap year.

runs orbis temporum ratio congrueret, inter Novembrem & Decembrem mensem adjecit alios duos fuitque is annus —ex mensium cum Intercalario, qui ex consuetudine in annum inciderat Suet I Cæs 40

Sun Hist N 18 25

descripte sibi M Fla vio

A Urb 707
Cic 61
Coſl
C Julius
Caſar III
M Æmilius
Lepidus

troduced *the Julian, or ſolar year*, with the commencement of the enſuing January, which continues in uſe to this day in all Chriſtian Countries, without any other variation, than that of *the old and new ſtile*—[z]

Soon after the affair of Marcellus, Cicero had another occaſion of trying both his eloquence and intereſt with Cæſar, in the cauſe of Ligarius, who was now in exil on the account of his having been in arms againſt Cæſar, *in the African war*, in which he had born a conſiderable command His two Brothers however had always been on Cæſar's ſide, and being recommended by Panſa, and warmly ſupported by Cicero, had almoſt prevailed for his pardon, of which Cicero gives the following account in a Letter to Ligarius himſelf.

Cicero to Ligarius

" I would have you be aſſured, that I em-
" ploy my whole pains, labor, care, ſtudy, in

---

to ſcriba, qui ſcriptos dies ſingulos ita ad Dictatorem detulit, ut & ordo eorum in veniri facillime poſſet, & invento, certus ſtatus perſeveraret — eaque re factum eſt, ut annus confuſionis ultimus in quadringentos quadraginta tres dies tenderetur Macrob Sat i 14 Dio 227

Macrobius makes this year to conſiſt of 443 days, but he ſhould have ſaid 445, ſince, according to all accounts, ninety days were added to the old year of 355

[z] This difference *of the old and new ſt l.* was occaſi

oned by a regulation made *by Pope Gregory A D* 1582 for it having been obſerved, that the computation of *the Vernal Equino* was fallen back ten days from the time of *the Council of Nice*, when it was found to be on *the 21ʃ of March*, according to which all the feſtivals of the Church were then ſolemnly ſettled, Pope Gregory, by the advice of Aſtronomers, cauſed ten days to be entirely ſunk and thrown out of the current year, between the 4th and 15th of October

" procuring

A Urb 707
Cc 61
CoſT
C Julius
Cæsar III
M Æmilius
Lepidus

"procuring your restoration · for as I have ever
"had the greatest affection for you, so the fin-
"gular piety and love of your Brothers, for
"whom, as well as yourself, I have always
"professed the utmost esteem, never suffer me
"to neglect any opportunity of my duty and fer-
"vice to you   But what I am now doing, or
"have done, I would have you learn from their
"Letters, rather than mine, but as to what I
"hope, and take to be certain in your affair,
"that I chufe to acquaint you with myfelf · for
"if any man be timorous in great and dangerous
"events, and fearing always the worst, rather
"than hoping the best, I am he, and if this be
"a fault, confefs myfelf not to be free from it,
"yet on the twenty feventh of November, when,
"at the defire of your Brothers, I had been
"early with Cæfar, and gone through the trou-
"ble and indignity of getting accefs and audi-
"ence, when your Brothers and relations had
"th own themfelves at his feet, and I had faid,
"what your caufe and circumftances required, I
"came away perfuaded, that your pardon was
"certain   which I collected, not onely from
"Cæfar's difcourfe, which was mild and gene-
"rous, but from his eyes and looks, and many
"other figns, which I could better obferve than
"deſcribe   It is your part therefore, to behave
"yourfelf with firmnefs and courage, and as
"you have born the more turbulent part pru-
"dently, to bear this calmer ftate of things
"chearfully   I fhall continue ftill to take the
"fame pains in your affairs, as if there was the
"greateft difficulty in them, and will heartily
"fupplicate in your behalf, as I have hitherto
"done, not onely Cæfar himfelf, but all his
"friends,

" friends, whom I have ever found more affecti-
" onate to me. Adieu [a]"

WHILE Ligarius's affair was in this hopefull
way, Q. Tubero, who had an old quarrel with
him, being defirous to obftruct his pardon, and
knowing Cæfar to be particularly exafperated
againft all thofe, *who through an obftinate averfion*
to him, had renewed the war in Afric, accufed
him, in the ufual forms, of an uncommon zeal
and violence in profecuting that war. Cæfar
privately encouraged the profecution, and ordered the caufe to be tried *in the Forum,* where
he fat upon it in perfon, ftrongly prepoffeffed
againft the Criminal, and determined to lay hold
on any plaufible pretence for condemning him.
but the force of Cicero's eloquence, exerted with
all his fkill in a caufe, which he had much at
heart, got the better of all his prejudices, and
extorted a pardon from him againft his will.

THE merit of this fpeech is too well known,
to want to be enlarged upon here thofe, who
read it, will find no reafon to charge Cicero with
flattery. but the free fpirit, which it breaths, in
the face of that power, to which it was fuing
for mercy, muft give a great idea of the art of
the fpeaker, who could deliver fuch bold truths
without offence, as well as of the generofity of
the Judge, who heard them not onely with patience, but approbation

" Obferve, Cæfar, fays he, with what fide-
" lity I plead Ligarius's caufe, when I betray
" even my own by it. O that admirable clemen-
" cy, worthy to be celebrated by every kind of
" praife, letters, monuments ! M. Cicero de-
" fends a criminal before you, by proving him

[a] Ep. fam 6 14

" not

" not to have been in thofe fentiments, in which
" he owns himſelf to have been, nor does he
" yet fear your fecret thoughts, or while he is
" pleading for another, what may occur to you
" about himſelf   See, I ſay, how little he is
" afraid or you   See with what a courage and
" gaiety of ſpeaking your generofity and wifdom
" in praiſe me   I will raiſe my voice to ſuch a
" pitch, that the whole Roman people may hear
" me   After the war was not onely begun,
" Cæſar, but in great meaſure finiſhed, when I
" was driven by no neceſſity, I went by choice
" and judgment to join myſelf with thoſe, who
" had taken arms againſt you   Before whom do
" I ſay this ? why before him, who, though he
" knew it to be true, yet reſtored me to the Re-
" public, before he had even ſeen me, who
" wrote to me from Egypt, that I ſhould be
" the ſame man, that I had always been, and
" when he was the onely Emperor within the
" dominion of Rome, ſuffered me to be the
" other, and to hold my laurelled Faſces, as long
" as I thought them worth holding—[*h*]   Do
" you then, Tubero, call Ligarius's conduct
" wicked ? for what reaſon ? ſince that cauſe
" has never yet been called by that name   ſome
" indeed call it miſtake, others fear, thoſe who
" ſpeak more ſeverely, hope, ambition, hatred,
" obſtinacy, or at the worſt, raſhneſs, but no
" man, beſides you, has ever called it wickedneſs.
" For my part, were I to invent a proper and ge-
" neral name for our calamity, I ſhould take it
" for a kind of fatality, that had poſſeſſed the un-
" wary minds of men, ſo that none can think it
" ſtrange that all human counfils were over-

[*h*] Pro Ligar 3

" ruled

" ruled by a divine neceffity. Call us then, if A Urb 707
" you pleafe, unhappy, though we can never Cic 61
" be fo, under this Conqueror, but I fpeak not Coff
" of us who furvive, but of thofe who fell, C Julius
" let them be ambitious, let them be angiy, Cæsar III
" let them be obftinate, but let not the guilt of M Æmilius
" crime, of fury, of parricide, ever be charged Lepidus
" on Cn Pompey, and on many of thofe who
" died with him   When did we evei hear any
" fuch thing from you, Cæfar ? or what other
" view had you in the war, than to defend
" yourfelf from injury ?—you confidered it from
" the firft, not as a war but a feceffion, not as
" an hoftile, but civil diffenfion   where both
" fides wifhed well to the Republic   yet through
" a difference, partly of counfils, partly of in-
" clinations, deviated from the common good
" the dignity of the Leaders was almoft equal,
" though not perhaps of thofe that followed
" them   the caufe was then dubious, fince there
" was fomething which one might appiove on
" either fide, but now, that muft needs be
" thought the beft, which the Gods have fa-
" vored, and after the experience of youi cle-
" mency, who can be difpleafed with that victoiy,
" in which no man fell, who was not actually in
" Arms [c] ?"

THE Speech was foon made public, and greedily bought by all : Atticus was extiemely pleafed
with it, and very induftrious in recommending it;
fo that Ciceio fays meriily to him by Lettei,
" You have fold my Ligarian fpeech finely :
" whatever I write for the future, I will make you
' the Publifher·" and again, " your authoity,
" I peiceive, has made my little oration famous :

[c] Ib 6

" for

A Urb 707
Cic 61
Coff
C JULIUS
CÆSAR III
M ÆMILIU.
LEPIDUS

" for Balbus and Oppius write me word, that
" they are wonderfully taken with it, and have
" sent a Copy to Cæsar [*d*] " The success,
which it met with, made Tubero ashamed of the
figure that he made in it, so that he applied to
Cicero, to have something inserted in his favor,
with the mention *of his wife, and some of his fa-*
mily, who were *Cicero's near relations* but Cicero
excused himself, *because the speech was got abroad,*
nor had he a mind, he says, *to make any apology for*
Tubero's conduct [*e*]

LIGARIUS was a man of distinguished zeal
for the liberty of his Country which was the
reason both of Cicero's pains to preserve, and of
Cæsar's averseness to restore him. After his return he lived in great confidence with Brutus,
who found him a fit person to bear a part in the
conspiracy against Cæsar ; but happening to be
taken ill near the time of it's execution, when
Brutus, in a visit to him, began to lament, *that*
he was fallen sick in a very unlucky hour ; Ligarius,
raising himself presently upon his elbow, and taking
Brutus by the hand, replied. yet still, Brutus, if
you mean to do any thing worthy of yourself, I am
well [*f*] nor did he disappoint Brutus's opinion
of him, for we find him afterwards in the list of
the conspirators

[*a*] Ligarianam præclare
reddidisti Posthac qu cquid
scripsero, tibi præconium de-
ferat Ad Att 13 12

Ligarianam uti deo, præ-
clare auctoritas tua commen-
davit Scripsit enim ad me
Balbus & Oppius, mirifice se
probare, ob eamque causam
ad Cæsarem eam se oratiun-
culam misisse Ib 19

[*e*] Ad Ligarianam de uxo-
ore Tuberonis, & privigna,
neque possum jam addere,
est enim res pervulgata, neque Tuberonem volo defen-
dere Mirifice est enim φι-
λαιτι❀. Ib 20

[*f*] Plutarch in Brut.

Iv

IN the end of the year, Cæfar was called away in great haft into Spain to oppofe the attempts of Pompey's Sons, who, by the credit of their father's name, were become mafters again of all that Province, and with the remains of the troops, which Labienus, Varus, and the other Chiefs, who efcaped, had gathered up from Afric, were once more in condition to try the fortune of the field with him . where the great danger, to which he was expofed from this laft effort of a broken party, fhews how defperate his cafe muft have been, if Pompey himfelf, with an intire and veteran army, had firft made choice of this country for the fcene of the war.

CICERO all this while paffed his time with lit-tle fatisfaction at home, being difappointed of the eafe and comfort, which he expected from his new marriage his children, as we may ima-gine, while their own mother was living, would not eafily bear with a *young mother in law* in the houfe with them The Son efpecially was pref-fing to get a particular appointment fettled for his maintenance, and to have leave alfo to go to Spain, and *make a Campaign under Cæfar*, whi-ther his Coufin Quintus was already gone Cice-ro did not approve this project, and endeavoured by all means to diffuade him from it, reprefent-ing to him *that it would naturally draw a juft reproach upon them, for not thinking it enough to quit their former party, unlefs they fought againft it too, and that he would not be pleafed to fee his Coufin more regarded there than himfelf*, and pro-mifing withal, if he would confent to ftay, *to make him an ample and honorable allowance* [g] This diverted

A Urb 708.
Cic 62
Coff
C Julius
Cæsar
Dictator III.
M Æmilius
Lepidus
Mag Equit.

[g] De Hifpania duo attuli, primum idem, quod tibi.
suc

A Urb 703
Cic 62
Coss
C Julius
Cæsar
Dictator III
M Æmilius
Lepidus
Mag Equit

diverted him from the thoughts of Spain , though not from the defire of removing from his Father, and taking a feparate houfe in the City, with a diftinct family of his own , but Cicero thought it beft to fend him to Athens, in order to fpend a few years in the ftudy of Philofophy, and polite Letters , and to make the propofal agreeable, offered him an appointment, *that would enable him to live as fplendidly as any of the Roman Nobility, who then refided there, Bibulus, Acidinus,* or *Meffala* [h] This fcheme was accepted, and foon after executed , and young Cicero was fent to Athens, with *two of his Father's Freedmen, L Tullus Montanus, and Tullius Mercianus,* as the Intendants and Counfellors of his general conduct, while the particular direction of his ftudies was left to the principal Philofophers of the place, and above all to Cratippus, the chief of *the Peripatetic* Sect [i].

IN this uneafy ftate both of his private and public life, he was oppreffed by a new and moft cruel affliction, the death of his beloved daughter Tullia , which happened foon *after her divorce* from Dolabella , whofe manners and humor were intirely difagreeable to her. Cicero had long been deliberating with himfelf and friends, *whether Tullia fhould not firft fend the divorce ,* but a pru-

me vereri vituperationem non fatis effe fi hæc arma reliquifemus ` etiam contraria ? deinde fore ut angeretur, cum a fratre familiaritate & omnia gratia vinceretur Vel in magis liberalitate uti mea quam fua libertate,——— Ad Att 12 7

[h] Præftabo nec Bibulum, nec Acidinum, nec Meffalam, quos Athenis futuros audio, majores fumptus facturos, quam quod ex eis mercedibus accipietur Ib 32

[i] L Tullium Montanum nofti, qui cum Cicerone profectus eft Ib 52, 53

Quanquam te, Marce fili, annum jam audientem Cratippum, &c De Off 1 1 it 2 2.

dential

dential regard to Dolabella's power and interest
with Cæsar, which was of use to him in these
times seems to have withheld him [k] The
case was the same with Dolabella, he was willing
enough to part with Tullia, but did not care to
break with Cicero, whose friendship was a credit
to him, and whom gratitude obliged him to observe and reverence; since Cicero had twice defended and preserved him in capital causes [l]
so that it seems most probable, that *the divorce*
was of an amicable kind, and executed at last by
the consent of both sides for it gave no appa-
rent interruption to the friendship between Cicero and Dolabella, which they carried on with
the same shew of affection, and professions of
respect towards each other, as if the relation had
still subsisted

TULLIA died in childbed, *at her husband's*
house [m], which confirms the probability of
their agreement in the divorce it is certain at
least, that she died in Rome, where Cicero *was*
detained, he says, *by the expectation of the birth, and*
to receive the first payment of her fortune back again
from Dolabella, who was then in Spain she was de-
livered, as it was thought, very happily, and suppo-
sed to be out of danger, when an unexpected turn
in her case put an end to her life, to the inexpres-
sible grief of her Father [n]   WE

A Urb 708
Cic 62
Coss
C JULIUS
CÆSAR
Dictator III.
M ÆMILIUS
LEPIDUS
Mag Equit.

[k] Te oro ut de hac mi-
sera cogite.—melius quidem
in pessimis mihi fuit discidio
—nunc quidem ipse videtur
denunciare—placet mihi igitur, & idem tibi nuncium re-
mitti, &c Ad Att xi 23
vid ib 3
Quod scripsi de nuncio re-
mittendo, qua sit istius vis
hoc tempore, & quæ conci-

tatio multitudinis, ignoro Si
metuendus iratus est, quies tamen ab illa fortasse nascetur
Ep fam 14 13
[l] Cujus ego salutem duobus capitis judiciis summa
contentione defendi——Ep
fam 3 x
[m] Plutarch in Cic
[n] Me Roma tenuit om
nino Tulliæ meæ partus, sed

cum

A Urb. 708
Cic 62
Coff
C Julius
Cæsar
Dictator III
M Æmilius
Lepidus
Mag Equit

WE have no account of the issue of this birth, which writers confound with that which happened three years before, when she was delivered at the end of seven months of *a puny male child* but whether it was from the first, or the second time of her lying in, it is evident, that she left *a Son by Dolabella*, who survived her, and whom Cicero mentions more than once in his Letters to Atticus, by the name of Lentulus [o] desiring him *to visit the Child*, and see a due care taken of him, and *to assign him what number of servants he thought proper* [p]

TULLIA was about two and thirty years old at the time of her death, and by the few hints, which are left of her character, appears to have been an excellent and admirable woman she was most affectionately and piously observant of her Father, and to the usual graces of her sex, hav-

cum ea quemadmodum spero, satis firma sit, tenor tamen, dum a Dolabellæ procuratoribus exigam primam pensionem — Ep fam 6 18

[o] The Father's names were Publius Cornelius Lentulus Dolabella, the two last being surnames acquired perhaps by adoption, and distinguishing the different branches of the Cornelian family

[p] Velim aliquando, cum erit tuum commodum, Lentulum puerum videas, eique de mancipiis quæ tibi videbitur, attribuas — ad A 12 28

Quod Lentulum invisis, valde gratum Ib 20 — vid etiam 18 ——

N B Mr Bayle declares himself surprized, *to find Asconius Pæd so ill informed of the History of Tullia, as to tell us, that after P so's death, she was named to P Lentulus, and died in child bed at his house* in which short account, there are contained, he says, *two or three lies* But Plutarch confirms the same account, and the mistake will rest at last, not on Asconius, but on Mr Bayle himself, who did not reflect, from the authority of those Ancients, that Lentulus was one of Dolabella's names, by which he was called indifferently, as well as by any of the rest See Bayl Diction Artic. Tullia, not k

ing

ing added the more folid accomplifhments of
knowledge and polite letters, was qualified to be
the companion as well as the delight of his age;
and was juftly efteemed not onely as one of *the*
beft, but the moft learned of the Roman Ladies.
It is not ftrange therefore, that the lofs of fuch a
daughter, in the prime of her life, and the moft
comfortlefs feafon of his own, fhould affect him
with all that grief, which the greateft calamity
could imprint on a temper naturally timid and
defponding.

A Urb 708,
Cic 62.
Coff
C Julius
Cæsar
Dictator III.
M Æmilius
Lepidus
Mag Equit

PLUTARCH tells us, *that the Philofophers came*
from all parts to comfort him, but that can hardly
be true, except of thofe, who lived at Rome,
or in his own family, for his firft care was, to
fhun all company as much as he could, by removing to Atticus's houfe, where he lived chiefly in the Library; endeavouring to relieve his
mind, *by turning over every book, which he could*
meet with on the fubject of moderating grief [q]:
but finding his refidence here too public, and a
greater refort to him than he could bear, he retired to Aftura, one of his feats near Antium;
a little ifland on the Latian fhore at the mouth of
a river of the fame name, covered with woods and
groves, cut out into fhady walks, a fcene of all
others the fitteft to indulge melancholy, and
where he could give a free courfe to his grief.
" Here, fays he, I live without the fpeech of
" man every morning early I hide myfelf in
" the thickeft of the wood, and never come
" out till the evening next to yourfelf, nothing
" is fo dear to me, as this folitude my whole
" converfation is with my books, yet that is

[q] Me mihi non defuiffe
tu teftis es, nihil enim de
marore minuendo ab ullo

fcriptum eft, quod ego non
domi tuæ legerim Ad Att
12 11

" fometimes

A Urb 708
Cic 62
Coſſ
C JULIUS
CÆSAR
Dictator III
M ÆMILIUS
LEPIDUS
Mag Equit

" ſometimes interrupted by my tears, which I
" reſiſt as well as I can, but am not yet able to
" do much [r] "

ATTICUS urged him to quit this retirement,
and divert himſelf with buſineſs, and the company of his friends, and put him gently in
mind, that, by afflicting himſelf ſo immoderately, he would hurt his character, and give people
a handle to cenſure his weakneſs to which he
makes the following anſwer.

" As to what you write, that you are afraid,
" leſt the exceſs of my grief ſhould leſſen my
" credit and authority, I do not know what
" men would have of me Is it, that I ſhould
" not grieve? that is impoſſible or that I
" ſhould not be oppreſſed with grief? who
" was ever leſs ſo? when I took refuge at
" your houſe, was any man ever denied ac-
" ceſs to me? or did any one ever come, who
" had reaſon to complain of me? I went from
" you to Altura where thoſe gay ſparks, who
" find fault with me, are not able even to
" read ſo much as I have written. how well,
" is nothing to the purpoſe, yet it is of a kind
" which no body could write with a diſordered
" mind—I ſpent a month in my gardens about
" Rome, where I received all who came, with
" the ſame eaſineſs as before At this very mo-
" ment, while I am employing my whole time
" in reading and writing, thoſe, who are with
" me, are more fatigued with their leiſure, than

[ ] In præſio red re cireo
omnium coloquio cumque
mane r faciam me abſtruſi
deniam & aperiam non cvo
inde ad te veperam Secun-
dum te, r nil mihi amicus

ſolitudine In ea mihi om
nis ſermo eſt cum litteris,
cum tamen interpellat fletus
cui repugno quoad poſſum,
ſed adhuc pares non ſumus
ID 15

" I with

" I with my pains. If any one afks, why I am
" not at Rome, becaufe it is vacation time why
" not in fome of my villa's, more fuitable to
" the feafon, becaufe I could not eafily bear fo
" much company I am, where he, who has
" the beft houfe at Baiæ, chufes to be, in this
" part of the year When I come to Rome, no-
" body fhall find any thing amifs, either in my
" looks or difcourfe. as to that chearfulnefs,
" with which we ufed to feafon the mifery of
" thefe times, I have loft it indeed for ever, but
" will never part with my conftancy and firm-
" nefs, either of mind or fpeech, &c [s] "

ALL his other friends were very officious likewife in making their compliments of condolence,
and adminiftring arguments of comfort to him
among the reft, Cæfar himfelf, in the hurry of
his affairs in Spain, wrote him a Letter on the
occafion, dated from *Hifpalis, the laft of April* [t].
Brutus wrote another, *fo friendly and affectionate,
that it greatly moved him* [u] Lucceius alfo, one
of the moft efteemed writers of that age, fent
him two, the firft to condole, the fecond to ex-
poftulate with him for perfevering, to cherifh an
unmanly and ufelefs grief [x] but the following
Letter of Ser Sulpicius is thought to be a mafter-
piece of the confolatory kind.

Ser. Sulpicius to M. T Cicero.

" I was exceedingly concerned, as indeed I
" ought to be, to hear of the death of your

Marginal note (top right):
A. Urb 708.
Cic 62.
Coff
C Julius
Cæsar
Dictator III
M Æmilius
Lepidus
Mag Equit.

---

[s] Ad Att 12 40
[t] A Cæfare litteras ac-
cepi confolatorias, datas p id
Kal Maii, Hifpali Ad Att
13 20
[u] Bruti litteræ fcriptæ

& prudenter & amice. multas
tamen mihi lacrimas attulerunt Ib 12 13
[x] Vid Ep, fam 5 13,
14

     " daughter

"daughter Tullia, which I looked upon as an
"affliction common to us both If I had been
"with you, I would have made it my business
"to convince you, what a real share I take in
"your grief   Though that kind of consola-
"tion is but wretched and lamentable, as it is
"to be performed by friends and relations, who
"are overwhelmed with grief, and cannot en-
"ter upon the task without tears, and seem to
"want comfort rather themselves, than to be
"in condition to administer it to others I re-
"solved therefore to write to you in short, what
"occurred upon it to my own mind   not that
"I imagined, that the same things would not
"occur also to you, but that the force of your
"grief might possibly hinder your attention to
"them   What reason is there then to disturb
"yourself so immoderately on this melancholy
"occasion? consider how fortune has already
"treated us, how it has deprived us of what
"ought to be as dear to us as children, our
"country, credit, dignity, honors   After so
"miserable a loss as this, what addition can it
"possibly make to our grief, to suffer one mis-
"fortune more? or how can a mind, after being
"exercised in such trials, not grow callous, and
"think every thing else of little or no value? but
"is it for your daughter's sake that you grieve?
"yet how often must you necessarily reflect, as
"I myself frequently do, that those cannot be
"said to be hardly dealt with, whose lot it has
"been in these times, without suffering any af-
"fliction, to exchange life for death   For
"what is there in our present circumstances that
"could give her any great inducation to live?
"what benefits? what hopes? what prospect
"of comfort before her? was it to pass her
"days

A. Urb - 8.
Cic 6.
Coss
Julius
Cæsar
Dictator III
M Æmilius
Lepidus
Mag Equit.

" days in the married state, with some young
" man of the first quality? (for you, I know,
" on the account of your dignity, might have
" chosen what son-in-law you pleased out of all
" our youth, to whose fidelity you might safely
" have trusted her,) was it then for the sake of
" bearing children, whom she might have had
" the pleasure to see flourishing afterwards, in
" the enjoyment of their paternal fortunes, and
" rising gradually to all the honours of the state,
" and using the liberty, to which they were
" born, in the protection of their friends and
" clients? but what is there of all this, which
" was not taken away, before it was even given
' to her? but it is an evil, you'll say, to lose
" our children It is so, yet it is much greater
' to suffer, what we now endure I cannot
' help mentioning one thing, which has given
" me no small comfort, and may help also per-
" haps to mitigate your grief On my return
' from Asia, as I was sailing from Ægina to-
" wards Megara, I began to contemplate the
" prospect of the countries around me Ægina,
" was behind, Megara before me, Piræeus on
" the right, Corinth on the left all which
" towns, once famous and flourishing, now lie
" overturned, and buried in their ruins upon
" this sight, I could not but think presertly
" within myself, alas! how do we poor mortals
" fret and vex ourselves, if any of our friends
" happen to die, or to be killed, whose life is
' yet so short, when the carcasses of so many
' noble cities lie here exposed before me in one
" view? Why wilt thou not then command
' thyself, Servius, and remember, that thou
" art born a man? Believe me, I was not a lit-
' tle confirmed by this contemplation try the

" force

" force of it therefore, if you pleafe, upon
" yourfelf, and imagine the fame profpect be-
" fore your own eyes. But to come nearer
" home, when you confider how many of our
" greateft men have perifhed lately at once;
" what deftruction has been made in the Em-
" pire, what havock in all the Provinces, how
" can you be fo much fhocked to be deprived
" of the fleeting breath of one little woman?
" who, if fhe had not died at this time, muft
" necefarily have died a few years after, fince
" that was the condition of her being born
" But recall your mind from reflections of this
" kind, to the confideration of yourfelf, and
" think rather on what becomes your character
" and dignity that your daughter lived, as
" long as life was worth enjoying, as long as
" the Republic ftood, had feen her Father
" Prætor, Conful, Augur, been married to the
" nobleft of our youth, had tafted every good
" in life, and when the Republic fell, then
" quitted it what ground is there then, either
" for you, or her, to complain of fortune on
" this account? In fhort, do not forget, that
" you are Cicero, one, who has been ufed al-
" ways to prefcribe and give advice to others,
" nor imitate thofe paultry Phyficians, who pre-
" tend to cure other people's difeafes, yet are
" not able to cure their own, but fuggeft rather
" to yourfelf the fame leffon, which you would
" give in the fame cafe There is no grief fo
" great, which length of time will not alle-
" viate but it would be fhamefull in you to
" wait for that time, and not to prevent it by
" your wifdom befides, if there be any fenfe
" in the dead, fuch was her love and piety to
" you, that fhe muft be concerned to fee, how
" muft

" much you afflict yourself Give this therefore to
' the deceased, give it to your friends, give it to
" your country, that it may have the benefit of
" your affistance and advice, whenever there fhall
" be occafion Laftly, fince fortune has now made
" it neceffary to us to accommodate ourfelves to
' our prefent fituation, do not give any one a
" handle to think, that you are not fo much
" bewailing your daughter, as the ftate of the
" times, and the victory of certain perfons   I
" am afhamed to write any more, left I fhould
" feem to diftruft your prudence, and will add
' therefore but one thing farther, and conclude
" We have fometimes feen you bear profperity
" nobly, with great honor and applaufe to your-
" felf, let us now fee, that you can bear ad-
" verfity with the fame moderation, and with-
" out thinking it a greater burthen than you
" ought to do left in the number of all your
' other virtues, this one at laft be thought to
" be wanting   As to myfelf, when I under-
" ftand that your mind is grown more calm and
" compofed, I will fend you word, how all
" things go on here, and what is the ftate of
" the Province   Adieu [y] "

His anfwer to Sulpicius was the fame in effect
with what he gave to all his friends, " that his
" cafe was different from all the examples,
" which he had been collecting for his own
" imitation, of men, who had born the lofs of
" children with firmnefs, fince they lived in
" times, when their dignity in the ftate was able
" in great meafure to compenfate their misfor-
" tune but for me, *fays he*, after I had loft all
' thofe ornaments, which you enumerate, and

Right margin annotation:

A Urb 708
Cic 62
Cofl
C Julius
Cæsar
Dictator III
M Æmilius
Lepidus
Mag Equit

[y] Ep fam 4 5

B b 3   " which

" which I had acquired with the utmoſt pains,
" I ſee now loſt the onely comfort that was
" left to me. In this ruin of the Republic,
" thoughts were not diverted by ſerving
" the intereſts of my country. I had no
" inclination to the Forum, could not bear the
" ſight of the Senate, took myſelf, as the caſe
" really was, to have loſt all the fruit of my
" induſtry and ſtudies: yet when I reflected,
" that theſe were common to you, and to ma-
" ny others, as well as to myſelf, and was for-
" cing my mind to bear it tolerably, I
" found ſome relief, more what always to recur
" to, and then I can acquieſce, and in whoſe
" ſweet company then I could drop all my cares
" and troubles: but by this laſt cruel wound,
" all theſe, which ſeemed to be healed, are
" broken out again freſh: for as I then could
" relieve the uneaſineſs, which the Republic
" gave me, by what I found at home, ſo I
" cannot now, in the affliction which I feel at
" home, find any remedy abroad, but am dri-
" ven as well from my houſe, as the Forum,
" ſince neither my houſe can eaſe my public
" grief, nor the public my domeſtic one [z]"

The remonſtrances of his friends had but little effect upon him, all the relief that he found,
was in reading and writing, in which he continually employed himſelf, and *did what to*
write that does good him, drew up a treatiſe
of cuſtom for himſelf, from which he pro-
feſſes to have received his greateſt comfort,
" Though he wrote it, he owns, at a time
" when, in the opinion of the Philoſophers, he
" was not ſo wiſe as he ought to have been

[z] Ep. fam. l. 6. it add. Vt. 12. 78

" but

" but I did violence, *says he*, to my nature, to
" make the greatness of my sorrow give place
" to the greatness of the medicine though I
" acted against the advice of Chrysippus, who
" dissuades the application of any remedy to
" the first assaults of grief [a] " In this work
he chiefly imitated Crantor, *whose work* , who
had left a celebrated piece on the same subject,
and he is said also whatever he is said , *whence any*
other authors also had written on it [b] , il-
lustrating his precepts all the way, by examples
from their own history, *of the most eminent Ro-*
mans of both sexes, who had born their own mis-
fortune with remarkable constancy This book
was much read by the *private philosophers, especially*
Lactantius , to whom we are obliged for *the few*
fragments , which remain of it, for, as the Critics have long since observed, that piece, which
we now see in the collection of his writings, under the title of *Consolation*, is undoubtedly spu-
rious.

[a] Tum, quod ante me
nemo ut ipse me per literas
consolarer —— affirmo tl
nullam consolationem esse talem Ad Att 12 14 it ib
28

Quid ego de consolatione
dicam? quæ mihi quidem
ipsi sane aliquantum mede-
tur, ceteris item multum illam profuturam puto De
Div 2 1

In consolationis libro, quem
in medio, (non enim sapien-
tes eramus) in œrore & dolore
conscripsimus quodque ve-
tat Chrysippus, ad recentes

quasi tumores animi reme-
dium adhibere, id nos etiam-
nunc, naturæque vim adtuli-
mus, ut magnitudini me-
dicinæ doloris magnitudo
concederet Tusc Disp 4
2)

[b] Crantorem sequor,
Plin Præf Hi N

Neque tamen progredior
longius, etiam in his doctissimi hominis se necdunt, quorum scripta omnia, quæcun-
que sunt in eam sententiam
non legendum —— sed in mea
etiam scripta transtuli Ad
Att 12 21 it 22

A Urb 708
Coſſ 62
Coſſ
C Julius
Cæſar
Dictator III
M Æmilius
Lepidus
Mag Equit

BUT the deſign of this treatiſe was, not onely to relieve his own mind, but to conſecrate the virtues and memory of Tullia to all poſterity nor did his fondneſs for her ſtop here; but ſuggeſted the project of a more effectual conſecration, *by building a Temple to her,* and erecting her into a ſort *of Deity* It was an opinion of the Philoſophers, which he himſelf conſtantly favored, and in his preſent circumſtances particularly indulged, " that the ſouls of men " were of heavenly extraction and that the " pure and chaſt, at their diſſolution from the " body, returned to the fountain from which " they were derived, to ſubſiſt eternally in the ' fruition and participation of the Divine Na‐ ' ture, whilſt the impure and corrupt were left " to grovel below in the dirt and darkneſs of " thoſe inferior regions." He declares there‐ fore, " that as the wiſdom of the antients had " conſecrated and deified many excellent per‐ " ſons of both ſexes, whoſe Temples were then " remaining, the progeny of Cadmus, of Am‐ " pnitryon, of Tyndarus, ſo he would perform " the ſame honour to Tullia, who, if any crea " ture had ever deſerved it, was of all the moſt " worthy of it I will do it therefore, *ſays he* " and conſecrate thee, thou beſt and moſt learn‐ " ed of women, now admitted into the aſſem‐ " bly of the Gods, to the regard and veneration " of all mortals [c] "

IN

In his Letters to Atticus we find the strongeft
expreffions of his refolution, and impatience to fee
this defign executed " I will have a Temple,
" *fays he*, it is not poffible to divert me from
" it— if it be not finifhed this fummer, I fhall
" not think myfelf clear of guilt— I am more
" religioufly bound to the execution of it, than
" any man ever was to the performance of his
" vow [*d*] " He feems to have defigned a Fabric of great magnificence; for he had fettled
the plan with his Architect, and contracted for
Pillars of Chian marble, with a fculptor of that
Ifle, where both the work and the materials
were the moft efteemed of any in Greece [*e*].
One reafon, that determined him to *a Temple*,
rather than *a Sepulchre*, was, that in the one he
was not limited in the expenfe, whereas in the
other he was confined by law to a certain fumm,

A Urb 708
Cic 62.
Coff
C Julius
Cæsar
Dictator III
M Æmilius
Lepidus
Mag Equit.

fimilem pervolare — Fragm
Confolat. ex Lactantio—

Cum vero & mares & fœ-
minas complures ex hominibus in Deorum numero effe
videamus, & eorum in urbi-
bus atque agris auguftiffima
templa veneremur, affentia-
mur eorum fapientie, quo-
rum ingeniis & inventis omnem vitam legibus & inftitu-
tis excultam conftitutamque
habemus Quod fi ullum
unquam animal confecran-
dum fuit, illud profecto fuit
Si Cadmi, aut Amphitrionis
progenies, aut Tyndari in
cælum tollenda fama fuit,
huic idem honos certe ci-
candus eft Quod quidem
faciam, teque omnium op
timam doctifimamque, up

probantibus Diis ipfis in eorum cœtu locatam, ad opi-
nionem omnium mortalium
confecrabo Ib —vid Tufc
Difp l 1 c xi 12, 30, 31

[*a*] Fanum fieri volo, neque mihi erui poteft [Ad
Att 12 36] Redeo ad Fa-
num, nifi hac æftate abfolu-
tum erit— fcelere me libera-
tum non putabo [b 41]
Ego me majore religione,
quam quifquam fuit ullius
voti, obftrictum puto Ib 43

[*e*] De Fano illo dico——
neque de genere dubito, placet enim mihi Cluatii ib.
18] Tu tamen cum Apella
Chio confice de columnis
[ib 19] vid Plin Hift N
36 5 6.

which

which he could not excede, without the forfeiture of the fame fum: allo to the public: yet
this, as he tells us, was not the chief motive,
but a refolution, that he had taken, of making
a pious apotheofis [f] The only difficulty
was

[text largely illegible — left column]

This fact feems to confirm
what the Author of the book
of ... obferves on the
origin of Idolatry, that it
is owing to the fond affection of Parents, defiring to
do honor to their deceafed
children *The Firft*, fays
he, ...

... [Wifd xiv 15] But
it was not Cicero's real
thought after all to exalt his
daughter into a Deity he
knew her to be a God, as he
often declares, to pay divine

[right column]

... and
... that P
had decided that quef-
... for when the
... Immortal G
... accepted out of their
... the left of the C
... denied, that ...
...
... defervedly ...
... de lording
... on Profperity,
... pirates with them
[de Nat Deor 3 19] Yet
in his political view he fometimes recommends the wor-
fhip of thofe fons of men,
whom their eminent fervices
to mankind had advanced to
the rank of inferior Gods,
as it inculcated, in a manner the moft fenfible, the
doctrine of *the Soul's Immortality* [de Leg 2 xi] And
fince a temple was the *nof
artis artis* of doing honor
to thofe dead, who had deferved it, [Plin Hift 27]
he confidered it as the moft
effectual method of perpetuating the memory and praifes of Tullia, and was willing to take the benefit of the
popular fuperftition, and
follow the example of thofe
Ancients who had polifhed
and civilized human life, by
confecrating

was to find a place that suited his purpose his
first thought was *to purchase certain gardens cross
the Tiber*, which lying near the city, and in the
public view, were the most likely to draw a resort of votaries to his new Temple " he pref-
" ses Atticus therefore to buy them for him at
" any rate, without regard to his circumstances,
" since he would sell, or mortgage, or be con-
" tent to live on little, rather than be disap-
" pointed Groves and remote places, *he says*,
" were proper onely for Deities of an establish-
" ed name and religion, but for the Deification
" of mortals, public and open situations were
" necessary, to strike the eyes, and attract the
" notice of the people ' But he found so many obstructions in all his attempts of purchasing,
that to save trouble and expence, Atticus advised
him, *to build at last in one of his own villa's*, to
which he seemed inclined, lest the summer
should pass without doing any thing yet he was
irresolute still, which of his villa's he should
chuse; and discouraged, by reflecting *on the
change of masters*, to which all private estates
were exposed, in a succession of ages, which
might defeat the end of his building, and destroy the honor of his temple, by converting
it to other uses, or suffering it to fall into
ruins [g].

BUT

A Uid 708.
Cic 62
Coss
C Julius
Cæsar
Dictator III
M Æmilius
Lepidus
Mag Equit

consecrating such patterns of
virtue to the veneration of
their fellow Citizens Vid
Mongault Not 1 ad Att
12 18

[g] Sed meenda nobis ra-
tio est, quemadmodum in
omni mutatione dominorum,
qui innumerabiles fieri pos-

sunt in infinita posteritate —
illud quod consecratum re-
manere posset Equidem jam
nihil egeo vectigalibus, &
parvo contentus esse possum
Cogito interdum trans Tibe-
rim hortos aliquos parare,
& quidem ob hanc causam
maxime, nihil enim video
quod

But after all his eagerness and follicitude about the Temple, it was never actually built by him; we find no mention of it in any of the antient writers, which could not have been omitted, if a fabric fo memorable had ever been erected [h] It is likely, that as his grief evaporated, and his mind grew more calm, he began to confider his project more philofophically, and to perceive the vanity of expecting any lafting glory from fuch monuments, which time itfelf, in the courfe of a few ages, muft neceffarily deftroy it is certain at leaft, that as he made no ftep towards building it this fummer, fo Cæfar's death, which happened before the next, gave frefh obftruction to it, by the hurry of affairs, in which it engaged him, and though he had not ftill wholly dropt the thoughts of it, but continued to make preparation, and to fet apart a fund for it [i], yet in the fhort and bufy fcene

quod tam celebre effe poffet [ad Att 12 19] De hort s, etiam atque etiam te rogo [o. 22] Et fæpe locati fumus, commutationes dominorum reformido [io 36] Celebritatem requiro io 37

[h] Cælius Rhodiginus tells us, that in the time of Sextus the 4th there was found near Rome on the Appian way, over againft the Tomb of Cicero, the body of a woman whofe hair was dreffed up in network of gold, and which from the infcription, was thought to be the body of Tullia It was intire, and fo well preferved by fpices, as to have fuffered no injury from time,

yet when it was removed into the City, it mouldered away in thrice days But this was only the hafty conjecture of fome learned of that time, which, for want of authority to fupport it, foon vanifhed of itfelf, for no infcription was ever produced to confirm it, nor has it been mentioned, that I know of, by any other author, that there was any fepulchre of Cicero, on the Appian way —— vid Cæl Rhod Lection antiq 1 3 c 24

[i] Quod ex iftis fructuofis rebus receptum eft, id ego ad illud fanum fepofitum putabam Ad Att 15 15

of

of life, which remained to him, he never had
leisure enough to carry it into execution

He was now grown so fond of solitude, that
all company was become uneasy to him, and
when his friend Philippus, the Father-in-law of
Octavius, happened to come to his villa in that
neighbourhood, he was not a little disturbed at
it, from the apprehension of being teized with
his visits, and he tells Atticus, with some pleasure, *that he had called upon him onely to pay a
short compliment, and went back again to Rome,
without giving him any trouble* [k] His wife
Publilia also wrote him word, *that her Mother
and Brother intended to wait upon him, and that
she would come along with them, if he would give
her leave*. which she begged in the most earnest
and submissive terms— but his answer was, *that
he was more indisposed than ever to receive company, and would not have them come* and lest they
should come without leave, he desires Atticus *to
watch their motions, and give him notice, that he
might contrive to avoid them* [l] A denial so
peremptory confirms what Plutarch says, *that
his wife was now in disgrace with him, on account
of her carriage towards his daughter, and for
seeming to rejoice at her death* a crime, which,
in the tenderness of his affliction, appeared to

A Urb 708.
C.c 62
Coss
C Julius
Cæsar
Dictator III.
M Æmilius
Lepidus
Mag Equit.

---

[k] Mihi adhuc nihil pri-
us fuit hac solitudine, quam
vereor, ne Philippus tollat
heri enim vesperi venerat
Ib 12 16

Quod eram veritus, non
obturbavit Philippus nam
u heri me salutavit statim
Romam profectus est Ib 18

[l] Publilia ad me scrip
suam matrem suam cum Pub-

lilio ad me venturam, & se
uná, si ego paterer orat
multis & supplicio s verbis
ut liceat, & ut sibi rescribam
——rescripsi, me etiam gravius esse affectum, quam tum,
cum illi dixissem, me solum
esse velle, quare nolle me
hoc tempore eam ad me ve-
nire—— te hoc nunc rogo
ut explores Ib 32

him

him fo heinous, that he could not bear the thoughts of feeing her any more, and though it was inconvenient to him, to part with her fortune at this time, yet he refolved *to fend her a divorce*, as a proper facrifice to the honor of Tullia [m]

BRUTUS likewife about this time took a refolution of putting away his wife Claudia, for the fake of taking Porcia, *Bibulus's widow, and his Uncle Cato's daughter* But he was much cenfured for this ftep, fince Claudia had no ftain upon her character, was nobly born, the Sifter of Appius Claudius, and nearly allied to Pompey. *fo that his Mother Servilia*, though Cato's Sifter, feems to have been averfe to the divorce, and ftrongly in the intereft of Claudia, againft her Niece Cicero's advice upon it was, *that if Brutus was refolved upon the thing, he fhould do it out of hand*, as the beft way to put an end to people's talking, by fhewing, that it was not done out of levity or complaifance to the times, but to take *the daughter of Cato*, whofe name was now highly popular [n] which Brutus foon after complied with, and made Porcia his wife

THERE happened another accident this fummer, which raifed a great alarm in the City, *the furprizing death of Marcellus*, whom Cæfar

---

[m] This affair of Pub[-] *lia*'s divorce is frequently re[-] ferred to, though with fome obfcurity in his Letters, and we find Atticus employed by him afterwards to adjuft with the Brother Publilius, the time and manner of paying back the fortune Vid ad Att 13 34, 47 16 2

[n] A te expecto aliquid

de Pruto quanquam Nicias confectum putabat, fed diffolutum non probari — Ad Att 13 9

Brutus si quid—curabis ut fciam Cui quidem quam primum agendum puto, prafertim fi ftatuit, firmunculum enim omnem aut refumye it aut fedant Ib 10

had

had lately pardoned He had left Mitylene, A Urb 708.
and was come as far as Piræcus, on his way to- Cic 62
wards Rome, where he spent a day, with his Coff
old friend and collegue, Serv Sulpicius, intend- C Julius
ing to pursue his voyage the day following by Cæsar
sea, but in the night, after Sulpicius had taken Dictator III.
leave of him, *on the twenty-third of May*, he M Æmilius
was killed by his friend and client, Magius, who Lipidus
stabbed himself presently, with the same poignard Mag Equit
of which Sulpicius sent the following account to
Cicero

Serv Sulpicius to M. T Cicero.

" Though I know that the news, which I
" am going to tell you, will not be agreeable,
" yet since chance and nature govern the lives
" of us all, I thought it my duty to acquaint
" you with the fact, in what manner soever it
" happened On the twenty-second of May I
" came by sea from Epidaurus to Piræcus, to
" meet my collegue Marcellus, and for the sake
" of his company, spent that day with him
" there The next day, when I took my leave
' of him, with design to go from Athens into
" Bœotia, to finish the remaining part of my
" jurisdiction, he, as he told me, intended to
" set sail at the same time towards Italy The
' day following, about four in the morning,
" when I was preparing to set out from Athens,
" his friend, P Postumius, came to let me
" know, that Marcellus was stabbed by his
" companion P Magius Cilo after supper, and
' had received two wounds, the one in his sto-
mach, the other in his head near the ear,
' but he was in hopes still, that he might live
' but that Magius presently killed himself, and
' that

A Urb 708
C.c 62
Coſſ
C Julius
Cæsar
Dictator III
M. Æmilius
Lepidus
Mag Equit.

"that Marcellus ſent him to inform me of the
"caſe, and to deſire, that I would bring ſome
"Phyſicians to him. I got ſome together im-
"mediately, and went away with them before
"break of day: but when I was come near Pi-
"ræeus, Acidinus's boy met me with a note
"from his maſter, in which it was ſignified, that
"Marcellus died a little before day   Thus a
"great man was murthered by a baſe villain,
"and he, whom his very enemies had ſpared
"on the account of his dignity, received his
"death from the hands of a friend   I went
"forward however to his tent, where I found
"two of his freedmen, and a few of his ſlaves,
"all the reſt, they ſaid, were fled, being in a
"terrible fright, on the account of their maſter's
"murther.   I was forced to carry his body with
"me into the City, in the ſame litter in which
"I came, and by my own ſervants: where I
"provided a funeral for him, as ſplendid as the
"condition of Athens would allow   I could
"not prevail with the Athenians, to grant a
"place of burial for him within the City, they
"ſaid, that it was forbidden by their religion,
"and had never been indulged to any man
"but they readily granted, what was the moſt
"deſirable in the next place, to bury him in
"any of their public Schools, that I pleaſed. I
"choſe a place therefore, the nobleſt in the
"Univerſe, *the School of the Academy*, where I
"burnt him, and have ſince given orders, that
"the Athenians ſhould provide a Marble Mo-
"nument for him in the ſame place   Thus I
"have faithfully performed to him, both when
"living and dead, every duty, which our part-
"nerſhip in office, and my particular relation
"to

" to him required. Adieu   The thirtieth of
" May from Athens [*o*]."

A Urb 708.
Cic 62
Coff
C Julius
Cæsar
Dictator III
M Æmilius
Lepidus
Mag Equit.

M. MARCELIUS was the head of a family,
which, for a succession of many ages had made
the first figure in Rome, and was himself adorned with all the virtues, that could qualify him to
sustain that dignity, which he derived from his
noble ancestors. He had formed himself in a
particular manner for the Bar, where he soon
acquired great fame, and, of all the Orators of
his time, seems to have approached the nearest
to Cicero *himself*, in the character of a complete
Speaker   His manner of speaking was *elegant,*
strong, and copious, with a sweetness of voice,
and propriety of action, that added a grace and lus-
ter to every thing that he said   He was a constant
admirer and imitator of Cicero, of the same prin-
ciples in peace, and on the same side in war; so
that Cicero laments his absence, as the loss *of a*
companion and partner, in their common studies
and labors of life.   Of all the Magistrates, he
was the fiercest opposer of Cæsar's power, and
the most active to reduce it : his high spirit, and
the ancient glory of his house, made him impatient under the thought of receiving a master;
and when the battle of Pharsalia seemed at last
to have imposed one upon them, he retired to
Mitylene, the usual resort of men of learning,
there to spend the rest of his days in a studious
retreat, remote from arms, and the hurry of
war, and determined neither to seek, nor to
accept any grace from the Conqueror   Here
Brutus paid him a visit, and found him, as he
gave an account to Cicero, *as perfectly easy and*
happy under all the misery of the times, from the

[*o*] Ep fam 4 12

A Urb 708.
Cic 62
Coff
C Julius
Cæsar
Dictator III
M Æmilius
Lepidus
Mag Equit

consciousness of his integrity, *as the condition of human life could bear* , surrounded with the principal Scholars and Philosophers of Greece, and eager in the pursuit of knowledge, so that in departing from him towards Italy, *he seemed*, he said, *to be going himself into exil, rather than leaving Marcellus in it* [p].

Magius, who killed him, was of a family which had born some of the publick offices, and had himself been *Questor* [q], and having attached himself to the fortunes of Marcellus, and followed him through the wars and his exil, was now returning with him to Italy. Sulpicius gives no hint of any cause, that induced him to commit this horrid fact which, by the immediate death of Magius, could never be clearly known.

[A] Mihi inquit, Marcellus satis est notus Qui igitur ... judicas —quod habiturus es similem tui—ita est & vehementer placet Nam & dictu & omnis cæteris studiis ... eget unum, seque ... quotidianis commentationibus acerrime exercuit Itaque & lectis utitur verbis & frequentibus, & splendore vocis, dignitate motus et specosum & ... quod ... omnia ... suppetunt, ut ... nullam deceret ... orationis ... Brut 567.

Dolebam, Patres conscripti, ... illo æmulo atque imitatore ... meorum, quasi quodam a me & co... ... ... aut obid... aut probitate, aut opti... ... ... ad proceris, ...

ullo genere laudis præstantior —pro Marcel 1.

Nostri enim sensus, ut in pace semper, sic tum etiam in bello congruebant Ib 6

Qui hoc tempore ipso—in hoc communi nostro & quasi fatali malo, consoletur se cum conscientia optimæ mentis, tum etiam usurpatione ac renovatione doctrinæ Vidi enim Mitylenis nuper virum, atque ut dixi, vidi plane virum Itaque cum eum antea tui similem in dicendo viderim, tum vero nunc doctissimo viro, tibique ut intellexi, amicissimo Cratippo, instructum omni copia, multo videbam similiorem Brut ibid vid Senec Consolat ad Hel p 79.

[q] Vid Pigh Annal A U 691

Cicero's conjecture was, that Magius oppressed with debts, and apprehending some trouble on that score at his return, had been urging Marcellus, who was his sponsor for some part of them, to furnish him with money to pay the whole, and by receiving a denial, was provoked to the madness of killing his Patron [r] *Others assign a different reason, as the rage of jealousy, and the impatience of seeing others more favored by Marcellus, than himself* [s].

As foon as the news reached Rome, it raifed a general confternation and from the fufpicious nature of the times, all people's thoughts were préfently turned on Cæfar, as if he were privately the contriver of it, and from the wretched fate of fo illuftrious a Citizen, every man began to think himfelf in danger. Cicero was greatly fhocked at it, and feemed to confider it, as the prelude of fome greater evil to enfue, and Atticus fignifying his concern upon it, advifes him to take a more particular care of himfelf, *as being the onely confular Senator left*, who ftood expofed to any envy [t] But Cæfar's friends foon cleared him of all fufpicion, as indeed the fact itfelf did, when the circumftances came to be known, and fixt the whole guilt of it on the fury of Magius.

A Urb 708.
Cic 62.
Coff
C JULIUS
CÆSAR
Dictator III
M ÆMILIUS
LEPIDUS
Mag. Equit.

[r] Quanquam nihil habeo quod dubitem, nifi ipfi Magio quæ fuert caufa amentiæ Pro quo quidem etiam Sponfor Sum factus eft Nimirim id fuit Solvendo enim non erat Credo eum a Marcello petiiffe aliquid, & illun, ut erat, conftantius refponaffe Ad Att 13 10

[s] Indigna us aliquem amicorum ab eo fibi præferri. Val Max 9 11

[t] Minime miror te & graviter ferre de Marcello & plura veteri periculi genera Quis enim hoc timere, quod neque accideret antea, nec videbatur utula ferre, ut accidere poffet Omnia ig tur metuenda, &c Ad Att 13 10

THERE

A Urb 708.
Cic. 62.
Coff.
C Julius
Cæsar
Dictator III.
M Æmilius
Lepidus
Mag Equit.

THERE appeared at this time a bold Impoſtor, who began to make a great noiſe and figure in Italy, by aſſuming the name, and pretending to be *the Grandſon of Caius Marius*: but apprehending that Cæſar would ſoon put an end to his pretenſions, and treat him as he deſerved, he ſent a pathetic Letter to Cicero, by ſome young fellows of his company, to juſtify his claim and deſcent, and to implore his protection againſt the enemies of his family, *conjuring him by their relation; by the poem, which he had formerly written in praiſe of Marius; by the eloquence of L Craſſus, his mother's Father, whom he had likewiſe celebrated, that he would undertake the defence of his cauſe*. Cicero anſwed him very gravely, *that he could not want a Patron, when his Kinſman Cæſar, ſo excellent and generous a man, was now the Maſter of all, yet that he alſo ſhould be ready to favor him* [u] But Cæſar, at his return, knowing him to be a cheat, baniſhed him out of Italy; ſince inſtead of being, what he pretended to be, he was found to be onely *a Farrier*, whoſe true name was Herophilus [x]

ARIARATHES the Brother and preſumptive heir of Ariobarzanes, *King of Cappadocia*, came

---

[ ] Heri—quidam Urbani, ut videbantur, ad me mandata a litteras attulerunt, a C Mario, C F C N multis verbis agere mecum per cognationem, quæ mihi ſecum eſſet, per eum Marium, quem ſcripſiſſem, per eloquentiam L Craſſi avi ſui, ut ſe defenderem—reſcripſi nihil eo Patrono opus eſſe, quoniam Cæſaris, propinqui ejus, omnis poteſtas eſſet, viri optimi & hominis liberaliſſimi; me tamen ei futurum—ad Att 12 49

[x] Herophilus Equarius medicus, C Marium ſepties Conſulem avum ſibi vendicando, ita ſe extulit, ut coloniæ veteranorum complures & municipia ſplendida, collegiaque fere omnia patronum adoptarent—cæterum decreto Cæſaris extra Italiam relegatus, &c Val. Max 9 15.

A Urb. 708.
Cic 62.
Coff
C Julius
Cæsar
Dictator III
M Æmilius
Lepidus
Mag Equit.

to Rome this year ; and as Cicero had a particular friendſhip with his family, and, when Conſul, had, by a decree of the Senate, conferred upon his Father the honor of *the Regal Title*, he thought proper to ſend a ſervant to meet him on the road, *and invite him to his houſe* · but he was already engaged by Seſtius, whoſe office it then was, to receive foreign Princes and Embaſſadors at the public expence ; which Cicero was not diſpleaſed with in the preſent ſtate of his domeſtic affairs . *he comes, ſays he, I gueſs, to purchaſe ſome kingdom of Cæſar, for he has not at preſent a foot of land of his own* [y].

CICERO's whole time during his ſolitude was employed in reading and writing this was the buſineſs both of his days and nights . *it is incredible, he ſays, how much he wrote, and how little he ſlept : and if he had not fallen into that way of ſpending his time, he ſhould not have known what to do with himſelf* [z]. His ſtudies were chiefly Philoſophical, which he had been fond of from his youth, and, after a long intermiſſion, now reſumed with great order, having taking a reſolution, to explain to his Countrymen in their own language, whatever the Greeks had taught on every part of Philoſophy whether ſpeculative or

---

[y] Ariarethes Ariobarzani filius Romam venit Vult, opinor, regnum aliquod emere a Cæſare nam, quo modo nunc eſt, pedem ubi ponat in ſuo non habet Omnino eum Seſtius noſter parochus publicus occupavit quod quidem facile patior Verumtamen quod mihi ſummo beneficio meo, magna ſum fratribus illius neceſſi-

tudo eſt, invito eum per litteras, ut apud me diver e ur. Ad Att 13 26

[z] Credibile non eſt, quantam ſcribam die, quin etiam noctibus Nihil enim ſomni. Ib 26

Niſi mihi hoc veniſſet in mentem, ſcribere iſta neſcio quæ, quo verterem me non haberem. Ib 10.

practical :

A Urb 705
Ct 62
Cot
C Julius
Cesar
Dictator III
M Æmilius
Lepidus
Mag Equit

practical. " For being driven, as he tells us, " from the public adminiftration, he knew no " way fo effectual of doing good, as by inftruct- " ing the minds, and reforming the morals of " the youth, which, in the licence of thofe " times, wanted every help to reftrain and cor- " rect them. The calamity of the City, *fays he*, " made this tafk neceffary to me fince in the " confufion of civil arms, I could neither de- " fend it after my old way, nor, when it was " impoffible for me to be idle, could I find any " thing better, on which to employ myfelf My " Citizens therefore will pardon, or rather thank " me, that when the government was fallen into " the power of a fingle perfon, I neither wholly " hid, nor afflicted myfelf unneceffarily, nor " acted in fuch a manner, as to feem angry at " the man, or the times, nor yet flattered or " admired the fortune of another fo, as to be " difpleafed with my own For I had learnt " from Plato and Philofophy, that thefe turns " and revolutions of ftates are natural, fome- " times into the hands of *a few*, fometimes of " *the many*, fometimes *of one*. as this was the " cafe of our own Republic, fo when I was de- " prived of my former poft in it, I betook my- " felf to thefe ftudies, in order to relieve my " mind from the fenfe of our common miferies, " and to ferve my country at the fame time in the " beft manner that I was able for my books " fupplied the place of my votes in the Senate, " and of my fpeeches to the people ; and I took " up philofophy, as a fubftitute for my manage- " ment of the ftate [*a*]."

[*a*] Divin 2 2 —de Fin 1 3

HE

HE now publifhed therefore, in the way of
dialogue, a book, which he called Hortenfius,
in honor of his deceafed friend, where in a debate of learning he did, what he had often done
in contefts of the Bar, *undertake the defence of*
Philofophy against Hortenfius, to whom he affigned
the part of arraigning it [b]. It was the reading
of this book, long fince unfortunately loft, which
firft inflamed St Auftin, as he himfelf fomewhere
declares, *to the ftudy of the Chriftian Philofophy ·*
and if it had yielded no other fruit, yet happy it
was to the world, that it once fubfifted, to be
the inftrument of raifing up fo illuftrious a convert and champion to *the Church of Chrift* [c]

HE drew up alfo about this time *in four books*,
a particular account and defence *of the Philofophy
of the Academy*, the fect, which he himfelf followed · being, as he fays, *of all others, the moft
confiftent with itfelf, and the leaft arrogant, as well
as moft elegant* [d] He had before publifhed
a work on the fame fubject in two books, the

---

[b] Cohorti fumus, ut
maxime potuimus, ad Philo-
fophiæ ftudium eo libro, qui
eft infcriptus, Hortenfius—
de Div 2 1

Nos autem univerfa Philo-
fophiæ vituperatoribus re-
fpondimus in Hortenfio Tul
Difp 2 2

[c] It is certain, that *all the
Latin Fathers* made great ufe
of *Cicero's writings*, and efpecially Jerom, who was not
fo grateful as Auftin, in ac-
knowledging the benefit,
for, having conceived fome
fcruples on that fcore in his
declining age, he endeavoured to difcourage his difciples
from reading them at all,
and declared, *that he had not
taken either Cicero or Maro,
or any heathen writer into his
hands for above fifteen years ·*
for which his adverfary Ruf-
finus rallies him very feverely
ly Vid Hieron, Op Tom
4 par 2 p 414 it par 1.
p 288 Edit Benedict —
[d] Quod genus philofo-
phandi minime arrogans,
maximeque & conftans, & e-
legans arbitraremur, quatuor
Academicis libris oftendimus,
De Divin 2 1.

A Urb 708
Cic 62
Coff
C Julius
Cæsar
Dictor III
M Æmilius
Lepidus
Mag Equit.

one called Catulus, the other Lucullus but considering *that the argument was not suited to the characters of the speakers*, who were not particularly remarkable for any study of that sort, he was thinking to change them to Cato and Brutus, when Atticus happening to signify to him, that *Varro had expressed a desire to be inserted in some of his writings*, he presently reformed his scheme, and enlarged it into *four Books*, which he addressed to Varro, taking upon himself *the part of Philo, of defending the principles of Academy*; and affigning to *Varro that of Antiochus*, of oppofing and confuting them, and introducing Atticus, as the moderator of the difpute He finifhed the whole with great accuracy, fo as to make it a prefent worthy of Varro, *and if he was not deceived*, he fays, *by a partiality and felf love too common in fuch cafes, there was nothing on the fubject equal to it, even among the Greeks* [e]. All thefe four books, excepting part of the firft, are now loft; whilft the fecond book of the firft edition, which he took fome pains to fupprefs, remains ftill intire, under it's original Title of Lucullus

HE publifhed likewife this year one of the nobleft of his works, and on the nobleft fubject in Philofophy, his treatife called, *de Finibus, or of the chief good and ill of man*, written *in Ariftotle's*

[e] Ego illam Ἀκαδημικήν, in qua homines nobiles illi quidam, fed nullo modo φιλόλογοι, nimis acute loquuntur, ad Varronem transferamus—Catulo & Lucullo alibi reponemus — Ad Att 13 12

Quod ad me de Varrone fcripferas, totam Academiam

ab hominibus nobiliffimis abftuli, tranftuli ad noftrum fodalem, & ex duobus libris contuli in quatuor—libri quidem ita exierunt (nifi me forte communis φιλαυτία decipit) ut in tali genere ne apud Græcos quidem quicquam fimile lb 13, vide it ib. 16 19

manner

A. Urb 708.
Cic 62.
Coff.
C Julius
Cæsar
Dictator III
M Æmilius
Lepidus
Mag Equit.

manner [*f*], in which he explained with great elegance and perfpicuity, the feveral opinions of all the ancient fects on that moft important quef-tion. *It is there inquired,* he tells us, *what is the chief end, to which all the views of life ought to be referred, in order to make it happy or what it is which nature purfues as the fupreme good, and fhuns as the worft of ills* [*g*] The work confifts of five books in the two firft, *the Epicurean doc-trine* is largely opened and difcuffed, being de-fended by Torquatus, and confuted by Cicero, in a conference fuppofed to be held in his *Cuman Villa,* in the prefence of Triarius, a young Gentleman, who came with Torquatus to vifit him The two next explane *the doctrine of the Stoics,* afferted by Cato, and oppofed by Cicero, in a friendly debate, upon their meeting acci-dentally in *Lucullus's Library.* The fifth con-tains the opinions *of the old Academy, or the Pe-ripateticks,* explaned by Pifo, in a third dialogue, fuppofed to be held at Athens, in the prefence of *Cicero, his Brother Quintus, Coufin Lucius, and Atticus.* The Critics have obferved fome im-propriety in this laft book, in making *Pifo refer to the other two dialogues,* of which he had no fhare, and could not be prefumed to have any knowledge [*h*]. But if any inaccuracy of that kind be really found in this, or any other of his

[*f*] Quæ autem his tem-poribus fcripfi Αρεςο] λsιον morem habent — ita confeci quinque libros περὶ τιλῶν— ib 19

[*g*] Tum id, quod his li-bris quæritur, quid fit finis, quid extremum, quid ulti-mum, quo fint omnia bene vivendi, recteque faciendi confilia referenda Quid fe-quatur natura, ut fummum ex rebus expetendis, quid fu-giat ut extremum malorum. De Fin 1 4

[*h*] Vid Præfat Davis in Lib de finib.

works,

A. Urb 708
Cic 62
Coſſ
C Julius
Cæſar
Dictator III
M Æmilius
Lepid
Mag Equit

works, it may reaſonably be excuſed by that multiplicity of affairs, which ſcarce allowed him time to write, much leſs to reviſe what he wrote : and in dialogues of length compoſed by piece-meal, and in the ſhort intervals of leiſure, it cannot ſeem ſtrange that he ſhould ſometimes forget his artificial, to reſume his proper character, and enter inadvertently into a part, which he had aſſigned to another. He addreſſed this work to Brutus, in return for a preſent of the ſame kind, which Brutus had ſent to him a little before, *a treatiſe upon virtue* [1]

Not long after he had finiſhed this work, he publiſhed another of equal gravity, called his *Tuſculan Diſputations*, in five books alſo, upon as many different queſtions in Philoſophy, the moſt important and uſeful to the happineſs of human life. The firſt teaches us, *how to contemn the terrors of death, and to look upon it as a bleſſing, rather than an evil*: the ſecond, *to ſupport pain and affliction with a manly fortitude*. the third, *to appeaſe all our complaints and uneaſineſſes under the accidents of life*: the fourth, *to moderate all our other paſſions*. the fifth, *to evince the ſufficiency of virtue to make man happy*. It was his cuſtom, in the opportunities of his leiſure, to take ſome friends with him into the country, where inſtead of amuſing themſelves with idle ſports or feaſts, their diverſions were wholly ſpeculative, tending to improve the mind, and enlarge the underſtanding. In this manner he now ſpent *five days at his Tuſculan Villa*, in diſcuſſing with his friends the ſeveral queſtions juſt mentioned: for after employing the mornings in declaming and rhetorical exerciſes, they uſed to retire in the after-

[1] De Finib. 1 3.

noon into a Gallery, called the *Academy*, which
he had built for the purpose of Philosophical con-
ferences· where, after the manner of the Greeks,
he held *a School*, as they called it, and invited
the company to call for any subject, that they
desired to hear explaned, which being proposed
accordingly by some of the audience, became
immediately the argument of that day's debate
These five conferences or dialogues he collected
afterwards into writing, *in the very words and
manner in which they really passed*, and published
them under the title of his *Tusculan Disputations*,
from the name of the Villa, in which they were
held [*k*].

Hr wrote also a little piece, in the way of *a
Funeral Encomium, in praise of Porcia, the sister
of Cato, and wife of Domitius Ahenobarbus*, Cæsar's mortal enemy; which shews how little he
was still disposed to court the times Varro and
Lollius attempted the same subject; and *Cicero
desires Atticus to send him their compositions* but
all the three are now lost. though Cicero took
the pains to revise and correct his, and sent
copies of it afterwards *to Domitius the Son, and
Brutus, the Nephew of that Porcia* [*l*].

A Urb 708.
Cic 62.
Coss
C Julius
Cæsar
Dictator III.
M Æmilius
Lepidus
Mag Equit.

[*k*] In Tusculano, cum
essent complures mecum Familiares — ponere jubebam,
de quo quis audire vellet, ad
id aut sedens aut ambulans
disputabam Itaque dierum
quinque Scholas, ut Græci
appellant, in totidem libros
contuli Tusc Disp 1 4

Itaque cum ante meridiem
dictioni operam dedissemus—
post meridiem in *Academiam*
descendimus in qua dispu-
tationem habitam non quasi
narrantes exponimus, sed eis-
dem fere verbis ut actum dis-
putatumque est Ib 2 3
3 3

[*l*] Laudationem Porciæ
tibi misi correctam ab eo
properavi, ut si forte aut
Domitio filio aut Bruto mitteretur hæc mitteretur Id
si tibi erit commodum, mag-
i opere cures velim, & velim
M Varronis, Lolliique mittas laudationem Ad Att
13 48 it ib 37

CÆSAR

A Urb 708.
Cic 62
Coss
C JULIUS
CÆSAR
Dictator III
M ÆMILIUS
LEPIDUS
Mag Equit

CÆSAR continued all this while in Spain, pursuing *the Sons of Pompey,* and providing for the future peace and settlement of the Province; whence he paid Cicero the compliment of sending him an account of his success with his own hand. Hirtius also gave him early intelligence *of the defeat and flight of the two Brothers,* which was not disagreeable to him, for though he was not much concerned about the event of the war, and expected no good from it on either side, yet the opinion, which he had conceived of the fierceness and violence *of the young Pompeys,* especially of *the elder* of them, Cnæus, engaged his wishes rather for Cæsar In a Letter to Atticus, Hirtius, says he, *wrote me word, that Sextus Pompey had withdrawn himself from Corduba into the hither Spain, and that Cnæus too was fled, I know not whither, nor in truth do I care* [m]: and this indeed seems to have been the common sentiment of all the Republicans as Cassius himself, writing to Cicero on the same subject, declares still more explicitely, " May I perish, *says he,* if I
" be not sollicitous about the event of things in
" Spain; and would rather keep our old and cle-
" ment master, than try a new and cruel one.
" You know what a fool Cnæus is , how he *takes*
" *cruelty for a virtue.* how he has always thought,
" that we laughed at him ; I am afraid left he
" should take it into his head to repay our jokes
" in his rustic manner with the sword [n]."

[m] Hirtius ad me scrip-
sit, Sex Pompeium Corduba
exisse, & fugisse in Hispaniam citeriorem , Cnæum
fugisse nescio quo, neque e-
nim curo Ad Att 12 37.
[n] Pereteam, nisi sollicitus
sam, ac malo veterem ac
clementem dominum habe-
re, quam novum & crudelem
experiri Scis, Cnæus quam
sit fatuus, scis quomodo cru-
delitatem virtutem putet ,
scis, quam se semper a nobis
derisum putet

A Urb 708.
Cic 62.
Coff.
C. Julius
Cæsar
Dictator III.
M Æmilius
Lepidus
Mag. Equit.

YOUNG Quintus Cicero, who made the campaign along with Cæfar, thinking to pleafe his company, and to make his fortunes the better among them, began to play over his old game, and to abufe his uncle again in all places. Cicero, in his account of it to Atticus, fays, " there is " nothing new, but that Hirtius has been " quarrelling in my defence, with our Nephew " Quintus, who takes all occafions of faying " every thing bad of me, and efpecially at pub- " lic feafts, and when he has done with me, " falls next upon his Father· he is thought to " fay nothing fo credible, as *that we are both ir-* " *reconcilable to Cæfar; that Cæfar fhould truft* " *neither of us, and even beware of me* this " would be terrible; did I not fee, that our King " is perfuaded that I have no fpirit left [o]."

ATTICUS was always endeavouring to moderate Cicero's *impatience* under the prefent government, and perfuading him, to comply more chearfully with the times; nor to reject the friendfhip of Cæfar, which was fo forwardly offered to him· and upon his frequent complaints of the flavery and indignity of his prefent condition, he took occafion to obferve, that Cicero could not but own to be true, *that if to pay a par-* *ticular court and obfervance to a man, was the mark* *of flavery, thofe in power feemed to be flaves rather*

Vereor, ne nos ruftice gladio velit τ.ημωπηρισα Ep fam 15 19

[o] Novi fare nihil, nifi Hirtium cum Quinto acerri- mo pro me litigaffe, omni- bus eum locis facere, maxi- meque in conviviis, cum multa de me, tum redire ad Patrem nihil autem ab eo tam αςιοπισως dici, quam a- lieniffimos nos effe a Cæfare, fidem nobis habendam non effe, me vero cavendum. φοβ οὖν ἢ, nifi viderem fcire Regem, me animi nihil ha- bere—Ad Att 13 37

4

A Urb 708
Cic 62
Coff
C Julius
Cæsar
Dictator III
M. Æmilius
Lepidus
Mag Equit

to him than he to them [p]. With the fame view he was now preffing him, among his other works, to think of fomething to be addreffed to Cæfar · but Cicero had no appetite to this tafk, he faw how difficult it would be to perform it without leffening his character, and defcending to flattery; yet being obliged to it alfo by other friends, he drew up a Letter, which was communicated to Hirtius and Balbus, for their judgement upon it, whether it was proper to be fent to Cæfar. The fubject feems to have been fome advice, about reftoring the peace and liberty of the Republic, and to diffuade him from *the Parthian war*, which he intended for his next expedition, till he had finifhed the more neceffary work of fettling the ftate of things at home · *there was nothing in it*, he fays, *but what might come from the beft of Citizens*. It was drawn however with fo much freedom, that though Atticus feemed pleafed with it, yet the other two durft not advife the fending it, unlefs fome paffages were altered and foftned, which difgufted Cicero fo much, that he refolved not to write at all, and when Atticus was ftill urging him to be more complaifant, he anfwered with great fpirit in two or three Letters [q].

---

[p] Et fi mehercule, ut tu mihi gis magis mini ifti ferviunt, fi obfervare fervire eft Ad Att 13 49

[q] Epiftolam ad Cæfarem mitti ideo tibi placere—mihi c dem hoc idem maxime placuit, & eo magis, quod nihil eft in ea nifi optimi est fed ita optimi, ut tempora, quibus parere omnes ita æqui præcipiunt Sed

fcis ita nobis effe vifum, ut illi ante legerent Tu igitur id curabis Sed nifi plane intelliges iis placere, mittenda non eft Ad Att 12 51

De Epiftola ad Cæfarem, *lex. 49* Atque id ipfum, quod ifti aiunt illum fcribere, fe, nifi conftitutis rebus, non iturum in Parthos, idem ego fuadebam in illa epiftola——
ib 13 31

" As

"As for the Letter to Cæfar, *says he,* I
"was always very willing, that they fhould firft
"read it · for otherwife I had both been want-
"ing in civility to them , and if I had happened
"to give offence, expofed myfelf alfo to dan-
"ger They have dealt ingenuoufly and kind-
"ly with me, in not concealing what they
"thought but what pleafes me the moft is,
"that by requiring fo many alterations, they give
"me an excufe for not writing at all As to the
"Parthian war, what had I to confider about
"it, but that which I thought would pleafe him;
"for what fubject was there elfe for a Letter,
"but flattery ? or if I had a mind to advife, what
"I really took to be the beft, could I have been
"at a lofs for words ? there is no occafion there-
"fore for any Letter . for where there is no
"great matter to be gained, and a flip, though
"not great, may make us uneafy, what reafon
"is there to run any rifk ? efpecially, when it is
"natural for him to think, that as I wrote no-
"thing to him before, fo I fhould have written
"nothing now, had not the war been wholly
"ended · befides, I am afraid left he fhould
"imagine, that I fent this, as a fweetner for
"my Cato . in fhort, I was heartily afhamed of
"what I had written ; and nothing could fall
"out more luckily, than that it did not pleafe
"[r] "

Again, "As for writing to Cæfar, I fwear
"to you, I cannot do it nor is it yet the fhame
"of it that deters me, which ought to do it the
"moft, for how mean would it be to flatter,
"when even to live is bafe in me ? but it is not,
"as I was faying, this fhame, which hinders

[r] Ad Att 13, 27

me,

A Urb 708.
Cic 62
Coff.
C Julius
Cæsar
Dictator III.
M Æmilius
Lepidus
Mag Equit.

A Urb. 708.
Cic 62.
Coſſ
C Julius
Cæsar
D.ctator III.
M Æ4ilius
Lepidus
Mag Equit.

" me, though I wiſh it did; for I ſhould then
" be, what I ought to be, but I can think of
" nothing to write upon As to thoſe exhorta-
" tions, addreſſed to Alexander, by the eloquent
" and the learned of that time, you ſee on what
" points they turn they are addreſſed to a youth,
" inflamed with the thirſt of true glory, and de-
" ſiring to be adviſed how to acquire it. On an
" occaſion of ſuch dignity, words can never be
" wanting, but what can I do on my ſubject?
" Yet I had ſcratched, as it were, out of the
" block ſome faint reſemblance of an image:
" but becauſe there were ſome things hinted in
" it, a little better than what we ſee done
" every day, it was diſliked. I am not at all ſor-
" ry for it, for had the Letter gone, take my
" word for it, I ſhould have had cauſe to re-
" pent For do you not ſee that very ſcholar
" of Ariſtotle, a youth of the greateſt parts, and
" the greateſt modeſty, after he came to be call-
" ed a King, grow proud, cruel, extravagant?
" Do you imagine, that this man, ranked in the
" proceſſions of the Gods, and inſhrined in the
" ſame Temple with Romulus, will be pleaſed
" with the moderate ſtile of my Letters? It is
" better that he be diſguſted at my not writing,
" than at what I write in a word, let him do
" what he pleaſes, for that problem, which I
" once propoſed to you, and thought ſo difficult,
" *in what way I ſhall manage him*, is over with
" me. and in truth, I now wiſh more, to feel
" the effect of his reſentment, be it what it will,
" than I was before afraid of it [*s*]." " I beg of
" you therefore, ſays he, in another Letter, let
" us have no more of this; but ſhew ourſelves

[ ] Ad Att 13 28.

A Urb 708
Cic 62
Coss
C Julius
Cæsar
Dictator III
M Æmilius
Lepidus
Mag Equit

" at leaft *half free*, by our filence and re-
" treat [*t*]."

FROM this little fact, one cannot help reflecting on *the fatal effects of arbitrary power*, upon
the ftudies and compofitions of men of genius,
and on the reftraint, that it neceffarily lays on the
free courfe of good fenfe and truth among men.
It had yet fcarce fhewn itfelf in Rome, when we
fee one of the greateft men, as well as the greateft
wits which that Republic ever bred, embarraffed in the choice of a fubject to write upon;
and for fear of offending, chufing not to write
at all . and it was the fame power, which, from
this beginning, gradually debafed the purity both
of the Roman wit and language, from the perfection of elegance, to which Cicero had advanced them, to that ftate of rudenefs and barbarifm,
which we find in the productions of the lower
Empire.

THIS was the prefent ftate of things between
Cæfar and Cicero, all the marks of kindnefs on
Cæfar's part, of coldnefs and referve on Cicero's.
Cæfar was determined never to part with his
power, and took the more pains, for that reafon,
to make Cicero eafy under it he feems indeed
to have been fomewhat afraid of him, not of
his engaging in any attempt againft his life, but
left by his infinuations, his railleries, and his authority, he fhould excite others to fome act of
violence but what he more efpecially defired
and wanted, was to draw from him fome public
teftimony of his approbation, and to be recommended by his writings to the favor of pofterity.

[*t*] Obfecro, abjiciamus mus, quod affequemur & ta-
ifta, & femiliberi faltem fi- cendo, & latendo— ib 31.

CICERO on the other hand, perceiving no step taken towards the establishment of the Republic, but more and more reason every day to despair of it, grew still more indifferent to every thing else the restoration of public liberty was the onely condition, on which he could entertain any friendship with Cæsar or think and speak of him with any respect without that, no favors could oblige him, since to receive them from a master, was an affront to his former dignity, and but a splendid badge of servitude books therefore were his onely comfort, for while he conversed with them, he found himself easy, and fancied himself free —— Thus in a Letter to Cassius, touching upon the misery of the times, he adds, " What is be- " come then, you'll say, of Philosophy? Why, " yours is in the kitchen but mine is trouble- " some to me for I am ashamed to live a slave, ' and feign myself therefore to be doing some- ' thing else, that I may not hear the reproach " of Plato [z] '

DURING Cæsar's stay in Spain, Antony set forward from Italy, to pay his compliments to him there or to meet him at least on the road in his return towards home, but when he had made about half of the journey, he met with some dispatches, which obliged him to turn back in all haste to Rome This raised a new alarm in the city, and especially among the Pompeians, who were afraid, that Cæsar, having now sub- dued all opposition, was resolved, after the ex- ample of former Conquerors, to take his revenge in cool blood on all his adversaries, and had sent

---

[z] Ubi igitur inquies, comre aliis res agere, ne P. ...p... l...... con.gium Platonis audiam ... ... Phil. Ep. fam. 15 18

Antony back, as the properest instrument to execute some orders of that sort. Cicero himself
had the same suspicion, and was much surprized at Antony's *sudden return*, till Balbus and Oppius eased him of his apprehensions, by sending
him *an account of the true reason of it* [x] which,
contrary to expectation, gave no uneasiness at last
to any body, but to Antony himself. Antony
had bought *Pompey's Houses in Rome* and the
neighbourhood, with all their rich furniture, *at
Cæsar's auction*, soon after his return from Ægypt,
but trusting to his interest with Cæsar, and to the
part, which he had born in advancing him to
his power, never dreamt of being obliged to
pay for them; but Cæsar, being disgusted by the
account of his debauches, and extravagancies in
Italy, and resolved to shew himself the sole master, nor suffer any contradiction to his will, sent
peremptory orders to L. Plancus, the Prætor,
to require immediate payment of Antony, or
else to levy the money upon his sureties, according to the tenor of their bond. This was the
cause of his quick return, to prevent that disgrace from falling upon him, and find some
means of complying with Cæsar's commands; it
provoked him however to such a degree, that in
the height of his resentment, he is said to have
entered into a design *of taking away Cæsar's life*,
of which Cæsar himself complained openly in the
Senate [y]

THE

A. Urb 708
Cic 62
Col
C Julius
Cæsar
Dictator III
M Æmilius
Lepidus
Mag Equit

[x] Heri cum ex aliorum
litteris cognovissem de Antonii adventu, admiratus sum
nihil esse in tuis. Ad Att
12 18

De Antonio Balbus quoque
ad me cum Opp o conscripsit,

id'que tibi placuisse, ne per-
turbarer. Illis egi gratias,
—ib 1,

[y] Appellatus es de pecunia quam pro domo, pro
hortis, pro sectione debebas --
& a te & ad prædes tuos milites

THE war being ended in Spain, by *the death of C. us Pompey, and the flight of Sextus,* Cæsar finished his answer to Cicero's *Cato, in two books,* which he sent immediately to Rome, in order to be published. This gave Cicero at last the argument of a Letter to him, to return thanks for the great civility, with which he had treated him in that piece, and to pay his compliments likewise in his turn, upon the elegance of the composition. This Letter was communicated again to Balbus and Oppius, who declared themselves extremely pleased with it, and forwarded it directly to Cæsar. In Cicero's account of it to Atticus, " I forgot, says he, to send you a copy of what " I wrote to Cæsar not for the reason, which " you suspect, that I was ashamed to let you see, " how well I could flatter for in truth, I wrote " to him no otherwise, than as if I was writing " to an equal, for I really have a good opinion " of his two books, as I told you, when we " were together, and wrote therefore both with-" out flattering him, and yet so, that he will " read nothing, I believe, with more plea-" sure [z] "

CÆSAR

literas misit —— [Phil. 2. 20.] Idcirco a terit more nocturno Italiam a literarum dierum metu peturba —— ne L. Pancus preces tuo vendicet —— [b. 5] Cur h. pris temporibus comiterni super c.. ab tro mihi depre her as a cesaar che cen ficr. De quo Cæsar in senat t, a.e e in te a ctiens que sit e.st —— b. 20 .. [z] Conscripsi ce ni h literas epistolam Cæsaris, que

deferretur ad Dolabellam sed ejus exemplum misi ad Balbum & Oppium, scripsique ad eo, ut tum deferri ad Dolabellam juberunt meas literas, si exemplum proba ent, ita mihi rescripserunt, nihil unquam se legisse melius. Ad Att. 13. 50.

Ad Cæsarem quam misi epistolam ejus exemplum fugit me tum tibi mittere, nec id quod suspicaris, ut me puderet tui —— nec mehercule scripsi

CÆSAR returned to Rome about *the end of September*, when divesting himself of the Consulship, he conferred it on *Q. Fabius Maximus, and C. Trebonius, for the three remaining months of the year* [a] His first care, after his arrival, was to entertain the City with *the most splendid triumph*, which Rome had ever seen but the people, instead of admiring and applauding it, as he expected, were sullen and silent, considering it, as it really was, a triumph over themselves, purchased by the loss of their liberty, and the destruction of the best and noblest families of the Republic They had before given the same proof of their discontent *at the Circensian games*, where *Cæsar's statue*, by a decree of the Senate, *was carried in the procession, along with those of the Gods* for they gave none of their usual acclamations to *the favorite Deities*, as they passed, *lest they should be thought to give them to Cæsar* Atticus sent an account of it to Cicero, who says in answer to him, *Your Letter was agreeable, though the shew was so sad — the people however behaved bravely, who would not clap even the Goddess Victory, for the sake of so bad a neighbour* [b] Cæsar however to make amends for the unpopularity of his triumph, and to put the people into good humor, entertained the whole City soon after with something more substantial than shews, *two*

A Urb 708
Cic 62
Coss
Q. FABIUS
MAXIMUS,
C TREBO-
NIUS

scripsi, aliter ac si πρὸς ισ- ουσιον quæ scriberem Bene enim existimo de illis libris, ut tibi coram Itaque scripsi & ακολαλυτως, & tamen sic, ut nihil eum existimem lecturum libentius Ib 51

[a] Utroque anno binos Consules substituit sibi in ter-

nos novissimos menses Suet J Cæi 76

[b] Suaves tuas litteras ' etsi acerbi pompa—populum vero præclarum, quod propter tam malum vicinum, ne Victoriæ quidem ploditur Ad Att 13 44

public

A Urb —cS
Cc 62
CoT
Q F..B\L\
M.. .. s,
C Trebj-
N'c.

p'bl'c di ners, with plenty of *the moſt eſteemed
and coſtly wines, of C ios and Fale.num* [c]

Soon after Cæſar's triumph, *the Conſul Fabius,*
one of his Lieutenants in Spain, was allowed to
tr pph too, for the reduction of ſome parts of
that province, which had revolted but the magnificence of Cæſar's made Fabius's triumph appear
contemptible, *for his models of the conquered
Towns. which were* always a part of the ſhew,
being made onely *of wood,* when Cæſar's *were of*
S ver or Ivory, Chryſippus merrily called them,
the caſes or cues of Cæſar's Towns [d]

Cicero reſided generally in the Country, and
withdrew himſelf wholly from the Senate [e]
but on Cæſar's approach towards Rome, Lepidus
began to preſs him by repeated Letters, to come
and give them his aſſiſtance, aſſuring him, *that
it both Cæſar would take it very kindly of him*
He could not gueſs, for what particular ſervice
they wanted him, except *the dedication of ſome Temple, to which the preſence of three Augurs* was neceſſary [f] But whatever it was, as his friends had
long been urging the ſame advice, and perſuading

---

[c] Quid ror & Cæſar
Dictator triumph. ſui cœna
vini Falerni amphoras, Chi
caeos in convicia diſtribuit?
idem in Hiſpanenſi triumpho Cnium & ı alernum dedit Plın Hiſt 14 15

Adjecit poſt Hiſpanienſem
victoriam duo prandia Sucton 38

[d] Ut Chryſippus cum in triumpho Cæſaris eborea oppida ferent tran lata & poſt dies paucosFeb navali lignea, theatra eſſe oppidorum Cæſaris dixit Quintil 6

3 Dio 234
[e] Cum his temporibus non ſane in ſenatum ventitarem— Ep fam 13 77

[f] Ecce tibi, orat Lepidus, ut veniam Opinor Augures nil habere ad Templum efferendum Ad Att 13 42

Lepidus ad me heri— litteras miſit Rogat magnopere ut ſim Kalend in Senatu, me & ſibi & Cæſari vehementer gratum eſſe facturum—
ib 4-

him

him to return to public affairs, he confented at laft, to quit his retirement and come to the City, where foon after Cæfar's arrival he had an oppor- tunity of employing his authority and eloquence, where he exerted them always with the greateft pleafure, in the fervice and defence of *an old friend, King Deiotarus*

A Urb -08
Cic 62
Col
Q Fabius
Maximus,
C Trebo-
nius

THIS Prince had already been deprived by Cæfar of part of his dominions, for his adhe- rence to Pompey, and was now in danger of lo- fing the reft, from an accufation preferred againft him by his Grandfon, of a defign pretended to have been formed by *him againft Cefer's life*, when Cæfar was entertained at his houfe, four years before, on his return from Egypt The charge was groundlefs and ridiculous, but under his prefent difgrace, any charge was fufficient to ruin him, and Cæfar's countenancing it fo far, as to receive and hear it, fhewed a ftrong preju- dice againft the King, and that he wanted onely a pretence for ftripping him of all that remained to him Brutus likewife interefted himfelf very warmly in the fame caufe, and when he went to meet Cæfar, on his road from Spain, *made an Oration to him at Nicæa, in favor of Deiotarus,* with a freedom, which ftartled Cæfar, and gave him occafion to reflect on what he had not per- ceived fo clearly before, the *venerable franknefs and vehemence of Brutus's temper* [g] The pre- fent trial was held in Cæfar's *houfe*, where Cice-

[g] Ad Att II 1 The Jefuit Catrou and Rouille, take Nice, where Brutus made this fpeech, to be the *Capital of Bulgaria*, Deiota- rus's kingdom but it was the City on the river coaft mof called Nice, where Bru- tus met Cæfar on his laft re- turn from Spain, and when he was not able to prevail for Deiotarus, Cicero was forced to undertake the caufe as foon as Cæfar came to Rome Vid Hift Tom 17 p 91 not

ro

A Urb 708
Cic 62.
Coss
Q. Fabius
Maximus,
C Trebonius

ro fo manifeftly expofed the malice of the accufer, and the innocence of the accufed, that Cæfar, being determined not to acquit, yet afhamed to condemn him, chofe the expedient of referving his fentence to farther deliberation, till he fhould go in perfon into the Faft, and inform himfelf of the whole affair upon the fpot Cicero fays, *that D ----, ---- prefent nor abfent, could ---- ---- ---- from Cæfar and that ---- as he pleaded for him, which he was always ---- to do, he could never perfuade Cæfar, to ---- a thing ----, that he afked for him* [b] He fent a copy of his oration *to the King* , and, at Dolabella's requeft, gave another likewife to him *excufing it, as a trifling performance, and hardly worth tranfcribing, but I had a mind, fays he, to m---- c flight prefent to my old friend ---- ----, of coarfe fluff indeed, yet fuch as his pre---- ---- are to me* [ ]

So e little time after this trial, Cæfar, to fhew his confidence in Cicero, invited himfelf to fpend a day with him, at his houfe in the country, and chofe *the third of the Saturnal a* for his vifit, a feafon always dedicated to mirth and feafting among friends and relations [k] Cicero gives

---

[b] Quærum cuiolan in mictior quam De t o Cal —a oto nec præfens rec aolers Rex Deotaris quidquar acui beu anje t aut—lle ninouem, fem per ea ---- ---- ---- Deo taro quiccuam fib quod no pro o po culure nus, ---- quam dat videri Philip 2 ----

[ ] O tu caiun pro Deotaro quam ---- ebas—— ---- m Quat ----m fc

legr, ut caufam tenveri & inopem, n c fcriptione mag ro opere dignam Sed ego hofpiti vetui & amico muru feulum nitret volui levi aunfe craffo fio, cujufmodi ipfius folent effe munera Li fam 9 1

[k] This Feftival after Cæfar's reformation of the Kalendar began on the 17th of December, and lafted three days Macrob Saturn 1 ----

Atticus

A Urb 708
Cic 62
Cofs
Q Fabius
Maximus,
C Trebo-
nius

Atticus the following account of the entertainment, and how the day paffed between them.
" O this gueft, fays he, whom I fo much dread-
" ed! yet I had no reafon to repent of him for
" he was well pleafed with his reception. When
" he came the evening before, on the eighteenth,
" to my neighbour Philip's, the houfe was fo
" crouded with foldiers, that there was fcarce a
" room left empty for Cæfar to fup in there
" were about two thoufand of them which gave
" me no fmall pain for the next day but Barba
" Caffius relieved me, for he affigned me a
" guard, and made the reft encamp in the field
" fo that my houfe was clear On the nine-
" teenth, he ftaid at Philip's till one in the after-
" noon, but faw nobody, was fettling accounts,
" I guefs, with Balbus, then took a walk on
" the fhore, bathed after two, heard the verfes
" on Mamurra [*l*], at which he never changed

[*l*] Mamurra was a Ro-
man Knight, and *General of
the Artillery to Cæfar in Gaul,*
where he raifed an immenfe
fortune, and is faid to have
been the firft man in Rome,
who *incrufted his houfe with
marble, and made all his pillars of folid marble* [Plin
Hift 36 6] He was fe-
verely lafhed, together with
Cæfar himfelf for his ex-
ceffive luxury, and more infamous vices by Catullus,
whofe verfes are ftill extant,
and the fame probably that
Cicero here refers to, as being firft read to Cæfar at his
houfe Vid Catull 27, 55

The reader perhaps will
not readily underftand the
time and manner of Cæfar's
paffing from Philip's houfe to

Cicero's in this fhort account
of it but it muft be remem
bred, that their villa's were
adjoining to each other on
the Formian coaft near Ca-
jeta, fo that when Cæfar
came out of Philip's houfe,
he took a walk on the fhore
for about an hour and then
entered into Cicero's, where
the bath was prepared for
him, and in bathing he heard
Catullas's verfes, not produced by Cicero, for that
would not have been agreeable to good manners, but by
fome of his own friends who
attended him, and who knew
his defire to fee every thing
that was publifhed againft
him, as well as his chracter
in flighting or forgiving it

" countenance

A Urb 708
Cic 62
Coss
Q FABIUS
MAXIMUS,
C TREBO-
NIUS

" countenance, was rubbed, anointed, sat down
" to table   Having taken a vomit just before,
" he eat and drank freely, and was very chear-
" full [*m*]   the Supper was good and well served.

" But our discourse at table, as we eat,
" For taste and seasoning still excell'd our meat [*n*]

" Besides Cæsar's table, his friends were plenti-
' fully provided for in three other rooms , nor
" was there any thing wanting to his freedmen
" of lower rank, and his slaves, but the better
" sort were elegantly treated   In a word, I ac-
" quitted myself like a man · yet he is not a
' guest to whom one would say at parting,
" pray call upon me again, as you return . once

[*m*] The custom of *taking*
a vomit both immediately before and after meals, which
Cicero mentions Cæsar to
have done on different occasions, [pro Deiot 7] was very common with the Romans,
and used by them as an instrument both of their luxury, and of their health   *the*
vomit, says Seneca, *treat the*
ra, eat ar eat that the, a
vomit [Consol ad Helo 9]
By this evacuation before
eating, they were prepared
to eat more plentifully , and
by empt ing themselves presently after it, prevented any
hurt from replexion   Thus
Vitellius, who was a famous
glutton *is said to have pre-*
served his life by constant vo-
mits, while he destroyed all
his companions, who did not
use the same caution   [Sue-
tonius 12 Dio 65 734] And
the practice was thought so
effectual for strengthening the
constitution that it was the
constant regimen of all the
Athletæ, or the professed
Wrestlers, trained for the
public shews, in order to
make them more robust   So
that Cæsars vomiting before
dinner was a sort of compliment to Cicero, as it intimated a resolution to pass the
day chearfully and to eat and
drink freely with him
[*n*] This is a citation from
Lucilius, of an Hexameter
verse, with part of a second,
which is not distinguished
from the text, in the editions
of Cicero's Letters

fille colio et
condito j m i L n, & f
quam li r m

" is

" is enough · we had not a word on bufinefs, A. Urb 708
" but many on points of literatuie in fhort, he Cic 62.
" was delighted with his entertainment, and paf- Coff
" fed the day agreeably   He talked of fpend- Q Fabius
" ing one day at Puteoli, another at Baiæ thus Maximus,
" you fee the manner of my receiving him, C Trebo-
" fomewhat tioublefome indeed, but not uneafy nius
" to me   I fhould ftay here a little longer, and
" then to Tufculum   As he paffed by Dolabel-
" la's villa, his troops marched clofe by his
" horfe's fide, on the right and left, which was
" done no where elfe I had this from Nicias [o]."

On the laft of December, when *the Conful
Trebonius* was abroad, his Collegue Q Fabius
died fuddenly, and his death being declared in
the morning, C. Caninius Rebilus was named by
Cæfar to the vacancy at one in the afternoon;
whofe office was to continue onely *through the remaining part of that day* This wanton profanation of the foveieign dignity of the Empire raifed a general indignation in the City, and a Confulate fo ridiculous gave biith to much raillery,
and many jokes which aie tranfmitted to us by
the ancients [p], of which Cicero, who was the
chief author of them, gives us the following fpecimen, in his own account of the faci

Cicero to Curius

" I no longer either advife or defire you to
" come home to us, but want to fly fome whi
" thei myfelf, where I may hear neither the
" names nor the acts of thefe fons of Pelops   It
" is incredible, how meanly I think of myfelf,

---

[o] Ad Att 13 52
[p] Macrob Sat n, 2 3   Dio p 256

" fo

A Urb 703
Cic 62
Cof
Q Fabius
Ma   us,
C Iacto
vit

" for being present at these transactions. You
" had surely an early foresight of what was com-
" ing on, when you ran away from this place
" for though it be vexatious to hear of such
" things, yet that is more tolerable than to see
" them It is well, that you were not in the
" field, when at seven in the morning, as they
" were proceeding to an election of Quæstors,
" the Chair of Q Maximus, whom they called
" Consul [q], was set in it's place but, his
" death being immediately proclaimed, it was re-
" moved , and Cæsar, though he had taken the
" auspices for an assembly of the Tribes,
" changed it to an assembly of the Centuries,
" and, at one in the afternoon, declared a new
" Consul, who was to govern till one the next
" morning I would have you to know there-
" fore, that whilst Caninius was Consul, *nobody*
" *died*, and that there was *no crime committed in*
" *his Consulship*, for he was so wonderfully *vigi-*
" *lant, that* through his whole administration *he*
" *never so much as slept* These things seem ri-
" diculous to you, who were absent, but were
" you to see them, you would hardly refrain
" from tears What if I should tell you the
" rest ? For these are numberless facts of the
" same kind , which I could never have born,
" if I had not taken refuge in the port of Philo-

[q] Cicero would not al-
low c Con   of the c m tns
so irregulari chosen to be
properly called a Consul nor
did the people themselves ac-
knowledge him for, as Suetonius tells us, [n J Cæl
80] when upon Fabius's en-

trance into the Theater, his
Once s, according to custom,
proclaimed his presence, and
ordered the people *to make*
way, for the Consul, the whole
assembl, cried out, *he is no*
Consul

3

" sophy,

" fophy, with our friend Atticus, the companion
" and partner of my ftudies, &c [*r*]"

CÆSAR had fo many creatures and dependents, who expected *the honor of the Confulfhip*
from him, as the reward of their fervices, that
it was impoffible to oblige them all in the regular
way, fo that he was forced to contrive the expedient of fplitting it, as it were, into parcels, and
conferring it for *a few months, or weeks, or even
days*, as it happened to fuit his convenience and
as the thing itself was now but a name, without
any real power, it was of little moment for what
term it was granted, fince the fhorteft gave the
fame privilege with the longeft, and a man once
declared Conful, enjoyed ever after the rank and
character of a confular Senator [*s*].

ON the opening of the new year Cæfar entered into his *fifth Confulfhip*, in partnerfhip with
M Antony he had promifed it all along to Dolabella, but, contrary to expectation, took it at
laft to himfelf. This was contrived by Antony,
who, jealous of Dolabella, as a rival in Cæfar's
favor, had been fuggefting fomewhat to his dif-
advantage, and laboring to create a diffidence of
him in Cæfar; which feems to have been the
ground of what is mentioned above, *Cæfar's
guarding himfelf fo particularly, when he paffed by
his Villa*. Dolabella was fenfibly touched with
this affront, and came full of indignation to the
Senate, where, not daring to vent his fpleen on
Cæfar, he entertained the affembly with a fevere
fpeech againft Antony, which drew on many
warm and angry words between them, till Cæfar,
to end the difpute, promifed to refign the Con-

A Urb 709
Cic 63
Coff
C Julius
Cæsar V.
M Anto-
nius

[*r*] Ep fam 7 30.   [*s*] Vid Dio p 240

fulfhip

A Urb 709
Cic 63
Coſ
C Julius
Cæsar
M Anto-
nius

fulſhip to Dolabella, before he went to *the Parthian war :* but *Antony proteſted, that by his authority as Augur, he would diſturb that election, whenever it ſhould be attempted* [t], and declared, without any ſcruple, that the ground of his quarrel with Dolabella was, *for having caught him in an attempt to debauch his wife Antonia,* the daughter of his Uncle, though that was thought to be a calumny, contrived to color his divorce with her, and his late marriage with Fulvia, the widow of Clodius [u]

CÆSAR was now in the height of all his glory, and *dreſſed, as* Florus ſays, *in all his trappings, like a victim deſtined to ſacrifice* [x] He had received from the Senate the moſt extravagant honors, both human and divine, which flattery could invent, *a Temple, Altar, Prieſt, his Image carried in proceſſion with the Gods, his Statue among the Kings, one of the months called after his name, and a perpetual Dictatorſhip* [y] Cicero endeavoured to reſtrain the exceſs of this complaiſance, within *the bounds of reaſon* [z], but in vain ſince Cæſar was more forward to receive, than they to give, and out of the gaiety of his pride, and to try, as it were, to what length their adulation would reach, when he was actu-

---

[t] Cum Cæſar oſtendiſſet ſe priuſquam profiſceretur Dolabellam Conſulem eſſe poſiturum—hic bonus Augur eo ſe ſacerdotio prædictum eſſe dixit, ut comitia auſpiciis vel impedire vel vitiare poſſet, idque ſe facturum eſſe erat Phil 2 32

[u] Frequentiſſimo ſenatu—harc uoi eſt cum Dolabella cauſam dicere au

fuſes, quod ab eo ſorori & uxori tuæ ſtuprum oblatum eſſe comperiſſes Phil 2 38

[x] Quæ omnia, velut inſulæ, in deſtinatam mort victimam congererentur l 4 2 92

[y] Flor ibid Sueton J Cæſ 76

[z] Plutarch in Cæſ

---

ally

ally poffeffed of every thing, which carried with
it any real power, was not content ftill without
a title, which could add nothing but envy, and
popular odium, and wanted *to be called a King*
Plutarch thinks it a ftrange inftance of folly in
the people to endure with patience all the real
effects *of Kingly government,* yet declare fuch an
abhorrence *to the name.* But the folly was not
fo ftrange in the people, as it was in Cæfar. it is
natural to the multitude to be governed by names
rather than things, and the conftant art of parties to keep up that prejudice, but it was unpar-
donable in fo great a man, as Cæfar, to lay fo
much ftrefs on a title, which, fo far from being
an honor to him, feemed to be a diminution rather of that fuperior dignity, which he already
enjoyed

AMONG the other compliments, that were paid
to him, there was *a new fraternity of Luperci* in-
ftituted to his honor, and called by his name,
of which Antony was the head. Young Quintus Cicero was one of this fociety, with the confent of his Father, though to the diffatisfaction
of his Uncle, who confidered it, not onely as a
low piece of flattery, but an indecency for a
young man of family, to be engaged in ceremonies fo immodeft of running *naked and frantic
about the Streets* [a] The Feftival was held
about the *middle of February,* and Cæfar, *in his
triumphal role, feated himfelf in the Roftra,* in a
golden Chair, to fee the diverfion of the running,
where, in the midft of their fport, the Conful
Antony, at the head of his naked crew, *made him*

[a] Quintus Pater quar-
tum vel potius millefimum
nihil fapit, qui latetur Lu-
perco filio & Stado, ut cer-
nat duplici dedecore cumu-
latam corum. Ad Att 15
5

the offer of a *Regal Diadem, and attempted to put it upon his head*, at the fight of which a *general groan iſſued from the whole Forum*, till upon Cæſar's flight refufal of it, the people loudly teftified their joy, *by an univerſal ſhout* Antony however ordered it to be entered in the public acts, *that by the command of the people, he had offered the Kingly name and power to Cæſar, and that Cæſar would not accept it* [b].

WHILE this affair of *the Kingly Title* amuſed and alarmed the city, two of the Tribuns, Marulius and Cæfetius, were particularly active in diſcouraging every ftep and attempt towards it they *took off the Diadem*, which certain perfons had privately put upon Cæfar's *Statue in the Roftre*, and committed thofe to prifon, who were fufpected to have done it , and publicly punifhed others for daring *to falute him in the ftreets by the name of King*, declaring, *that Cæfar himſelf refuſed and abhorred that title* This provoked Cæfar beyond his ufual temper, and command of himfelf, ſo that he accufed them to the fenate, *of a deſign to raiſe a ſedition againſt him, by perſuading the City, that he really affected to be a King*; but when the affembly was going to pafs the fevereft fentence upon them, he was content *with depoſing them from their Mag ſtracy, and expelling*

<hr />

[b] Sedebat in Roſtris collega ſua, amictus toga purpurea in ſella aurea, coronatus adſcendis accedis ad ſellam — diadema oſtendis geminus toto roro—tu d adema imponebas cum plangore populi ile cum plauſu reiiciebat — at enim adſeriori juſfit in Faſtis ad Lupercalia, C Cæfari, Dictatori perpetuo M Antonium Conſulem populi jaſſu regnum detuliſſe, Cæfarem uti noluiſſe [Phil 2 34] Quod ab eo ita repulſum erat, ut non offenſus videretur Ⅴell P 2 56

them from the Senate [c]. which convinced people ftill the more, of his real fondnefs for a name,
that he pretended to defpife.

Hr had now prepared all things for his expedition againft the Parthians, had fent his legions
before him into Macedonia, fettled the fucceffion
of all the Magiftrates *for two years to come* [d],
appointed Dolabella to take his own place, as
Conful of the current year, named A. Hirtius
and C Panfa, for confuls of the next, and D.
Brutus, and Cn Plancus, for the following year:
but before his departure, he refolved to have *the
Regal Title* conferred upon him by the Senate,
who were too fenfible of his power, and obfequious to his will, to deny him any thing and
to make it the more palatable at the fame time to
the people, he caufed a report to be induftrioufly
propagated through the city, *of ancient prophecies
found in the Sibylline books, that the Parthians
could not be conquered, but by a King,* on the
ftrength of which, *Cotta, one of the Guardians of
thofe books, was to move the Senate, at their next
meeting, to decree the title of king to him* [e]
Cicero fpeaking afterwards of this defign, fays,
*it was expected that fome forged teftimonies would
be produced, to fhew, that he, whom we had felt
in reality to be a King, fhould be called alfo by that
name, if we would be fafe but let us make a bargain with the keepers of thofe Oracles, that they
bring any thing out of them, rather than a King,*

---

[c] Sueton J Cæf 73
Dio p 247 App l 2 p
496 Vell P 2 68

[d] Ltu nne Confules &
Tribunos pleb in biennium,
quos ille voluit? Ad Att
14 0

[e] Proximo autem Senatu,

L Cottam Quindecim virum
fententiam dicturum, ut quoniam libris fatalibus contine-
retur, Parthos non nifi a Rege poffe vinci, Cæfar Rex
appellaretur Sueton c 79
Dio p 247

A. Urb. 710
Cic. 63
Coſſ.
C. Julius
Cæſar V
M. Anto-
nius.

— *whether the Gods nor men will ever endure againſt Rome* [f]

ONE would naturally have expected, after all the fatigues and dangers through which Cæſar had made his way to Empire, that he would have choſen to ſpend the remainder of a declining life in the quiet enjoyment of all the honors and pleaſures, which abſolute power, and a command of the world could beſtow but in the midſt of all this glory, he was a ſtranger ſtill to eaſe he ſaw the people generally diſaffected to him, and impatient under his government; and though amuſed a while with the ſplendor of his ſhews and triumphs, yet regretting ſeverely in cool blood the price, that they had paid for them, the loſs of their liberty, with the lives of the beſt and nobleſt of their fellow Citizens This expedition therefore againſt the Parthians ſeems to have been a political pretext for removing himſelf from the Murmurs of the City, and leaving to his Miniſters the exerciſe of an invidious power, and the taſk of taming the ſpirits of the populace, whilſt he, by employing himſelf in gathering freſh laurels in the Eaſt, and extending the bounds, and retrieving the honor of the Empire, againſt its moſt dreaded enemy, might gradually reconcile them to a reign, that was gentle and clement at home, ſucceſsfull and glorious abroad

But his impatience to be *a King* defeated all

[f] Quorum Interpres nuper falſo quædam hominum fama diéturus in Senatu paratro tr eam quem revera regem habuerunt explanda in cito at eſſe Regem ſi vere ſe ſe eos—cum An tiſtibus agamus, ut quidvis poéius ex illis libris quam regem proferant, quem Ro mt poſthac nec Du nec ho mines eſſe patientur De Divin. 2.54

his

his projects, and accelerated his fate, and pushed
on the nobles, who had conspired against his life,
to the immediate execution of their plot, that
they might save themselves the shame of being
forced to concur in an act, which they heartily
detested [g] and the *Two* Brutus's in particular,
the honor of whose house was founded in the
extirpation of *Kingly Government*, could not but
consider it as a personal infamy, and a disgrace to
their very name, to suffer the restoration of it

THERE were *above sixty persons* said to be engaged in *this conspiracy* [b], the greatest part of
them of the Senatorian rank, but M. Brutus,
and C Cassius were the chief in credit and authority, the first contrivers and movers of the whole
design

M JUNIUS BRUTUS was about one and forty
years old, of the most illustrious family of the
Republic, deriving his name and descent in a
direct line from that first Consul, L Brutus, who
expelled Tarquin, and gave freedom to the Roman people [i]. Having lost his Father when
very

A Urb 70
Cic 63
Coss
C Julius
CÆSAP V.
M ANTO-
NIUS

[g] Quæ causa conjuratis fuit maturandi destinata negotia, ne assentiri necesse esset Suet J Cæs 80 Dio p 247

[b] Conspiratum est in eum a Sexaginta amplius, C Cassio, Marcoque & Decimo Bruto principibus conspirationis Suet 18

[i] Some of the ancient writers call in question this account of Brutus's descent, particularly Dionysius of Halicarnassus, the most judicious and critical of them, who alledges several arguments a-

gainst it, which seem to be very plausible Yet while Brutus lived, it was universally allowed to him Cicero mentions it in his public speeches, and other writings, as a fact, that nobody doubted, and often speaks of the *Image of old Brutus*, which Marcus kept in his house among those of his Ancestors and Atticus, who was peculiarly curious in the antiquities of the Roman families, drew up *Brutus's genealogy* for him and deduced his succession from that old

Hero

A Urb. 709
Cic. 43
Coss.
C. Iulius
Caesar V.
M. Anto-
nius.

very young, he was trained with great care by his uncle Cato, in all the studies of polite letters, especially of eloquence and Philosophy, and under the discipline of such a Tutor, imbibed a warm love for liberty and virtue. He had excellent parts, and equal industry, and acquired an early fame at the bar, where he pleaded several causes of great importance, and was esteemed the most eloquent and learned of all the young nobles of his age. His manner of speaking was correct, elegant, judicious, yet wanting that force and copiousness, which is required in a consummate Orator. But Philosophy was his favorite study, in which, though he professed himself of the more moderate sect of *the old Academy*, yet from a certain pride and gravity of temper, he affected the severity of *the Stoic*, and to imitate his uncle Cato, to which he was wholly unequal, for he was of a mild, mercifull, and compassionate disposition, averse to every thing cruel; and was often forced by the tenderness of his nature to confute the rigor of his principles. While his mother lived in the greatest familiarity with Cæsar, he was constantly attached to the

---

Hero, in a direct line through all the intermediate ages from father to son. Corn. Nep. vit. Att. 18. Tuscul. Disp. 4. 1.

He was born in the Consulship of L. Cornelius Cinna III. and Cn. Papirius Carbo, A. U. 668. which full, confutes the vulgar story of his being commonly believed to be Cæsar's son, since he was but fifteen years younger than Cæsar himself, whose familiarity with his mother Ser-

vilia, cannot be supposed to have commenced, till many years after Brutus was born, or not till Cæsar had lost his first wife Cornelia, whom he married when he was very young, and always tenderly loved, and whose *funeral oration* he made when he was *Quæstor*, and consequently *thirty years old*. Vid. Sueton. J. Cæs. c. 1, 6. 50. it. Brut. p. 343. 447. & Corradi natos

opposite

oppofite party, and firm to the interefts of liber- ty for the fake of which he followed Pompey, whom he hated, and acted on that fide, with a diftinguifhed zeal At the battel of Pharfalia, Cæfar gave particular orders to find out and pre- ferve Brutus being defirous to draw him from the purfuit of a caufe, that was likely to prove fatal to him fo that when Cato, with the reft of the Chiefs, went to renew the war in Afric, he was induced by Cæfar's generofity and his mo- ther's prayers, to lay down his arms, and return to Italy Cæfar endeavoured to oblige him by all the honours, which his power could beftow . but the indignity of receiving from a Mafter, what he ought to have received from a free peo- ple, fhocked him much more than any honors could oblige , and the ruin, in which he faw his friends involved by Cæfar's ufurped dominion, gave him a difguft, which no favors could com- penfate He obferved therefore a diftance and referve through Cæfar's reign , afpired to no fhare of his confidence, or part in his counfils, and by the uncourtly vehemence, with which he defend- ed the rights of *King* Deiotarus, convinced Cæ- far, that he could never be obliged, where he did not find himfelf free. He cultivated all the while the ftricteft friendfhip with Cicero, whofe principles, he knew, were utterly averfe to the meafures of the times , and in whofe free conver- fation, he ufed to mingle his own complaints on the unhappy ftate of the Republic, and the wretched hands, into which it was fallen , till animated by thefe conferences, and confirmed by the general difcontent of all the honeft, he form- ed the bold defign of freeing his Country by the deftruction of Cæfar He had publicly defend- ed Milo's act of *killing Clodius*, by a maxim,

E e 3 which

which he maintained to be univerſally true, *that those, who live in defiance of the laws, and cannot be brought to a trial, ought to be taken off without a trial.* The caſe was applicable to Cæſar in a much higher degree than to Clodius, whoſe power had placed him above the reach of the law, and left no way of puniſhing him, but by an aſſaſſination. This therefore was Brutus's motive; and Antony did him the juſtice to ſay, that he *was the only one of the conſpiracy, who entered into it out of principle, that the reſt, from private malice, roſe up againſt the man, he alone againſt the Tyrant* [k]

C CASSIUS was deſcended likewiſe from a family, not leſs honorable or ancient, nor leſs zealous for the public liberty, than Brutus's; whoſe Anceſtor, Sp Caſſius, after a triumph of three conſulſhips, is ſaid to have been condemned, and put to death, by his own Father, for aiming at a dominion. He ſhewed a remarkable inſtance, when a boy, of his high ſpirit and love of liberty, for *he gave Sylla's Son, Fauſtus, a box on the ear, for bragging among his ſchool-*

---

[k] Natura admirabilis & exculta doctrina, & ſingulari induſtria Cum enim in maximis cauſis verſatus eſſes —[Brut 26] quo magis tuum Brute judicium probo, cui eorum, deſt, exacte neſcio philoſophorum ſectam ſecutus es, quorum in doctrina & præceptis differend ratio conjungitur cum ſuavitate ⟨…⟩ & copia [Brut 219] Nam cum in Academia Xyſto—M ad re Bruti conſueverat, cum T Pomponio venerat—

[Brut 15] tum Brutus—itaque doleo & illius conſilio & tua voce populum Rom carere tamdiu Quod cum per ſe dolendum eſt, tum multo magis conſiderantı, ad quos iſta non tranſlata ſint, ſed neſcio quo pacto devenerint [Brut 269

Ἀλλ' Ἀντώνιός γε καὶ πολλάκις ἀκούεται λέγων, ὡς μόνον οἴοιτο Βροῦτον ἐπιτεθεῖσθαι Καίσαρι, τῇ λαμπρότητι καὶ τῷ δοκοῦντι νῦν καλῷ τῆς πράξεως—vid Plut in Brut p 997 it App p 498

fellows,

A Urb 700
Cic 63
Coff
C Julius
Cæsar V
M Antro-
nius

fellows, of his Father's greatness and absolute power; and when Pompey called the boys before
him, to give an account of their quarrel, he declared in his presence, *that if Custus should dare
to repeat the words, he wou'd repeat the blow*   He
was Quæstor to Crassus, in the Parthian war,
where he greatly signalized both his courage and
skill, and if Crassus had followed his advice,
would have preserved the whole army, but after
their miserable defeat, he made good his retreat
into Syria with the remains of the broken legions and when the Parthians, flushed with success, pursued him thither soon after, and blocked him up in Antioch, he preserved that City
and Province from falling into their hands, and,
watching his opportunity, gained a considerable
victory over them, with the destruction of their
General.   In the civil war, after the battel of
Pharsalia, he sailed with *seventy Ships* to the
coast of Asia to raise fresh forces in that country,
and renew the war against Cæsar, but, as the
Historians tell us, happening to meet with Cæsar crossing *the Hellespont* in a common passage-
boat, instead of destroying him, as he might
have done, he was so terrified by the sight of
the Conqueror, that he begged his life in an abject manner, and delivered up his fleet to him.
But Cicero gives us a hint of a quite different
story, which is much more probable, and worthy of Cassius, that having got intelligence
where Cæsar designed to land, he lay in wait for
him, in *a Bay of Cilicia*, at the mouth of the
river Cydnus, with a resolution to destroy him,
*but Cæsar happening to land on the opposite shoar be-
fore he was aware,* so that seeing his project
blasted, and Cæsar secured in a country where
all people were declaring for him, he thought it

best

A. Urb. 709
Cic 63.
Coss
C Julius
Cæsar V
M Anto-
nius

beſt to make his own peace too, by going over to him with his fleet   He married Tertia, the Siſter of Brutus, and though differing in temper and philoſophy, was ſtrictly united with him in friendſhip and politics, and the conſtant partner of all his counſils   He was brave, witty, learned, yet paſſionate, fierce, and cruel, ſo that *Brutus was the more amiable friend, he the more dangerous enemy*   in his later years he deſerted the Stoics, and became a convert to Epicurus, whoſe doctrine he thought more natural and reaſonable   conſtantly maintaining, *that the pleaſure, which their maſter recommended, was to be found only in the habitual practice of juſtice and virtue*, while he profeſſed himſelf therefore an Epicurean, he lived like a Stoic, was moderate in pleaſures, temperate in diet, and a water-drinker through life   He attached himſelf very early to the obſervance of Cicero, as all the young Nobles did, who had any thing great or Laudable in view   this friendſhip was confirmed by a conformity of their ſentiments in the civil war, and in Cæſar's reign, during which, ſeveral Letters paſſed between them, written with a freedom and familiarity, which is to be found only in the moſt intimate correſpondence   In theſe letters though Cicero rallies his Epicuriſm, and change of principles, yet he allows him to have acted always with the greateſt honor and integrity, and pleaſantly ſays, *that he ſhould begin to think it ſafe to have more nerves, than he imagined, ſince C——d embraced it*   The old writers aſſign ſeveral frivolous reaſons of diſguſt, as the motives of his killing Cæſar   *that Cæſar took a number of Lions from him, which he had provided for a public ſhow*, *that he would not give him the Conſulſhip*   *that he gave Brutus the more honorable Prætorſhip*

torſhip *in preference to him.* But we need not look farther for the true motive, than to his temper and principles for his nature was singularly impetuous and violent, impatient of contradiction, and much more of ſubjection, and paſſionately fond of glory, virtue, liberty it was from theſe qualities, that Cæſar apprehended his danger . and when admoniſhed to beware of Antony and Dolabella, uſed to ſay, *that it was not the gay, the curled, and the jovial, whom he had cauſe to fear, but the thoughtful, the pale, and the lean, meaning Brutus and Caſſius* [*l*]

A Urb 709.
Cic 63.
Coſſ
C Julius
Cæsar V
M Anto-
nius.

THE

[*l*] C Caſſius in ea familia natus, quæ non modo dominatum, ſed ne potentiam quidam cujuſquam ferre potuit [Phil 2 11] Quem ubi primum magiſtratu adiit, damnatumque conſtat Sunt qui patrem actorem ejus ſupplicii ferant Eum cognita domi cauſa verberaſſe ac necaſſe, peculiumque filii Cereri conſecraviſſe. [Liv 2 41] Cujus filium, Fauſtum, C Caſſius condiſcipulum ſuum in ſchola, proſcriptionem paternam laudantem — colapho percuſſit [Val Max 3 1 vid Plutar in Brut] Reliquias legionum C Caſſius — Quæſtor conſervavit, Syriamque adeo in populi Romani poteſtate retinuit, ut tranſgreſſos in eum Parthos, felici rerum eventu fugaret ac funderet [Vell Pat 2 46 it Phil xi 14] οὐδε ἔργον ἕτερον ἡγημαι τυχης εν ἀπορω κλιρω γειεθαι μᾶλλον, ἢ Χαςςιον τὸν πολεμικωτατον - τι τει ιρῶν εδδομη-

ρεια ἀπαρατνυω Χαςαρος ςυιγυήᾳ, υπὸ ες χειρας ελθειν ανωςωηναι, ὁ δ᾽ οὕτω εαυτων αισχεως υπὸ ὀριες μονα παρατλλημι παραδος, υςερον εν Ρωμη δυναςευς ε ι τι ηςα κατεχλαιεν [App 2 483 it. Dio 1 42. 188 Sueton J. Caſ 63] C Caſſius—ſine his clariſſimis viris hanc rem in Cilicia ad oſtium fluminis Cydni confeciſſet, ſi ille ad eam ripam, quam conſtituerat, non ad contrariam naves appuliſſet [Phil 2 11] e quibus Brutum amicum habere malles, inimicum magis timeres Caſſium [Vell P 2 72] ἰδοτι vero, & αταραξια virtute, juſtitia, τῷ ραλῷ parari, & verum & probabile eſt Ipſe enim Epicurus — dicit ακ εςιν ἡδεως ζι-ι τε ραλῶς και δικαιως, ζην [Ep fam 15 19] Caſſius tota vita æquam bibit [Senec 547] Quanquam quicum loquor ? cum viro fortiſſimo viro, qui poſtea quam forum att giſti, nihil

A Urb 709.
Cic 63
Coſſ
C Julius
Cæſar V
M Anto-
nius

THE next in authority to Brutus and Caſſius though very different from them in character, were Decimus Brutus, and C Trebonius they had both been conſtantly devoted to Cæſar, and were ſingularly favored, advanced, and entruſted by him in all his wars; ſo that when Cæſar marched fiſt into Spain, he left them to command *the ſiege of Marſeilles, Brutus by ſea, Trebonius by land*, in which they acquitted themſelves with the greateſt courage and ability, and reduced that ſtrong place to the neceſſity of ſurrendering at diſcretion   Decimus was of the ſame family with his nameſake, Marcus, and Cæſar, as if jealous of a name, that inſpired an averſion to Kings, was particularly ſolicitous to gain them both to his intereſt, and ſeemed to have ſucceded to his wiſh in Decimus, who forwardly embraced his friendſhip, and accepted all his favors; being named by him *to the command of Ciſa'pine Gaul, and to the Conſulſhip of the following year, and the ſecond heir even of his eſtate, in failure of the firſt*   He ſeems to have had no peculiar character of virtue, or patriotiſm, nor any correſpondence with Cicero, before the act of killing Cæſar, ſo that people, inſtead of expecting it from him, were ſurprized at his doing it. yet he was brave, generous, magnificent, and lived with great ſplendor, in the enjoyment of an immenſe fortune, for he kept *a numerous band of Gladiators*, at his own expence, for the diverſion of the City, and after Cæſar's death, ſpent *about four hundred thouſand pounds* of his own

---

nihil feceri niſi pleniſſimum amplſſma dignitaui. In iſta pla atreſi neuo re plus . horum ſi, quam ego putarur, ſi modo eam tu probas

[Ep fam 15 16] Differen do conſulatum Caſſium offenderat [Vell P 2 56 it Plut in Brut App 408]

money,

money, in maintaining an army againſt Antony [*m*]

TREBONIUS had no family to boaſt of, but
was wholly a new man, and the creature of Cæſar's power, who produced him through all the
honors of the State, to his late conſulſhip of three
months Antony calls him *Son of a Buffoon*,
but Cicero, *of a ſplendid Knight*. he was a man
of parts, prudence, integrity, humanity was
converſant alſo in the politer arts, and had a peculiar turn to wit and humor. for, after Cæſar's
death, he publiſhed *a volume of Cicero's ſayings*,
which he had taken pains to collect, upon
which Cicero compliments him, for having explained them with great elegance, and given them
a freſh force and beauty, by his humorous manner of introducing them.   As the Hiſtorians
have not ſuggeſted any reaſon that ſhould move
either him or Decimus to the reſolution of killing
a man, to whom they were infinitely obliged. ſo
we may reaſonably impute it, as Cicero does, to
a greatneſs of ſoul, and ſuperior love of their
country, which made them *prefer the liberty of
Rome to the friendſhip of any man*, *and chuſe rather to be the deſtroyers, than the partners of a
Tyranny* [*n*].

THE

[*n*] Adjectis etiam confi-
liariis cædis, familiariſſimis
omnium, & fortuna partium
ejus in ſummum evectis faſti-
gium, D Bruto & C Trebo-
nio, aliiſque clari nominis viris [Vell P 2 56] Plureſ-
que percurſorum in tutoribus
filii nominavit Decimum
Brutum etiam in ſecundis he-
redibus [Sueton Cæf 83]

Vid Cæf Comm de Bell
civil l 2 Plat in Brut App
p 497, 518 Dio l 44 247
&c D Brutus—cum Cæſaris
primus omnium amicorum
fuiſſet, interfector fuit Vell
P 2 64
[*r*] Scuræ filium appellat
Antonius Quaſi vero ignotus nobis fuerit ſplendidus
Eques Romanus Trebonii pater

A Urb 709.
Cc 63
Coss
C. Julius
Cæsar V
M A TO-
nius

THE reft of the confpirators were partly *young men,* of noble blood, eager to revenge the ruin of their fortunes and families, *partly men obfcure, and unknown to the publc* [*o*], yet whofe fidelity and courage had been approved by Brutus and Caffius It was agreed by them all in council to execute their defign in the Senate, which was fummoned to meet *on the Ides,* or fifteenth of March they knew that the Senate would applaud it when done, and even affift, if there was occafion, in the doing it [*p*], and there was a circumftance, which peculiarly encouraged them, and feemed to be even ominous, that it happened to be *Pompey's Senate Houfe,* in which their attempt was to be made, and where Cæfar would confequently fall *at the foot of Pompey's Statue,* as a juft facrifice to the *manes* of that great man [*q*] They took it alfo for granted, that the City would be generally on their fide, yet for their greater fecurity, *D. Brutus gave orders, to arm his Gladiators that morning, as if for fome public fhew,* that they might be ready, on the firft no-

---

ter [Phil 13 10] Trebonii — confilium ingenium, humanitatem, innocentiam, magnitudinem animi in patria liberanda quis ignorat? [Phil xi 4] liberifce, quem mihi mififti, quantam habet declarationem amoris tui? primum, quod tibi facetum videtur quicquid ego dixi, quod alus fortaffe non item deinde, quod illa, five faceta funt, five fic fiunt narrante te venuftiffima Quin etiam antequam ad me veniatur, rifus omnis pæne confumitur, &c. Ep fam 15 21 it 12.

16} Qui libertatem populi Romani unius amicitiæ præpofuit, depulforque dominatus, quam particeps effe maluit Phil 2 11

[*o*] In tot hominibus, partim obfcuris, partim adolefcentibus, &c Phil 2 11

[*p*] ως των βελευτων, ει και μη προμαθοιει, προθυμως, οτι ιδοιεν το εργον, συνεπιλη ξομεναν App 499

[*q*] Poftquam Senatus idibus Martiis in Pompeii curiam edictus eft, facile tempus & locum prætulerunt [Sueton 80]

tice to fecure the avenues of the Senate, and de- A Urb 709.
fend them from any fudden violence ; and *Pom-* Cic 63
pey's Theater, which adjoined *to his Senate-houfe*, Coff
being the propereft place for the exercife of the C Julius
Gladiators, would cover all fufpicion, that might Cæsar V.
otherwife arife from them The onely delibera- M Anto-
tion that perplexed them, and on which they nius
were much divided, was whether they fhould not
kill *Antony alfo,* and *Lepidus, together with Cæfar* ;
efpecially Antony, the more ambitious of the
two, and the more likely to create frefh danger to the Commonwealth Caffius, with a majority of the company, was warmly for killing
him but the *two Brutus's* as warmly oppofed,
and finally over ruled it they alledged, " that
" to fhed more blood, than was neceffary, would
" difgrace their caufe, and draw upon them an
" imputation of cruelty, and of acting not as
" Patriots, but as the Partifans of Pompey, not
" fo much to free the City, as to revenge them-
" felves on their enemies, and get the dominion
" of it into their hands " But what weighed with
them the moft, was a vain perfuafion, that Antony would be tractable, and eafily reconciled, as
foon as the affair was over but this lenity proved
their ruin and by leaving their work imperfect,
defeated all the benefit of it , as we find Cicero afterwards often reproaching them in his Letters [*r*].

MANY prodigies are mentioned by the Hifto-
rians to have given warning of Cæfar's death [*s*],
which having been been forged by fome, and

[*r*] Plutar in Cæf App   frm x 28 12 4 ad Brut
2 99 502 Dio 247, 248   2 7
Quam vellem ad illas pul-   [*s*] Sed Cæfari futura cæ
cheirimas epulas me Idibus   des er deptibus prodigii de
Martiis invitates Reliqui- nunciata eft, &c Sueton di
arum nihil habeiemus Ep   flut n v t

cre luloufly

A Urb 705
Cic 63
Coff
C Julius
Cæsar
M Antro-
nius

credulously received by others, were copied, as usual, by all, to strike the imagination of their readers, and raise an awful attention to an event, in which the Gods were supposed to be interested Cicero has related one of the most remarkable of them, " that as Cæsar was sacrificing a little be-
" fore his death, with great pomp and splendor,
" in *his triumphal robes and golden chair,* the vic-
" tim, which was a fat Ox, was found to be
" *without a heart* and when Cæsar seemed to be
" shocked at it, Spurinna, the Haruspex, admo-
" nished him to beware, lest through a failure
" in *counsil,* his *life* should be cut off, since the
" heart was the seat and source of them both
" The next day he sacrificed again, in hopes to
" find the entrails more propitious ; but the liver
" of the bullock appeared to *want its head,*
" which was reckoned also among the direfull
" omens [t] " These facts, though ridiculed

[t] De Divin 1 52 2 16 These cases of victims found sometimes *without a heart or liver,* gave rise to a curious question among those who believed the reality of this kind of *augurations,* as the *Stoics generally* did, how to account for the cause of so strange a phænomenon The common solution was, that the Gods made such changes instantaneously in the moment of sacrificing by annihilating or creating the condition of the entrails so, as to make them correspond with the circumstance of the Sacrificer and the admonition which they intended to give [De Div ibid] But this was laughed at by the Naturalists, as wholly unphilosophical, who thought it absurd to imagine, that the Deity could either annihilate, or create , either reduce any thing to nothing, or form any thing out of nothing What seems the most probable, is, that if the facts really happened, they were contrived by Cæsar's friends, and the heart conveyed away by some artifice, to give them a better pretence of enforcing their admonitions, and putting Cæsar upon his guard against dangers, which they really apprehended, from quite different reasons, than the pretended denunciations of the Gods

by

by Cicero, were publicly affirmed and believed at the time, and feem to have raifed a general rumor through the City, of fome fecret danger that threatened Cæfar's life, fo that his friends being alarmed at it, were endeavouring to inftil the fame apprehenfion into Cæfar himfelf and had fucceeded fo far, as to fhake his refolution of going that day to the Senate. when it was actually affembled by his fummons in Pompey's Senate-houfe, till D Brutus, by rallying thofe fears, as unmanly and unworthy of him, and alledging, that his abfence would be interpreted as an affront to the affembly, drew him out againft his will to meet his deftined fate [u]

A Urb 709.
Cic 63
Coff
C Julius
Cæsar V.
M Anto-
nius

In the morning of the fatal day, M Brutus and C Caffius appeared, according to cuftom, in the Forum fitting in their *Prætorian Tribunals*, to hear and determine caufes, where, though they had daggers under their gowns, they fat with the fame calmnefs as if they had nothing upon their minds, till the news of Cæfar's coming out to the Senate, called them away to the performance of their part in the tragical act, which they executed at laft with fuch refolution, that through the eagernefs of ftabbing Cæfar, they wounded even one another [x]

Thus fell Cæfar on *the celebrated Ides of March*, after he had advanced himfelf to a height of power, which no Conquerer had ever attained before him, though to raife the mighty Fabric, he had made more defolation in the world than any man perhaps, who ever lived in it. He ufed to fay, *that his conquefts in Gaul had coft o-*

[u] Plutar in J Cæf
[v] Ib in Brut App 2 sc

A. Urb. 709
Cc 65
Coſſ
C. JULIUS
CÆSAR I.
M. ANTO-
NIUS

beat a million, and two hundred thouſand lives [y], and if we add the civil wars to the account, they could not coſt the Republic much leſs, in the more valuable blood of it's beſt Citizens: yet when through a perpetual courſe of faction, violence, rapine, ſlaughter, he had made his way at laſt to Empire, he did not enjoy the quiet poſſeſſion of it above five months [z].

HE was endowed with every great and noble quality, that could exalt human nature, and give a man the aſcendant in ſociety, formed to excell in peace, as well as war provident in counſil; fearleſs in action, and executing what he had reſolved with an amazing celerity generous beyond meaſure to his friends, placable to his enemies, and for parts, learning, eloquence, ſcarce inferior to any man His orations were admired for two qualities which are ſeldom found together, *ſtrength and elegance.* Cicero ranks him among the greateſt orators, that Rome ever bred and Quintillian ſays, *that he ſpoke with the ſame force with which he fought, and if he had devoted himſelf to the bar, would have been the onely man capable of rivalling Cicero.* Nor was he a maſter onely of the politer arts, but converſant alſo with the moſt abſtruſe and critical part of learning, and among other works which he publiſhed, addreſſed *two books to Cicero, on the Analogy of language*, or the art of ſpeaking and writing correctly [a]. He was a moſt liberal Patron of

wit

---

[y] Undecies centena & ſexagi ſta duo hominum millia occiſa præliis ab eo—quod ita eſſe confeſſus eſt ipſe, bellorum civilium ſtragem non prodendo Plin. Hiſt. ~ 25

[z] Neque illi tanto viro—pluſquam quinque menſium principalis quies contig ~—Vell. Pat. 2 56

[a] It was in the dedication of this piece to Cicero, that

wit and learning, wheresoever they were found, and out of his love of those talents, would readily pardon those, who had employed them against himself rightly judging, *that by making such men his friends, he should draw praises from the same fountain, from which he had been aspersed*. His capital passions were *ambition and love of pleasure*, which he indulged in their turns to the greatest excess yet the first was always predominant, to which he could easily sacrifice all the charms of the second, and draw pleasure even from toils and dangers, when they ministred to his glory For *he thought Tyranny*, *as* Cicero says, *the greatest of Goddesses*, and had frequently in his mouth a verse of Euripides, which expressed the image of his soul, *that if right and justice were ever to be violated, they were to be violated for the sake of reigning*. This was the chief end and purpose of his life the scheme that he had formed from his early youth, so that, as Cato truly declared of him, *he came with sobriety and meditation to the subversion of the Republic*. He used to say, *that there were two things necessary, to acquire and to support power, soldiers and money*; which yet depended mutually on each other. with money therefore he provided soldiers, and with soldiers extorted money and was of all men the most rapacious in plundering, both friends and foes, sparing neither *Prince nor State, nor Temple, nor even private persons*, who were known to possess any share of treasure His great abilities would necessarily have made him one of the first Citizens of Rome, but disdaining

A. Urb. 709. Cic. 63. Coss. C. Julius Cæsar V. M. Antonius.

that Cæsar paid him the compliment, which Pliny mentions, of his having *acquired a laurel, superior to that of all triumphs, as it was more glorious to extend the bounds of the Roman wit, than of their Empire*. Hist. N. 7. 30.

the condition of a fubject, he could never reft, till he had made himfelf *a Monarch*. In acting this laft part his ufual prudence feemed to fail him, as if the height, to which he was mounted, had turned his head, and made him giddy for, by a vain oftentation of his power, he deftroyed the ftability of it, and as men fhorten life, by living too faft, fo by an intemperance of reigning, he brought his reign to a violent end [b]

It was a common queftion after his death, and propofed as a problem by Livy, *whether it was of juft to the Republic, that he had ever*

[b] De Cæfaris … … … … Orationum … … … legent … … … It… … … … referendi… … … … … f … … … … cutu — … … … … vero Cæf… … … … non … … contra … … … non … … … … … eo … … id … … … … animo … … quo … … apparet [Quintil … 1] C Cæfar in libris quos ad M Ciceronem de Analogia co ferp… —[a Gell 10 8] Q n… … … … … … … … … … … … fum, … … … … … … … … … … … … … me … … … —[Brut … … … … Sueton c6] in Cefare … … … … … … … … … … … … … … fæ inge… s excellentibus, … … … tum e^a, deleftatur— … … n fonte … … … in-

tell … … … … … uas, e quo fit … … … alperius [Ep … m 6 C] … … … … … … … … … … [Ad Att 7 11] pf … tem in ore fem- … … græco … verius de Phæniffis … … ba—

Nam … … … jus, … … … gratia
*J … … … alus rebus pie-
ta… … slas*

[Offic 3 21]

Cato dixit, C Cæfarem ad evertendam rempublicam, fobriam acceffiffe [Quintil 1 8 2] Abftinentiam neque in Imperiis neque in Magiftratibus præftitit— in Gallia fana, templaque Deum donis referta expilavit urbes diruit, fæpius ob prædam quam delictum — evidentiffimis rapinis, ac Sacrilegiis onera bellorum civilium — fuftinuit. [Sueton c 54 vid it Dio p 209]

2   *been*

A U'b 700
Cic 63
Coff
C Julius
C T..ar V
M A T.
..ius

been born [c] The queſtion did not turn on the ſimple merit of his acts, for that would bear no diſpute, but on the accidental effects of them, their producing the ſettlement under Auguſtus. and the benefits of that government, which was the conſequence of his Tyranny Suetonius, who treats the characters of the Cæſars with that freedom, which the happy reigns, in which he lived, indulged, upon balancing the exact ſumm *of his virtues and vices*, declares him, on the whole, *to have been juſtly killed* [d] · which appears to have been the general ſenſe of the beſt, the wiſeſt and the moſt diſintereſted in Rome, at the time when the fact was committed

The onely queſtion which ſeemed to admit any diſpute, was, whether it ought to have been committed by thoſe, who were the leaders in it [e]. ſome of whom owed their lives to Cæſar, and others had been loaded by him with honors, to a degree, that helped to encreaſe the popular odium; particularly D Brutus, who was the moſt cheriſhed by him of them all, *and left by his will, the ſecond Heir of his Eſtate* [f] For, of *the Two Brutus's*, it was not Marcus, as it is commonly imagined, but Decimus, who was *the favorite, and whoſe part in the conſpiracy ſurprized people the moſt* [g] But this circumſtance ſerved onely for a different handle to the different parties, for aggra-

---

[c] Vid Senec Natur Quæſt l 5 18. p 766

[d] Prægravant tamen cætera facta, dictaque ejus, ut & abuſus dominatione & jure cæſus exiſtimetur Sueton c 76

[e] Diſputari de M Bruto ſolet, an debuerit accipere a D Julio vitam cum occi-

dendum eum judicaret Senec de Benef l 2 20

[f] Appian 2 518.

[g] Etſi et eum Brutorum commune ſit & laudis ſocietas æqua, Decimo tamen enarationes erant, quid factum dolebant, quo minus ab eo rem ill m dicebant fieri debuiſſe Philip 7

F f 3 *juſting*

vating either their crime, or their merit　Cæsar's friends charged them with *base ingratitude*, for killing their Benefactor, and abusing the power which he had given to the destruction of the giver　The other side gave a contrary turn to it, extolled the greater virtue of the men, for not being diverted by private considerations, from doing an act of public benefit　Cicero takes it always in this view, and says, " That the Re-
" public was the more indebted to them, for
" preferring the common good, to the friend-
" ship of any man whatsoever, that as to the
" kindness of giving them their lives, it was the
" kindness onely of a Robber, who had first
" done them the greater wrong, by usurping
" the power to take it　that, if there had been
" any it n or ingratitude in the act, they could
" never have acquired so much glory by it, and
" though he wondered indeed at some of them
" for doing it, rather than ever imagined, that
" they would have done it, yet he admired
" them so much the more, for being regardless
" of favors, that they might shew their regard to
" their Country [*I*] "

So me of Cæsar's friends, particularly Pansa and Hirtius, advised him always to keep a stand-ing guard of Prætorian Troops, for the defence of his person　alledging *that a power acquired by arms, could only be maintained by arms*　but his

[*I*] Quod si hac one
iouim — Tironi n ut
commemorare possit, v le
dedi te man, quibus ion de-
cnerint　quod si eret be-
neficium n aquem a n il-
lum interuicerum, a quo e
rant servo ,— anium efficit
gioria i commecti　Phil 2　7

Quo etiam majorem er
Refpub gratiam debet, qui
liberiatem populi Romani u-
nius imicitie præposuit, depulforque dominatus quam
particeps esse maluit— admiratus fum ob eam causam, quod
immemor beneficiorum, me-
mor patria fuisset — ib 11

common

common anſwer was, *that he had rather die once by* A Urb 709.
treachery, than live always in fear of it [*i*]. He
uſed to laugh at Sylla for reſtoring the liberty of
the Republic, and to ſay in contempt of him,
that he did not know his letters [*k*]. But, as a judicious writer has obſerved, Sylla *had learnt a*
better Grammar than he, which taught him to re-
ſign his guards, and his government together where-
as Cæſar, by diſmiſſing the one, yet retaining the
other, committed a dangerous ſoleciſm in politics [*l*];
for he ſtrengthened the popular odium, and conſequently his own danger, while he weakened his
defence.

A Urb 709.
Cic 63.
Coſſ.
C Julius
Cæsar V.
M Anro-
nius.

HE made ſeveral good laws during his adminiſtration, all tending to enforce the publick diſcipline, and extend the penalties of former laws.
The moſt conſiderable, as well as the moſt uſefull
of them was, *that no Prætor ſhould hold any Province*
more than one year, nor a Conſul more than two [*m*].
This was a regulation, that *had been often wiſhed*
for, as Cicero ſays, *in the beſt of times*, and what
one of the ableſt *Dictators of the Republic* had
declared to be it's chief ſecurity, *not to ſuffer great*
and arbitrary commands to be of long duration, but
to limit them at leaſt in time, if it was not con-

[*i*] Laudandum experien-
tia conſilium eſt Panſa atque
Hirtii qui ſemper prædixe-
rant Cæſari, ut principatum
nimis quæſitum armis tene-
ret Ille dictitans, mori ſe
quam timeri malle Vel P
2 57
Inſidias undique imminen-
tes ſubire ſemel confeſſum ſatis eſſe, quam cavere ſemper
Sueton c 86

[*k*] Nec minoris impoten-
tiæ voces propalam edebat—
Syllam neſciſſe litteras, qui
Dictaturam depoſuerit Sueton 77
[*l*] Vid Sir H Saviles
Diſſertat de *Militia Rom* at
the end of his tranſlation of
Tacitus
[*m*] Phil 1 8 Sueton J
Caſ 42, 43

venient

vement to limit them in power [n]. Cæsar knew by experience, that the prolongation of these extraordinary commands, and the habit of ruling Kingdoms was the readiest way, not onely to inspire a contempt of the laws, but to give a man the power to subvert them, and he hoped therefore by this law, to prevent any other man from doing what he himself had done, and to secure his own possession from the attempts of all future invaders.

[n] Quæ lex melior utilior optima etiam Repub sæpius pagnata, quam ne Prætoriæ provinciæ plus quam annum, neve plus quam biennium consulares obtinerentur —Phil 1 8

Mamercus Æmilius—maximam autem, ait, ejus custodiam esse, si magna imperia diuturna non essent, & temporis modus imponeretur, quibus juris imponi non posset Liv 1 4 24

The End of the SECOND VOLUME.

Lightning Source UK Ltd.
Milton Keynes UK
UKHW030616240719
346734UK00007B/593/P